Transitive - has a direct object

E = e/a
I = i, ı, u, ü } p. 26

writing - p. 59
79
~~101~~/89

30
68
40
59
92

Review begins

Lesson 15
16 - 169
17 - 181

p. 157

~~ne~~ - what?
Neden - why? niçin / niye } why?
neye - why (dative)
neler - what things

nereye - where
ondan - from him ~~therefore~~
burada } here
buraya } here
orada - there
nerelere - where
onun için - therefore

fazla = too much

-I the (~~definite~~ objective case) definite noun, etc.
-E/a to, for (dative)
-dE in, at, on (~~ablative~~ locative)
-DEN from (~~locative~~ ablative)

I - i, ı, u
E - a

vakit, zaman, sefer
süre, mühlet
kere, defa, kez
} 'time' (189 - usage)

Transitive Verb - a verb that takes an object. 'John read a book.'

kimin 'whose'
kimden 'from whom' or 'who from'
kimler 'what people' 'who'

bunlar these
şunlar these (here)
buna to this
şundan from this (here)
onu that (obj)
bunun
bunu this (obj.)

-ken } 'while'
iken }
-mIş-ken 'having done'
-(y)EcEk-ken 'while being about to do'

Vocab. 100%

13 - 7/28/91

11 - 7/28/91

5 - 7/28/91

6 - 7/28/91

8 - 7/28/91

Vocab:

Eng./Turk.	Turk/Eng
3	3
	5
	6
	8
	11
	13

Review the following daily: 27,

TURKISH GRAMMAR

TURKISH GRAMMAR

Robert Underhill

The MIT Press
Cambridge, Massachusetts, and London, England

Fifth printing, 1987

Printed and bound in the United States of America

Library of Congress Cataloging in Publication Data

Underhill, Robert.
Turkish grammar.

Includes index.
1. Turkish language--Grammar. I. Title.
PL123.U45 494'.35'82421 75-46535
ISBN 0-262-21006-1

CONTENTS

PREFACE xvi

LESSON 1: PRONUNCIATION AND SPELLING 1

1. Spelling and transcription 1
2. Consonants 4
2.1. The letters k, g, and l 7
2.2. Yumuşak ge 10
2.3. Aspiration of stops 12
3. Vowels 13
3.1. Long vowels 17
4. Accent 18
5. Summary of the alphabet 19

LESSON 2: VOWEL HARMONY 23

1. The Turkish vowel system 23
2. Vowel harmony rules 25
3. Exceptions to vowel harmony rules 26

LESSON 3: BASIC SENTENCE PATTERNS 29

1. Variation in suffixes: buffer consonants 29
2. Variation in suffixes: consonant harmony 30
3. Basic sentence patterns 30
4. Pronouns 32
5. The suffix -DIr 32
6. Plurals 33
7. Accent: unaccented suffixes 34
8. Usage 34

LESSON 4: THE NOUN PHRASE AND NEGATIVES 37

1. The noun phrase 37

1.1. Definite and indefinite nouns 38
1.2. Adjectives 38
1.3. Noun phrases as predicates 39
2. The negative değil 40
3. Variation in stems: final voiced stops 41
3.1. Final g 42
3.2. Additional notes on final stops 43
3.3. A note on spelling 43
4. Usage 43

LESSON 5: THE DEFINITE PAST OF VERBS AND THE OBJECTIVE CASE 47

1. The infinitive 47
2. Definite past tense 48
3. The verb phrase 49
4. The objective case 50
5. Obligatory objects 52
6. Usage 52

LESSON 6: VERBAL NEGATIVES AND QUESTIONS 57

1. The verbal negative 57
2. Yes-or-no questions 58
3. Yes and no 60
4. Accent: proper nouns 61
5. The words çok, az, and pek 62
6. Usage 63

LESSON 7: THE DATIVE AND ABLATIVE CASES 67

1. The dative case 67
2. The ablative case 68

3. Interrogatives: *ne* 69
4. Rules of order 70
5. Usage 73

LESSON 8: THE LOCATIVE CASE 79

1. The locative case 79
2. Additional uses of the ablative 80
3. Interrogatives: *hangi* 81
4. 'And' 81
5. Usage 84

LESSON 9: THE GENITIVE CASE AND POSSESSIVE SUFFIXES 89

1. Variation in suffixes: vowel dropping 89
1.1. Variation in stems: pronominal -*n*- 90
2. The possessive relation 90
2.1. The genitive suffix 91
2.2. The possessive suffixes 92
3. Possessive compounds 93
4. Omission of possessives 96
5. Two possessives 96
6. Usage 97

LESSON 10: *VAR* AND *YOK* 101

1. Existential particles 101
2. Questions with *var* and *yok* 103
3. 'To have' 104
4. Variation in stems: *su* and *ne* 105
5. Variation in stems: final clusters 105
6. Interrogatives: *kim* 107
7. Usage 108

LESSON 11: THE PROGRESSIVE TENSE 111

1. Variation in stems: *y* conditioning 111
2. The progressive tense 112
3. Questions with -*Iyor* 113
4. Possessive and predicative endings 114
5. *DE* 116
6. Accent: compounds 117
7. Usage 117

LESSON 12: DEMONSTRATIVES AND NUMBERS 121

1. Demonstratives 121
1.1. Use of demonstratives 123
2. Numbers 124
2.1. Uses of numbers 125
2.2. Counting words 126
3. Interrogatives: *kaç* 129
4. Usage 129

LESSON 13: THE FUTURE TENSE 135

1. The future tense 135
2. Adverbs of place 136
3. Numerical expressions: fractions 139
4. Usage 140

LESSON 14: THE PRESENT TENSE 145

1. The present tense 145
2. Uses of the present 147
3. The verb *olmak* 149
4. Numerical expressions: dates 151
5. Usage 152

LESSON 15: POSTPOSITIONS 157

1. Postpositions 157
2. Postpositions with the nominative/genitive 158
3. The words böyle, şöyle, öyle 160
4. Interrogatives 161
5. Numerical expressions: times 162
6. Usage 163

LESSON 16: THE NARRATIVE PAST AND POSTPOSITIONS WITH THE DATIVE 169

1. The narrative past 169
2. Postpositions with the dative 171
3. Numerical expressions: prices 172
4. Variation in stems: final long vowels 174
5. Usage 175

LESSON 17: THE PAST AUXILIARY 181

1. The past auxiliary 181
1.1. Forms of the past auxiliary 183
1.2. Meaning of the past auxiliary 185
1.3. Auxiliaries 185
2. Numerical expressions: ordinals 187
3. Usage 188

LESSON 18: THE DUBITATIVE AUXILIARY 195

1. The dubitative auxiliary 195
1.1. Forms of the dubitative auxiliary 196
1.2. Meaning of the dubitative auxiliary 198
2. Numerical expressions: distributive 199
3. Names 201

4. Usage 202

LESSON 19: USES OF -DIr AND THE RELATIVE -ki 207

1. The suffix -DIr 207
2. The "relative" suffix -ki 209
3. Adjectives as adverbs 212
4. Usage 214

LESSON 20: POSTPOSITIONS WITH THE ABLATIVE 219

1. Postpositions with the ablative 219
2. Comparative and superlative of adjectives 224
2.1. Comparative 224
2.2. Superlative 226
3. Partitive ablative 226
4. Usage 227

LESSON 21: POSTPOSITIONAL CONSTRUCTIONS 233

1. Postpositional constructions 234
1.1. Nouns used in postpositional constructions 235
1.2. Use of possessive suffixes 239
2. Usage 240

LESSON 22: COMPOUND VERBS 245

1. Variation in stems: double final consonants 246
2. Compound verbs 246
3. Additional postpositional constructions 248
4. Directional adverbs 250
5. Usage 251

LESSON 23: INDEFINITE AND NEGATIVE EXPRESSIONS 257

1. Indefinite expressions 257
2. Negative expressions 262
3. Possessive suffixes 265
4. Usage 267

LESSON 24: RELATIVE CONSTRUCTIONS AND SUBJECT PARTICIPLES 273

1. The nature of relative constructions 273
2. Subject participles 276
3. The present participle 279
4. The past participle 279
5. The future participle 280
6. The aorist participle 281
7. Usage 282

LESSON 25: OBJECT PARTICIPLES 287

1. Object participles 287
2. Examples of head nouns 288
3. The future participle 290
4. 'When' 291
5. A translation procedure 291
6. Usage 292

LESSON 26: PARTICIPLES FROM POSSESSIVES 297

1. Participles from possessives 297
1.1. Cases involving <u>var</u> and <u>yok</u> 299
1.2. Cases involving postpositional constructions 300
2. Adjectives with possessive suffix 302

3. Additional uses of object participles 302
4. Usage 303

LESSON 27: VERBAL NOUNS AND INFINITIVES 307

1. Verbal noun constructions 307
2. Turkish verbal nouns 309
2.1. The infinitive 310
2.2. The "short infinitive" 311
2.3. The suffix -(y)Iş 312
3. The suffix -mEktEdIr 313
4. The adjective lâzım 314
5. Usage 315

LESSON 28: NOMINALIZATIONS 321

1. Nominalizations 321
2. The difference between nominalizations and verbal nouns 323
3. Nominalizations with postpositions 324
4. Indirect questions 325
5. Usage 326

LESSON 29: THE PASSIVE 331

1. The passive verb 331
2. The passive of transitive verbs 332
3. The "impersonal" passive 334
4. Transitive and intransitive pairs 336
5. Derivation: -CE 337
6. Usage 338

LESSON 30: THE CAUSATIVE 343

1. The causative verb 343

2. Meanings of the causative 345
3. Grammar of the causative 347
4. Causative and passive 349
5. Multiple causatives 349
6. Derivation: -CI 350
7. Usage 351

LESSON 31: THE REFLEXIVE 355

1. The reflexive pronoun 355
2. The reflexive verb 357
3. Reflexive, causative and passive 358
4. Nominal derivation: -lIk 359
5. Usage 361

LESSON 32: THE RECIPROCAL 365

1. The reciprocal pronoun 365
2. The reciprocal verb 366
3. Reciprocal and other suffixes 369
4. Derivation: -lE 370
5. Usage 372

LESSON 33: ADVERBIAL CONSTRUCTIONS AND SUFFIXES 377

1. Adverbial constructions 377
2. Adverbial suffixes 379
3. Variation in stems: glottal stops 382
4. Usage 383

LESSON 34: COMPOUND ADVERBIAL CONSTRUCTIONS 387

1. Compound adverbial suffixes 387
2. Nominal derivation: -lI and -sIz 391

3. Usage 393

LESSON 35: THE ADVERBIAL AUXILIARY AND POSSIBILITY 399

1. The adverbial auxiliary -*ken* 399
2. Uses of -*ken* 401
3. 'Impossible' 402
4. 'Possible' 403
5. Other periphrastic constructions 404
6. Usage 405

LESSON 36: THE CONDITIONAL 411

1. The conditional 411
1.1. The conditional tense 411
1.2. The conditional auxiliary 412
1.3. Uses of the conditional 413
2. Usage 416

LESSON 37: IMPERATIVES, THE OPTATIVE, AND THE NECESSITATIVE 421

1. Imperatives 421
2. The optative 423
3. The necessitative 425
4. '-Ever' constructions 426
5. Usage 428

LESSON 38: SUBORDINATING CONJUNCTIONS 431

1. *Diye* 431
1.1 Writing direct quotations 432
2. *Ki* complements 433

3. Other subordinating conjunctions 435
4. Reduplication 436
5. Usage 438

GLOSSARY OF SUFFIXES 443

GLOSSARY 447

INDEX 471

PREFACE

The objective of this book is not only to provide a comprehensive grammar for teaching Turkish but also to demonstrate the relevance of modern linguistics, particularly generative grammar, to language teaching. I have intentionally avoided as far as possible the terminology and formalism of transformational grammar, since these would serve only to confuse and alarm students whose specialty is not linguistics. But the description of Turkish presented here rests throughout on the conceptual framework of generative grammar. I believe, and hope to have shown, that much of Turkish grammar can be explained more simply and incisively with the use of generative concepts—for example, the relations between relative clauses (and other types of subordination) and simple sentences, and the derivation of variants of stems and suffixes from more abstract phonological forms. Thus there are extensive and fundamental differences between the analysis of Turkish presented here and that found in most textbooks, in ways that are partially disguised by the use of traditional terminology. In most areas, the presentation here rests on a thorough reanalysis of Turkish grammar.

The book is designed to be used at the rate of one or two lessons a week, depending on the speed of the course. Each lesson is concerned primarily with one major grammatical point, but sometimes a group of related points is presented. In addition, the lessons contain much information on phraseology and idiomatic usage, so that students should not only learn the grammar but also be able to form colloquial sentences. I have tried to break down the material as much as possible into separate teaching topics and have arranged these subjects sequentially through the lessons in a reasonably logical order. My experience is that it is easier to teach grammar in small doses than large ones, and I have therefore tried to keep the lessons constant in length and difficulty and to avoid overloading any one lesson with too much information on a single topic.

Teachers will presumably supplement the text with readings, exercises, and drills according to their own preferences in methods of language teaching. Simple readings, such as those in the primers (_Okuma Kitapları_) used in the Turkish schools, can be introduced as early as Lesson 9, since Lessons 1 through 9 contain the minimum essential information necessary for understanding a simple Turkish text.

The vocabulary introduced in this grammar has intentionally been kept to a minimum. The students in a beginning Turkish course normally have a wide variety of reasons for learning Turkish, and no single vocabulary can be appropriate for all purposes. I have therefore chosen to present only a small basic, common vocabulary, and expect that each student can learn whatever additional vocabulary he needs for his own purposes. In choosing the words to be introduced, I have made use of the frequency data given in Joe E. Pierce's _Turkish Frequency Counts_.

In preparing this book, I have made use of a number of references on Turkish grammar, by Turkish, European, and American scholars. The two most useful of these are Geoffrey L. Lewis's _Turkish Grammar_ and A. N. Kononov's _Grammatika sovremennogo turetskogo jazyka_. The assistance of these books and Lewis's _Teach Yourself Turkish_ (from which I first started to learn Turkish) is particularly acknowledged.

Work on this grammar goes back more years than I care to remember, and it would be impossible to thank by name all those who have contributed to the final result in one way or another. These include the many native speakers who have assisted me during all phases of my work on Turkish and the students who served as experimental subjects in Turkish classes. A primary debt is owed to my teachers in Turkish and linguistics, particularly Omeljan Pritsak and Calvert Watkins. Anthony Arlotto, Engin Sezer, and Grace Smith used early versions of this text in Turkish classes and provided invaluable suggestions; Sezer also wrote a number of exercises. A number of native speakers have helped me in verifying the accuracy of the examples, including Sezer, Şinasi Tekin, and particularly Ayşegül Underhill, who responded with extraordinary patience to years of questions on all aspects of the language.

San Diego, California
March 1975

TURKISH GRAMMAR

LESSON 1: PRONUNCIATION AND SPELLING

1. Spelling and transcription

It is well known that English spelling does not adequately reflect English pronunciation. If you were trying to teach English to Turkish students, you would have difficulty explaining why the three words pare, pear, and pair are all pronounced exactly the same way, while the words lead 'conduct' and lead 'metal' are spelled the same way but pronounced differently.

Every language has a small number of distinctive sound elements, or "units of pronunciation," that are strung together to form words. The technical term for these is "phonemes." The phonemes and letters of a word frequently fail to correspond, especially in English. The word pin contains three phonemes corresponding exactly to its three letters. The word chin contains four letters, but only three phonemes, since the two letters ch are used together to indicate a single sound. The word pane also contains only three phonemes: the final letter e has no sound value of its own but serves merely to indicate that the preceding vowel /ē/ is long. The word pine contains four phonemes, but these do not correspond to the letters: the pronunciation of pine is /payn/ (say it over to yourself until you become convinced, remembering to pronounce /a/ as in father).

Ideally, the spelling system should correspond to the phonemic system in such a way that each letter always represents a single phoneme, and always the same phoneme. This would be a "phonetic alphabet" in the traditional sense of the term. Unfortunately, this rarely happens in natural languages, for a variety of reasons. Therefore, in discussing pronunciation, it is frequently convenient to write words in "phonemic transcription" instead of in conventional spelling. Phonemes are normally enclosed by slant lines, to distinguish them from letters. The three words pare, pear, and pair could all be transcribed /pēr/, while the words lead and lead could be transcribed:

lead	'conduct'	/līd/ (or /liyd/ in some systems)
lead	'metal'	/led/

In Turkish, the situation is considerably better, since the Turkish spelling system is much more nearly phonemic than that of English. For this reason, we shall normally be able to dispense with special symbols or transcriptions. However, there are some cases where Turkish spelling is not adequate to indicate the correct pronunciation of a word. Compare the following two words, as spoken by a native speaker:

sakın	'beware'
sakin	'quiet'

Nothing in the spelling indicates that the *a* of the first word is short, while the *a* of the second word is long. (Ignore the difference between the second vowels for the moment.) Turkish has a set of four phonemic long vowels that are distinctly different from the corresponding short vowels. Since vowel length is not usually indicated in the spelling, we shall have to indicate it in transcription; and we transcribe the second word of the preceding example as /sākin/.

Again, compare the following two words, as spoken by a native speaker:

bal	'honey'
hal	'condition'

Nothing in the spelling indicates that the *l* of the first word is a "dark" or velar *l*, while that of the second word is a "light" or palatal *l*. These two sounds are distinctively different in Turkish—that is, they are different phonemes—as they are, for example, in Russian. In transcription, we shall indicate the "light" l as follows: /l̲/. We transcribe the second word as /hal̲/.

Another use for phonemic transcription, especially important in Turkish, is to indicate the ways in which a word can change its form. Consider, for example, the following words:

sanat	'art'	kanat	'wing'
sanatlar	'arts'	kanatlar	'wings'
sanatı	'his art'	kanadı	'his wing'

If you know German or Russian, you will remember that the phoneme /d/ (along with all other voiced consonants) is pronounced [t] at the end of a word. (We use square brackets [] for "phonetic" transcriptions, which indicate the specific ways that phonemes are pronounced in specific positions.) Thus the German word Hund 'dog' is pronounced [hunt]. The basic /d/ reappears, however, when a vowel is added to the end, as in the plural Hunde, pronounced [hunde].

Almost the same situation exists in Turkish. The word for 'wing' is basically /kanad/, but the final /d/ is pronounced [t] at the end of a word, as in kanat alone, or before a consonant, as in kanatlar (with plural -lar). Before a vowel, however, the basic /d/ reappears, as in kanadı (with possessive -ı). The word sanat 'art', on the other hand, has a basic /t/ that appears in all forms of the word.

The only difference between Turkish and German in this respect is that in Turkish this change of /d/ to [t] is reflected in the spelling, while German spelling preserves the basic form. This makes Turkish spelling somewhat hard to work with. If you are given, for example, the word maksat 'purpose', there is no way of knowing whether the possessive should be maksatı or maksadı, since the spelling does not indicate whether the word ends basically in /t/ or /d/. However, if these words are given in transcription, you should be able to tell immediately that the possessive of the first word is maksadı and that of the second word is suratı:

maksat	/maksad/	'purpose'
surat	/surat/	'face'

Turkish stems and suffixes tend to be highly changeable, even though the changes usually take place according to very regular rules. It will frequently be useful to use phonemic transcription to pin down the basic forms of words, in order to see more clearly exactly what changes are taking place.

2. Consonants

b, f, m, p, s, y, z These consonants are pronounced as in English.

c As English 'j' in 'judge'. English 'jazz' is caz in Turkish.

ç As English 'ch'. The English name Churchill is spelled Çörçil in Turkish.

j As English 'z' in 'azure' or 'g' in 'rouge'. This is the sound that is normally spelled 'j' in French (as in 'jour') or 'zh' in transliterations of Russian (as in 'Zhukov'). French 'jalousie' ('Venetian blind') is jaluzi in Turkish.

ş As English 'sh'. The English name Washington is spelled Vaşington in Turkish. In the poorly-designed IBM type face used here, the mark under ş looks like a comma; it should actually be a cedilla, the same mark that is used under ç.

v At the beginning of a word, v is pronounced as 'v' in English. In the middle or at the end of a word, the pronunciation of v varies from speaker to speaker, but in almost all cases it is "weaker" than English 'v'. After a vowel and before a consonant, v is frequently pronounced as a bilabial fricative: that is, it is formed by friction between the two lips (English 'v' is formed by friction between the upper teeth and lower lip). It is thus much like the Spanish 'b' in 'Habana'; it resembles English 'w' but is stronger and has more friction. Practice with a native speaker:

tavşan	'rabbit'
yavru	'young animal'
havlu	'towel'

Between vowels, v may be pronounced as the sound just described or as a sound closely approximating English 'w'. Between a and u, v may be pronounced as 'w' or may disappear entirely in colloquial speech. Practice with a native speaker:

övünmek	'boast'
dövüş	'fight'
tavuk	'chicken'
kavun	'melon'
Arnavut	'Albanian'
davul	'drum'

r This sound is made with tip of the tongue against the ridge behind the upper teeth, in approximately the position where English 't' is made. Between vowels, or after a consonant and before a vowel, r is either a single tap of the tongue against this ridge or a short trill. Practice with a native speaker:

kere	'time'
kara	'black'
kuru	'dry'
yavru	'young animal'
sivri	'pointed'

At the beginning of a word or before a consonant, r may also be a fricative, in which the tongue is held briefly close to the ridge and sound is formed by the air escaping through the resulting narrow passage. Practice with a native speaker:

ruh	'soul'
radyo	'radio'
renk	'color'
gırtlak	'throat'

Turkish r should not be pronounced like English 'r', which is a continuant: the tip of the tongue is held upright in the mouth, and a vowellike sound is produced. For Turkish r (and English 't') the tongue is considerably farther forward in the mouth than it is for English 'r'.

In final position, r is frequently unvoiced. Practice with a native speaker:

var	'there is'
bir	'one'
ver	'give'
Burdur	place name
gör	'see'

h The sound of English 'h' at the beginning of a word, as in 'here', is used for Turkish h not only at the beginning but also at the end of a word and between vowels. Medial h should therefore be pronounced as in English 'behind', not as in 'vehicle'; and you should be careful to avoid the English-speaking habit of ignoring h at the end of a word. Practice the following examples with a native speaker:

ruh	'soul'
siyah	'black'
Allah	'God'
tuhaf	'strange'
saha	'area'

In colloquial speech, h before a consonant is often elided, and a long vowel results. Practice with a native speaker:

kahve		'coffee'
Mehmet		proper name
kahvaltı		'breakfast'
mahsus	/máhsus/	'on purpose'

d, t Turkish d and t are made with the tip of the tongue against the back of the upper teeth. They therefore differ from English 't' and 'd', which are made with the tip of the tongue farther back, against the hard ridge behind the upper teeth.

n In most positions, n is pronounced like t and d, with the tongue immediately behind the upper teeth.
Before certain consonants, n assimilates to the following consonant. Before b and p, n is pronounced [m]. Practice with a native speaker:

penbe or pembe	'pink'
tenbel or tembel	'lazy'
İstanbul	place name
en büyük	'biggest' (when spoken as one word)

Before g and k, n is pronounced as the sound normally written 'ng' in English, as in 'sing'; it is therefore pronounced like English 'n' in 'sinker'. Practice:

renk	'color'
Ankara	place name
çünkü	'because'
en güzel	'prettiest' (when spoken as one word)

Before c and ç, n is pronounced like French 'gn' in 'campagne' or Spanish 'ñ' in 'mañana'. Practice:

pencere	'window'
dinç	'vigorous'
en çirkin	'ugliest' (when spoken as one word)

2.1. The letters k, g, and l

The Turkish letter k actually stands for two distinct sounds. One of these is the "front k" (as in English 'key'), found before or after front vowels (e, i, ö ü). The other is the "back k" (as in English 'cool'), found before or after back vowels (a, ı, o, u). The difference between these is most noticeable when the sound stands at the end of a word. Compare these pairs, as pronounced by a native speaker:

ek 'affix' (front k)
ak 'white' (back k)

ekmek 'bread'
çakmak 'cigarette lighter'

In the pairs below, the first word contains the front k, and the second word contains the back k:

kere 'time'
kara 'black'

kir 'dirt'
kır 'plain'

kürk 'fur'
kurt 'wolf'

In some words, the front k is found before the back vowels a or u; the vowel is then usually written with a circumflex accent. Compare:

kar 'snow' (back k)
kâr 'profit' (front k)

The spelling indicates the difference between these words with a mark over the vowel, although the difference is actually in the preceding consonant. Furthermore, the vowel following /k/ in words of this type is frequently long, and the circumflex accent interferes with the placing of a long mark. In transcription, therefore, we will indicate a front k before a back vowel with a special symbol: /k̭/. We will not bother to mark a front k before a front vowel, since its occurrence in this position is predictable. Practice the following words with a native speaker:

kâtip /k̭ātib/ 'secretary'
hikâye /hik̭āye/ 'story'

imkân	/imk̭an/	'possibility'
mefkûre	/mefk̭ūre/	'ideal'

The letter *g* also stands for two sounds in exactly the same way as does *k*. In the following pairs of words the first word contains the "front *g*," and the second word contains the "back *g*":

gece	'night'
gaga	'beak'
girdi	'entered'
gırtlak	'throat'

When front *g* stands before back *a* or *u*, the orthography uses a circumflex over the vowel, but we will transcribe it with the symbol /ĝ/. Compare:

gâvur	/ĝavur/	'infidel'
gaga		'beak'

(Remember to pronounce *v* like [w].)

The letter *l* also stands for two sounds, a front or "light *l*" with front vowels, and a back or "dark *l*" with back vowels. Compare the following pairs:

bel	'waist'
bal	'honey'
göl	'lake'
kol	'arm'
eşekler	'donkeys'
ayaklar	'feet'

Front *l* before *a* or *u* is indicated with a circumflex over the vowel; we shall transcribe it /ḽ/. At the beginning of a word, *l* is almost always front. Practice:

lâle	/ḽāle/	'tulip'

lâzım	/l̂āzım/	'necessary'
lûtfen	/l̂utfen/	'please'

Front /l̂/ can also appear at the end of a word, after a back vowel. Compare the following words, as spoken by a native speaker:

hal	/hal̂/	'condition'
bal		'honey'
kabul	/kabul̂/	'reception'
kul		'slave'

Turkish spelling has no way of indicating whether l at the end of a word is front or back. The presence of front /l̂/ in these words is important, however, not only for correct pronunciation but also because it affects the form of the suffixes that may be added. Phonemic transcription is therefore especially important in these cases.

2.2. Yumuşak ge

The Turkish letter g (that is, the two sounds /g/ and /ĝ/) is normally found only at the beginning of a word or after a consonant. The letter g does not occur after vowels or between vowels, except for a very short list of exceptions, mainly words of European origin (sigara 'cigarette', sigorta 'insurance', gaga 'beak'). What occurs instead of g in this position is the letter called yumuşak ge or "soft g"—the letter ğ. The sound that this letter represents is thus simply a variant of the phoneme /g/. Because its pronunciation is very different from the normal sound of the letter g, however, it was given a separate letter in the Turkish alphabet.

When ğ is between back vowels, it is not pronounced at all and should simply be ignored. The two vowels before and after it remain separate, however; they should not be merged. Practice with a native speaker:

ağaç	'tree'
ağır	'heavy'

uğur 'good luck'
soğuk 'cold'
doğar 'is born'
sığır 'ox'
sığar 'it fits'

After a back vowel, before a consonant, or at the end of a word, ğ is dropped, and the preceding vowel is lengthened. Practice:

dağ 'mountain'
tuğ 'banner'
çığ 'avalanche'
doğ 'be born'

doğru 'right'
tuğla 'brick'
bağla 'tie'
sığmak 'fit'

In some dialects, ğ between and after front vowels is treated in the same way as ğ with back vowels. In other dialects, it is pronounced as [y] in these positions. The two words in each pair below will therefore be pronounced in exactly the same way by some speakers but will differ for others.

eğer 'if'
eyer 'saddle'

öğle 'noon'
öyle 'thus'

Practice with a native speaker:

diğer 'other'
söğüt 'willow'
değirmen 'mill'

düğün	'wedding'
çiğ	'raw'
değ	'touch'
iğne	'needle'
öğren	'learn'
eğlen	'enjoy oneself'

Be sure to distinguish a long vowel, which arises when ğ is dropped before a consonant or at the end of a word, from a double vowel, which arises when ğ is dropped between two vowels. A long vowel is a single syllable, pronounced longer than a short vowel; a double vowel is a sequence of two short vowels and is two syllables. Compare:

dağ	[dā]	'mountain'
dağa	[daa]	'mountain (dat)'
da	[da]	'also'
düğme	[dǖme] or [düyme]	'button'
düğüme	[düüme] or [düyüme]	'knot (dat)'

In some Turkish dialects, especially in Anatolia, ğ does not drop but is pronounced as a velar fricative, that is, as a spirant made in the same tongue position as [g] but without complete closure. This is the same sound as γ in Modern Greek. This sound is not used in Standard Turkish.

2.3. Aspiration of Stops

In English, the stop consonants /p/, /t/, and /k/, when they occur at the end of a word after a vowel, may either be released or unreleased. A stop that is released, like the 't' in 'crypt', is followed by a small burst of air; an unreleased stop, like the 't' in 'butler', is not. The 't' in English 'bet' is optionally released (or "aspirated"); many speakers tend to release it when they pronounce the word in isolation but to leave it unreleased when they speak the word in a sentence.

In Turkish, however, the consonants p, t, and k (both varieties) must always be released in all positions.

3. Vowels

a As English 'a' in 'father' but somewhat shorter. Be sure to give the vowel this sound even when it appears at the end of a word; do not lengthen it, as in Pa, or pronounce it [ə] ('uh'). Practice:

baba	'father'
kara	'black'
boğa	'bull'
at	'horse'
baş	'head'

e As English 'e' in 'bet'. Be sure to give the vowel this sound even when it appears at the end of a word. Practice:

kere	'time'
gebe	'pregnant'
ne	'what'
beyaz	'white'

Before ğ, e has a sound more like French 'é', or English 'ay' but without the final [y] glide of this vowel. Practice:

eğer	'if'
beğen	'like'
değirmen	'mill'
değiş	'change'
eğlen	'enjoy'
değnek	'stick'

Another variant of _e_ is found in some dialects, especially in the speech of Istanbul, and more commonly in the speech of women than of men. This sound is similar to, but somewhat higher than, English 'a' of 'bat'. It is found in closed syllables (syllables ending in a consonant) before _l_, _m_, _n_, and _r_. Practice:

ben	'I'
gel	'come'
gelen	'coming'

(In _gelen_ the first vowel is a normal _e_, the second vowel a lowered _e_.)

_i_ As English 'i' in 'bit'.

bit	'louse'
siz	'you'
bin	'thousand'

English-speaking students should be particularly careful to give the vowel this sound even when it appears at the end of the word. In English, final /i/ (which is normally spelled 'y', as in 'city') is pronounced higher than medial /i/; it has the same quality as the 'i' of 'machine', but is slightly shorter. In Turkish, _i_ has the value of the first vowel of 'city' in all positions (except before _ğ_). Using a native speaker, compare the pronunciation of English 'city' with Turkish _gitti_ 'he went'. Practice also:

kedi	'cat'
gibi	'like'
yedi	'seven'
kişi	'person'
indi	'descended'

Before _ğ_, _i_ has a sound like French 'i', or the English 'i' of 'machine' but without a final [y] glide. Practice:

diğer	'other'
iğne	'needle'
iğri	'crooked'
çiğ	'raw'

ı This letter is an i without the dot. The corresponding capital letters are distinguished in the same way: the capital of ı is I, and the capital of i is İ. I is a high, unrounded, back vowel, somewhat similar to the English 'i' of 'fir' but without r coloring. It is also similar to the somewhat elusive sound of the second vowel of 'roses'. Try pronouncing u with the lips unrounded and drawn as far back as possible. Practice:

kız	'girl'
altı	'six'
kısım	'part'

Learn to distinguish ı from i with the following pairs:

çiğ	'raw'
çığ	'avalanche'
sinir	'nerve'
sınır	'border'

o In an open syllable and before ğ, o is pronounced like English 'o' in 'note' but without the slight [w] glide of this vowel. Practice:

boğa	'bull'
soğuk	'cold'
doğru	'right'
olur	'becomes'
hoca	'teacher'
oda	'room'

In a closed syllable, o has the sound of the vowels of English 'law' or 'ought' but considerably shorter. Practice:

ot	'grass'
on	'ten'
çok	'much'
hoş	'agreeable'

ö This is the front rounded vowel of French 'peur'; it is distinctly lower than the vowel of French 'peu'. If you do not have experience with this vowel in French or German, try pronouncing Turkish e with the lips rounded.

dört	'four'
göz	'eye'
köy	'village'

u In open syllables not at the end of a word, and before ğ, u is pronounced like 'oo' of English 'boot' but shorter and without the final [w] glide.

uzak	'far'
tuhaf	'strange'
buğday	'wheat'

In closed syllables and at the end of a word, this vowel has the sound of English 'u' in 'put'.

su	'water'
buz	'ice'
kuru	'dry'
nutuk	'speech'
uzun	'long'

ü This is Turkish i with the lips rounded; it is distinctly lower than the vowel of French 'pu'.

üzüm	'grape'

yüz	'hundred'
üç	'three'
ütü	'iron'

3.1. Long vowels

Turkish has four long vowels /ā/, /ē/, /ī/, and /ū/, which are distinctively different from the corresponding short vowels. The presence of the long vowels is not normally indicated in Turkish spelling, although in some cases a circumflex accent may be used. We will indicate these vowels in transcription with a long mark.

Long /ā/ is pronounced as a lengthened version of Turkish a, like English 'a' in 'Pa'; long /ē/ is pronounced as a lengthened version of Turkish e, like English 'e' in bed' but slightly longer. Long /ī/ is pronounced like the vowel of English 'beet' but without the final [y] glide; long /ū/ is pronounced like the vowel of English 'boot' but without the final [w] glide.

Compare the following pairs with the aid of a native speaker:

sakin	/sākin/	'quiet'
sakın		'beware'
memur	/mēmur/	'official'
meme		'breast'
iman	/īman/	'faith'
imam		'imam'
suret	/sūret/	'manner'
surat		'face'

Practice also:

mavi	/māvi/	'blue'
imza	/imzā/	'signature'
ilân	/īlan/	'notice'

ciddî	/ciddī/	'serious'
itibar	/ītibar/	'esteem'
mevzu	/mevzū/	'topic'
malûmat	/māḽūmat/	'information'

4. Accent

There is no doubt that accent plays a distinctive role in Turkish, since there are many pairs of words that are distinguished from each other only by the placement of accent. There is much less agreement about the precise phonetic nature of Turkish accent. In English, accent consists of dynamic stress, together with a rise in pitch on the stressed syllable. In Turkish, accent seems to consist of a rise in pitch on the accented syllable alone, without the accompanying increase in force that is characteristic of English. Compare the following pairs with the aid of a native speaker:

adamím		'my man'
adámım		'I am a man'
gitmé		'going'
gítme		'don't go'
vardí		'he arrived'
várdı		'he existed'
razí	/rāzí/	'willing'
bázı	/bā́zı/	'some'

The general rule is that accent is on the last syllable of a word; assume, therefore, that accent is on the last syllable unless told otherwise. There are numerous exceptions to this rule. Some of these exceptions are grammatically conditioned and will have to be discussed later.

Other exceptions are particular: there are some words with exceptional, "inherent" accent on some syllable other than the last. For example:

évet	'yes'
háyır	'no'
násıl	'how?'
yálnız	'only'
lokánta	'restaurant'
mása	'table'

Inherent accent will be indicated in transcription; thus we would transcribe the word masa as /mása/.

When suffixes are added to a regular noun, the suffixes are accented; that is, the general rule that accent is on the last syllable is obeyed:

odá	'room'
odalár	'rooms'
odalardá	'in the rooms'

But when suffixes are added to a noun with inherent accent, the accent remains in place on the stem, although there may be a slight secondary accent on the last syllable:

mása	'table'
másalar	'tables'
másalarda	'on the tables'

5. Summary of the alphabet

Turkish alphabetical order corresponds to that of English. The "dotted letters" are each added immediately after the corresponding undotted letter. Thus ç follows c, ğ follows g, ö follows o, ş follows s, and ü follows u. Notice especially that i is considered to be the dotted correspondent of ı; therefore, i follows ı in Turkish alphabetical order.

The spoken names of the letters are, for vowels, the sound of the vowel, and for consonants, the consonant followed by e: thus a, be, ce, çe, etc.

The following table gives the Turkish letters, the corresponding international phonetic symbol, and the English letter that most frequently corresponds to the sound of the Turkish letter.

Turkish	Phonetic	English
a	a	a
b	b	b
c	ǰ	j
ç	č	ch
d	d	d
e	e	e
f	f	f
g	g	g
ğ	(see text)	—
h	h	h
ı	ɨ	—
i	i	i
j	ž	zh
k	k	k
l	l	l
m	m	m
n	n	n
o	o	o
ö	ö	—
p	p	p
r	r	r
s	s	s
ş	š	sh
t	t	t
u	u	u

Turkish	Phonetic	English
ü	ü	—
v	v	v
y	y	y
z	z	z

EXERCISES

Practice the following words, with a native speaker if possible:

A.

kal	'stay'	böl	'divide'
kel	'bald'	kör	'blind'
kıl	'hair'	gül	'rose'
kil	'clay'	göl	'lake'
kül	'ashes'	gel	'come'
kul	'slave'	gar	'station'
kol	'arm'		

B.

renk	'color'	kalp /kaḽp/	'heart'
zamk	'glue'	kalp	'counterfeit'
zevk	'pleasure'	sulh /suḽh/	'peace'
kalk	'get up'	tarz	'manner'
park	'park'	ölç	'measure'
köşk	'villa'	harç	'fee'
aşk	'love'	ört	'cover'
zarf	'envelope'	art	'back'

C.

oda	'room'	odda	'fire (loc)'
keçe	'felt'	geççe	'little late'
kafa	'head'	affa	'amnesty (dat)'

takı	'affix'	hakkı	'his right'
eli	'his hand'	elli	'fifty'
yere	'place (dat)'	zerre	'particle'
kese	'pouch'	hisse	'share'
katı	'solid'	kattı	'he combined'
eve	'house (dat)'	evvel	'before'

D.

yağlı	'greasy'	yalı	'villa'
dağlı	'mountainous'	dalı	'its branch'
iğri	'crooked'	iri	'big'
düğmen	'your button'	dümen	'steering wheel'

E.

dağ	'mountain'	dağa	'mountain (dat)'
tığ	'needle'	tığı	'his needle'
sat	'sell'	saat	'hour'
buğ	'leader'	buğu	'steam'
tuğ	'banner'	tuğu	'his banner'

LESSON 2: VOWEL HARMONY

The following table gives the objective and dative case forms of certain Turkish nouns. Study these endings:

Nominative	Objective	Dative	Meaning
el	eli	ele	'hand'
it	iti	ite	'dog'
göz	gözü	göze	'eye'
kül	külü	küle	'ashes'
at	atı	ata	'horse'
kız	kızı	kıza	'girl'
kol	kolu	kola	'arm'
kul	kulu	kula	'slave'

Turkish suffixes change according to the rules of vowel harmony, which have the effect of causing the vowels of a word to assimilate to one another. In order to understand how vowel harmony works, it is first necessary to analyze the Turkish vowel system.

1. The Turkish vowel system

Try pronouncing the (Turkish) vowels i, e, a, o, u in sequence, concentrating your attention on your tongue as you do so. You should notice that the tongue moves steadily backward during the pronunciation of this sequence; it is well forward in the mouth for i, well back in the mouth for u. Vowels made with the tongue in the front of the mouth are called "front vowels"; those made with the tongue in the back of the mouth are called "back vowels." Turkish has four front and four back vowels, matched in pairs as follows:

Front	Back
e	a
i	ı
ö	o
ü	u

Pronounce the pairs i-e, ı-a, or u-o, concentrating your attention on your tongue; you should notice that for the first member of each of these pairs (i, ı, u) the tongue is close to the roof of the mouth, the jaw is high, and the mouth relatively closed, while for the second member (e, a, o) the tongue and jaw are low, and the mouth is relatively open. Vowels made with the tongue high and close to the roof of the mouth are called "high vowels"; those made with the tongue low and jaw open are called "low vowels." Turkish has four high and four low vowels, matched in pairs as follows:

High	Low
i	e
ı	a
u	o
ü	ö

Pronounce the pairs i-u or a-o, concentrating your attention on your pronunciation; you should notice that for the first member of each of these pairs (i, a) the lips are drawn back, while for the second member (u, o) the lips are forward and rounded. Vowels made with the lips forward and rounded are called "rounded vowels"; those made with the lips drawn back are called "unrounded vowels." Turkish has four rounded and four unrounded vowels, matched in pairs as follows:

Rounded	Unrounded
o	a
ö	e
u	ı
ü	i

The system can be summed up with a diagram in the

form of a cube. In Figure 1, we have put front vowels in the front of the cube, high vowels on top, and rounded vowels to the right.

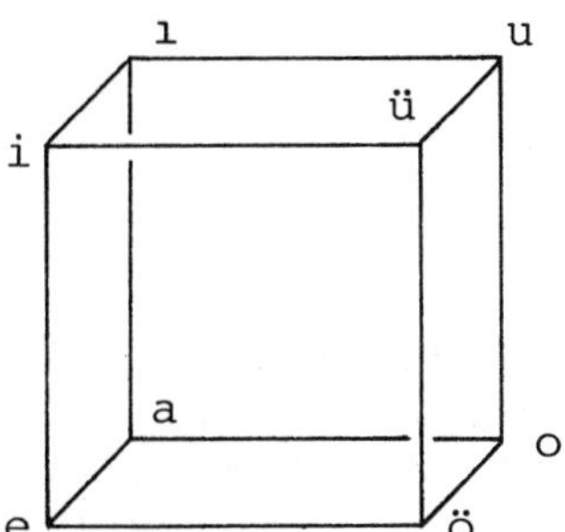

Figure 1

2. Vowel harmony rules

Any one of the eight Turkish vowels may appear in the first syllable of a word. But each following vowel is conditioned by the vowel immediately preceding it, according to these rules:

A. The following vowel assimilates to the preceding vowel in frontness; that is, front vowels must be followed by front vowels, and back vowels must be followed by back vowels.
B. A following high vowel assimilates to the preceding vowel in rounding; that is, high vowels are rounded after a rounded vowel, unrounded after an unrounded vowel.
C. A following low vowel must be unrounded; that is, *o* and *ö* may not appear in any syllable except the first in a Turkish word.

If we work out the possibilities, it turns out that after any given Turkish vowel, there are only two vowels that may appear in the following syllable:

Preceding Vowel	Following Vowel
e	e, i
i	e, i

Preceding Vowel	Following Vowel
ö	e, ü
ü	e, ü
a	a, ı
ı	a, ı
o	a, u
u	a, u

That is, the following vowel may be "low" (e or a according to the circumstances) or "high" (i, ı, u, or ü according to circumstances). For suffixes, we need to state merely whether the vowel is high or low. For example, the objective suffix is a high vowel, alternating according to the environment, while the dative suffix is a low vowel.

We shall henceforth use the symbols E and I in the transcription of suffixes. The symbol E stands for the alternation between e and a; I stands for the alternation between i, ı, u, and ü. Thus, if we write a certain suffix -Er, the suffix has the form -er or -ar depending on the environment; while if we write another suffix -sIn, the suffix has the form -sin, -sın, -sun, or -sün depending on the environment.

3. Exceptions to vowel harmony rules

There are many Turkish words that do not obey the rules of vowel harmony. Some of these are borrowed from Arabic or Persian, for example, memur (/mēmur/) 'official' or insan 'person'. Others are of European origin, such as kamyon 'truck' or otobüs 'bus'. But suffixes attached to these words are still conditioned by the immediately preceding vowel, that is, by the last vowel of the stem:

Nominative	Objective
memur	memuru
insan	insanı
kamyon	kamyonu
otobüs	otobüsü

In addition, there are nonharmonic suffixes, whose vowel does not alternate. For example, the verbal progressive suffix -*Iyor* has a harmonic *I* in the first syllable but an invariable *o* in the second.

geliyor	'he is coming'
açıyor	'he is opening'
duruyor	'he is standing'
gülüyor	'he is laughing'

Because vowel harmony in Turkish progresses strictly from syllable to syllable, the invariable *o* in this suffix conditions back rounded harmony in any vowels that follow: *geliyorsunuz* 'You are coming'.

Finally, there are some nouns that contain back vowels but require front vowel suffixes. Among these are all nouns that end in front *l* (/l̂/): *kabul* 'reception', objective *kabulü*, dative *kabul̂e*. Others cannot be predicted in any regular fashion: *saat* 'hour', objective *saati*; *harf* 'letter', dative *harfe*. Whenever words of the latter group are introduced in this grammar, we shall use the notation (-*i*) following the word in the vocabulary.

EXERCISES

A. The plural suffix in Turkish is -*lEr*: *et* 'meat', *etler* 'meats'. Make the plural of the following nouns:

1. gül 'rose'
2. yer 'place'
3. yan 'side'
4. söz 'word'
5. son 'end'
6. zil 'bell'
7. kıl 'hair'
8. kuş 'bird'
9. köprü 'bridge'
10. köpek 'dog'
11. çocuk 'child'

12. hayvan 'animal'

13. radyo 'radio'

14. otomobil 'automobile'

15. politika 'politics'

16. kitap 'book'

17. cumhuriyet 'republic'

B. The suffix -*sIz* is added to nouns to form adjectives meaning 'without': *et* 'meat', *etsiz* 'without meat'. Make the -*sIz*-form of all the nouns in Exercise A.

C. The following nouns are cited both in spelling and in transcription. Make both the plural and the -*sIz*-forms of each:

1. hal	/haḽ/	'condition'
2. mal	/mal/	'property'
3. kıral	/kıral/	'king'
4. hayal	/hayaḽ/	'fantasy'
5. yol	/yol/	'road'
6. rol	/roḽ/	'role'
7. okul	/okul/	'school'
8. usul	/usuḽ/	'method'
9. sual	/suaḽ/	'question'

LESSON 3: BASIC SENTENCE PATTERNS 

Study the following sentences:

Ben açım (or: Açım)	'I am hungry'
Sen tembelsin (or: Tembelsın)	'You are lazy'
O yorgundur or yorgun	'He (she, it) is tired'
Biz hastayız (or: Hastayız)	'We are sick'
Siz çalışkansınız (or: Çalışkansınız)	'You are hardworking'
Onlar kötüdürler, kötüdür, kötüler	'They are bad'
Orhan iyidir or iyi	'Orhan is well (or good)
Adam tembeldir or tembel	'The man is lazy'
Kızlar hoştur or hoş	'The girls are pleasant'
Atlar yorgundur or yorgun	'The horses are tired'

1. Variation in suffixes: buffer consonants

Many suffixes in Turkish vary in form according to whether they are attached to a vowel or a consonant. In general, two vowels may not come together in Turkish, except in some loan words and except in the case where ğ drops out between vowels. When a suffix basically beginning in a vowel is to be attached to a preceding vowel, either one of the vowels drops out, or a consonant ("buffer consonant") is inserted between the two vowels. This consonant is nearly always y.

For example, the suffix meaning 'I am' has the form -Im after a consonant, but the form -yIm after a vowel. Compare:

aç	'hungry'	açım	'I am hungry'
hasta	'sick'	hastayım	'I am sick'
tembel	'lazy'	tembelim	'I am lazy'
iyi	'good'	iyiyim	'I am good (well)'
yorgun	'tired'	yorgunum	'I am tired'
kötü	'bad'	kötüyüm	'I am bad'

We can transcribe this suffix as -(y)Im, where the (y) in parentheses is present after a vowel but drops after a consonant.

2. Variation in suffixes: consonant harmony

The initial consonant of some suffixes assimilates to the preceding consonant with respect to voicing; that is, if the suffix is attached to a voiceless consonant, the suffix-initial consonant becomes voiceless, while if the suffix is attached to a voiced consonant or vowel, the suffix-initial consonant is voiced. The voiceless consonants are ç, f, h, k, p, s, ş, and t; all others are voiced.

For example, the suffix meaning 'he is' (more or less) has the form -tIr after a voiceless consonant but -dIr after a voiced consonant or a vowel. Compare the following examples:

aç	'hungry'	açtır	'he is hungry'
çalışkan	'hardworking'	çalışkandır	'he is hardworking'
hasta	'sick'	hastadır	'he is sick'
hoş	'pleasant'	hoştur	'he is pleasant'
yorgun	'tired'	yorgundur	'he is tired'

There are also suffixes that begin with k after a voiceless consonant but g elsewhere; and suffixes that begin with ç after a voiceless consonant but c elsewhere.

We shall use the symbol D for the alternation between d and t, the symbol G for the alternation between k and g, and the symbol C for the alternation between ç and c. Thus we can transcribe this suffix -DIr, where the D is realized as d or t depending on the nature of the preceding phoneme.

3. Basic sentence patterns

The sentence Orhan iyidir 'Orhan is well' contains three elements, which are the three basic elements of the Turkish sentence; each of these three must be present (sometimes implicitly) in every sentence. These are: subject (Orhan), predicate (iyi), and what we may

(to be)
call an auxiliary (-dir). It may be useful to represent this information graphically, as in Figure 2.

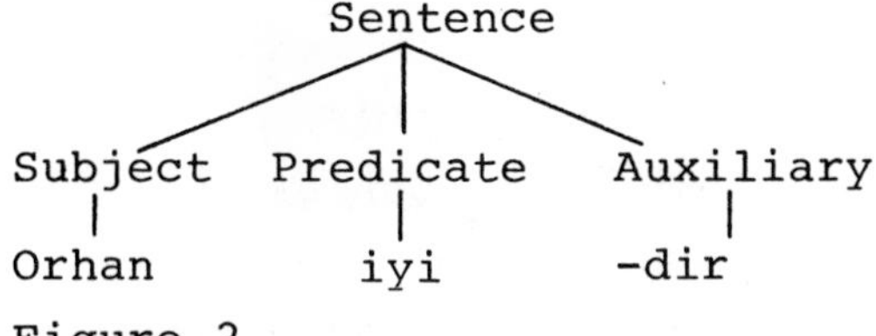

Figure 2

The auxiliary has a function roughly similar to the English verb 'to be' in such sentences as 'George is hungry', 'George is at home', 'George is running'. We may say that it links the subject with the predicate and is necessary for a complete sentence. In Turkish, this element is not a separate word but is a suffix or group of suffixes attached to the predicate.

We shall see later that the auxiliary can be quite complex and can consist of a number of elements. At the moment, however, we are interested only in the personal endings, or suffixes that indicate the person and number of the subject. These are:

'I'	-(y)Im	'we'	-(y)Iz
'you (sg)'	-sIn	'you (pl)'	-sInIz
'he, she, it'	(-DIr)	'they'	(-DIr)(lEr)

In all the sentences in this lesson, the predicate is an adjective (hasta, iyi, etc.). We shall see later that the predicate can be one of a number of things, such as a noun or one of several types of adverbial construction. All of these are sentences where English would have some form of the verb 'be' (such as 'Orhan is a fool', 'Orhan is on the fence'). We shall see that the predicate can also be a verb; in such cases, however, the sentence construction is slightly different. We shall therefore find it useful to speak of two types of sentences: those in which the predicate is a verb ("verbal sentences") and those, like the sentences in this lesson, where it is something else ("nonverbal sentences").

4. Pronouns

The Turkish pronouns are the following:

'I'	ben	'we'	biz
'you (sg)'	sen	'you (pl)'	siz
'he, she, it'	o	'they'	onlar

Turkish has no grammatical gender, that is, no distinction between 'he', 'she', and 'it', and the pronoun o serves for all three.

We have used the traditional terms "singular" and "plural" for sen and siz, although the difference between them is actually similar to that between French tu and vous, or German du and Sie. Sen, along with the corresponding personal ending -sIn, is used for close friends and relatives, children, servants, and inferiors, and for only one person; siz, along with the corresponding personal ending -sInIz, is used for more distant acquaintances, superiors, strangers, and people to whom one wishes to be polite, and is used for two or more people of any type. Turkish sen is probably used more frequently than French tu or German du, since Turks tend to use the familiar forms more readily.

In a sentence such as (Ben) iyiyim 'I am well', the pronoun ben is unnecessary, since the suffix -yim indicates the person and number of the subject adequately. The pronoun may therefore be omitted; İyiyim is a grammatical sentence by itself. In colloquial speech, the pronoun would almost invariably be omitted from sentences of this type. It may be present, however, for stylistic reasons, notably for emphasis—for example, if there is a contrast between two subjects:

Ben iyiyim, amma sen hastasın	'I am well, but you are sick'

5. The suffix -DIr

The suffix -DIr is a complicated element, and it is probably best to postpone a detailed discussion of its uses. Although it may be used with suffixes of any person, it is most common with the third person ('he, she, it') and for the moment may be considered as a third person suffix. It is used when the speaker wishes to emphasize the truth or definiteness of the statement. One common use is for statements of general validity:

Atlar tembeldir	'Horses are lazy' (a general statement about horses)
Atlar tembel	'The horses are lazy' (at the moment)

The suffix -DIr is common in written or newspaper Turkish but relatively much less common in the colloquial language.

6. Plurals

The suffix -lEr, added after the noun, forms the plural.

at	'horse'	atlar	'horses'
adam	'man'	adamlar	'men'

It may follow -DIr to form a third person plural ending. There is a tendency, however, to omit this suffix wherever it is not felt to be necessary. In general, if the subject is animate, and especially human, -lEr is used, while if the subject is inanimate, the suffix is omitted.

When the predicate is an adjective, -lEr is rare unless preceded by -DIr; thus Yorgundurlar is preferable to Yorgunlar for 'They are tired'. If -lEr is present on the subject, it may not be repeated in the auxiliary unless -DIr precedes:

Kızlar çalışkan	'The girls are hardworking'
Kızlar çalışkandırlar	'Girls are hardworking'

But we cannot have *Kızlar çalışkanlar.

In a compound sentence, -lEr may be omitted from the first predicate but present in the second; the same is also true of -DIr:

At çalışkan, amma yorgundur	'The horse is industrious, but tired'

Atlar çalışkan, amma yorgundurlar	'Horses are industrious, but tired'

7. Accent: unaccented suffixes

We said in Lesson 1 that accent falls on the last syllable of a word unless we have an exception. One group of exceptions includes the "unaccented suffixes," which may not be accented and which normally come at the end of the word. When one of these is present, accent falls on the syllable immediately preceding the unaccented suffix—that is, on the last possible syllable.

As a general rule, to be slightly modified later, all suffixes that are part of the auxiliary are unaccented. Therefore, when one of the personal endings of Section 3 (except -lEr) is used, accent falls on the last vowel of the predicate:

yorgúnum	'I am tired'
tembéliz	'We are lazy'
hastásınız	'You are sick'

Note that -lEr, the plural suffix, is accented normally even when it is used as a personal ending, although -DIr is unaccented:

hoşlár	'They are pleasant'
hóşturlar	'They are pleasant'

8. Usage

In this section, in each lesson, we will discuss some particular problems of usage of the words introduced in the lesson.

When ama 'but' (/áma/) is pronounced with strong emphasis, it comes out amma (/ámma/).

İyi corresponds to English 'good' in the general sense and 'well' in reference to health. Thus İyiyim 'I am well' is an answer to the question 'How are you?' But kötü means only 'bad' in a general sense or in reference to character; it cannot be used for 'unwell', which is fena.

Hoş corresponds to 'pleasant, nice, agreeable' and may be used of persons or objects, especially places.

It may also be used for 'attractive' in reference to people.

Kız usually means 'girl', but with a possessive suffix it means 'daughter'.

VOCABULARY

aç		hungry
adam		man
ama, amma	/áma, ámma/	but
at		horse
çalışkan		hardworking, industrious
hasta		sick
hoş		pleasant, nice, agreeable (see "Usage")
iyi		good, well (see "Usage")
kız		girl, daughter (see "Usage")
kötü		bad
Orhan		man's name
tembel		lazy
yorgun		tired

EXERCISES

A. Translate into English:

1. Açız.
2. Tembelsin.
3. Hastadırlar.
4. İyisiniz.
5. Kötüdür.
6. Kızlar hoş.
7. Adamlar çalışkan, ama yorgun.
8. Orhan tembeldir.

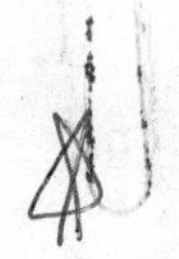

9. Adamlar hasta, ama kızlar iyidir

B. Translate into Turkish:

1. You (pl) are nice.
2. We are tired.
3. You (sg) are lazy.
4. She is hungry.
5. I am hardworking.
6. We are well.
7. They are tired.
8. You (pl) are bad.
9. The girl is sick but hungry.
10. I am sick.
11. The men are good, but Orhan is bad.

LESSON 4: THE NOUN PHRASE AND NEGATIVES

Study the following sentences:

Büyüğüm	'I am big'
Biz Türküz	'We are Turks'
Küçük çocuk daima hasta	'The small child is always sick'
Sen genç bir çocuksun	'You are a young man'
Büyük adam, eski bir kâtiptir	'The big man is a former clerk'
Mehmet kasap değil	'Mehmet is not a butcher'
Küçük köpek aç değil	'The little dog is not hungry'
Mehmet hoş bir adam değil	'Mehmet is not a pleasant man'
Ağaçlar büyük değil, küçüktür	'The trees are small, not large'
Gençler değil, ihtiyarlar yorgundur	'The old people, not the young people, are tired'
Müdür çalışkan, fakat ben değilim	'The director is industrious, but I am not'

1. The noun phrase

The subject of a sentence in Turkish may be:
A. a pronoun:

Ben gencim	'I am young'

B. a single noun:

Ağaç büyüktür	'The tree is big'
Orhan Türktür	'Orhan is a Turk'

C. a construction with a noun as principal member:

Küçük çocuk yorgundur	'The small child is tired'
Küçük bir çocuk daima yorgundur	'A small child is always tired'

Constructions of these three types—that is, anything that can serve as the subject of a sentence—are called noun phrases.

1.1. Definite and indefinite nouns

In Turkish, as in English, we can distinguish three uses of the noun: generic ('Man is mortal'), definite ('The man was late'), and indefinite ('A man is at the door'). When a noun is the subject of a sentence, however, there is no grammatical distinction between the generic and definite uses, since Turkish does not have a definite article corresponding to English 'the':

Atlar çalışkandır	'Horses are hardworking' 'The horses are hardworking'
Küçük çocuklar tembeldir	'Small children are lazy' 'The small children are lazy'

The word for 'one', bır, is frequently found in indefinite uses corresponding to English 'a':

Bir köpek açtır	'A dog is hungry'

The correspondence is only partial, however, since bir is still basically the number 'one'; we shall show later that there are many cases where English would use 'a' but where Turkish does not use bir.

1.2. Adjectives

When an adjective modifies a noun, it precedes that noun, as in English; but if there is a bir before the noun, the adjective precedes bir:

eski ağaç	'the old tree'
iyi adam	'the good man'
eski bir ağaç	'an old tree'
iyi bir adam	'a good man'

Some adjectives can be used as nouns. In such a case, the noun 'person' should always be understood or, if the adjective is followed by -lEr, the noun 'people'.

Küçük hoştur	'The small one (small person) is pleasant'
Gençler tembeldir	'The young people are lazy'

Some adjectives frequently used in this way have acquired an idiomatic meaning:

hasta	'patient (sick person)'
büyükler	'grown-ups (big people)'
ihtiyar	'old man (or woman)'

1.3. Noun phrases as predicates

In English, when a noun is used as the predicate of a sentence, it is customary to use the article 'a', as in 'Mehmet is a butcher'. In Turkish, however, it is customary to omit bir and use simply the noun.

Mehmet kasaptır	'Mehmet is a butcher'

If bir is included, its use places more emphasis on the statement. This emphasis may be favorable or unfavorable, depending on the nature of the statement. Thus, while the preceding sentence is simply a statement of Mehmet's profession, the following sentence underscores the fact that he is a butcher and nothing else; if butcher is considered to be a lowly occupation, it means that he is a butcher and nothing more.

Mehmet bir kasaptır	'Mehmet is (just) a butcher'

Compare also:

Ben adamım	'I am a man'
Ben bir adamım	

The first of these means simply 'I am a man'; the second emphasizes that I am a man and not an animal.

If the noun phrase includes an adjective, however, the normal usage is reversed; in this case it is normal to include bir, although it may be omitted. The first of the following two possibilities would therefore be more common:

Ben büyük bir adamım	'I am a big man'
Ben büyük adamım	

A noun phrase used as predicate is always singular even if the subject is plural. Thus:

Biz kasabız	'We are butchers' (not *kasaplarız)
Onlar kasaptır or kasaptırlar	'They are butchers' (not *kasaplardır)

Do not be misled by the fact that the predicate is plural in English.

2. The negative

The negative of nonverbal sentences is made with the word değil, pronounced either /deil/ or /diil/. Değil follows the predicate as a separate word, and personal endings are attached to it. Accent is on the last syllable of değil.

Ben yorgun değílim	'I am not tired'
Siz çalışkan değílsiniz	'You are not hardworking'
Orhan iyi değil or değildir	'Orhan is not well'
Genç kâtipler hasta değil (değildir, değiller, değildirler)	'The young clerks are not sick'

Değil may also be placed in the middle of a sentence; in this case, it has the effect of negating the word or phrase immediately before it.

Çocuklar değil, kızlar calışkandır	'The girls, not the children, are hardworking'
Ben değil, siz çalışkansınız	'You, not I, are hardworking'
Atlar küçük değil, büyüktür	'The horses are big, not small'

3. Variation in stems: final voiced stops

In Turkish, the voiced stops b, d, and c may not appear at the end of a word; furthermore, in words of Turkic origin these consonants may not appear in the middle of a word before another consonant. Many words and stems, however, end basically in one of these consonants. When the word stands alone without a suffix, or when a suffix beginning with a consonant is added, the final stop changes to its unvoiced counterpart: b becomes p, d becomes t, and c becomes ç. When a suffix beginning with a vowel is added, however, the basic voiced stop is retained.

For example, the word for 'butcher' is basically /kasab/; when the word stands alone, however, it appears as kasap. The plural is kasaplar; but in 'I am a butcher' the basic /b/ appears before the vowel: kasabım. Compare this word with top 'ball', basically /top/ with a final /p/, which appears in all forms: toplar 'balls', topum 'I am a ball'.

Similarly, the adjective genç 'young' is basically /genc/, with a final /c/, which appears in gencim 'I am young'; while aç 'hungry' ends in /ç/, as in açım 'I am hungry'.

Remembering from Lesson 2 that the objective case suffix is -I after a consonant, compare the subject and object forms of the following nouns:

Nominative	Objective	Meaning
kitap	kitabı	'book'
top	topu	'ball'
Mehmet	Mehmedi	name
sepet	sepeti	'basket'
armut	armudu	'pear'
at	atı	'horse'
ağaç	ağacı	'tree'
saç	saçı	'hair'

It is important to notice that in many cases the basic form of a Turkish word is not the form in which the word appears in isolation—not, for example, the form in which you would find the word in the dictionary. If you were to find in a dictionary the word kâtip 'clerk', you would still be unable to say 'I am a clerk', since the form could be either kâtipim or kâtibim. If you were given the word in transcription as /k̂ātib/, however, you would know that 'I am a clerk' is kâtibim and also that the word in isolation must be kâtip. For this reason, whenever a word ends basically in /b/, /d/, or /c/, we shall give the word in the vocabulary both in spelling and in transcription.

3.1. Final g

The phoneme g is also a voiced stop and also may not appear at the end of a word or before another consonant. The alternations that it undergoes, however, are somewhat different.

At the end of a word after a consonant, g becomes k under the same conditions that b becomes p, and so forth. Thus /reng/ 'color' appears as renk alone, renkler in the plural, but rengi in the objective case. Compare this with Türk 'Turk', Türkler, Türkü.

After a vowel, g again becomes k, but remains /g/ when a suffix beginning with a vowel is added. We have seen, however, that the sound represented by g does not appear between vowels; what we get instead is the letter ğ, which represents a sound that we know to be another variant of the phoneme /g/.

Thus we have çocuk 'child', basically /çocug/, plural çocuklar, but çocuğum 'I am a child'; also büyük 'big', basically /büyüg/, plural büyükler, but büyüğüm 'I am big'.

Any word of more than one syllable that is found in the dictionary with final k almost always ends basically with /g/. For this reason, we will normally not need to indicate final /g/ in transcription: if you see, for example, the word küçük 'small', you can assume that its basic form is /küçüg/. On the other hand, words of one syllable with final k normally really end in /k/. There are three one-syllable words with final /g/: çok (/çog/) 'much', gök (/gög/) 'sky', and yok (/yog/) 'nonexistent'.

3.2. Additional notes on final stops

There are a few words that are sometimes actually pronounced with a final voiced stop. These include ad 'name', öd 'bile', uc 'end', hac 'pilgrimage', and ab 'water'. Individual speakers will vary widely in their treatment of these words: some speakers will pronounce all of them with a voiced stop, others will substitute the corresponding voiceless stop in all cases, and others will pronounce some of these words with a voiced stop and others with an unvoiced stop.

Notice that the rule requiring final stops to be unvoiced takes precedence, so to speak, over the rule of Lesson 3, Section 2, stating that initial consonants become unvoiced when attached to an unvoiced consonant. For example, consider the form for 'It is a book':

Basic form: kitab + Dır

b becomes p before a consonant: kitap + Dır

D becomes t after p: kitaptır

3.3. A note on spelling

When suffixes are added to a proper noun, an apostrophe is sometimes written after the stem; in addition, if the final consonant of the stem changes, either the voiced or voiceless consonant may be written. Thus the objective of Mehmet may be written Mehmedi, Mehmed'i, or Mehmet'i, although it is always pronounced /mehmedi/. Suffixes are always written in the form in which they are pronounced, thus the objective of Fatma is Fatma'yı.

4. Usage

Eski corresponds to English 'old' when used to describe things but to 'former' when used to describe people: eski müdür 'the former director'. 'Old' for people is only ihtiyar: ihtiyar müdür 'the old director'.

A çocuk in Turkish may be older than a 'child' in English; the word çocuk may be used of young people, especially young men, up to their twenties. Thus we have küçük çocuk 'small child' but genç çocuk 'young man'.

Fakat and *ama* (*amma*) both mean 'but' and are more or less interchangeable. Pairs of words meaning the same thing are quite common in Turkish; the reason is that the Turkish vocabulary is drawn from many different sources, and there may frequently be an Arabic and a Turkic word, or a European and a Turkic word, either meaning exactly the same thing or differing only slightly in meaning or usage. *İhtiyar* (Arabic) and *yaşlı* (Turkic) are another such pair; both mean 'old' and are used for people or animals. *İhtiyar* can be used without a noun in the idiomatic meaning 'old man'; *yaşlı* may be used only with a noun following.

VOCABULARY

ağaç	/agac/	tree
büyük		big
çocuk		child
daima	/dā́imā/	always
eski		old; former
fakat	/fákat/	but
genç	/genc/	young
ihtiyar		old
kasap	/kasab/	butcher
kâtip	/k̭ātib/	clerk
köpek		dog
küçük		small
Mehmet	/Mehmed/	man's name
müdür		director
Türk		Turk
yaşlı		old

EXERCISES

A. Translate into English:

1. İyi bir kâtipsiniz.
2. Hasta, adamdır.

3. Orhan kâtip değil, kasaptır.
4. Atlar yorgun, fakat köpekler yorgun değil.
5. Sen çalışkan değil, tembelsin.

B. Translate into Turkish:

1. Old trees are large.
2. Mehmet is a young Turk.
3. The young person is sick.
4. The large horse is not hungry.
5. The old dog is always hungry.
6. The little ones are not tired.
7. Orhan is a clerk, not a director.
8. You (sg) are a man, not a child.
9. The men, not the girls, are lazy.
10. He is a small child, but she is a big girl.

C. Translate into Turkish:

We are ...

1. ... bad
2. ... big
3. ... children
4. ... clerks
5. ... girls
6. ... hardworking
7. ... men
8. ... small
9. ... Turks
10. ... young

D. Give the objective case form of the following nouns and adjectives:

1. ak 'white'

2. bacak 'leg'
3. dik 'upright'
4. ek 'affix'
5. eşek 'donkey'
6. ıslak 'wet'
7. kelebek 'butterfly'
8. ok 'arrow'
9. parlak 'shiny'
10. tek 'solitary'

E. The following nouns are cited in transcription; give the nominative form of each in Turkish spelling and the plural and objective case forms of each:

1. /çöp/ 'trash'
2. /cevab/ 'answer'
3. /derd/ 'pain'
4. /dib/ 'bottom'
5. /harc/ 'expense'
6. /kat/ 'layer'
7. /koç/ 'ram'
8. /kuvvet/ 'strength'
9. /söğüd/ 'willow'
10. /uc/ 'tip'

LESSON 5: THE DEFINITE PAST OF VERBS AND THE OBJECTIVE CASE

Study the following sentences:

Geldim	'I came'
Gittin	'You (sg) went'
Mektup dün geldi	'The letter came yesterday'
Halil mektup yazdı	'Halil wrote letters'
Et yedik	'We ate meat'
Ekmek yediniz	'You (pl) ate bread'
Yemek yediler	'They ate (food)'
Halil kızı gördü	'Halil saw the girl'
Kız adamları gördü	'The girl saw the men'
Çocuk beni gördü	'The child saw me'
Dün yeni bir kitap satın aldım	'Yesterday I bought a new book'
Bugün yeni kitabı okudunuz	'Today you (pl) read the new book'
Eski müdür kitap yazdı	'The former director wrote a book/books'
Eski müdür bir kitap yazdı	'The former director wrote a book'
Eski müdür kitaplar yazdı	'The former director wrote books'

1. The infinitive

The infinitive or "citation form" of a verb is the form normally used for referring to the verb, and it is the form in which the verb is found in a dictionary. In English, this form is made by preposing the word 'to'; in Turkish, by attaching the suffix -mEk (/-mEg/) to the verb stem.

görmek	'to see'
yazmak	'to write'

The suffix -mEk also has a grammatical function as a verbal noun, which will be discussed later.

2. Definite past tense

The definite past tense is formed by adding the suffix -DI to the verb stem. Personal endings are then added to -DI. This tense is used when (1) the action described took place in the past, and (2) the speaker knows, from his own personal observation, that the action took place. We shall see later that there is another tense used when the speaker did not observe the action directly but only knows about it from report or hearsay. We will discuss the difference between these two tenses in more detail when the other tense is introduced.

The personal endings used with -DI differ somewhat from the personal endings we have seen previously. They are:

'I'	-m	'we'	-k
'you (sg)'	-n	'you (pl)'	-nIz
'he, she, it'	nothing	'they'	nothing or -lEr

Notice that the suffix -DIr cannot be used with this tense. These endings are accented.

Remember that the general principle governing the use of -lEr is that it is omitted whenever it is not necessary. Thus 'They have come' would be Geldiler if there is no other indication of the plurality of the subject; but Onlar geldi or Adamlar geldi 'The men have come'.

By way of illustration, we give the full set of forms for two verbs, gitmek 'go' and okumak 'read':

	'go'	'read'
(ben)	gittim	okudum
(sen)	gittin	okudun
(o)	gitti	okudu
(biz)	gittik	okuduk
(siz)	gittiniz	okudunuz
(onlar)	gittiler	okudular

3. The verb phrase

We know that the predicate of a sentence may be an adjective or a noun phrase; we see now that it may also be a verb, or a construction with a verb as principal member, that is, a verb with its object and various adverbial elements. Such a construction is called a "verb phrase." Notice that the personal endings, which belong to the auxiliary, are attached to a verbal predicate in the same way that they are added to a nonverbal predicate, even though the actual form of the endings differs. In other words, the sentences *Ben gencim* and *Ben geldim* are constructed according to the same pattern, which we may represent graphically in Figure 3.

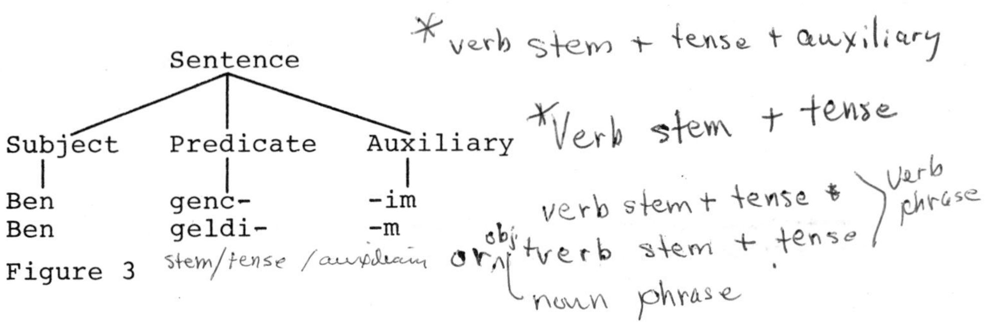

Figure 3

The verb phrase, in turn, consists basically of two elements, and in some cases must have three. The parts of the verb phrase are as follows:

1. There is a verb stem, for example, *gel-* 'come' or *gör-* 'see'. This may be a single unit or built up from several elements.
2. There is a tense marker, added after the stem. Turkish has eight tenses, one of which is the definite past *-DI*.
3. If the verb is transitive, that is, a verb that takes an object, then there must be an object, which precedes the stem. The object is a noun phrase.

There may also be various adverbial elements sprinkled throughout the verb phrase and the sentence; we do not attempt to keep track of these, since their order and position in the sentence is not fixed.

As an example, we may represent the construction of the sentence Ben mektubu okudum 'I read the letter' in graphic form, as shown in Figure 4.

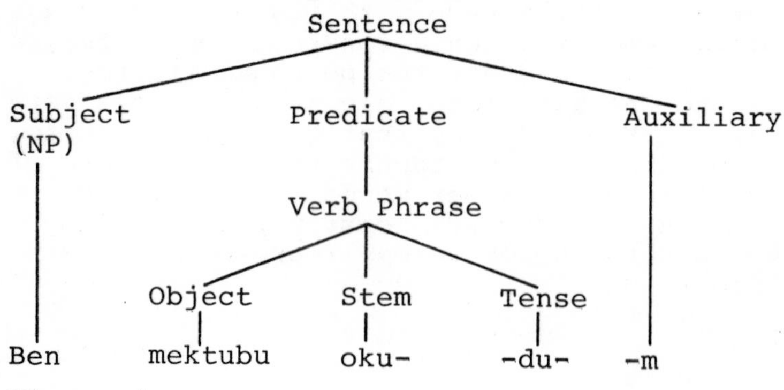

Figure 4

4. The objective case

A noun is definite if it refers to some particular thing or things that have either been mentioned previously in the conversation or are otherwise clearly identified by the context. In English, definite nouns are normally marked with the article 'the'. In Turkish, if a definite noun is the object of a verb, it is marked with the suffix -(y)I, which we may call the "objective case." This suffix is not used if the object is indefinite.

Halil kitap okudu	'Halil read a book'
Halil kitabı okudu	'Halil read the book'
Çocuk et yedi	'The child ate meat'
Çocuk eti yedi	'The child ate the meat'
Köpekler gördüm	'I saw some dogs'
Köpekleri gördüm	'I saw the dogs'

If the object of the verb is a proper noun, the suffix -(y)I is required; a proper noun refers to a single person and is therefore definite. The suffix -(y)I must also be used if the object is a pronoun. The objective form of the pronoun o is onu.

Mehmedi gördüm	'I saw Mehmet'
Seni gördüm	'I saw you'

We saw in the last lesson that Turkish frequently omits bir where English would use the article 'a'. When an indefinite noun is the object of a verb, the use of bir indicates specifically that only one thing is involved. Compare these sentences:

Ekmek aldım	'I bought bread'
Bir ekmek aldım	'I bought a loaf of bread'

Compare also:

Kitap okudum	'I read a book'
Bir kitap okudum	'I read a (one) book'

A speaker would use the second of these sentences if he wanted specifically to stress the fact that he read only one book. Normally, he would use the first of these sentences, which states merely what activity he engaged in and is noncommittal about the number of books involved.

The plural suffix is also frequently omitted under similar conditions. Compare:

Halil mektup yazdı	'Halil wrote letters (or a letter)'
Halil mektuplar yazdı	'Halil wrote some letters'

A speaker would use the second of these sentences if he wanted specifically to stress the fact that Halil wrote more than one, or several, letters. Normally, he would use the first of these sentences. This simply states what activity Halil engaged in (letter writing) and is noncommittal about the number: Halil may have written one letter or several.

In English, we are forced by the rules of English grammar to specify the number of every noun: 'I read a book' or 'I read books', but we cannot say 'I read book'. In Turkish, however, the simple form Kitap okudum is the normal form, and the number of the noun is usually left unspecified. In short, do not use either bir or -lEr with an indefinite object of a verb unless you have some special reason to state the number of things involved.

If the noun is modified by an adjective, the situation is again somewhat reversed; bir is more common:

Yeni bir kitap aldım	'I bought a new book'
Yeni kitap aldım	'I bought new books'
	'I bought a new book'
Yeni kitaplar aldım	'I bought some new books'

5. Obligatory objects

A transitive verb is one that takes an object ('John saw the cat'); an intransitive verb does not ('John came'). In English, most transitive verbs may be used either with or without an object: 'John read a book' or 'John read', 'The child played tennis' or 'The child played'. In Turkish, however, a transitive verb must always have an object, except in colloquial speech. Thus we cannot say *Mehmet okudu 'Mehmet read' but must specify what he read: Mehmet kitap okudu, Mehmet mektup okudu. In some cases, nouns that have little meaning of their own are used to fill the position of the required object. For example in the expression Orhan yazı yazdı 'Orhan wrote', yazı is a noun meaning 'writing', 'something written', or 'article'. Similarly, Adam yemek yedi, with the noun yemek 'meal, food', may be translated 'The man ate a meal', 'The man ate food', or simply 'The man ate'.

6. Usage

Almak corresponds to English 'get, take, buy, receive'; in short, it is used for the process of receiving in the widest sense. For 'buy' in particular, either almak or satın almak (satın 'by sale') may be used.

Yemek means cooked food: either a meal or an individual dish. Uncooked food, or food in the generic sense, is yiyecek.

VOCABULARY

almak		get, receive, take, buy
bugün	/búgün/	today
dün		yesterday
ekmek		bread, loaf of bread
et		meat
gelmek		come
gitmek	/gid-/	go
görmek		see
Halil		man's name
kitap	/kitab/	book
mektup	/mektub/	letter
okumak		read
satın almak		buy
yazı		piece of writing, article
yazmak		write
yemek (n)		meal, food
yemek (v)		eat
yeni		new

EXERCISES

A. Translate into English:

1. Mehmet'i değil, Orhan'ı gördüm.
2. Genç kız bugün bir mektup aldı.
3. İhtiyar adam gitti, et aldı, geldi; ama eti köpek yedi.
4. Geldim, gördüm, aldım.
5. Dün bir kitap aldık, bugün okuduk.
6. Yeni kâtip eski müdürü bugün gördü.

7. Dün Mehmet yazıyı yazdı.
8. Dün Mehmet yazı yazdı.
9. Dün Mehmet bir yazı yazdı.
10. Et değil, ekmek aldım.

B. Translate into Turkish:

1. They saw horses.
2. You (sg) ate meat.
3. We wrote (several) books.
4. I ate the meat.
5. They read the books.
6. I wrote a (one) letter.
7. We ate the bread.
8. You (sg) read the letters.
9. She wrote.
10. I saw the trees.
11. You (sg) wrote the letter.
12. I read a book.
13. You (pl) saw a (one) child.
14. We saw the horses.
15. You (pl) wrote books.
16. They ate.
17. She saw (several) horses.
18. We got a (one) dog.
19. He read letters.
20. You (sg) saw (several) trees.
21. They bought the bread.
22. You (pl) saw (several) children.
23. He got the dog.
24. You (pl) bought bread.

C. Translate into Turkish:

1. The old man got a letter.
2. The small child ate a big horse.
3. The children came, but the grown-ups went.
4. We read the new book, but it isn't good.
5. Yesterday you ate bad meat; today you are sick.
6. Today I bought bread, but the dog ate it.
7. Mehmet wrote books, not Halil.
8. Halil saw you, not me.

LESSON 6: VERBAL NEGATIVES AND QUESTIONS

Study the following sentences:

Elmaları beğenmedim, az aldım	'I didn't like the apples, and bought few'
Kitabı değil, gazeteyi okumadım	'I didn't read the newspaper, not the book' ('It was the newspaper, not the book, that I didn't read')
Mehmet genç mi? —Değil	'Is Mehmet young? —No'
İstanbulu sevdiniz mi? —Sevdim	'Did you like Istanbul? —Yes'
Meyvaları siz mi yediniz?	'Did you eat the fruit?'
Hasta mısınız, yorgun musunuz?	'Are you sick or tired?'
Pek mi meşgulsünüz? —Pek değilim	'Are you very busy?' —Not very'

1. The verbal negative

The negative of verbal sentences is not made with değil, but with the suffix -mE, which follows the verb stem and precedes the tense. The suffix -mE is, in fact, part of the stem, and the infinitive suffix -mEk may be added to it:

gör-	'see'	görmek	'to see'
görme-	'not see'	görmemek	'not to see'

The suffix -mE is unaccented in the sense in which this term was defined in Lesson 3; that is, accent falls on the preceding syllable:

gítmedim	'I didn't go'
okúmadınız	'you (pl) didn't read'
Bugün çok çalíşmadım	'Today I didn't work very much'
Kitabı okuduk, ama beğénmedik	'We read the book, but we didn't like it'

2. Yes-or-no questions

The particle *mI* is used for asking yes-or-no questions. It follows the word to which it applies, normally the predicate. Although it is written as a separate word, it behaves like an unaccented suffix: it changes according to vowel harmony, and accent falls on the preceding syllable.

If the predicate is a verb in the definite past tense, *mI* follows the verb form and thus stands alone at the end of the sentence:

Gittí mi?	'Did he go?'
Geldiníz mi?	'Did you come?'
Onu gördünüz mü?	'Did you see him?'
Onu görmediniz mi?	'Didn't you see him?'
Gazete geldi mi?	'Did the newspaper come?'
Meyva aldık mı?	'Did we buy fruit?'

If the predicate is nonverbal, *mI* follows the predicate but precedes the personal ending; the ending is then attached to *mI* and continues to be affected by vowel harmony. We shall see later that other verb tenses follow the same pattern.

Yorgún musunuz?	'Are you tired?'
Hastá mıyım?	'Am I sick?'
Áç mıyız?	'Are we hungry?'
Kasáp mısın?	'Are you a butcher?'
İstanbul güzél mi? (or midir?)	'Is Istanbul beautiful?'
İstanbul güzel bir yer mi? (or midir?)	'Is Istanbul a beautiful place?'

Among the personal endings, only the third person plural *-lEr* precedes *mI*:

İyiler mi?	'Are they well?'

If *değil* is present, *mI* follows *değil* (since *değil* is also part of the predicate):

Kâtip değil misiniz?	'Aren't you a clerk?'
Mehmet tembel değil mi?	'Isn't Mehmet lazy?'
İyi değil miyim?	'Aren't I well?'

The particle mI may be used not only at the end of the sentence but also within the sentence; it may be placed after a noun, noun phrase, or adverb inside the sentence. It then has the effect of questioning the word that immediately precedes.

Mehmet mi geldi?	'Did Mehmet come?' ('Was it Mehmet who came?')
Elma mı aldınız?	'Did you buy apples?' ('Was it apples that you bought?')
Orhan çok mu çalışkan?	'Is Orhan very industrious?'
Şimdi mi geldiniz?	'Did you come just now?'

The questioned word and mI always immediately precede the verb:

Kitabı sen mi aldın?	'Did you buy the book?'

The question may ask for a choice between two alternatives; the second choice is placed after the sentence, followed by mI:

Halil mi geldi, Orhan mı?	'Did Halil come, or Orhan?'
Gazeteyi mi okudunuz, kitabı mı?	'Did you read the newspaper or the book?'

Note carefully:

Gitti mi, gitmedi mi?	'Did he go or not?' ('Did he go, or did he not go?')
Kitabı okuduk mu, okumadık mı?	'Did we read the book or not?' ('Did we read the book, or did we not read?')

Tembel misiniz, değil misiniz?	'Are you lazy or not?'

The expression <u>değil mi</u> means 'is it not so?'; it corresponds to French 'n'est-ce pas' or German 'nicht wahr'. It is placed at the end of the sentence and has no grammatical connection with it.

İstanbul güzel, değil mi?	'Istanbul is beautiful, isn't it?'
Kitabı okumadınız, değil mi?	'You didn't read the book did you?'
Yemek aldınız, değil mi?	'You bought food, didn't you?'

Distinguish carefully between these questions:

Halil tembel değil mi?	'Isn't Halil lazy?'
Halil tembel, değil mi?	'Halil is lazy, isn't he?'
Halil tembel mi, değil mi?	'Is Halil lazy or not?'

<u>3. Yes and no</u>

The words for 'yes' and 'no' are <u>evet</u> (/évet/) and <u>hayır</u> (/háyır/), respectively. In practice, however, the answer to a yes-or-no question in Turkish is usually a repetition of the main verb, either in the positive or the negative. <u>Evet</u> or <u>hayır</u> may be added for reinforcement.

Yemek aldınız mı? —Aldım or Evet, aldım	'Did you buy food? —Yes, (I did)'
Kitabı sevdiniz mi? —Sevmedim or Hayır, sevmedim	'Did you like the book? —No, (I didn't)'
Mehmet tembel mi? —Tembeldir or Evet, tembeldir	'Is Mehmet lazy? —Yes, (he is)'
Yorgun musunuz? —Değilim or Hayır, değilim	'Are you tired?' —No, (I am not)'

4. Accent: proper nouns

Place names are normally accented on the first syllable.

Ánkara

Kónya

Búrsa

Notice that when a common noun is used as the name of a place, accent shifts from the last syllable to the first.

bebék	'baby'
Bébek	suburb of Istanbul
ordú	'army'
Órdu	province on the Black Sea

Some place names are irregularly accented on some syllable other than the first.

İstánbul

Antálya

Irregular accent of this type will be noted in transcription in the vocabularies.

The accent on a place name does not shift when suffixes are added:

İstánbulu gördüm	'I saw Istanbul'
Ánkarayı gördüm	'I saw Ankara'

Personal names are normally accented on the last syllable: Mehmét, Orhán. But when they are used as vocatives—that is, for calling someone—accent shifts to the first syllable. The same is true of kinship terms like baba 'father', anne 'mother', and so on.

Mehmét geldi	'Mehmet came'
Méhmet!	'Mehmet!'

Babâ yorgundur	'Father is tired'
Bâba!	'Father!'

5. The words çok, az, and pek

Çok, which may be used as an adjective, adverb, or noun, means 'much', 'very much', or 'too much (excessively much)'. Turkish does not make the distinction between these meanings which is found in English. Az means 'little' or 'few', or 'too little' or 'too few'. The plural suffix is never used with either çok or az.

Halil çok çalıştı	'Halil worked very hard' 'Halil worked too hard'
Çocuk çok genç	'The child is very young' 'The child is too young'
Çok yemek yedim	'I ate too much'
İstanbulu çok sevdim	'I liked Istanbul very much'
Az kitap aldım	'I bought few books'
Köpek az yedi	'The dog ate very little' 'The dog ate too little'

When it is important, for some reason, to stress the meaning 'too much', and when the context does not provide this meaning adequately, fazla may be used, either alone or in combination as çok fazla.

Çok fazla çalıştınız Fazla çalıştınız	'You worked much too hard'
Köpek çok fazla yemek yedi Köpek fazla yemek yedi	'The dog ate much too much'

Fazla is much less common in Turkish than 'too much' is in English; native speakers of English, accustomed to making a clear distinction between 'very much' and 'too much' should avoid a very strong tendency to try to preserve this distinction by using fazla indiscriminately in Turkish. Note that fazla may not be used with az.

Pek is an adverb and simply means 'very'; it is less strong and less frequently used than çok. It may be combined with çok with no change in meaning.

Orhan pek iyi bir adamdır	'Orhan is a very good man'
Pek hastasınız	'You are very sick'
Pek çok çalıştınız	'You worked very hard'

6. Usage

Güzel has a number of meanings, beginning with 'pretty' or 'beautiful', extending to 'attractive' or 'good looking' in a more general sense, and often simply 'nice' or 'good'.

güzel bir kız	'a pretty girl, a beautiful girl'
güzel bir ağaç	'an attractive tree'
güzel bir yer	'a beautiful place, a nice place'
güzel bir elma	'a nice (good-looking) apple'
güzel bir kitap	'a good book'

Meyva means strictly 'piece of fruit', and the plural meyvalar corresponds to English 'fruit', but can also mean 'kinds of fruit'.

Sevmek means 'love' when used to refer to persons, but it is not so strong when used to refer to things (books, places, and so on) and often corresponds simply to 'like'.

Şimdi normally corresponds to English 'now'. But with a past tense it may mean 'just now'; that is, it may correspond to English 'just' used as an adverb.

Şimdi yorgunum	'I am tired now'
Şimdi Orhan geldi	'Orhan has come now'

Orhan şimdi geldi 'Orhan has just come'

<u>Yer</u> also corresponds to a number of meanings: 'place, ground, floor', and so on.

VOCABULARY

Ankara		place name
az		few, etc. (see Section 4)
beğenmek		like
çalışmak		work
çok	/çog/	much (see Section 4)
elma		apple
gazete	/gazéte/	newspaper
güzel		pretty, beautiful (see "Usage")
İstanbul	/istánbul/	place name
meşgul	/meşgul̂/	busy, occupied
meyva		piece of fruit (see "Usage")
pek		very
sevmek		love, like (see "Usage")
şimdi	/şímdi/	now (see "Usage")
yer		place, etc. (see "Usage")

EXERCISES

A. Compose an answer, in the form of a grammatical and meaningful Turkish sentence, to each of these questions:

1. Çok mu çalışkansınız?
2. İstanbul mu güzel, Ankara mı?
3. Halil Türk mü?
4. Bugün ekmek yediniz mi?

5. Dün çok mu meşguldünüz?

B. Translate into English:

1. Halil tembel mi? Çok değil.
2. Ben mi tembelim, sen mi?
3. Atlar yorgun, değil mi?
4. Atlar yorgun değil mi?
5. Ben İstanbulu görmedim. Siz gördünüz mü?
6. Ankaraya gittim, ama pek sevmedim.
7. Ahmet Anita Ekberg'i beğenmedi mi?
8. Anita Ekberg'i Ahmet mi beğenmedi?
9. Ahmet Anita Ekberg'i mi beğenmedi?
10. Müdür hasta değil, ama çok meşgul. Bugün yemek yemedi.

C. Make the following sentences interrogative. Remember that there are several possibilities for each sentence depending on where mI is placed.

Example:

Ahmet gazeteyi okudu

Answers:

Ahmet gazeteyi okudu mu?

Ahmet gazeteyi mi okudu?

Gazeteyi Ahmet mi okudu?

1. Ankara çok güzel.
2. Hastasınız.
3. Çocuklar dün çok çalıştılar.
4. Elma bir meyvadır.
5. Ahmet hasta değil.

D. Make the following sentences both negative and interrogative, putting mI after the predicate.

Example:

Ahmet gazeteyi okudu

Answer:

Ahmet gazeteyi okumadı mı?

1. Dün gazete aldık.
2. Kızlar çok hoş.
3. Ahmet iyi bir adamdır.
4. Yazıyı beğendiniz.
5. İhtiyarlar daima hastadır.

E. Translate into Turkish:

1. Isn't she pretty?
2. Orhan is not a very pleasant man.
3. I am very busy now.
4. Are we children or men?
5. Didn't you eat today?
6. Is the dog always hungry?
7. Is the fruit good or not?
8. Mehmet worked yesterday, didn't he?
9. Are you tired, or am I?
10. Did you read the books? Did you like them?

LESSON 7: THE DATIVE AND ABLATIVE CASES

Study the following sentences:

Otobüs İstanbuldan Ankaraya gitti	'The bus went from Istanbul to Ankara'
Adam evden çıktı, lokantaya girdi	'The man left the house and entered the restaurant'
Orhan eve erken geldi	'Orhan came home early'
Çocuk ağaçtan indi	'The child descended from the tree'
Kasaptan et aldık, köpeğe verdik	'We bought meat from the butcher and gave it to the dog'
Ev sokağa yakın, ama lokantadan uzaktır	'The house is near the street but far from the restaurant'
Ders bugün başladı	'The course began today'
Yeni bir kitaba başladım	'I began a new book'
Ona ne söylediniz?	'What did you tell him?'
Dün nelere baktınız?	'What (things) did you look at yesterday?'
Orhan yemeği köpeğe verdi	'Orhan gave the food to the dog'
Orhan köpeğe yemek verdi	'Orhan gave food to the dog'
Köpek yemeği yedi	'The dog ate the food'
Yemeği bir köpek yedi	'A dog ate the food'

1. The dative case

The dative case suffix is -(y)E. This suffix normally corresponds to the English words 'to' and 'for'. Some of its uses are the following:

A. The dative indicates the place to or toward which motion is directed:

Eve girdik	'We entered the house'
Mehmet bugün Ankaraya gitti	'Mehmet went to Ankara today'

Otobüse bindim	'I got on the bus'

B. The dative indicates the person (or thing) to or for whom the action is directed; in this use, it corresponds to the English "indirect object":

Adama yemek verdim	'I gave the man food' ('I gave food to the man')
Halil kıza bir mektup yazdı	'Halil wrote the girl a letter' ('Halil wrote a letter to the girl')
Size bir kitap aldım	'I bought you a book' ('I bought a book for you')

C. There are some verbs in Turkish that "take the dative"; these are actually Turkish intransitive verbs whose English counterparts are transitive. These include <u>başlamak</u> 'begin' and <u>bakmak</u> 'look at, watch'. They may be used as simple intransitive verbs:

Ders bugün başladı	'The course began today'

As intransitives, they may not take a direct object but may appear with a noun in the dative instead:

Derse geç başladık	'We began the lesson late'
Sokağa baktım	'I looked at the street'

Do not be misled by the fact that the English verbs 'begin' and 'look at' take a direct object.

D. Some adjectives are regularly used with a noun in the dative:

Ev sokağa yakındır	'The house is near the street

Note: Three pronouns have irregular dative forms. The datives of <u>ben</u> and <u>sen</u> are <u>bana</u> and <u>sana</u>, and the dative of <u>o</u> is <u>ona</u>.

2. The ablative case

The ablative case suffix is <u>-DEn</u>. This suffix normally corresponds to the English word 'from'. Some of its uses are the following:

A. The ablative indicates the place from which motion proceeds:

Lokantadan çıktım	'I went out of the restaurant'
Mehmet İstanbuldan geldi	'Mehmet came from Istanbul'
Otobüsten indik	'We got off the bus'

B. The ablative indicates the person (or thing) from whom the action proceeds:

Kasaptan et satın aldım	'I bought meat from the butcher'
Kitabı Halilden aldım	'I took (or got) the book from Halil'

C. Some Turkish verbs "take the ablative"; these are intransitive verbs that may not take a direct object but may appear with a noun in the ablative instead. They include <u>korkmak</u> 'fear, be afraid of':

Fatma attan korktu	'Fatma was afraid of the horse'

D. Some adjectives are regularly used with a noun in the ablative:

Lokanta, evden uzaktır	'The restaurant is far from the house'

Note: The ablative of the pronoun <u>o</u> is <u>ondan</u>.

3. Interrogatives: ne

The most important point about all Turkish interrogative words (except, of course, <u>mI</u>) is that the declarative, not the interrogative, form of the verb is used. Thus we have:

Ne aldınız?	'What did you buy?'

We do not have *<u>Ne aldınız mı?</u>

The word ne is used as a noun and means 'what'.

Otobüs nedir?	'What is a bus?'
Ne geldi?	'What came?'

As an object, ne is usually found in the indefinite form.

Ne gördünüz?	'What did you see?'
Orhana ne söylediniz?	'What did you tell Orhan?'
Mehmet ne yazdı?	'What did Mehmet write?'

The definite neyi is possible if both speakers have some definite object in mind. For example, if one says Onu aldım 'I bought it', and the hearer is not sure what the pronoun refers to, he may ask Neyi aldınız? The answer to this question must contain a definite objective noun, for example, Gazeteyi.

Ne may be used in the dative and ablative cases; it is restricted here, however, to appearing with the verbs that take the dative or ablative. Otherwise, the forms neye (/niye/) and neden mean 'why' and will be discussed later.

Fatma neye baktı?	'What did Fatma look at?'
Kız neden korktu?	'What was the girl afraid of?'

The plural neler means 'what things' or 'what' when the speaker expects several things to figure in the reply.

Bugün neler gördünüz?	'What (things) did you see today?'

Ne may also be used as an adjective:

Ne yemek aldınız?	'What food did you buy?'

4. Rules of order

Turkish word order, like that of English, is not strictly fixed, and many variations are possible, with corresponding subtle differences of style. In addition, the suffixes on Turkish words are often sufficient to indicate the grammatical function of the word, so that Turkish is not as dependent as English on strict word order to indicate grammatical relations. It is possible, however, to formulate a number of general principles of word order.

A. The principal member of a construction comes at the end of the construction. Thus a noun, the principal member of a noun phrase, comes at the end of the phrase, preceded by adjectives, articles, and other modifiers.

çok küçük bir çocuk	'a very small child'

A verb, the principal member of a verb phrase, comes at the end of the phrase, preceded by its object and adverbial modifiers.

Elmaları lokantadan aldı	'He got the apples from the restaurant'

B. An indefinite object of a verb must come immediately before the verb; a definite object need not. We shall see later that the same is true of definite and indefinite possessors of a noun; thus this is a general statement about definiteness in Turkish. Therefore, with indefinite objects, we have:

Kasaptan et aldım	'I bought meat from the butcher'
Kıza bir mektup yazdım	'I wrote a letter to the girl'

But with definite objects, we have two possibilities each:

Eti kasaptan aldım Kasaptan eti aldım	'I bought the meat from the butcher'
Mektubu kıza yazdım Kıza mektubu yazdım	'I wrote the letter to the girl'

These two possibilities differ in emphasis; see Rule D. The first sentence of each pair has the usual order: direct before indirect object.

C. An indefinite subject of a verb comes immediately before the verb; a definite subject does not.

Haber Mehmet'ten geldi	'The news came from Mehmet'
Mehmet'ten haber geldi	'News came from Mehmet'
Adam eve girdi	'The man entered the house'
Eve bir adam girdi	'A man entered the house'

Rule B takes precedence over Rule C; thus if both the object and the subject are indefinite, the object comes next to the verb:

Lokantadan bir adam yemek aldı	'A man bought food from the restaurant'

D. The position of emphasis in Turkish is the position immediately before the verb; thus, place in that position any word that you wish to emphasize. In conversation, emphasis is also indicated by increased stress on the emphasized word (as in English).

Halil kitabı dün okudu	'Halil read the book <u>yesterday</u>'
Halil dün kitabı okudu	'Halil read <u>the book</u> yesterday'
Kitabı dün Halil okudu	'<u>Halil</u> read the book yesterday'

There is secondary emphasis on the word at the beginning of the sentence; and anything in the middle is not emphasized at all. In the following translations, we have tried to indicate degrees of emphasis by capitals and underlining, but these are not to be taken too seriously:

Kitabı Halil dün okudu	'Halil read <u>the book</u> YESTERDAY'
Dün Halil kitabı okudu	'Halil read THE BOOK <u>yesterday</u>'
Dün kitabı Halil okudu	'HALIL read the book <u>yesterday</u>'

If a sentence contains an interrogative word or a word followed by _mI_, the interrogative is always considered to be emphasized and therefore comes immediately before the verb:

Kitapları sen mi aldın?	'Did _you_ buy the books?'
Sen kitap mı aldın?	'Did you buy _books_?'
Sen kitapları mı aldın?	'Did you buy _the books_?'
Haberi Orhan'a mı söylediniz?	'Did you tell the news _to Orhan_?'
Orhan'a haberi mi söylediniz?	'Did you tell Orhan _the news_?'
Gazeteyi Halil'e verdiniz	'You gave the newspaper to Halil'
Halil'e ne verdiniz?	'What did you give to Halil?'

5. Usage

The ablative is used in the time expressions _çoktan_ 'a long time ago', _eskiden_ 'formerly', _şimdiden_ 'henceforth', and _yeniden_ 'anew'.

Ata binmek means 'to mount the horse' but also means 'take a ride on a horse' or 'go horseback riding'.

Dün ata bindik	'Yesterday we went horseback riding'

We saw the intransitive verb _çalışmak_ 'work' used in the last lesson (_Bugün çalıştınız mı_ 'Did you work today?'); it may also be used with the dative, with the meanings 'work at', 'work on', or 'try'.

Bugün derse çalıştım	'Today I worked on the lesson'

There is also the idiom _ders çalışmak_ 'study' (intransitive).

Çıkmak has a number of meanings, most of them centering around the motion 'go out' (or 'come out', depending on the position of the speaker); an important secondary meaning is 'go up'.

Adam evden çıktı	'The man went out (came out, got out) of the house'
Adam lokantadan sokağa çıktı	'The man went out (came out) of the restaurant to the street'
Yeni bir kitap çıktı	'A new book appeared (came out)'
Yeni bir mesele çıktı	'A new problem appeared (came forth)' (mesele 'problem')
Elmalar kötü çıktı	'The apples turned out to be bad (came out bad)'

Ev means 'house' but also can mean, idiomatically, 'home':

Adam eve gitti	'The man went to the house'
	'The man went home'

When in doubt, translate söylemek as 'tell'; but sometimes English 'say' or 'speak' fit better. This is a transitive verb and can be used only with an object; at the moment, the only words we have that can go with it are haber and ne.

VOCABULARY

bakmak (dat)	look (at), look after, watch
başlamak (dat)	begin
binmek (dat)	mount, get on
çıkmak	go out, leave, go up (see "Usage")
ders	lesson
erken	early
ev	house, home
Fatma	girl's name
geç	late
girmek (dat)	enter

haber		news, piece of news; message
inmek		descend, go down
korkmak (abl)		fear, be afraid (of)
lokanta	/lokânta/	restaurant
otobüs		bus
sokak		street
söylemek		tell; say, speak
uzak (abl)		far (from)
vermek		give
yakın (dat)		near (to)

EXERCISES

A. Compose an answer, in the form of a grammatical and meaningful Turkish sentence, to each of these questions:

1. Bugün neye başladık?
2. Fatma neden korktu?
3. Çocuk neye bindi?
4. Kasaptan ne aldım?
5. Orhan kıza ne verdi?
6. Halil ne yazdı?
7. Dersi beğendiniz mi?
8. Bugün ders çalıştınız mı, çalışmadınız mı?
9. Bugün Mehmet lokantaya gitti mi?
10. Eve yakın mısınız?

B. Translate into English:

1. Ahmet dün evden çok erken çıktı, otobüse bindi, Ankaraya gitti.
2. Ahmet mektubu müdüre verdi.
3. Müdür mektubu okudu, ama beğenmedi.

4. Kızlar dün lokantaya gittiler, ama Ayşe yemek yemedi, sokağa baktı.
5. Kasap bugün bize et vermedi.
6. Ağaca çıktım, elmayı aldım.
7. Fatmaya ne söylediniz? Bugün eve gelmedi.
8. Haberi gazeteden okuduk, ama Ayşeye söylemedik.
9. Size söylemedim mi? Elmaları bakkaldan aldık.
10. Köpekten korktum, eve uzaktan baktım.

C. Complete the following with the correct form of the objective, dative, or ablative suffix (changing the noun stem where necessary), and the correct form of the past tense:

1. Ben kitap___ dün al___.
2. Kâtip otobüs___ bin___.
3. Halil yazı___ çok beğen___.
4. Müdür ev___ çık___, değil mi?
5. Biz ev___ gör___.
6. Fatma mektup___ Ahmet___ verme___.
7. Ben gazete___ oku___.
8. Siz sokak___ bakma___.
9. Sen yemek___ ye___.
10. Fatma köpek___ korkma___.
11. Siz ders___ calış___.
12. Et___ kasap___ mı al___?
13. Siz İstanbul___ mu sev___?
14. Onlar Ankara___ dün mü gel___?
15. Kızlar dün lokanta___ gir___.

C. Translate into Turkish:

1. The newspaper came early today.
2. A newspaper came from Ankara today.
3. The old man got off the bus.

4. An old man got off the bus.
5. We gave the bread to Fatma.
6. We gave bread to Fatma.
7. Did you eat the meat?
8. Did _you_ eat the meat?
9. Did you buy the fruit from the restaurant?
10. What did you buy from the restaurant?

D. Translate into Turkish:

1. The clerk wrote me a letter yesterday.
2. Today the girl left home late.
3. The restaurant is near Istanbul.
4. Today the lesson began early.
5. Fatma got off the horse; she was afraid of it.
6. The tree is far from the street.
7. The children began a new book.
8. She bought meat for the dog, but the meat turned out bad.
9. The small child was very much afraid.
10. They told him the news, but he didn't like it.
11. What did the butcher give you?
12. What did you buy from the butcher?
13. Didn't Fatma get on the bus?

LESSON 8: THE LOCATIVE CASE

Study the following sentences:

Bir lokantadayım	'I am in a restaurant'
Arabada oturduk	'We sat in the car'
Otobüs köşede durmadı	'The bus didn't stop at the corner'
Evi tahtadan yaptılar	'They made the house out of wood'
Taştan bir evde oturduk	'We lived in a stone house'
Otomobil sağdan gitti	'The car went to the right'
Halil pencereden çıktı	'Halil went out through the window'
Ekmekle eti yedim	'I ate the bread and the meat'
Fatmayla Ayşe evde kaldı	'Fatma and Ayse stayed at home'
İhtiyar kadın yemeği masaya koydu ve oturdu	'The old woman put the food on the table and sat down'

1. The locative case

The locative case suffix is -DE. This suffix is used to indicate the place at which an action occurs, or the place at, in, or on which an object is located.

Otobüs köşede durdu	'The bus stopped at the corner'
Adam İzmirde oturdu	'The man lived in Izmir'
Bir lokantada yemek yedik	'We ate in a restaurant'
Kadın evde kaldı	'The woman stayed at home'
Mehmet pencerede durdu, sokağa baktı	'Mehmet stood at the window and looked at the street'

A noun in the locative may serve as the predicate of a sentence:

Ankaradayım	'I am in Ankara'

Meyvalar masada (masadadır) — 'The fruit is on the table'

Çocuklar arabada — 'The children are in the car'

With some verbs, such as oturmak 'sit', it is important to distinguish between the significance of the dative and the locative. Briefly, when an object moves to a certain position, the dative is used; when an object remains in a certain position, the locative is used. Compare:

Masaya oturduk — 'We sat (down) at the table'

Masada oturduk — 'We sat at the table'

The first of these sentences describes the act of sitting down, the second describes the state of being seated. Notice also:

Kitabı masaya koydum — 'I put the book on the table'

Here the sentence describes the action of placing the book on the table, and therefore the Turkish dative is appropriate, even though the English translation uses 'on'. As a general rule, always use the dative, not the locative, with koymak.

Note: The locative of the pronoun o is onda.

2. Additional uses of the ablative

A. With the verb yapmak 'make', and other verbs similar in meaning, the ablative may be used to indicate the material out of which something is made:

Tahtadan bir masa yaptım — 'I made a table out of wood (from wood)'

The ablative construction may also be used without the verb, in the same meaning. It may serve as predicate of a sentence or may modify another noun:

Sokak taştandır — 'The street is (made) of stone'

Masa tahtadandır — 'The table is of (from) wood'

taştan bir ev	'a stone house'
tahtadan bir masa	'a wooden table'

B. The ablative may be used to indicate the direction 'through' or 'by way of' which motion proceeds.

Adamlar yoldan geldi	'The men came down (along) the street'
Ayşe kapıdan girdi	'Ayse entered by the door'
Kız pencereden sokağa baktı	'The girl looked through the window at the street'

The following sentence is ambiguous when removed from context:

Ankaraya Bursadan gittim	'I went to Ankara by way of Bursa' 'I went to Ankara from Bursa'

Similarly, in Araba soldan gitti 'The car went by way of the left', soldan may mean 'on the left', if the car used the left lane, or 'to the left', if the car made a left turn. Thus in some cases English 'to' must be translated with the ablative in Turkish.

3. Interrogatives: hangi

Hangi (/hángi/) means 'which'. It is used as an adjective. Remember that the phrase containing hangi is considered to be emphasized and must be placed immediately to the left of the verb.

Hangi gazeteyi okudunuz?	'Which newspaper did you read?'
Bunu hangi kâtip yazdı?	'Which clerk wrote this?'
Kitabı hangi masaya koydunuz?	'Which table did you put the book on?'

4. 'And'

There are a number of different methods of conjunction in Turkish; we shall discuss some of the constructions here and save others for later. In particular, we shall discuss two of the words for 'and', ve and ile, which are used in different ways and under different conditions.

Ve, when it is used, simply means 'and'. İle is also a postposition meaning 'with' and will be discussed again with the other postpositions. İle may be used as a separate word, or it may be a suffix to the word preceding it. If the word to which it is suffixed ends in a consonant, the i drops; if it ends in a vowel, the i becomes y. In either case, the final e becomes subject to vowel harmony, that is, becomes E. We thus end up with a suffix that we may transcribe -(y)lE. This suffix is unaccented. Some examples follow:

Mehmet ile Orhan	'Mehmet and Orhan'
Mehmétle Orhan	
Orhan ile Mehmet	'Orhan and Mehmet'
Orhánla Mehmet	
Fatmayla Ayşe	'Fatma and Ayse'
Ayşeyle Fatma	'Ayse and Fatma'

A. To join nouns or noun phrases, ile is preferred, but ve may also be used.

Bir adam ile bir kadın lokantaya girdi	'A man and a woman entered the restaurant'
Bir adamla bir kadın lokantaya girdi	
Bir adam ve bir kadın lokantaya girdi	
Büyük bir at ile küçük bir köpek yemeği yedi	'A big horse and a small dog ate the food'
Büyük bir atla küçük bir köpek yemeği yedi	
Büyük bir at ve küçük bir köpek yemeği yedi	

B. If the nouns being joined have case suffixes, and if ile is used, the case suffix must be omitted from the first noun. The suffix on the second noun is assumed to apply to both. If ve is used, the omission of the suffix is optional.

Evle sokağa baktım	'I looked at the house and the street'
Ev ve sokağa baktım	
Eve ve sokağa baktım	
Gazeteyle kitabı okudum	'I read the newspaper and the book'
Gazete ve kitabı okudum	
Gazeteyi ve kitabı okudum	

C. To join adjectives, use ve.

eski ve büyük bir ev	'an old and large house'

D. When two adjectives that are serving as predicates are conjoined, the auxiliary (personal ending) may be omitted from the first; the suffix on the second adjective is assumed to apply to both.

Gencim ve büyüğüm	'I am young and big'
Genç ve büyüğüm	
Müdür ihtiyar ve yorgundur	'The director is old and tired'
Müdür ihtiyardır ve yorgundur	

E. To join verbs, use ve for the moment. We shall see later, however, that this usage is not particularly idiomatic and that there are better ways of doing it. In colloquial usage, especially in narrative, the verbs may simply be juxtaposed, with a pause between them in speech, a comma in writing.

Mehmet geldi ve gitti	'Mehmet came and went'
Mehmet geldi, gitti	

F. To join sentences, it is possible to use ve. But it is much more common and idiomatic for conjoined sentences simply to be juxtaposed, as in the preceding example.

Mehmet geldi ve Orhan gitti	'Mehmet came, and Orhan went'
Mehmet geldi, Orhan gitti	
At hasta ve köpek açtır	'The horse is sick, and the dog is hungry'
At hasta, köpek açtır	

5. Usage

The locative is used in the time expression yakında 'soon'.

Araba, the word for 'cart' or 'carriage', now means also 'automobile'. There is the European word otomobil as well. Both words are equally common; individual speakers tend to prefer one or the other.

Fena and kötü both mean 'bad'. Only fena can be used for health: fenayım 'I am unwell'.

The idiom geç kalmak means 'to be late'. The past tense of this idiom corresponds to the present tense in English; thus geç kaldım may be translated either 'I was late' or 'I am late'. The expression takes the dative ('for'):

Mehmet yemeğe geç kaldı	'Mehmet is/was late for dinner'

Oturmak means 'live' only in the sense of 'reside'; otherwise, it means 'sit'.

Kadın güzel bir evde oturdu	'The woman lived in an attractive house'

Sağ 'right' and sol 'left' may be used either as nouns or as adjectives, as in English.

Yol has a large number of meanings; most concretely 'road' or 'path', it can also be used for 'way', 'trip', or 'journey'.

İstanbula yeni bir yol yaptılar	'They built a new road to Istanbul'
Yolda kitap okudum	'On the way I read a book'

Notice also the expression yola çıkmak 'set out (on a journey)'.

Orhan dün yola çıktı	'Orhan set out yesterday'

VOCABULARY

araba		car, cart, coach, carriage
Ayşe		woman's name
Bursa		place name
durmak		stand, stop
fena	/fenā/	bad, unwell (see "Usage")
hangi	/háŋgi/	which
İzmir		place name
kadın		woman
kalmak		stay, remain, be left
kapı		door
koymak		put, place
köşe		corner
masa	/mása/	table
otomobil		automobile
oturmak		sit, live (see "Usage")
pencere		window
sağ		right
sol		left
tahta		wood, board
taş		stone

yapmak	do, make
yol	road, path, way, journey (see "Usage")

EXERCISES

A. Compose an answer, in the form of a grammatical and meaningful Turkish sentence, to each of these questions:

1. Bugün ne yaptınız?
2. Köşede ne durdu?
3. Masaya ne koydum?
4. İzmirde neler gördünüz?
5. Adam lokantada ne yaptı?
6. Hangi kitabı beğendiniz?
7. Dün hangi lokantada yemek yediniz?
8. Otobüs hangi sokaktan gitti?
9. Ahmet hangi kıza baktı?
10. Evde hangi çocuk kaldı?

B. Complete the following with the correct form of the objective, dative, or ablative suffix (changing the noun stem where necessary):

1. Yazı gazete___ çıktı.
2. Yemek___ lokanta___ yedik.
3. Sokak___ bir araba geldi.
4. Bugün ev___ misiniz?
5. Otobüs___ bindik, bir yer___ oturduk.
6. Adam sokak___ durdu, kapı___ baktı.
7. Mektuplar___ masa___ koydum.
8. Çocuklar pencere___ girdiler.
9. Siz ders___ çalışmadınız.
10. Kapı___ taş___ mı yaptılar, tahta___ mı?
11. Ahmet___ haber geldi.

C. Translate into English:

1. Elmalar yerde.
2. Gazetede fena bir haber gördüm.
3. Masada ne kaldı?
4. Orhan evde durdu, pencereden baktı.
5. İstanbula İzmirden mi geldiniz? 
6. Ayşe otobüste pencereden yola baktı.
7. Orhan mektubu sağ köşede, masada yazdı.
8. İzmir'de otelde kaldık, yemekleri lokantada yedik.
9. İzmir'de Efes'e gitmediniz mi?
10. Otobüs köşede, araba kapıda durdu.

D. Translate into Turkish:

1. The restaurant is on the corner.
2. The house is on the left, Halil is on the right.
3. We got into the car and went to Izmir.
4. Ayse is not very late today.
5. The youths made a table out of wood.
6. The bus went through Bursa, but it didn't stop.
7. The child put a small stone in the food.
8. An old woman sat at the window and watched the street and the cars.
9. Yesterday Mehmet stayed home and wrote.
10. The man came home early, and Mehmet and Orhan left through the window.
11. Has the director gone? Yes, he set out yesterday.

LESSON 9: THE GENITIVE CASE AND POSSESSIVE SUFFIXES

Study the following phrases and sentences:

(benim) köyüm	'my village'
(senin) elin	'your hand'
(onun) başı	'his (her, its) head'
(bizim) babamız	'our father'
(sizin) anneniz	'your mother'
(onların) odası, odaları	'their room'
Halilin eski evi şimdi Mehmedin	'Halil's old house is now Mehmet's'
Yeni kitabını okudum	'I read his new book'
Orhan, kızından bir mektup aldı	'Orhan got a letter from his daughter'
Evleri, bizim evimize yakın	'Their house is near our house'
Orhanın babasının evinde oturduk	'We lived in Orhan's father's house'
bakkalın dükkânı	'the grocer's store'
bakkal dükkânı	'grocery store'
Lokantanın yemekleri pek iyi değil	'The meals of the restaurant are not very good'
Lokanta yemekleri pek iyi değil	'Restaurant meals are not very good'
Otel, Ankara Sokağının köşesindedir	'The hotel is at the corner of Ankara Street'

1. Variation in suffixes: vowel dropping

We saw in Lesson 3 that two vowels may not come together in Turkish, except under certain conditions. When a suffix beginning with a vowel is to be attached to a preceding vowel, a buffer consonant is sometimes inserted, as in the case of the first person singular personal ending -(y)Im. In other cases, the first vowel of the suffix simply drops. For example the suffix meaning 'my' has the form -Im after a consonant but -m after a vowel. Compare:

el	'hand'	elim	'my hand'
anne	'mother'	annem	'my mother'
baş	'head'	başım	'my head'
baba	'father'	babam	'my father'

We can transcribe this suffix as *-Im*. If a suffix begins with a vowel, and if no buffer consonant is indicated in the transcription, assume that this vowel drops when the suffix is being added to a preceding vowel.

1.1 Variation in stems: pronominal *-n-*

You will have noticed by this time that the pronoun *o* adds an *n* before any case suffix (*onu*, *ondan*) and the plural suffix (*onlar*). That is, all case forms and the plural are built on an "oblique stem" *on-*, although the final *n* is missing when the word stands alone. This *n* is also found in the forms of certain other pronouns, which are to be introduced later; in addition, the suffix meaning 'his (her, its)' has the same variation: it has the form *-(s)I* at the end of a word, but *-(s)In* before any case suffix. For example:

baba	'father'	ev	'house'
babası	'his father'	evi	'his house'
babasına	'to his father'	evine	'to his house'
babasından	'from his father'	evinden	'from his house'

Note that this *n* does *not* appear before a suffix that is part of the auxiliary:

odur	'it is he'
babasıdır	'it is his father'

2. The possessive relation

Consider this English expression:

John's hand

Here the relationship of possession between 'John' and 'hand' is expressed by a suffix '-'s' attached to 'John'. In Turkish, the same relationship is expressed by *two* suffixes:

Mehmed*in* el*i*

These are the genitive case suffix -*in* attached to *Mehmet*, and the possessive suffix -*i* attached to *el* 'hand'.

The genitive suffix indicates that the noun to which it is attached is the possessor of some other noun. Clearly, ordinary physical possession is not implied: this would be absurd in the light of such examples as 'John's father' or 'John's idea'. But it should be clear what the term "possessor" means, since this relationship is found in all languages, although expressed differently in each language.

The possessive suffix indicates that the noun to which it is attached is possessed by some other noun, in the same sense in which we used the term "possess" earlier. The possessive suffixes indicate the person and number of the possessor and thus may be considered to be a kind of personal ending, although they are used with nouns rather than with predicates.

The genitive and possessive suffixes refer to one another, and both are necessary (unless the possessor is a pronoun: see Section 2.2). A noun in the genitive in a Turkish sentence normally means that there must be a noun with a possessive suffix somewhere later in the sentence; a noun with a possessive suffix means that there must be an explicit or implied noun in the genitive somewhere earlier.

2.1. The genitive suffix

The form of the genitive suffix is -*(n)In*. Several pronouns, however, have irregular forms. The genitive forms of the pronouns are the following:

benim	bizim
senin	sizin
onun	onların

The most common use of the genitive is in possessive constructions, but a noun in the genitive may also be the predicate of a sentence:

Beyaz ev Mehmedin(dir)	'The white house is Mehmet's'
Oda benim mi, senin mi?	'Is the room mine, or yours?'

2.2. The possessive suffixes

These are:

'I'	-Im	'we'	-ImIz
'you (sg)'	-In	'you (pl)'	-InIz
'he, she, it'	-(s)I(n)	'they'	-lErI(n)

By way of illustration, we give the forms for *el* 'hand' and *baba* 'father':

(benim)	elim	babam
(senin)	elin	baban
(onun)	eli	babası
(bizim)	elimiz	babamız
(sizin)	eliniz	babanız
(onların)	elleri	babaları

These suffixes are accented: *elím*, *elimíz*, etc.

These suffixes are used in combination with a noun in the genitive; but if the possessor is a pronoun, it may be omitted. In an expression such as *(Benim) odam* 'my room', the pronoun is unnecessary, since the suffix *-m* indicates the person and number of the possessor adequately. In expressions of this simple nature the pronoun would almost always be omitted; it might be retained, however, for stylistic reasons or for emphasis.

In the third person plural, *-lEr* may precede the third person *-(s)I(n)*, giving the combination *-lErI(n)*. As we have seen before, *-lEr* is used only when there is no other indication of the plurality of the possessor: *odaları* 'their room'. If there is an explicitly plural possessor, -lEr is omitted: çocukların odası 'the children's room'. The possessed noun may itself be plural: çocukların odaları 'the children's rooms'. Even if both the possessor and possessed nouns are plural, only one -lEr is permitted; thus odaları can mean 'his rooms', 'their room', or 'their rooms'. Odalarına can mean 'to his rooms', 'to their room', 'to their rooms', or 'to your (sg) rooms'.

Possessive suffixes follow the plural and precede the case suffixes:

Elinizde ne tuttunuz?	'What did you hold in your hand?'
Dükkânımıza girdi	'He entered our shop'
Otobüsün pencerelerinden baktılar	'They looked through the windows of the bus'
Orhanın başına bir elma düştü	'An apple fell on Orhan's head'
Halilin çocuklarının odasında bir kadın oturdu	'A woman sat in the room of Halil's children'

3. Possessive compounds

Compare the following pairs of expressions in English:

the children's book	(as in 'the children's book is in their room')
a children's book	(as in 'Dr. Seuss wrote a new children's book')
Hilton's hotel	
Hilton Hotel	

The first member of each of these pairs is a possessive construction of the type that we have just been studying. The second expressions, however, are constructions of a different type: they are like compounds, since the two nouns function together to make a single unit.

Notice that in the first member of each of the preceding pairs, the two words have approximately equal stress, while in the second members, the first word has distinctly stronger stress than the second.

(Pronounce the pairs to yourself until you become convinced of this.) Notice also that the two words of a normal possessive construction may be separated by any number of other words:

The children's tattered and torn book

Hilton's newly built hotel

But nothing may come between the two words in a possessive compound: we cannot say:

*children's smudgy book	(*Dr. Seuss wrote a new children's smudgy book)
*Hilton new Hotel	

In Turkish, there is also a difference between normal possessive constructions and possessive compounds: in compounds, the genitive suffix is omitted from the first noun, although the possessive suffix is still attached to the second noun. Compare:

çocuğun kitabı	'the child's book'
çocuk kitabı	'children's book'
Halil, çocuğun kitabını odasından aldı	'Halil took the child's book from his room'
Halil, çocuk kitabını yazdı	'Halil wrote the children's book'
Hiltonun oteli	'Hilton's hotel'
Hilton Oteli	'Hilton Hotel'

Nothing may come between the two members of a possessive compound; the indefinite article bir and any adjectives or other modifiers come before the entire group:

bir çocuk kitabı	'a children's book'
yeni bir çocuk kitabı	'a new children's book'
büyük bir Hilton Oteli	'a big Hilton Hotel'

In the case of normal genitive-possessive constructions,

however, bir and adjectives may precede either noun and apply only to the noun that they precede:

bir çocuğun kitabı	'a child's book'
çocuğun yeni kitabı	'the child's new book'
küçük bir çocuğun yeni kitabı	'the new book of a small child'

In a possessive compound, the accent of the first word is reinforced, as in English:

çocúk kitabı	'children's book'
át arabası	'horse cart'

Compound groups of this sort are very common in Turkish, and we give some more examples:

elma ağacı	'apple tree'
bakkal dükkânı	'grocery store'
at eti	'horse meat'
ev kadını	'housewife'
ders kitabı	'textbook (lesson book)'
sokak köşesi	'street corner'
yemek masası	'dinner table (food table)'
köy odası	'town hall (village room)'
otel odası	'hotel room'
yemek odası	'dining room (food room)'
Türk sigarası	'Turkish cigarette'
ekmek tahtası	'bread board'
el yazısı	'handwriting (manuscript)'

Notice also the use of this construction in proper names and titles:

İstanbul Üniversitesi	'Istanbul University'
Ankara Sokağı	'Ankara Street'
Bebek köyü	'Town of Bebek'

İzmir Lokantası	'Izmir Restaurant'
Bebek Oteli	'Bebek Hotel'
"Bizim Köy" kitabı	'the book Bizim Köy'
"Yeni İstanbul" gazetesi	'the newspaper Yeni Istanbul'

In summary, when you put two nouns together to form a compound group:
1. the second noun must have a possessive suffix
2. the accent falls on the first noun
3. articles and adjectives precede the first noun and apply to the whole group
When you form a normal possessive construction:
1. there must be two suffixes, genitive on the first and possessive on the second noun
2. the two nouns are independent: each has its own accent and modifiers

4. Omission of possessives

In colloquial speech, it is possible to omit the possessive suffix if there is a noun in the genitive present. For example, the title of the popular book Bizim Köy 'Our Village' ought to be (Bizim) Köyümüz according to our rules.

The possessive is also frequently omitted from place names, when the place name is used as a unit and its grammatical structure has been forgotten:

Çengelköy	'Village of the Hook' (we should except Çengelköyü)
Ankara Sokak	'Ankara Street' (we should expect Ankara Sokağı)

Students should remember that when a native Turk omits the possessive suffix, it is assumed that he is speaking colloquially; but when a foreigner omits the suffix, it is assumed that he is making a mistake.

5. Two possessives

It is possible for a possessive compound to become itself possessed by another noun or become the second member of another compound:

Mehmedin ders kitabı	'Mehmet's textbook'
üniversite ders kitabı	'university textbook'

Here *kitap* ought to have two possessive suffixes: one because it is in a compound with *ders*, and another because the group *ders kitabı* is possessed by Mehmet in one case and forms a compound with *üniversite* in the other. However, there may not be more than one possessive suffix on a word; whenever there ought to be more than one, all but the last are dropped. Consider this example:

Benim otel odam	'my hotel room'

Here *benim* in the genitive is the possessor of the group *otel odası*; the suffix -*sı* is dropped and the suffix -*m*, going with *benim*, replaces it.

6. *Usage*

Anne is the regular word for 'mother'. The variant *ana* is used rhetorically and in expressions such as *ana yurdu* (*ana yurt*) 'motherland'. It may also be used as an adjective, meaning 'main' or 'principal', in certain expressions such as *ana yol* 'main road'.

Baş means 'head'; but like English 'head', it can be used in a variety of metaphorical uses, expecially 'chief': *kasap başı* 'head butcher' (a possessive compound: 'butcher chief'). It may also be used adjectivally: *baş kâtip* 'chief clerk', *baş müdür* 'chief director'.

VOCABULARY

anne, ana		mother; main (see "Usage")
baba		father
bakkal		grocer; grocery
baş		head; chief (see "Usage")
beyaz		white
dükkân	/dük̭k̭an/	shop, store

düşmek		fall
el		hand
köy		village
oda		room
otel		hotel
sigara	/sigâra/	cigarette
tutmak		hold
üniversite		university

EXERCISES

A. Compose an answer, in the form of a grammatical and meaningful Turkish sentence, to each of these questions:

1. Masadan ne düştü?
2. Bakkal dükkânından ne aldınız?
3. Elinizde ne tuttunuz?
4. Siz hangi üniversiteye gittiniz?
5. İstanbul'un dükkânlarını sevdiniz mi?

B. Translate into English:

1. Lokanta, otelinizden çok uzak.
2. Mehmedin evinde yemek yedik.
3. Halilin kızı bugün odasından çıkmadı.
4. Kızın annesi yemeği elinde tuttu; onu ona vermedi.
5. Başıma neler düştü!
6. Dün Mehmedi yeni arabasında gördüm.
7. Babam beyaz taş masayı evin bir köşesine koydu.
8. Ankara otobüsü sizin evinizin sağında durdu.
9. Ahmedin arabasını dün evin kapısında gördüm.
10. Orhanın eski dükkânından güzel çocuk kitapları aldık.

C. Complete the following with the correct case and possessive suffixes:

1. Bakkalın çocuk___ çok hoş.
2. Hangi otel___ kaldınız?
3. Köy oda___ köy___ çok uzaktır.
4. Siz___ kitap___ çok güzeldir.
5. Ahmet___ sigara___ yer___ düştü.
5. Ayşe Fatma___ bir yemek kitap___ verdi.
7. Bizim eski müdür___ şimdi Ankara___ çalışıyor.
8. Ahmet sigara___ sağ el___ tuttu.
9. Mehmet, el___ kız___ baş___ koydu.
10. Bügün sen oda___ kaldın mı?

D. Translate into Turkish:

1. Fatma studied at Ankara University.
2. I bought Turkish cigarettes from the shop.
3. The man came from his village.
4. They lived near my father's house.
5. Village houses are not big.
6. The Bebek bus didn't stop at the corner today.
7. The child's mother put her hand on his head.
8. We bought apples from a small grocery store.
9. Orhan's daughter stayed in her room yesterday.
10. We stayed at the Divan Hotel, but we didn't like it; its rooms are too small.
11. The book fell from his hand to the floor.
12. He looked through the car window at a white horse.
13. Is the newspaper mine or yours?

LESSON 10: VAR AND YOK

Study the following sentences:

Bugün su yok	'Today there is no water'
Köyde neler var?	'What things are there in the village?'
Hayvanın ağzında ne var?	'What is (there) in the animal's mouth?'
Mehmedın odasında eski bir sandalye var	'There is an old chair in Mehmet's room'
Siz resimde yoksunuz, amma biz varız	'You are not in the picture, but we are'
Ankara şehrinde çok geniş sokaklar var	'There are very wide streets in the city of Ankara'
Bakkalda meyva yok, kalmadı	'There is no fruit at the grocery; it ran out'
Siyah bir köpeğimiz var	'We have a black dog'
Ahmedin oğlu yok, kızı var	'Ahmet does not have a son; he has a daughter'
Arkadaşımın küçük bir oğlu var, ismi Mehmet'tir	'My friend has a small son; his name is Mehmet'
Adınız yok mu?	'Don't you have a name?'
Kimin sigarası var?	'Who has cigarettes?'

1. Existential particles

The particles var and yok are used as predicates; they mean 'it exists' and 'it does not exist', respectively. They are used for sentences corresponding to English expressions with 'there is' and 'there are':

Odada hayvan var	'There is an animal in the room (An animal exists in the room)'
Odada hayvan yok	'There is no animal in the room (An animal does not exist in the room)'

Var and *yok*, as nonverbal predicates, are used with the same endings that we have seen already in use with adjectives and other nonverbal constructions. This means, for example, that the suffix *-DIr* may be used, under the same conditions that determine its use in other cases:

Ankarada çok otel var or vardır	'There are many hotels in Ankara'
Bursada çok otel yok or yoktur	'There are not many hotels in Bursa'

These particles are almost always used with the third person subject; under exceptional conditions, however, they may appear with first or second person:

Evde kim var? —Biz varız	'Who is there in the house? —We are'
Sen resimde yoksun	'You are not in the picture'
Biz resimde yokuz	'We are not in the picture'

The subject of a sentence with *var* or *yok* is nearly always indefinite, and therefore, in accordance with the rules of order, it comes next to the predicate particle:

Orhanın odasında şimdi genç bir kadın var	'There is a young woman in Orhan's room now'

As usual, Turkish normally does not use either *bir* or *-lEr* with this indefinite noun:

Odada iskemle var	'There is a chair in the room'
	'There are chairs in the room'
Bakkalda elma var	'There are apples at the grocery'
Sandalyemde su var	'There is water on my chair'

The indefinite article or the plural suffix would be used only if the speaker had some particular reason to stress the singularity or plurality of the subject:

Odada bir iskemle var — 'There is a (one) chair in the room'

Odada iskemleler var — 'There are some chairs in the room'

If there is an adjective, however, -lEr and bir are more common:

Sokakta siyah bir araba var — 'There is a black car in the street'

Şehirde güzel evler var — 'There are beautiful houses in the city'

With the negative yok, bir and -lEr are even rarer:

Bakkalda elma yok — 'There are no apples at the grocery'

Otelde lokanta yok — 'There is no restaurant in the hotel'

Bir in this context has the connotation of 'not even one':

Bakkalda bir elma yok — 'There is not a single apple at the grocery'

2. Questions with var and yok

Var and yok are nonverbal predicates, and questions with them are formed in the normal manner:

Resimde var mıyız? — 'Are we in the picture?'

Otobüste yer var mı? — 'Is there any room on the bus?'

Evimizde yemek yok mu? — 'Isn't there any food at our house?'

Remember that, according to the principle that the answer to a yes-or-no question in Turkish is a repetition of the predicate, either in the positive or the negative, the answer to a question with *var* or *yok* is *var* or *yok*:

Dükkânda ekmek var mı? —Var	'Is there any bread in the store? —Yes'

In addition, *yok* is widely used in the colloquial language as the general word for 'no', instead of *hayır*.

3. 'To have'

Turkish does not have a verb corresponding to English 'have'; instead, it uses a possessive construction as subject of a sentence with *var* or *yok*. For example, *(Benim) oğlum var* means literally 'My son exists' and is used for 'I have a son'. Similarly, *Ahmedin oğlu yok*, literally 'Ahmet's son does not exist', is used for 'Ahmet does not have a son'. Some other examples follow:

Halilin geniş bir odası var	'Halil has a large (spacious) room'
Çocuğun arkadaşı yok	'The child has no friends'
Sigaranız var mı?	'Do you have any cigarettes?'
Evin kapısı yok mu?	'Doesn't the house have a door?'
Otelin çok güzel odaları var, ama lokantası yok	'The hotel has very nice rooms but no restaurant'

It is important to distinguish between the use of the genitive and the locative in this construction:

(Benim) sigaram yok	'I have no cigarettes'
Bende sigara yok	'There are no cigarettes on me'

Although the two constructions frequently mean the same thing in practice, basically there is a difference between permanent and immediate possession; compare:

Evde sigaram var, ama şimdi bende yok — 'I have cigarettes at home but none on me now'

As a general rule, English constructions with 'to have' correspond to Turkish constructions with the genitive, while English 'there is/there are' correspond to Turkish expressions with the locative.

4. Variation in stems: *su* and *ne*

The two nouns *su* 'water' and *ne* 'what', before a suffix beginning with a vowel (or a buffer consonant), add the consonant *y* to the stem. Compare the following forms of *su* and *ne* with the regular forms of *anne* 'mother':

Nominative	su	ne	anne
Genitive	suyun	neyin	annenin
3rd sg possessive	suyu	neyi	annesi
1st sg possessive	suyum	neyim	annem

But in the colloquial language, "regular" forms of *ne* are also possible—for example, *nem*, *nenin*.

5. Variation in stems: final clusters

In Turkish, a word may end in two consonants only under certain conditions: there are restrictions on what combinations may be used. The same restrictions apply to groups of two consonants in the middle of a word preceding another consonant. In general, a word may end in two consonants only if (1) the first is *l*, *m*, *n*, or *r*, and (2) the second is *ç*, *k*, *p*, or *t*. The following words therefore meet these requirements:

Türk	'Turk'	semt	'direction'
genç	'young'	alp	'brave'
korkmak	'to fear'	borç	'debt'
renk	'color'	harp	'war'
halk	'people'	dört	'four'

There are some examples of words with other final clusters, such as <u>ders</u> 'lesson', <u>aşk</u> 'love', <u>üst</u> 'top', <u>harf</u> 'letter'.

Many stems in Turkish end basically in clusters of consonants that are not permitted by the rule just given. For example, the word for 'city' is basically /şehr/. When this word stands alone, or when it is followed by a suffix beginning with a consonant, the vowel <u>I</u> is inserted between the two final consonants in order to break up the cluster. Thus we get <u>şehir</u> 'city', plural, <u>şehirler</u>. When the word is followed by a suffix beginning with a vowel, however, the <u>I</u> is not needed, since the two consonants are no longer at the end of the word. Thus we get <u>şehre</u> 'to the city', <u>şehrim</u> 'my city'. Notice also:

oğul (/ogl/) pl. oğullar	'son'	oğlu	'his son'
ağız (/agz/) pl. ağızlar	'mouth'	ağzı	'his mouth'
isim (/ism/) pl. isimler	'name'	ismi	'his name'

These words therefore basically consist of a single syllable but become two-syllable words when they stand alone. By way of contrast, there are also words that genuinely consist of two syllables and that never lose their second vowel even when a vowel is added. Compare:

boyun (/boyn/)	'neck'	boynu	'his neck'
koyun	'sheep'	koyunu	'his sheep'

This means that, when we have the dictionary form of a word, we are in the same difficulty as in the case of words like <u>armut</u> or <u>ağaç</u>: we have no way of knowing what the form of the word before a vowel will be. Consider these examples:

deniz	'sea'
resim	'picture'

Here we cannot tell whether 'to the sea' should be

denze or _denize_, or whether 'his picture' should be _resmi_ or _resimi_. With transcription, however, the difficulty is resolved:

deniz		'sea'
resim	/resm/	'picture'

We can now predict _denize_ 'to the sea' and _resmi_ 'his picture'. For this reason, whenever a word ends basically in a cluster of two consonants, we shall indicate this cluster in transcription in the vocabulary.

6. Interrogatives: _kim_

Kim means 'who':

Buğün kim geldi?	'Who came today?'
Fatma kimdir?	'Who is Fatma?'
Kimin evinde oturdunuz?	'Whose house did you live in?'
Kitabı kimden aldınız?	'Who did you get the book from?'

Kimler means 'what people', or 'who' when the speaker expects several people to figure in the answer.

Üniversitede kimler gördünüz?	'Who (all) did you see at the university?'

The interrogative _ne_ (but not _kim_) may appear with possessive suffixes. A word such as _neyim_ means 'what of mine'. If this seems hard to comprehend, observe the exact parallelism between:

Kitabımı aldı	'He took my book'
Neyimi aldı	'He took my what?' ('What of mine did he take?')

Similarly:

Çocuğa neyini verdi?	'What of his did he give the child?'
Neyiniz var?	'What's wrong with you?' ('What do you have?')

7. Usage

Notice that deniz corresponds to both 'sea' and 'shore' or 'seashore'. The idiom for 'go in (swimming)' is denize girmek.

Kalmadı, literally 'it did not remain', is used for 'there is none left'. It is a favorite expression in shops and restaurants in Turkey.

Ne var ne yok is a colloquial form of address, used instead of Nasılsınız? 'How are you?'

The idiom for 'go downtown' is şehre inmek.

Siyah and kara both mean 'black', but siyah is much more common; kara is used in names like Karadeniz 'Black Sea' and in set expressions like kara köpek 'black dog'.

VOCABULARY

ad		name
ağız	/agz/	mouth
Ahmet	/Ahmed/	man's name
arkadaş		friend
deniz		sea, seashore
geniş		wide, spacious
hayvan		animal
isim	/ism/	name
iskemle	/iskémle/	chair
kara		black
kim		who?
oğul	/ogl/	son
resim	/resm/	picture
sandalye	/sandályе/	chair
siyah		black
su		water; juice
şehir	/şehr/	city
var		it exists
yok		it does not exist

EXERCISES

A. Compose an answer to the following questions:

1. İstanbul şehrinde neler var?
2. Köyünüzde neler var?
3. Evinizde kim var?
4. Resimde kimleri gördünüz?
5. Kimin sigarası var?
6. İsminiz ne?
7. Elimde ne var?
8. Sizde ne hayvanlar var?

B. Complete the following with the correct case and possessive suffixes:

1. Otobüs___ benim bir arkadaş___ gördüm.
2. Baba___ büyük bir otomobil___ var.
3. Siz___ çok arkadaş___ var mı?
4. Lokanta___ yemek___ kalmadı.
5. Fatma___ çok güzel el yazı___ var.
6. Otel___ yemek oda___ yok mu?
7. "Bizim Köy" kitap___ kim yazdı?
8. Gazete___ kim___ resim___ var?

C. Translate into English:

1. Halil'in küçük oğlunun adı Orhan (Orhan'dir).
2. Bakkalda elma kalmadı.
3. Evde hayvanınız var mı?
4. Kara köpek kimin?
5. Gazetede Ayşenin yeni evinin bir resmi var.
6. Bu resimde ben yokum, ama Ayşenin babası var.
7. Ankara'da deniz var mı, yok mu?
8. İstanbul Üniversitesinde bir oğlumuz var, adı Ahmet.
9. Benim adım Fatma. Sizin isminiz ne?

10. Bugün İstanbul'dan Ankara'ya otobüs yok.

D. Translate into Turkish:

1. The girls went to the seashore, but Fatma didn't go in.
2. The dog doesn't have a name.
3. We have good bread today.
4. There is good meat in the butcher shop today.
5. In Ahmet's room there is a picture of his son.
6. I have many friends in Izmir.
7. There was no food left at the restaurant.
8. The child put the fruit in his mouth.
9. Halil's friend made apple juice at home, but it turned out bad.
10. There is a black animal in the road; what is it?
11. You sat on my chair.

LESSON 11: THE PROGRESSIVE TENSE

Study the following sentences:

Şimdi derse başlıyoruz	'Now we are beginning the lesson'
Sigaraları yeni kutuma koyuyorum	'I am putting the cigarettes in my new box'
Kardeşiniz hâlâ odasında oturuyor, pencereden bakıyor	'Your brother is still sitting in his room and looking out the window'
Attilanın mektubunu anlıyor musunuz?	'Do you understand Atilla's letter?'
Çay mı içiyorsunuz, kahve mi?	'Are you drinking tea or coffee?'
Onu istiyor musunuz, istemiyor musunuz?	'Do you want it or not?'
Orhan eve gitti, biz de eve gidiyoruz	'Orhan went home, and we are going home too'
Fatma daima yorgundur, az tembel de değil	'Fatma is always tired, and she is not a little lazy too'

1. Variation in stems: y conditioning

Under some circumstances, the vowel _E_ at the end of a stem or a suffix becomes _I_ when a _y_ immediately follows. The progressive suffix -_Iyor_, when it follows a vowel, loses its initial _I_; the suffix then begins with a _y_, and the preceding vowel becomes _I_. Thus:

iste + Iyor	'he wants'
iste + yor	(with dropping of _I_)
istiyor	(with raising of _e_ to _i_)

Similarly:

anlıyorum	'I understand' (anla + Iyor + (y)Im)
okumuyoruz	'we are not reading' (oku + mE + Iyor + (y)Iz)
görmüyor	'he does not see' (gör + mE + Iyor)

yiyor	'he is eating' (ye + Iyor)

(If you prefer, you may simply learn that the suffix -Iyor causes a preceding vowel to drop; but remember that this is not true of any other suffix beginning with -I.)

The conditions under which y conditioning takes place are hard to define; not only are the rules complex, but there is a certain amount of free variation as well. Individual speakers may differ not only in whether they make the change but also in whether they represent it in writing.

The change almost never takes place in nouns, except for niye 'why', an archaic dative of ne. It is much more common with certain verb suffixes. We shall discuss individual cases as they come up. For the moment, remember that with -Iyor the change always takes place and always is represented in writing.

2. The progressive tense

The progressive tense sign is -Iyor. This tense is used when the subject is in the process of performing some action or when the action is going on at the moment of the utterance. It normally corresponds to the English 'is -ing' tense but sometimes corresponds to the English present, including the narrative present:

Ne yapıyorsunuz? Pencereyi açıyorum	'What are you doing? I am opening the window'
Kahvede oturuyor, çay içiyorlar	'They are sitting in the coffeehouse and drinking tea'
Hayvanlar yemek istiyor	'The animals want food'
Otobüs şimdi geliyor	'The bus is coming now'
Adam eve geliyor, oturuyor, gazetesini açıyor	'The man comes home, sits down, and opens his newspaper'

The suffix -Iyor is used with the same endings that are used with adjectives and other nonverbal predicates. The suffix -DIr, however, is extremely rare with this tense; it appears mainly in a use that will be introduced much later. As a rule of thumb, do not use it. Notice that -Iyor is a nonharmonic suffix: the second vowel o does not change with vowel harmony, although the first vowel I does change. The vowels of the personal endings are governed harmonically by the o.

korkuyorum	'I am afraid'
içiyorsun	'you (sg) are drinking'
istemiyor	'he does not want'
söylüyoruz	'we are telling'
açıyorsunuz	'you (pl) are opening'
başlıyorlar, başlıyor	'they are beginning'

Accent may be on either the o or the I of -Iyor. The personal endings used with this suffix are unaccented; accent ought, therefore, to be on the preceding vowel, which is o. At a historically earlier period, however, accent was on the I. These two rules compete in modern Turkish, so that it is possible to hear the accent either way.

gelíyorum, geliyórum	'I am coming'

Remember that this suffix begins with a vowel; therefore, any verb stem that ends basically in a voiced stop will actually have this stop when -Iyor is added. So far we have had one such verb, gitmek 'to go', stem /gid-/. Compare:

gidiyor	'he is coming'
gitmiyor	'he is not going'

3. Questions with -Iyor

Questions with -Iyor are formed in the same way as with adjectives and other nonverbal predicates. In such questions, mI follows the tense suffix but precedes the personal ending; it is written as a separate word but is affected by vowel harmony (it is thus mu after -Iyor). Personal endings (except -lEr) are attached to mu and are also affected by vowel harmony:

Çalışıyor musun?	'Are you working?'

Anlamıyor musunuz? 'Don't you understand?'

Kalıyor muyuz? 'Are we staying?'

But notice:

Gidiyorlar mı? 'Are they going?'

4. Possessive and predicative endings

We have seen by this time that there are basically two sets of personal endings in Turkish. One of these is the set used with adjectives, nouns, and other non-verbal predicates, with the progressive -Iyor, and with several other tenses to be introduced later. We may call these the "predicative" endings.

The other set is used with nouns in possessive constructions. Also, the endings used with the past definite tense -DI, and with one other tense to be introduced later, are basically the same as the possessive suffixes. Notice that the ending -m of a past tense form such as geldim 'I came' is actually the possessive -Im, with the vowel I dropped after the vowel of -DI. Thus we have:

gel + DI + Im	becomes	geldim	'I came'
içki + Im	becomes	içkim	'my liquor'

Similarly, we have geldin 'you came', köşen 'your corner', açtınız 'you opened', kapınız 'your door'. There are, however, some differences: the ending for 'we' is -k after -DI but -ImIz as a possessive, and the ending for 'he' is -(s)I as a possessive but zero after -DI. These differences are, however, simply irregularities; essentially there is one set of endings with some variation, and we may call these the "possessive" endings.

We may sum up these endings with the following chart:

	Predicative (unaccented)	Possessive (accented)	
		true possessive	after -DI
ben	-(y)Im	-Im	-Im
sen	-sIn	-In	-In
o	(-DIr)	-(s)I	zero
biz	-(y)Iz	-ImIz	-k
siz	-sInIz	-InIz	-InIz
onlar	-(DIr)(lEr)	-(lEr)I	(-lEr)

In the light of this analysis, we can now explain some irregularities about the endings.

The predicative endings are unaccented, but the possessive endings are accented normally. Thus we have:

çalışkánsınız	'you are industrious'
tembélim	'I am lazy'
açtınín	'you opened'
kapınín	'your door'
geldím	'I came'
kâtibím	'my clerk'

The interrogative mI follows possessive endings but precedes predicative endings. Thus we have:

Yorgun musun?	'Are you tired?'
İçiyor musunuz?	'Are you drinking?'
Okudun mu?	'Did you read?'
Sevdiniz mi?	'Did you like?'

Arkadaşın mı geldi?	'Did your friend come?'

5. DE

We have seen that the particles mI and değil may be placed after almost any word in a Turkish sentence to question or negate the word or phrase that immediately precedes. There are several other particles of this sort in Turkish, and one of the most common is DE 'also'. Like mI, DE is written as a separate word in the literary language but alternates according to both vowel and consonant harmony with the preceding word:

sen de	'you too'
Ahmet te	'Ahmet too'
ağaç ta	'and the tree'
Orhan sigara aldı, içki de aldı	'Orhan bought cigarettes and also liquor'
Ahmet kahve içiyor, ben de kahve istiyorum	'Ahmet is drinking coffee, and I want coffee too'
Halilin kız kardeşi güzel değil, hoş ta değil	'Halil's sister is not attractive, and she isn't pleasant either'
Benim de sigaram yok	'I don't have any cigarettes either'

When DE refers to the entire sentence, it follows the first words, or the first noun phrase, in the sentence:

Annesi de ona küçük bir kutu yaptı	'And his mother made him a small box'

DE is extremely common in the colloquial language, in a multiplicity of uses that it would be impossible to formalize here. The expression bir de is used colloquially as a conjunction meaning 'and':

Kahve istiyorum, bir de su	'I want coffee and water'

Ama 'but' may be placed at the beginning of its

clause, as we have used it until now; or, more idiomatically, it may follow the first word of the clause:

Ben çalışkanım, sen ama çok tembelsin	'I am hard working, but you are very lazy'

6. Accent: compounds

Compounds in Turkish are accented on the last syllable of the first member. Thus búgün 'today', a compound of bu 'this' and gün 'day', is accented on bu; Karádeniz 'Black Sea' is accented on the last syllable of kara.

We have seen several examples of this principle in the grammar already. For example, when the word ile 'and' is suffixed to a preceding noun, accent falls on the last syllable of the noun:

Orhánla Mehmet	'Orhan and Mehmet'

The accent on Orhánla can be accounted for, since it is a compound of Orhan and ile.

Similarly, the particles mI and DE are written as separate words but pronounced as suffixes, since they are affected by vowel harmony. Accent falls on the last syllable of the word to which they are attached, and can be accounted for by the compounding rule:

Sén mi geldin?	'Did you come?'
Sén de geldin	'You came too'

The principle also applies in the case of phrases that are not written as single words; for example, in the case of possessive compounds:

yemék masası	'dinner table'
él yazısı	'manuscript'

There will be many more applications of this principle in the course of this grammar.

7. Usage

İçmek means not only 'drink' but also 'smoke' when a cigarette or pipe is referred to; it is also used for the taking of medicine or pills. It is also used for soup where English would use 'eat'.

Kahve içtim	'I drank coffee'
Sigara içtim	'I smoked a cigarette'
İlacı içtim	'I took (drank) the medicine' (ilaç 'medicine')
Hapları içtim	'I took the pills' (hap 'pill')
Çorba içtim	'I ate soup' (çorba 'soup')

İçmek is another transitive verb that requires an object (see Lesson 5, Section 5). When no more specific object is to be expressed, the noun içki 'drink' is used. When içki is used separately as a noun, it normally refers to an alcoholic drink.

Çay içiyorlar	'They are drinking tea'
İçki içiyorlar	'They are drinking'

İstemek corresponds to 'want' but also to 'ask for' or 'order' (for example, in a restaurant).

Kardeş properly means 'sibling'; that is, it does not distinguish between 'brother' and 'sister'. The terms kız kardeş and erkek kardeş may be used when it is important to make this distinction.

VOCABULARY

açmak		open
anlamak		understand
Attila		man's name
çay		tea
erkek		man, male
hâlâ	/hā́lā/	still
içki		(alcoholic) drink
içmek		drink, smoke (see "Usage")
istemek		want

kahve	coffee, coffeehouse
kardeş	brother, sister (see "Usage")
kutu	box

EXERCISES

A. Compose an answer to the following questions:

1. Kardeşiniz var mı?
2. Ne istiyorsunuz?
3. Pencereden ne görüyorsunuz?
4. Dersi anladınız mı?
5. Dersi hâlâ mı anlamadınız?

B. Translate into English:

1. Kutudan sigara aldı, şimdi içiyor.
2. Kardeşiniz erkek mi?
3. İçki mi içiyorsun, su mu?
4. Dersi okuyorum, ama anlamıyorum.
5. Denizde bir adam görüyorum, ağzında bir sigara var.
6. Görmüyor musun? Çocuk seni anlamıyor.
7. Beni mi istediniz? Şimdi geliyorum.
8. Fatma dün gitti, hâlâ gelmedi. Korkuyorum.
9. Onlar sigara içmiyorlar, biz de içmiyoruz.
10. Size yeni kitaplar verdim, ama onları hâlâ okumadınız.

C. Change the following sentences into the progressive tense:

1. Bizden ne istediniz?
2. İçki içmediniz, çay da mı içmediniz?
3. Kardeşimin resmini beğenmediniz mi?
4. Fatmanın köpeğinden korkmadınız mı?
5. Ayşe ile Orhan evde oturdular, çocuklar denize girdi, biz de kitap okuduk.

D. Supply the appropriate tense and person suffixes:

1. Orhanın babası şimdi Efes Otelinde çalış___.
2. Dün arkadaşımın oğlundan bir mektup al___.
3. Ali Ankara'dan dün gel___, hâlâ evde otur___.
4. Ahmet şimdi evde yok, siz ne iste___?
5. Çok hastasınız, ama içki iç___.
6. Dün senden bir kitap iste___, hâlâ verme___.

E. Translate into Turkish:

1. Yesterday, at your house, Mehmet drank too much.
2. The child took an old box and is putting his books in it.
3. You want tea, don't you? No, I don't; I want coffee.
4. Have you seen my cigarette box?
5. Is Attila busy today? Yes, he is writing letters to his sisters and brothers.
6. Are you coming or going?
7. Ahmet is a bad man, and his brother is not very nice either.
8. Are the Turks <u>always</u> sitting in the coffeehouse?
9. I still don't understand the lesson.

LESSON 12: DEMONSTRATIVES AND NUMBERS

Study the following sentences:

Bu kim?	'Who is this?'
O insan kim?	'Who is that person?'
Şu kalemi buldum	'I found this (here) pen'
Bunu gördünüz mü?	'Did you see this?'
Sokakta iki koca at var	'There are two large horses in the street'
O dükkânın dört büyük penceresi var	'That store has four big windows'
İstanbulda iki milyon kişi oturuyor	'Two million people live in Istanbul'
Bugün üç paket sigara içtim	'Today I smoked three packs of cigarettes'
İyi bir çeşit portakal arıyorum	'I am looking for a good kind of oranges'
Alinin kitaplarını saydınız mı?	'Did you count Ali's books?'
Kaç tane var?	'How many are there?'
Alinin dokuz bin yedi yüz otuz beş (tane) kitabı var	'Ali has 9735 books'
On dördünü okudu, öbürlerini okumadı	'He read 14 of them, he didn't read the others'

1. Demonstratives

Turkish has three demonstrative pronouns: bu, şu, and o. Bu 'this' and o 'that' correspond to the English demonstratives; they indicate the location of an object with respect to the speaker.

Şu, which may be translated 'this' or 'that', contains the additional notion of a gesture; the use of şu points more strongly to the object. The speaker may or may not actually make a gesture; but the object referred to must normally be in sight and in a location where it can be pointed to with a gesture.

Some nonstandard forms of English have the expressions 'this here' and 'that there' ('That there house

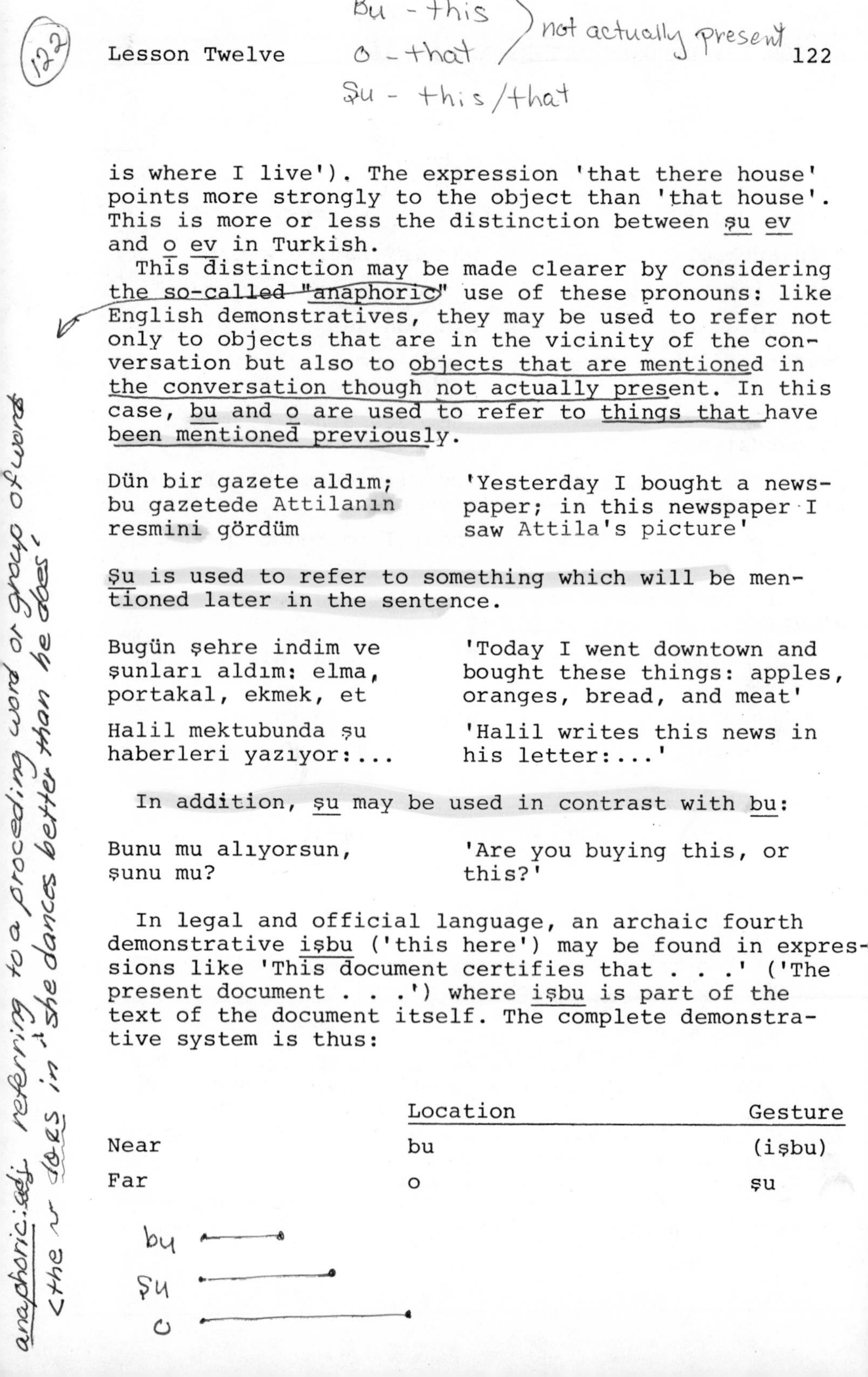

is where I live'). The expression 'that there house' points more strongly to the object than 'that house'. This is more or less the distinction between şu ev and o ev in Turkish.

This distinction may be made clearer by considering the so-called "anaphoric" use of these pronouns: like English demonstratives, they may be used to refer not only to objects that are in the vicinity of the conversation but also to objects that are mentioned in the conversation though not actually present. In this case, bu and o are used to refer to things that have been mentioned previously.

Dün bir gazete aldım; bu gazetede Attilanın resmini gördüm	'Yesterday I bought a newspaper; in this newspaper I saw Attila's picture'

Şu is used to refer to something which will be mentioned later in the sentence.

Bugün şehre indim ve şunları aldım: elma, portakal, ekmek, et	'Today I went downtown and bought these things: apples, oranges, bread, and meat'
Halil mektubunda şu haberleri yazıyor:...	'Halil writes this news in his letter:...'

In addition, şu may be used in contrast with bu:

Bunu mu alıyorsun, şunu mu?	'Are you buying this, or this?'

In legal and official language, an archaic fourth demonstrative işbu ('this here') may be found in expressions like 'This document certifies that . . .' ('The present document . . .') where işbu is part of the text of the document itself. The complete demonstrative system is thus:

	Location	Gesture
Near	bu	(işbu)
Far	o	şu

The meaning of *şu* has not been well understood in most traditional grammars, and the pronoun is often defined as indicating a "middle distance" between *bu* and *o*. The reason for this misinterpretation is probably that objects that can be referred to with a gesture tend to be closer to the speaker than objects that can be referred to generally with 'that'.

1.1. Use of demonstratives

An *n* is added to the stem of these pronouns before any noun suffix: plural, possessive, or case. (See Lesson 9, Section 1.1.)

bunlar	'these'
şunlar	'these (here)'
buna	'to this'
şundan	'from this (here)'
onu	'that (obj)'

An *n* is *not* added before a suffix that is not a noun suffix; that is, before suffixes belonging to the auxiliary:

budur	'it is this'
şudur	'it is this (here)'

These words may be used as pronouns:

Bu ne (nedir)?	'What is this?'
O kim (kimdir)?	'Who is that?'
Şu, kalem (kalemdir)	'This is a pen'
O Ali (Alidir)	'That is Ali'
Şunu buldum	'I found this'
Bundan korktum	'I was afraid of this'

They may also be used as adjectives:

Bu kitabı beğendim	'I liked this book'
Şu bardaklar pek temiz değil	'These glasses are not very clean'
Portakalları o kutuya koydum	'I put the oranges in that box'

If there is an adjective present, the demonstrative precedes the adjective:

Bu ihtiyar adam dün bize geldi	'This old man came to (visit) us yesterday'
Ahmedin babası, o beyaz evde oturuyor	'Ahmet's father lives in that white house'

2. Numbers

bir	one	on	ten
iki	two	yirmi	twenty
üç	three	otuz	thirty
dört (/dörd/)	four	kırk	forty
beş	five	elli	fifty
altı	six	altmış	sixty
yedi	seven	yetmiş	seventy
sekiz	eight	seksen	eighty
dokuz	nine	doksan	ninety

Number words from 11 to 99 are formed by compounding, with the tens figure first, then the units. From 11 to 19, the accent is on the first member (<u>on</u>); from 21 to 99, the accent is on the second member.

ón bir	'eleven'
ón sekiz	'eighteen'
yirmi bír	'twenty-one'
otuz dö́rt	'thirty-four'
doksan dokúz	'ninety-nine'

Yüz is 'one hundred'; bin is 'one thousand'. Bir is not used with these numbers. Other numbers are formed by compounding:

yüz on dokuz	119
altı yüz elli iki	652
bin yedi yüz otuz beş	1735
beş bin altı yüz doksan	5690
üç yüz bin yüz on	300,110
dört yüz yirmi iki bin dokuz yüz seksen bir	422,981

Bir milyon is 1,000,000, bir milyar is 1,000,000,000.

bir milyon üç yüz yirmi bir bin yedi yüz otuz	1,321,730
dört milyon	4,000,000
yüz milyon	100,000,000

Sıfır is 'zero'.

2.1. Uses of numbers

The plural suffix is not normally used with a noun when a number precedes:

yedi adam	'seven men'
yirmi beş kalem	'twenty-five pens'
Üç kitap getirdim	'I brought three books'
Üç kitabı getirdim	'I brought the three books'

The plural suffix may be added to the noun to refer to particular collections of people: Yedi Cüceler 'the Seven Dwarfs', Kırk Haramiler 'the Forty Thieves'. The suffix may be added to the number itself: Beşler 'The Five', if there is some group of five people who go by that name. An example is Şikagolu Yediler 'The Chicago Seven'.

Numbers precede adjectives but follow demonstratives:

yedi koca taş	'seven large stones'

o yedi taş	'those seven stones'
bu on altı çok aç çocuk	'These sixteen very hungry children'

Notice that, in accordance with this rule, bir meaning 'one' precedes an adjective, while bir meaning 'a' follows. Notice also that a noun with bir 'a' must be indefinite, while a noun with bir 'one' may be definite or indefinite.

boş bir kutu	'an empty box'
bir boş kutu	'one empty box'
Bir gazete aradım	'I looked for a newspaper'
Bir gazeteyi aradım	'I looked for the one newspaper'

2.2. Counting words

Some nouns, which we shall call "counting words," may be placed between a number and a following noun.

bir bardak su	'one (a) glass of water'
iki çeşit ekmek	'two kinds of bread'
üç kutu kalem	'three boxes of pens'
dört paket sigara	'four packs of cigarettes'
beş parça kâğıt	'five pieces of paper'

The most common counting word is tane (/tāne/), which literally means 'grain', but which has no independent meaning in these expressions. Tane may be placed freely between a number and any noun, with no change in the meaning:

İki elim var	'I have two hands'
İki tane elim var	
Kaç elma istiyorsunuz?	'How many apples do you want?'
Kaç tane elma istiyorsunuz?	

When the number stands alone, however, as in the answer to a question, the counting word *must* be present after it; the counting word may be omitted only in very colloquial conversation:

Kaç (tane) elma istiyorsunuz? —Beş tane	'How many apples do you want?' 'Five'
Kaç bardak su içti? —Yedi bardak	'How many glasses of water did he drink?' 'Seven'
Mehmede kaç parça kâğıt verdiniz? —İki parça	'How many pieces of paper did you give Mehmet?' 'Two'

A counting construction can exist only with a number; we can say *bir bardak su* 'a (one) glass of water', but we cannot say 'the glass of water' with this construction. The construction may, however, be definite or indefinite:

Yedi kutu kalem aldım	'I bought seven boxes of pens'
Yedi kutu kalemi aldım	'I bought the seven boxes of pens'

Notice the difference in the use of a noun such as *bardak* as a counting word and as an ordinary noun. When *bardak* is a counting word, it may not be preceded by *tane* (because, as a counting word, it replaces *tane*); thus we cannot have:

*Kaç tane bardak su içti?

*Yedi tane bardak

When *bardak* is used as an ordinary noun, without another noun following, it may be preceded freely by *tane*:

Kaç bardak düştü?	'How many glasses fell?'
Kaç tane bardak düştü?	
Yedi tane	'Seven'

Notice also the difference between a counting

construction such as bir bardak su and a possessive compound such as su bardağı 'waterglass'. In the counting construction, bardak does not modify su, nor does it form a compound; it merely gives the unit of measure. The two nouns remain independent; either one may be modified by an adjective, but there is no way by which the entire construction may be modified:

iki büyük paket sigara	'two big packs of cigarettes'
iki paket büyük sigara	'two packs of big cigarettes'

The noun kişi 'person' functions somewhat like a counting word; it may not precede another noun, but it is always used with a number and may not be preceded by tane:

Bugün kaç kişi geliyor?	'How many people are coming today?'
Otuz kişi	'Thirty'

Aded 'item' may be used as a counting word in place of tane, but it is much less common in ordinary usage; it is used mainly in formal documents (customs declarations and the like). Baş 'head' may be used as a counting word for certain kinds of animals, like 'head' in English.

Study the following additional examples of the use of tane. Notice that the third person possessive, 'of them', is frequently used, referring to the original noun. This suffix is normally omitted when the phrase is the subject of var.

O elmaları saydım: üç yüz tane var	'I counted those apples: there are 300'
Yüz ellisini yedim	'I ate 150 of them'
Yüz elli tanesini yedim	
Yetmiş beşini Mehmede verdim	'I gave Mehmet 75 of them'
Yetmiş beş tanesini Mehmede verdim	

Otuz tane (tanesi) kötü, öbürleri iyi	'Thirty (of them) are bad, the rest are good'
Köyümüzde bes (tane) araba var; ikisi Halil'in	'In our village there are five cars; two of them are Halil's'

3. Interrogatives: kaç

Kaç means 'how many'; it is the question word used when the speaker expects the answer to be a number.

Attilanın kaç (tane) oğlu var?	'How many sons does Attila have?'

There are many additional examples of kaç in the preceding sections.

4. Usage

Besides 'look for' and 'search', aramak means 'call (on the telephone)'.

Çeşit and cins, which have a variety of meanings centering around 'kind' ('sort', 'type', 'variety', and so on) are unusual among counting words in that they do not require a preceding numeral:

Bu çeşit meyvayı sevmiyorum	'I don't like this kind of fruit'

İnsan is the regular word for 'person', while kişi is used with a number:

Otelde çok insan var	'There are too many people at the hotel'

Compare:

Köşede bir kişi duruyor	'There is one person standing on the corner'
Köşede bir insan duruyor	'There is a person standing on the corner'

İnsan is also used for 'human being', or English 'man' in the generic sense.

Öbür means 'the other', not simply 'other'; it is always definite and always refers to some object that has previously been mentioned. Therefore, it may not be used with bir, and when it is used as a noun, it always has a possessive suffix.

Bir kadın lokantaya girdi, öbür kadın kapıda durdu	'One woman entered the restaurant, the other woman stopped at the door'
Bir kadın lokantaya girdi, öbürü kapıda durdu	'One woman entered the restaurant, the other stopped at the door'
Portakalların birini yedim, öbürlerini yemedim	'I ate one of the oranges, not the others (of them)'

When öbür is used with a number, the expression is turned around; the number functions as a noun, and öbür is treated as an adjective:

Öbür ikisi kapıda durdu	'The other two (of them) stopped at the door'
Öbür üçünü yemedim	'I didn't eat the other three (of them)'

VOCABULARY

aded		item
Ali		man's name
aramak		search, look for
bardak		glass
boş		empty
bulmak		find
cins		kind, sort
çeşit	/çeşid/	kind, sort
getirmek		bring
insan		person, human (see "Usage")
kaç		how many?

kâğıt	/k̂āgıd/	paper
kalem		pen
kişi		person
koca (adj)		large, huge
koca (n)		husband
öbür		the other (see "Usage")
paket		pack, package
parça		piece
portakal		orange
saymak		count
tane	/tāne/	grain (see Section 2.2)
temiz		clean

EXERCISES

A. Compose an answer to the following questions:

1. O ne?
2. Kaç kitabınız var?
3. O kadının kaç tane kocası var?
4. O kutuların kaç tanesi boş?
5. Bir pakette kaç tane sigara var?
6. Siz kaç kardeşsiniz?
7. Orhan bakkaldan kaç tane ekmek aldı?

B. Translate into English:

1. Masada on iki bardak var. Birini aldım. Kaç kaldı?
2. Bir kişi kapıda duruyor ve çocukları sayıyor.
3. Ben beş tane elma aldım, Orhan sekiz tane portakal aldı. Şimdi kaç tane meyvamız var?
4. Ali kitapları saydı ve onları boş bir kutuya koydu.
5. Bugün yemeğe altı kişi geliyor, ama dört tane sandalyemiz var.

6. Kalemim var, bir kâğıt istiyorum.
7. Kalemleri saydım: dokuz tane. Birini siz mi aldınız?
8. Bu bardaklar temiz değil, iki tane temiz bardak istiyorum.
9. Biz beş kişiyiz, siz kaç kişisiniz?
10. Bir pakette yirmi tane sigara var, iki pakette kaç tane sigara var?

C. Translate into Turkish:

1. eight boxes of books
2. five kinds of paper
3. four glasses of tea
4. six packages of letters
5. two pieces of meat
6. nine boxes of pens
7. one pack of cigarettes
8. three glasses of orange juice
9. ten pieces of wood
10. seven kinds of trees

D. Translate into Turkish:

1. these ninety husbands
2. those fifty hungry people
3. sixty clean windows
4. these seventy women
5. those (there) twenty hardworking clerks
6. these thirty pens
7. forty empty packages
8. those ten sick children
9. those (there) eighty tables
10. one hundred lazy horses

E. Translate into Turkish (in words, not figures):

1. 1001
2. 1100
3. 100,000
4. 30,000
5. 1,698,789

F. Translate into Turkish:

1. The pen of my father is on the table.
2. He is a clean old man.
3. Halil has two left hands.
4. Did you look at this? What is it?
5. I found five stones in my chair. —How many? —Five!
6. I am looking for oranges, but I don't like that kind.
7. Mehmet brought me two pieces of letter paper from that store; I am writing one letter to Ali, and I am writing the other to you.
8. In that (over there) village there are four hundred forty-six people; I counted them. Fifty-four of them are old men, one hundred twenty are women, and the rest are children. The young men are working in Istanbul.

LESSON 13: THE FUTURE TENSE

Study the following sentences:

Yarın inşallah yeni kitabıma başlıyacağım	'Tomorrow I will begin my new book (God willing)'
Buradan şimdi kalkacağım, akşam İzmire varacağım	'I will leave here now, and in the evening I will arrive in Izmir'
Köpeğe yemek vermiyecek misiniz?	'Aren't you going to give food to the dog?'
Kalemini o odada bulmıyacaksın; oraya baktım	'You won't find your pen in that room; I looked there'
Neredesiniz? Buradayım	'Where are you? I am here'
Ankaranın neresinde oturuyorsunuz?	'What part of Ankara do you live in?'
Bir büyük şişede dört buçuk bardak içki var	'There are four and a half glasses of liquor in one big bottle'
Bardağın yarısını içti	'He drank half the glass'
Şişenin tam üçte ikisini içti	'He drank exactly two-thirds of the bottle'
Şişelerin yüzde ellisini (%50) açtı	'He opened fifty percent of the bottles'
Kasaptan yarım kilo et alacağım	'I will buy a half kilo of meat from the butcher'

1. The future tense

The suffix of the future tense is -(y)EcEk (/-(y)EcEg/). It is used with predicative endings:

bulacağım	'I will find'
bineceksin	'you (sg) will get on'
varacak	'he (she, it) will arrive'
kalkacağız	'we will get up'
döneceksiniz	'you (pl) will return'

gidecekler	'they will go'

When the verb stem ends in a vowel, this suffix is preceded by y; the preceding vowel is almost always raised in pronunciation, and this raising is usually (but not always) reflected in the writing. The raised vowel, however, is not subject to rounding harmony.

başlıyacağım	'I will begin'
yapmıyacaksın	'you will not make'
gelmiyecek	'he will not come'
yiyeceğiz	'we will eat'
dönmiyeceksin, dönmeyeceksin	'you will not return'
korkmıyacak, korkmayacak	'he will not be afraid'

This tense corresponds in meaning to the English future: it is used to describe an action that is expected to happen but that has not yet happened.

Otobüs bu akşam İstanbuldan kalktı, yarın sabah Ankaraya varacak	'The bus left Istanbul this evening; it will arrive in Ankara tomorrow morning'
Yarın erken kalkacağım	'Tomorrow I will get up early'
Biz denize gidiyoruz; sen de gelecek misin?	'We are going to the seashore; will you come too?'

Notice that, as in English, the progressive tense may also be used with future meaning to describe an action that has not yet happened:

Yarın denize gidiyoruz	'Tomorrow we are going to the seashore'

2. Adverbs of place

'Here', 'there', 'where?' and similar expressions are formed in Turkish with the suffix -rE- meaning 'place'. It is added to the three demonstrative pronouns and the interrogative to form the noun stems bura- 'this place', *şura-* 'this/that place', *ora-* 'that place', *nere-* 'what place?'. These stems may not be used alone; they must be followed by either a possessive or a case suffix. The dative, locative, and ablative cases are most frequent in this use. Since the suffix -*rE*- is unaccented, accent falls on the pronoun, and the vowel *E* is often elided in speech:

burada [búrda] — 'here (in this place'

şuraya — 'to there (to this/that place)'

oradan [órdan] — 'from there (from that place)'

nerede? [nérde] — 'where? (in what place?)'

Orada kalacak — 'He will stay there'

Buraya döndüm — 'I came back here'

Şuradan geldik — 'We came from there (near)'

Oradan gitti — 'He went from there'

Neredeyiz? — 'Where are we?'

Nereye gidiyorsun? — 'Where are you going?'

The genitive, objective, and possessive suffixes are possible here but much less frequent:

Bu nerenin resmi? — 'What place is this the picture of?' ('This is the picture of what place?')

Oranın sokakları pek temiz değil — 'The streets there are not very clean' ('The streets of that place . . .')

Orayı görmedim — 'I didn't see that place'

Doktor burama baktı — 'The doctor looked at this part of me'

When no other suffix is to be used, the third person possessive (-*sI*) is added to the stem, and the result is simply a noun:

Burası güzel — 'This place is nice'

Orası İzmire yakın — 'That place is near Izmir'

Case - Objective, ablative, locative

Burası neresi?	'What place is this?' ('This place is what place?')

Case suffixes may then be added to the stem with -*sI*, and the result has about the same meaning as though -*sI* were not there:

Orasını görmedim	'I didn't see that place'

Similarly, expressions such as *burasına baktım* 'I looked at this place' are possible but rare, since *buraya baktım* means the same thing.

The use of the plural suffix in these constructions does not necessarily imply plurality but simply makes the spatial reference vaguer. A form such as *burada* 'here' refers to a particular place. This place need not be small; in a sentence such as *Burada otel var mı?* 'Is there a hotel here?' *burada* may refer to an entire town or city. *Buralarda*, on the other hand, refers not to a particular place but to a less specifically defined area. Thus:

Buralarda otel var mı?	'Is there a hotel around here?'
	'Is there a hotel in these parts?'

Compare also:

Oraya baktım	'I looked there'
Oralara baktım	'I looked around there; I looked in that general area'
Kitabım nerede?	'Where is my book?'
Kitabım nerelerde?	'Where on earth is my book?'

We might try to define the difference between this second pair of sentences in this way: the speaker saying *Kitabım nerelerde?* has (or claims to have) less knowledge of where his book might be than the speaker saying *Kitabım nerede?*; that is, the range of possible places is greater.

In some cases, the plural here actually has a plural meaning:

Nereye gittiniz?	'Where did you go (what place)?'
Nerelere gittiniz?	'Where did you go (what places)?'

3. Numerical expressions: fractions

A. Buçuk means 'and a half'; it is always used with another number preceding:

iki buçuk	'two and a half'
bir buçuk	'one and a half'
Üç buçuk şişe su içti	'He drank three and a half bottles of water'

B. Yarım means 'half' and is used as an adjective:

Bir yarım şişe su içti	'He drank a half bottle of water'
Yarım şişe suyu içti	'He drank the half bottle of water'
Köşede yarım gün durdum	'I stood on the corner half a day'

C. Yarı means 'half' and is normally used as a noun; when it is an object, it is always definite:

Şişenin yarısını içtı	'He drank half of the bottle'
Bir şişenin yarısını içti	'He drank half of a bottle'
Bu adamların yarısı Türktür	'Half of these men are Turks'

Note also the expression gece yarısı 'midnight' used as an adverb:

Ankaraya gece yarısı varacağım	'I will arrive in Ankara at midnight'

Distinguish between:

Bir buçuk elma yedi	'He ate one and a half apples'

Bir yarım elma yedi	'He ate a half apple'
Bir elmanın yarısını yedi	'He ate half of an apple'

D. Çeyrek means 'quarter' and is used as an adjective (like yarım); it is normally used, however, only with expressions of time (see Lesson 15).
E. Other fractions are expressed in the form üçte bir 'one in three' or 'one-third':

yedide beş	5/7
altmış dörtte yedi	7/64
yüzde on	10/100 or 10%
Şişenin üçte birini içti	'He drank one-third of the bottle'
Bunların yüzde doksanı Türktür	'Ninety percent (90/100) of these (men) are Turks'

In the expression of percentages, yüzde may be replaced in writing by the sign "%"; since yüzde is the first member of the construction, the percent sign also precedes in Turkish: %50.

4. Usage

The nouns sabah 'morning', akşam 'evening', and gece 'night' may be combined with dün 'yesterday', bu 'this' and yarın 'tomorrow':

dün sabah	'yesterday morning'
yarın akşam	'tomorrow evening'
bu sabah	'this morning'
bu gece	'tonight'
dün gece	'last night'
yarın gece	'tomorrow night'

These constructions may be used as nouns; in expressions of time, however, they are normally used as adverbs:

Müdür, yarın sabah evde kalacak	'The director will stay at home tomorrow morning'
Akşam çalışacak	'He will work in the evening'

There is also sabahleyin 'in the morning', and akşamleyin 'in the evening'.

The European metric terms gram and kilo are used as counting words (see Lesson 12):

Bakkal, bana tam beş yüz gram ekmek verdi	'The grocer gave me exactly 500 grams of bread'
İki buçuk kilo kahve istedim	'I asked for two and a half kilos of coffee'

Miktar 'amount' or 'quantity' is used like a counting word, but it is not preceded by numbers but by adjectives, especially az and çok:

Az bir miktar portakal aldım	'I bought a small quantity of oranges'

The basic meaning of kalkmak is 'get up' or 'arise'; it can also be used for 'leave' or 'depart', but only in the sense of 'leave for an extended journey'. The ordinary words for 'leave' are gitmek or çıkmak.

Evden kalktı, Ankaraya gitti	'He left home and went to Ankara'
Evden çıktı, lokantaya gitti	'He left home and went to the restaurant'

İnşallah, 'God willing', is frequently used with statements pretending to predict the future. It is pronounced /inşallah/ or /işallah/.

Yarın İstanbula varacağız, inşallah	'Tomorrow we will arrive in Istanbul, (God willing)'

VOCABULARY

akşam	evening

buçuk		half
doktor		doctor
dönmek		turn, return
gece		night
gün		day
gram		gram
inşallah	/înşallah/	God willing
kalkmak		get up, arise, leave, depart
kilo		kilogram
miktar		amount, quantity
sabah		morning
şişe		bottle
tam		exactly
varmak (dat)		arrive, reach
yarı		half
yarım		half
yarın		tomorrow

EXERCISES

A. Compose an answer to the following questions:

1. Bu otobüs nereye gidecek?
2. Buranın neresinde oturuyorsunuz?
3. Halil kitaplarının yüzde kaçını okudu?
4. Yarın ne yapacaksınız?
5. Fatmanın neresi güzel?
6. Altının yarısı kaç?

B. Translate into English:

1. Müdür burada mı? Hayır, şimdi gitti.
2. Buranın insanlarının yüzde kaçı erkek?
3. Çocuğun başı döndü de, ağaçtan indi.
4. Yarın erken üniversiteye gideceğim, akşam döneceğim

5. Orhanın eski odasında kim oturacak?
6. Göreceksin, yarın mektupları yazacağım.
7. Bu gece çok oturmayacağım, yarın sabah erken kalkacağım.
8. Sabah bir kitap aldım, şimdi okuyorum, akşam size vereceğim.
9. Ahmet hâlâ oturuyor, üniversiteye geç kalacak.
10. Şimdi küçüksün, anlamıyorsun, ama bir gün anlayacaksın.

C. Supply the correct future form for each verb, and then make each sentence negative, then interrogative.
Example:

Doktor akşam dön___.

Answers:

Doktor akşam dönecek.

Doktor akşam dönmiyecek.

Doktor akşam dönecek mi?

1. Orhan bugün eve gel___.
2. Siz bu dersi anla___.
3. Arkadaşlarım bu akşam kahveye git___.
4. Bakkal yarın yeni dükkânını aç___.
5. Sen yarın erken kalk___.
6. Bardakları ben say___.
7. Sen yarın sabah çay iste___.
8. Siz köyümüzü gör___.
9. Portakallar yere düş___.
10. Ben mektubunuzu oku___.

D. Translate into Turkish:

1. Didn't the doctor get up late today?
2. I will give this food to the dog, but he won't eat it.
3. Orhan will leave Istanbul tomorrow morning; in the evening he will reach Ankara. The bus will go by way of Bursa; it will stop there, but he will not get off.

4. Tomorrow (God willing) we will go to Şile. That place is not very far from Istanbul, and there is a small hotel there.
5. Halil found the bottle last night; he drank half of it and gave the other half to his brother. This morning the two of them are sick.
6. What percentage of Orhan's writings are here? —Six-sevenths; he wrote three and a half books.
7. I will return here tomorrow and stay three days.
8. I brought exactly 650 grams of bread and a small amount of tea in a water bottle.

LESSON 14: THE PRESENT TENSE

Study the following sentences:

Orhanın çocukları Bebekte mektebe gider	'Orhan's children go to school in Bebek'
Otobüs her akşam İstanbuldan kalkar, Ankaraya gider	'The bus leaves Istanbul every evening and goes to Ankara'
Hoca dersleri anlar, biz ama anlamayız	'The teacher understands the lessons, but we don't'
Mehmet hep aynı şey yapar: gece çalışır, sabah yorgun olur	'Mehmet always does the same thing: he works at night and is tired in the morning'
Bana bir parça ekmek verir misiniz?	'Will you give me a piece of bread?'
Halil her sene Temmuz ayında İzmire gider, orada on beş gün kalır	'Halil goes to Izmir in the month of July every year and stays there 15 days'
Yarın, Kasımın yirmi biri olacak	'Tomorrow will be the 21st of November'
955te (955 senesinde) Alinin oğlu öğretmen oldu	'In (the year) 1955 Ali's son became a teacher'
Halile ne oldu?	'What happened to Halil?' ('What became of Halil?')

-Ir/-Er

1. The present tense

The present tense has the following forms:
A. Verbs of more than one syllable take the suffix -Ir:

çalışmak	'to work'	çalışır	'he works'
oturmak	'to sit'	oturur	'he sits'

B. Verbs of one syllable that do not end in l or r take the suffix -Er:

gitmek	'to go'	gider	'he goes'
çıkmak	'to go out'	çıkar	'he goes out'
binmek	'to go up'	biner	'he goes up'
tutmak	'to hold'	tutar	'he holds'

C. A short list of verbs of one syllable that end in *l* or *r* take the suffix -*Ir*. These are:

almak	'to take'	alır	'he takes'
bilmek	'to know'	bilir	'he knows'
bulmak	'to find'	bulur	'he finds'
durmak	'to stand'	durur	'he stands'
gelmek	'to come'	gelir	'he comes'
görmek	'to see'	görür	'he sees'
kalmak	'to stay'	kalır	'he stays'
olmak	'to be'	olur	'he is'
ölmek	'to die'	ölür	'he dies'
varmak	'to arrive'	varır	'he arrives'
vermek	'to give'	verir	'he gives'
vurmak	'to hit'	vurur	'he hits'

In addition, passives of monosyllabic verbs ending in a vowel take the suffix -*Ir*: *denir* 'it is said', *yenir* 'it is eaten', *konur* 'it is placed'. The verbs *sanmak* 'think, consider', and *konmak* 'alight' sometimes are found with the -*Ir* suffix but more generally take -*Er*.

Any verb of one syllable ending in *l* or *r* which is not on the above list takes the normal -*Er*:

girmek	'to enter'	girer	'he enters'
sürmek	'to last'	sürer	'it lasts'

D. If the verb ends in a vowel, the *E* or *I* of the suffi drops, and the ending is simply -*r*:

yemek	'to eat'	yer	'he eats'
başlamak	'to begin'	başlar	'he begins'
okumak	'to read'	okur	'he reads'

The present tense takes predicative endings.

In the negative, the forms of the present are somewha irregular. The suffix of the present after the negative is -z, which remains in the second and third persons.

In the first person, -z drops; it is replaced by y in the plural and drops entirely, together with the following vowel, in the singular. The accent is also irregular. Study the following paradigms:

	bilmek	satmak
(ben)	bilmém	satmám
(sen)	bilmézsin	satmázsın
(o)	bilméz	satmáz
(biz)	bilméyiz	satmáyız
(siz)	bilmézsiniz	satmázsınız
(onlar)	bilmezlér, bilmézler	satmazlár, satmázlar

The missing -z of the first person reappears in the interrogative:

Bilmez miyim?	'Don't I know?'
Satmaz mıyız?	'Don't we sell?'

2. Uses of the present

The present tense (sometimes called the "aorist") has two important uses. One of these, the most common in the written or literary language, is to express habitual or repeated actions, or to make statements that are considered to be always true, without restriction as to time.

Halil çok çalışır	'Halil works very hard'
Erzuruma seyahat üç gün sürer	'The trip to Erzurum takes (lasts) three days'
Mehmet her gün aynı lokantada yemek yer	'Mehmet eats in the same restaurant every day'
Bu çocuk hep yemek ister	'This child always wants food'
Köpekler meyva yemez	'Dogs don't eat fruit'
Her şeyi bilmez misiniz?	'Don't you know everything?'

O adam ne yapar? —Sokakta elma satar	'What does that man do? —He sells apples on the street'

The other important use, more common in the spoken language, is to express the willingness of the subject to perform the given action:

Yarın ona bir mektup yazarım	'Tomorrow I'll write him a letter'
Bu sabah gazeteyi aldım; onu okurum, sana veririm	'This morning I bought the newspaper; I'll read it and give it to you'
Halil o kitabı okumaz; çok meşguldür	'Halil won't read that book; he is too busy'
Çay mı istersiniz, kahve mi?	'Would you like tea or coffee'

The present tense in this use frequently seems to mean almost the same thing as the future. But there is a difference in that the future in all cases simply states a fact, while the present frequently indicates that the subject acts voluntarily.

Geleceğim	'I am going to come, I will come'
Gelirim	'I'll come'
Halil gelmiyecek	'Halil will not come, is not going to come'
Halil gelmez	'Halil won't come (refuses to come)'

The present in this sense is frequently used as a polite imperative:

Bana bir sigara verir misiniz?	'Will (would) you give me a cigarette?'
İsminizi buraya yazar mısınız?	'Will you write your name here?'
Ahmet, derse başlar mısın?	'Ahmet, will you start the lesson?'

In the spoken language, the progressive -Iyor is in the process of replacing the present in its habitual or "aorist" sense. In letters, conversations, and other informal texts, one normally finds the progressive used when the present ought to be found according to the grammar books:

Mehmet Ankara Üniversitesine gidiyor	'Mehmet goes to Ankara University'
Kasabımız hep iyi et satıyor	'Our butcher always sells good meat'
Ankara otobüsleri Boludan gidiyor, Bursadan gitmiyor	'The Ankara buses go through Bolu; they don't go through Bursa'
Öğretmenimiz her şeyi biliyor	'Our teacher knows everything'

This means that in the spoken language the present is becoming restricted to its "voluntative" use.

3. The verb olmak

We have seen that Turkish has no need of a verb 'to be' in the present tense, since predicative endings are added directly to the predicate: Hocayım 'I am a teacher'. We shall see later that a similar mechanism is available for the past and certain other tenses. But there are still other tenses—for example, the future—for which a verb 'to be' is needed; this verb is olmak.

At the same time olmak also means 'become', and in this meaning it may be used in any tense. The uses of olmak are therefore the following:

A. 'become', in any tense or construction:

Arkadaşım mektebe gitti, doktor oldu	'My friend went to school and became a doctor'
Çocuğun elleri siyah oluyor	'The child's hands are becoming black'
Attila hep kötü elma yer, hasta olur	'Attila keeps eating bad apples and getting sick' ('Attila always eats bad apples and gets sick')

B. 'be', in the future tense and in other constructions to be introduced later. Olmak in the future is thus either 'be' or 'become':

Oğlum öğretmen olacak	'My son will be (become) a teacher'
Bu resim güzel olacak	'This picture will be beautiful'
Yarın evde olacağım	'Tomorrow I will be at home'

Olur, in the "habitual" use of the present, is more or less synonymous with -DIr:

Antalyanın portakalları çok büyük olur	'Oranges of Antalya are very large'
Antalyanın portakalları çok büyüktür	

C. 'happen', normally in certain standard expressions:

Ne oldu?	'What happened?'
Şimdi ne olacak?	'What will happen now?'
Attilanın oğluna ne oldu?	'What happened to Attila's son?'
	'What became of Attila's son

The two words olur 'all right' or 'it will be' and olmaz 'it cannot be' are among the most common expressions in Turkish:

Bana bir paket sigara alır mısınız? Olur	'Will you buy me a pack of cigarettes? All right'
Yarın bize gelir misiniz? Yarın olmaz, çok meşgulüm	'Will you come to (visit) us tomorrow? Tomorrow is impossible, I am too busy'
Bu arabada yedi kişi olmaz	'Seven people cannot get int this car' ('Seven people in this car is impossible')
Bu olmaz	'This cannot be'

4. Numerical expressions: dates

In English we can say 'the fifth of August', with an ordinal number, or 'August five', with a cardinal number. In Turkish, there are also two choices, but both involve the cardinal number; ordinals are not used for dates. If the number precedes, the number and the name of the month are simply in apposition: beş Ağustos 'August five'. If the number follows, a genitive construction is made: Ağustosun beşi 'the five of August'.

Üç Mart (3 Mart) güzel bir gün olacak	'March 3 will be a nice day'
Martın üçü (Martın 3ü) güzel bir gün olacak	'The third of March will be a nice day'
Orhanın babası, on Ekimde (10 Ekimde) öldü	'Orhan's father died on October 10'
Orhanın babası, Ekimin onunda (10unda) öldü	'Orhan's father died on the tenth of October'

Dates may be followed by the noun gün, which adds nothing to the meaning, or by such nouns as sabah, akşam, gece. In each case a possessive compound is formed.

on beş Ocak günü	'January 15'
Şubatın yedisi sabahı	'the morning of the seventh of February'
yirmi sekiz Nisan gecesi	'the night of April 28'

Names of months may be followed optionally by the noun ay 'month', and years may be followed by sene or yıl 'year':

Aralıkta (aralık ayında) Fatmanın kocası kalktı, gitti	'In (the month of) December Fatma's husband got up and left'
1965te (1965 senesinde) Orhanın annesi öldü	'Orhan's mother died in (the year) 1965'

These constructions may be used with the locative

ending, as in the case of the two preceding examples. The locative is normally used if a specific month or year is mentioned, but it is normally omitted in the expression of days or parts of days. It is rare with sabah or akşam, somewhat more common with gece:

Dokuz Kasım gecesinde Mehmet'ten haber geldi	'A message came from Mehmet in the night of November 9'
Sekiz Temmuz sabahı Ankaraya vardık	'We arrived in Ankara on the morning of July 8'
Dört Eylûl akşamı Mehmetle ben bir lokantaya gittik	'On the evening of September 4, Mehmet and I went to a restaurant'

The locative is not used if a specific date is not mentioned, and it is also not used if the reference is to a period of time:

Bu kitaba iki sene çalıştı	'He worked on this book for two years'
Seyahat beş gün sürdü	'The trip lasted five days'

In the expression of dates, remember that the English practice of expressing the first two figures of the date as 'hundred' may not be followed in Turkish; that is, 1950 ('Nineteen hundred and fifty') is not *on dokuz yüz elli but bin dokuz yüz elli. In writing, the figure 1 (for thousand) may be omitted from the year (950), and the names of months may be written with capital or small letters.

5. Usage

Hep does not mean exactly the same thing as daima, although both are normally translated 'always'; hep means 'on every occasion' or 'repeatedly' and daima means 'continuously'.

Hoca and öğretmen are both translated 'teacher', but for many speakers, öğretmen is restricted to designating primary school teachers, while a hoca may be a teacher at any level (or outside the school system). There is the same distinction for okul and mektep: okul is a primary school, mektep a school of any kind.

Sürmek can be used transitively in the meaning 'drive (animals, automobiles). But it is more common in the intransitive meaning 'last' (over a period of time).

Şey 'thing' is one of the most common words in Turkish. In addition to the wide variety of uses of the word for 'thing' in any language, it may be used at the beginning of an utterance as an expression of hesitation and may be used within an utterance in place of any noun that the speaker has momentarily forgotten.

Vurmak, in its most common meaning 'hit, strike', takes the dative:

Araba adama vurdu	'The car hit the man'

It also may mean 'shoot' or 'stab' and in these senses takes the objective.

VOCABULARY

ay		moon, month
aynı	/áynı/	same
bilmek		know
hep		always (see "Usage")
her		every
hoca		teacher
mektep	/mekteb/	school
okul		school
olmak		be, become
öğretmen		teacher
ölmek		die
satmak		sell
sene		year
seyahat	(-i)	journey
sürmek		drive; last (see "Usage")
şey		thing
vurmak (dat)		strike, hit; shoot, stab (see "Usage")
yıl		year

Ocak		January
Şubat		February
Mart		March
Nisan	/nīsan/	April
Mayıs		May
Haziran	/hazīran/	June
Temmuz		July
Ağustos		August
Eylûl	/eyl̂ul̂, eyl̂ül̂/	September
Ekim		October
Kasım		November
Aralık		December

EXERCISES

A. Compose an answer to the following questions:

1. Dün gece ne oldu?
2. Halil ne yapar?
3. Yarın ne yaparsınız?
4. 1950 senesinde ne oldu?
5. Seyahatinizde nereye gideceksiniz?

B. Translate into English:

1. Bu dükkân kalemle kâgıt satar, sigara satmaz.
2. Bu sene aynı yerde kalmayız; orasını sevmem.
3. Yirmi üç Aralık gecesinde Halil'in köyü yok oldu.
4. Ali her yıl Mart'ta İstanbul'a gelir, bir ay kalır, gider.
5. İyiler ölür, kötüler kalır.
6. Okullar hep Eylûlde başlar, Haziranda biter.
7. Ali Haziranın beşinde müdür olacak, şimdi hâlâ öğretmen.
8. Jules Verne'in romanı "Aya Seyahat"i okudunuz mu? Bizim çocuklar onun romanlarını çok severler.

9. Seyahat 1 Temmuz başlıyacak ve tam üç ay sürecek.
10. Ayın on beşinde evde olmıyacağım.

C. Supply the correct present tense form for each verb, and then make each sentence negative, then interrogative, then negative interrogative:

1. Biz köyde ata bin___.
2. Köpeğiniz hep küçük hayvan tut___.
3. Biz bu bakkaldan hep ekmek al___.
4. Ben sizi İstanbul'da bul___.
5. Gençler hep şu köşede dur___.
5. Ben Ankara'da iki gün kal___.
7. Arabayı siz sür___.
8. Dersler Eylülde başla___.
9. Fatma mektuplarını el ile yaz___.
10. Ahmet İstanbul'a Şubatta gel___, Mayısta git___.
11. Bu lokanta çok iyi et suyu yap___.
12. Orhan çok yemek ye___.
13. Sen denizi çok sev___.
14. Ahmet akşam hep yorgun ol___.
15. Fatma her gece pencereyi aç___.
16. Küçük hayvan hep annesini ara___.

D. Translate into Turkish:

1. the morning of September 9
2. January 25
3. the evening of June 11
4. the night of February 23
5. the fourth of May
6. the evening of the thirteenth of March
7. the night of the twelfth of December
8. the morning of the sixth of July
9. the night of April 1

10. November 3
11. the evening of October 22
12. the morning of August 30

E. Translate into Turkish:

1. The bus goes by way of our street; it stops at the corner. I get on there every morning.
2. The grocer sold me a bad apple; I'll give it to the child. —He'll die! —No, he won't die; he eats everything.
3. The same man comes to this place every day.
4. School begins here in the month of November. The school director will not be here this year; he left on a trip.
5. What became of Orhan's daughter? She went to the university for three years; now she is a teacher in Erzurum. His son is becoming a doctor.
6. What happened at Orhan's house last night? I don't know; they won't tell me.

LESSON 15: POSTPOSITIONS

Study the following sentences:

Saatler dakika gibi geçti	'The hours passed like minutes'
Ahmet ekmek için dükkâna gitti	'Ahmet went to the store for bread'
Müdür için büyük bir masa koyduk	'We set up (placed) a big table for the director'
Buraya uçakla mı geldiniz, vapurla mı?	'Did you come here by plane or by steamer?'
Ahmetle şimdi kim oturuyor?	'Who is living with Ahmet now?'
Halil, kahvesiyle beraber hep su içer	'Halil always drinks water with his coffee'
O çocuk, at kadar (çok) yemek yer	'That child eats as much as a horse'
Türkler daima öyle	'The Turks are always like that'
Türkler daima öyle yapar	'The Turks always act like that'
Kaç saat çalıştınız?	'How many hours did you work?'
Tayyare saat kaçta kalkar? —İkiyi yirmi beş geçe	'At what time does the airplane depart? —At twenty-five past two'
Pazartesi sabahları mektep dokuza çeyrek kala başlar	'On Monday mornings school begins at quarter of nine'
Salıları tam saat sekiz buçukta başlar	'On Tuesdays it begins exactly at eight-thirty'

1. Postpositions

English has prepositions, which precede the noun to which they refer; Turkish has postpositions, which follow the noun.

Mehmet için 'for Mehmet'

Turkish postpositions, like the prepositions of many other languages, require a certain case suffix on the noun. There are three groups: postpositions requiring the nominative or genitive (under conditions to be explained in the next section), those requiring the dative, and those requiring the ablative.

bunun için	'for this'
buna göre	'according to this'
bundan dolayı	'because of this'

We shall consider the postpositions with the dative and ablative in subsequent lessons.

Postpositional phrases are accented according to the compounding rule (Lesson 11, Section 6). Although the postposition is written as a separate word, the phrase is pronounced with the main accent on the last syllable of the noun, as though the phrase were a compound:

bunún için

buná göre

bundán dolayı

2. Postpositions with the nominative/genitive

These postpositions require the genitive of personal and demonstrative pronouns, except the pronouns that end in -lEr. Otherwise, they are used with the nominative.

benim için	'for me'
senin için	'for you'
onun için	'for him, for that'
bizim için	'for us'
kimin için	'for whom?'
onlar için	'for them'
bunlar için	'for these'
Mehmet için	'for Mehmet'
ev için	'for the house'

For the pronoun kim, kimin için is "correct", but

colloquially kim için is also possible.

Some of the more common postpositions of this group are the following:

A. gibi: 'like'

Kahve su gibi	'The coffee is like water'
Benim gibi yaptı	'He did as I did (He did like me)'
At gibi bir köpek gördüm	'I saw a dog like a horse'

B. için: 'for'

Bunu senin için yaptım	'I did this for you'
Ali, kardeşi için çalışıyor	'Ali works for his brother'

Sometimes için means more or less the same thing as the dative case:

Bu kutuyu sana getirdim	'I brought you this box'
Bu kutuyu senin için getirdim	'I brought this box for you'

The idiom onun için means 'therefore'.

C. ile:

We have seen this word already in the meaning 'and'; more generally it means 'with'. Like English 'with', it has two senses: 'by means of' and 'together with'.

Ankaraya tren ile (trenle) gideceğim	'I will go to Ankara by train'
Köpek ağzıyla kapıyı açtı	'The dog opened the door with his mouth'
Ankaraya Ahmet ile (Ahmetle) gideceğim	'I will go to Ankara with Ahmet'

The adjective beraber 'together' may be used freely with ile in its 'together with' sense and may also be used alone:

Şimdi beraberiz	'Now we are together'

Ahmetle beraber Ankaraya gittik	'We went to Ankara together with Ahmet'
Halille Mehmet beraber geldi	'Halil and Mehmet arrived together'

Other adjectives are regularly used with ile, including meşgul 'occupied (with)':

Attila her akşam dersleriyle meşgul	'Attila is busy with his lessons every evening'

D. kadar:
As a postposition with the nominative or genitive, kadar has a meaning that can be roughly represented as 'as'; X kadar Y means 'as Y as X'.

at kadar büyük bir köpek gördüm	'I saw a dog as big as a horse'
Ali'nin oğlu, babası kadar tembel oldu	'Ali's son became as lazy as his father'

Kadar may also be used as a noun, usually as a counting word with demonstratives: o kadar 'that much'. Distinguish carefully between:

Bu kadar içki isterim	'I would like this much liquor'
Bunun kadar içki isterim	'I would like as much liquor as this'

With a phrase indicating quantity, kadar may mean 'almost' or 'about':

İki şişe kadar su içti	'He drank almost two bottles of water'
İki üç şişe kadar su içti	'He drank about two or three bottles of water'

3. The words böyle, şöyle, öyle

The phrases bunun gibi 'like this', şunun gibi, onun gibi are theoretically possible in Turkish but extremely rare. Instead, we get the words böyle 'like this,

this way, thus', şöyle, öyle 'like that'. These may be used as adjectives, adverbs, or predicates.

Kutuyu böyle açtım	'I opened the box like this (this way)'
Böyle bir araba isterim	'I should like a car like this'
Halil öyledir	'Halil is like that'
Halil öyle bir adamdır	'Halil is that sort of man'

4. Interrogatives

Ne may be combined with gibi in the literal sense: 'like what':

Halil ne gibi bir adamdır	'What sort of man is Halil?'

But the word nasıl 'how', the interrogative counterpart of böyle, şöyle, öyle, is much more common:

Kutuyu nasıl açtınız?	'How did you open the box'
Halil nasıl bir adamdır?	'What sort of man is Halil?'
Halil nasıl?	'How is Halil?'
Nasılsınız?	'How are you?'

Turkish nasıl corresponds to English 'how' only in its interrogative sense; 'how' in exclamations should be translated by ne: Ne güzel! 'How beautiful!'

Ne may be combined with için in the literal sense: ne için 'for what'. But the compound niçin is much more common and means 'why' ('what for?'). Niçin, neden, and niye are the three most common of the many Turkish words for 'why':

Bu kitabı niçin beğenmediniz?	'Why didn't you like this book?'

Ne kadar means 'how much'; it is the question phrase used when the speaker expects the answer to be a unit of measure. Be careful to distinguish ne kadar from kaç, which means 'how many' and for which the answer is a number.

Ne kadar ekmek yediniz? —İki parça 'How much bread did you eat? —'Two pieces'

Kaç portakal yediniz? —İki tane 'How many oranges did you eat?' —'Two'

Ne kadar may also be used with adjectives and corresponds to English 'how' with adjectives:

Şu otel ne kadar eski? 'How old is that hotel?'

5. Numerical expressions: times

The noun saat means 'clock', 'watch', or 'hour'. It is used in expressions of time of the form saat beş (more rarely, saat beştir) 'It is five o'clock'.

Saat üç 'It is three o'clock'

Saat on bir 'It is eleven o'clock'

Saat dört buçuk 'It is four-thirty (four and a half)'

Saat yarım 'It is twelve-thirty (one-half)'

Saat kaç? 'What time is it?' ('It is how many?')

Be sure to distinguish Saat kaç? 'what time is it?' from kaç saat 'how many hours', and saat yarım 'twelve-thirty' from bir yarım saat 'a half hour'.

The noun dakika (pronounced /dakīka/ or /dakka/) means 'minute'. In expressions of time, minutes before the hour are expressed in the form 'There are ten minutes to five', using var and the dative case ('to') for the hour: Saat beşe on dakika var or Beşe on var. Minutes after the hour are expressed in the form 'Ten minutes pass five', using geçiyor 'it passes' and the objective case for the hour, which is the object of geçiyor: Saat beşi on dakika geçiyor or Beşi on geçiyor

Saat dörde kaç var? 'How many minutes before four is it?'

Saat dördü kaç geçıyor?	'How many minutes after four is it?'

'At five o'clock' is expressed with the locative case added to the hour:

Saat beşte eve geldi	'He came home at five o'clock'
Saat yedi buçukta kalktım	'I got up at seven-thirty'
Saat kaçta kalktınız?	'At what time did you get up?'

'At ten before five' is expressed in the form 'ten minutes remaining to five', using kalmak 'remain' and an adverbial suffix -E, to be discussed later. The dative case ('to') is added to the hour: Saat beşe on dakika kala or Beşe on kala. 'At ten after five' is expressed in the form 'ten minutes passing five', with geçmek, the same suffix -E, and the objective case for the hour, which is the object of geçe: Saat beşi on dakika geçe or Beşi on geçe.

Ona yirmi kala otobüs geldi	'The bus came at twenty to ten'
On biri beş geçe şehre vardı	'It arrived in the city at five after eleven'

The fraction çeyrek 'quarter' is used in all these expressions:

Saat ikiye çeyrek var	'It is quarter to two'
Saat ikiyi çeyrek geçiyor	'It is quarter after two'
Saat ikiye çeyrek kala geldi	'He came at quarter to two'
Saat ikiyi çeyrek geçe geldi	'He came at quarter after two'

6. Usage

The names of the days are treated like dates; they may be used as nouns or used adverbially. They may be followed by <u>sabah</u>, <u>akşam</u>, <u>gece</u>, or <u>gün</u> in a possessive compound construction.

Bugün Pazartesi	'Today is Monday'
Salı günü güzel olacak inşallah	'Tuesday will be beautiful, hopefully'
Çarşamba günü denize gideriz	'We'll go to the seashore on Wednesday'
Perşembe akşamı buraya döneriz	'We'll return here Thursday evening'

Notice especially the use of the plural and possessive suffixes in these examples:

Cuma günleri Halil okula gitmez	'Halil doesn't go to school on Fridays'
Cumartesi sabahları geç kalkar	'He gets up late on Saturday mornings'
Pazarları evde kalır	'He stays home on Sundays'

The familiar way to say 'What time is it?' is <u>Saat kaç</u>?; the polite way is <u>Saatiniz kaç</u>? 'What time do you have?'

VOCABULARY

beraber	/berāber/	together
böyle		this way, like this, thus
çeyrek		quarter
dakika	/dakīka/	minute
geçmek		pass
gibi (nom/gen)		like
hafta		week
için (nom/gen)		for
ile (nom/gen)		with
kadar (nom/gen)		amount; as (much) as
nasıl	/násıl/	how?

neden		why?
niçin	/níçin/	why?
niye		why?
öyle		that way, like that
saat	(-i)	watch, clock, hour
şöyle		that way, like that
tayyare	/tayyāre/	airplane
tren		train
uçak		airplane
vapur		steamship
Pazar		Sunday
Pazartesi		Monday
Salı		Tuesday
Çarşamba		Wednesday
Perşembe		Thursday
Cuma	/Cumā/	Friday
Cumartesi		Saturday

EXERCISES

A. Compose an answer to the following questions:

1. Nasılsınız?
2. Halil nasıl bir adam?
3. Yarın bize (saat) kaçta geleceksiniz?
4. Türkiye'ye ne ile gideceksiniz?
5. İstanbul'da ne kadar kalacaksınız?
6. Bir saatte kaç dakika var?
7. Bunun gibi kaç tane kitabınız var?
8. Günde kaç saat ders çalışıyorsunuz?
9. Uçak buraya kaçta varır?
10. Bu üniversitede bir ders kaç dakika sürer?
11. Saat şimdi kaç?

B. Translate into English:

1. Öbürleri benim kadar çalışmıyor.
2. Çocuk, senin kadar bunları yapmaz.
3. Bakkaldan iki kilo kadar ekmek aldım.
4. Sen benim kadar bilmiyorsun.
5. Kahvenizi nasıl istersiniz?
6. Bunun gibi fena bir yerde nasıl çalışırım! Pazartesi yeni bir yer arayacağım.
7. Benim için değil, oğlum için bir kitap arıyorum.
8. Ankara'ya sizinle beraber gitmiyeceğiz. Biz Salı günü sabah beş treni ile gidiyoruz.
9. Saat tam altı. Bu saatte niçin eve gidiyorsunuz?
10. Günler, dakikalar gibi geçiyor. Biz hâlâ yazıları yazmadık.

C. Supply the correct case suffix where necessary:

1. Ben siz___ gibi çalışkan bir insan görmedim.
2. Sen___ kadar büyük bir çocuk böyle şeyler yapar mı?
3. Cumartesi gecesi___ için ne yapıyorsunuz?
4. Sen ben___ kadar biliyor musun?
5. Ayşenin oğlu kızı___ gibi çok çalışkan.
6. Saat üçü beş geçe, kadın kocası___ ile kapıdan çıkacak.
7. Kâğıt, kalem, kitap___ gibi şeyleri sizler___ için aldık.
8. Matematik dersi___ için ne___ gibi kitaplar aldınız?
9. Ali şimdi ben___ ile çalışıyor; o___ için yemekleri beraber yiyoruz.
10. Bu akşam kim___ ile ders çalışacaksın?

D. Translate into Turkish:

1. It is eleven (minutes) to five.
2. It is quarter after seven.
3. It is six-thirty.

4. It is five (minutes) after eight.
5. We went home at ten-thirty.
6. We went home at quarter of nine.
7. We went home at twenty after twelve.
8. We went home at twelve-thirty.

E. Translate into Turkish:

1. How much did you drink? —This much.
2. How did you do that? —I did it like this.
3. Fatma is not as beautiful as Attila's sister.
4. The man eats like an animal.
5. These things too will pass, but it will be too late for you.
6. Attila is very busy with his writing this week.
7. How near is this place to Istanbul?
8. Did you come here by plane or by train? —I came together with Mehmet, in his new car. Therefore, I am late. We stopped for a half hour at Bolu for food.

LESSON 16: THE NARRATIVE PAST AND POSTPOSITIONS WITH THE DATIVE

bekleyormuş - supposedly waiting

Study the following sentences:

Halil bizi saat altıya kadar beklemiş	'Halil supposedly waited for us until six o'clock'
Saat dördü on geçeden beşe yirmi kalaya kadar bekledik	'We waited from ten after four to twenty of five'
Mehmet Bebeğe kadar yürümüş, şehre dönmüş	'Mehmet supposedly walked as far as Bebek and returned to the city'
Ev işi, kadınlara göredir	'Housework is suitable for women'
Akşam gazetesine göre, Yunanistana karşı harp çıkacak	'According to the newspaper Akşam, war will break out against Greece'
Resmi güneşe karşı çektiniz	'You took the picture into (facing) the sun'
Bu yol, Bebeğe doğru gidiyor	'This road goes toward Bebek'
Bu meyvalar kaça? —Yetmiş beş kuruşa	'How much is this fruit? —Seventy-five kuruş'
Bu meyvalar kaça? —Tanesi yetmiş beş kuruşa	How much is this fruit? —Seventy-five kuruş apiece'
Bu meyvaları üç liraya aldım	'I bought this fruit for three liras'
Arabanızı çok ucuza almışsınız	'They say you bought your car very cheaply'

1. The narrative past

The suffix of the narrative past is -mIş, used with predicative endings. This tense differs from the definite past -DI in that while -DI is used when the speaker has personally witnessed the action that he describes, the use of -mIş does not make this claim. It is used, therefore, when the speaker knows of the action only through hearsay. It is the tense used for narratives and tales when the speaker has no firsthand knowledge of the events described.

Orhan köşede iki saat beklemiş	'Orhan supposedly waited on the corner for two hours'
Halil mektubumuzu almamış; onun için cevabı gelmedi	'Halil supposedly didn't get our letter; therefore, his answer hasn't come'
Nasrettin Hoca bir gün erken kalkmış, ata binmiş, köye gitmiş	'Nasrettin Hoca (they say) got up early one day, mounted his horse, and went to the village'

This tense may be translated into English with expressions such as 'supposedly', 'allegedly', or 'they say'. These translations are deceptive, however, because the suffix -mIş is more common in Turkish than these expressions are in English, and because these expressions imply that -mIş has some special meaning of doubtfulness. In Turkish, it is the definite past that has the special meaning—namely, the claim that the speaker personally witnessed the action. It is a more serious mistake to use the definite past when you did not witness the action than to use the narrative past when you did witness it. Therefore, it might be better to use the qualifying expressions for the definite past: to translate Gelmiş as 'He came' and Geldi as 'He definitely came'. It is even better, however, to omit the qualifying expressions and simply remember what these tenses mean and when they can be used.

The nondefinite nature of -mIş comes out clearly only in the first, and in some cases the second, person

Ağustos ayında denize gitmişsiniz; doğru mu?	'They say you went to the seashore in August; is that right?'
Öğretmene göre, ders çalışmamışım	'According to the teacher, I didn't study'

In the first person, this tense sometimes indicates that the action was performed inadvertently or without conscious attention on the part of the speaker:

İyi et almamışım	'It seems I didn't buy good meat'
Sizi orada görmemişim	'I didn't see you over there'

An utterance like Saat iki olmuş! 'It is two o'clock already!' ('It seems it has become two o'clock') carries the connotation 'I didn't realize it was so late'.

2. Postpositions with the dative

Some of the most common postpositions with the dative are the following:

A. kadar

We have seen kadar already, in the meaning 'as much as'; with the dative, this postposition means 'until' or 'up to':

Bu otobüs, Bebeğe kadar gidiyor	'This bus goes as far as Bebek'
Şimdiye kadar öyle bir şey görmedim	'Up until now I haven't seen such a thing'
Ankaraya kadar yol güzel	'The road is fine as far as Ankara'
Cevabı yarına kadar bulurum	'I'll find the answer by tomorrow'

With expressions denoting a period of time, kadar corresponds to 'within':

Bir haftaya kadar geliyorlar	'They are coming within a week'

B. göre

This postposition means 'according to', 'suitable for', 'fitting for':

Tam bize göre bir yer bulduk	'We found a place exactly suitable for us'
Bu kitap, çocuklara göre değildir	'This book is not suitable for children'
Halile göre, Mehmet Ankaraya gitmiş	'According to Halil, Mehmet went to Ankara'

Notice the idiom ona göre 'accordingly'.

C. karşı

This postposition means 'against', or 'toward' in the sense of 'facing', that is 'toward' with no motion involved:

Yüzü güneşe karşı döndü	'His face turned toward the sun'
Yunanistana karşı yürüdüler	'They marched against Greec
Kardeşine karşı döndü	'He turned against his brother'

The idioms karşı gelmek or karşı durmak (rare) mean 'go against' or 'contradict'.

Çocuk annesine karşı geldi	'The child talked back to his mother (disobeyed his mother)'

D. doğru

This word is basically an adjective meaning 'straight or 'right'. As a postposition it means 'toward' when motion is involved.

Yunanistana doğru yürüdüler	'They walked (marched) towa Greece'
Çocuk sokağa doğru gitti	'The child went toward the street'
Araba, ihtiyar adama doğru geldi	'The car came (straight) toward the old man'

Be careful about the distinction between doğru and karşı. Both frequently correspond to English 'toward' but doğru is used only when there is motion involved (or implied motion, as in the case of a road).

Pencereye karşı oturdu	'He sat toward (facing) the window'
Sandalyeyi pencereye doğru çekti	'He pulled the chair toward the window'

3. Numerical expressions: prices

In Turkish, the price for which something is bought (or sold) is expressed with the dative:

Bu elmaları iki liraya aldım	'I bought these apples for two liras'

Bakkal bu elmaları 75 kuruşa sattı	'The grocer sold these apples for 75 kuruş'
Bu kitaplar on liraya	'These books are ten liras'
Ekmeğin kilosu iki liraya	'The bread is two liras a kilo' ('A kilo of the bread is two liras')

The basic unit of money is the *lira*, made up of 100 *kuruş*; the *kuruş* used to be composed, in turn, of 40 *para*. The *para* has been wiped out by inflation, but its name survives as the word for 'money'.

In asking prices, 'how much' may be expressed by the dative of *kaç*:

Bu elmalar kaça?	'How much are these apples?' ('For how much are these apples?')

The answer would then also be in the dative—for example, *otuz beş kuruşa*. But a variety of expressions in the nominative may also be used for asking the price:

Bu elmalar ne kadar?	'How much are these apples?'
Bu elmalar kaç para?	'How much money (how many *para*) are these apples?'
Bu elmalar kaç kuruş?	'How many *kuruş* are these apples?'

The answer in these cases would also be in the nominative—for example, *otuz beş kuruş*.

The word for 'price' is *fiat*.

Bu elmaların fiatı kaça? —Elli kuruşa.	'How much is the price of these apples? —Fifty *kuruş*'
Bu elmaların fiatı ne kadar (kaç para, kaç kuruş)? —(Fiatı) elli kuruş.	'How much (money) is the price of these apples? —(Their price is) fifty *kuruş*'

Ucuz and *pahalı* mean 'cheap' and 'expensive', respectively:

Bu bardaklar ucuz	'These glasses are cheap'

O kitap çok pahalı	'That book is too expensive'

These adjectives may also be used in the dative meaning 'cheaply' and 'expensively':

Meyvaları ucuza aldım	'I bought the fruit cheaply'
Kitabı pahalıya sattı	'He sold the book at an expensive price'

Note that the dative is used for prices only with the verbs almak and satmak; with other verbs, the price is the object of the verb, and the item for which the price is given or wanted is expressed with için or the dative:

Bu meyvalar için iki lira verdim	'I gave two liras for this fruit'
Bu meyvalara iki lira verdim	
Bakkal, bunlar için iki lira istedi	'The grocer wanted two liras for these'
Bakkal, bunlara iki lira istedi	

4. Variation in stems: final long vowels

In Turkish, a long vowel may appear only in an open syllable—at the end of a word or before a consonant that is followed, in turn, by a vowel. The following words contain examples of long vowels in open syllables:

tāne

kātip

cumā

dāima

Some words contain basic long vowels in the last syllable followed by a consonant: zaman /zamān/ 'time'. If the word stands alone, or if a suffix beginning with a consonant is added, the syllable is "closed" and the long vowel shortened. If a suffix beginning with a vowel is added, the basic long vowel is not shortened and should be pronounced.

zaman	'time', pronounced [zaman]
zamanda	'in time', pronounced [zamanda]
zamanı	'its time', pronounced [zamānı]

Similarly *cevap* /cevāb/ 'answer': the long vowel is not pronounced in the word alone but appears (along with the basic final /b/) in *cevabı* /cevābı/ 'his answer'.

5. Usage

Beklemek most frequently means 'wait for'; it is a transitive verb, and the person (or thing) waited for is in the objective case. It may also mean 'watch' or 'look after' or 'expect'.

Ahmet bizi odasında bekliyecek	'Ahmet will wait for us in his room'
Kasabımız köyüne gidiyor; oğlu dükkânı bekliyecek	'Our butcher is going to his village; his son will watch the store'
Bugün Fatmayı bekliyorum	'I am expecting Fatma today'

Çekmek basically means 'pull'; it also appears in a large number of idioms—for example, *resim çekmek* 'take a picture'.

'To answer' is *cevap vermek*.

İş has a number of meanings, including 'work, business, affair, job':

Çok işiniz var mı?	'Do you have much work?'
İşiniz nasıl gidiyor?	'How is your work going?'
Burada ne işiniz var?	'What business do you have here?'
Halil iş için İzmire gidiyor	'Halil is going to Izmir on (for) business'

Halil iş buldu	'Halil found a job (work)'

The possessive compound iş adamı means 'businessman', and the idiom iş görmek means 'do work' or 'do business':

Annem her sabah ev işi görür	'My mother does housework every morning'

Rum is the word for Greeks living in Turkey or Cyprus, or, in historical writings, for Greeks before the fall of Constantinople (that is, Byzantines). The word for Greeks living in modern Greece is Yunanlı, and Greece is Yunanistan.

Tutmak can be used to mean 'amount (to)' in the expression of prices and other quantities:

Kitap on lira tuttu	'The book came to (amounted to) ten liras'
Paket üç kilo tuttu	'The package came to three kilos'

Zaman and vakit 'time' are used in the interrogative ne zaman 'when' (less frequently, ne vakit) and in a number of other expressions:

Vaktiniz var mı?	'Do you have time?'
Bu iş çok vakit (zaman) alıyor	'This job takes too much time'
Bu iş çok vaktimi (zamanımı) alıyor	'This job takes too much of my time'
Doktor vaktinde gelmiyecek	'The doctor will not come in time'

Her zaman means 'every time'; o zaman may mean 'at that time' but also 'in that case':

O zaman ne yapacaksınız?	'What will you do in that case?'

VOCABULARY

beklemek	wait, watch, expect (see "Usage")

cevap	/cevāb/	answer
çekmek		pull
doğru (adj)		straight, right, correct
doğru (postp) (dat)		toward
fiat		price
göre (dat)		according to, suitable for
güneş		sun
harp	/harb/(-i)	war
iş		work, business, job (see "Usage")
kadar (dat)		until, up to
karşı (dat)		against
kuruş		unit of money
lira	/líra/	unit of money
pahalı		expensive
para		money
Rum		Greek (see "Usage")
ucuz		cheap
vakit	/vakt/(-i)	time
Yunanistan		Greece
Yunanlı		Greek (see "Usage")
yürümek		walk, march
yüz		face
zaman	/zamān/	time

EXERCISES

A. Compose an answer to the following questions:

1. Ders çalısmamışsınız; doğru mu?
2. Sabahları ne zaman kalkarsınız?

3. Bu yol nereye kadar gidiyor?
4. Neden böyle yüzünüz siyah?
5. Bu gece kaça kadar oturacaksınız?
6. Hasan Salı günü kaça kadar çalışıyor?
7. Kaç liranız kaldı?
8. Attila sabaha kadar ne yapar?
9. Üniversiteye kaç para verdiniz?
10. Sigaranın fiatı kaç kuruş oldu?

B. Translate into English:

1. Kissinger Çin'e gitmiş; gazetede okudum.
2. Hiç sigaram kalmamış; bir tane verir misiniz?
3. Elmaları çok ucuza almışsın; ben bunların kilosuna beş lira verdim.
4. Ayşe'nin babası pencereye karşı oturmuş, hasta olacak.
5. Öğretmen olmuşsunuz, ama hâlâ adam olmamışsınız.
6. Müdürden bir haber bekliyorum, ona göre size beş yüz liraya kadar bir iş vereceğim.
7. Otobüs hep geç kalıyor, onun için sabahları okula yürüyoruz.
8. Buraya çok güneş geliyor, masayı öbür köşeye çekeceğim.
9. Kitaplar 125,00 lira tuttu. Param kalmamış, onun için çek yazdım.
10. Hep bana bakıyorsunuz; yüzümde bir şey mi var?

C. Supply the correct case suffixes:

1. Mustafa at___ gibi yürüyor.
2. Bu kalemi kim___ için aldınız?
3. Fatma her şeyi fiatı___ göre alır.
4. Ben siz___ gibi bir adam görmedim.
5. Derslerimiz___ için sabah 7:00 de kalkıyoruz.
6. Adamlar hayvanları köy___ kadar sürdü.

hiç - ever never not at all öbür - the other hep - continually

7. Ankara'ya Mehmet___ ile mi gideceksiniz, Ahmet___ ile mi?
8. Benim sen___ kadar bir oğlum var.
9. Orhan biz___ karşı geldi.
10. Mehmet biz___ ile beraber oturuyor.
11. Bu ders___ kadar kötü şey görmedim.
12. Yol deniz___ doğru gidiyor.

D. Translate into Turkish:

1. We went by car as far as Şile. From there we walked by a small path to the seashore.
2. Mehmet's new job is not suitable for him; he is a teacher, not a clerk.
3. We sat down facing the table.
4. The steamers set out toward Greece.
5. Our butcher sells meat very cheaply, but his meat isn't very good.
6. I bought a loaf of bread for two and a half liras in Bursa; in Istanbul, it is three liras.
7. Are you still expecting Fatma's letter? —No, she won't write now; she doesn't have time.
8. What is the price of this liquor? —Six liras, seventy-five kurus a bottle. —That's too expensive; I won't buy it.
9. Ahmet writes for the newspapers; according to him, war will not break out. They are too afraid of us.
10. Halil (says he) arrived at the coffeehouse exactly at one-thirty; he waited for us for forty-five minutes. At quarter past two he (supposedly) returned home.
11. Man will go to the sun within a year, but the journey won't be very pleasant.
12. It seems I didn't bring my money.

LESSON 17: THE PAST AUXILIARY

Study the following sentences:

Üniversitede beraber talebeydik	'We were students together at the university'
Paket senin içindi. Açtım ama boştu	'The package was for you. I opened it, but it was empty'
Dün neredeydiniz? —Hastaydım, yatakta yatıyordum	'Where were you yesterday? —I was sick and in bed'
Eski evimiz tahtadandı	'Our former house was made of wood'
O ev bizimdi; şimdi Halilin oldu	'That house used to be ours; now it became Halil's'
O zaman Ankarada oturuyorduk. Babam her sabah şehre inerdi, annem ev işi görürdü	'At that time we were living in Ankara. My father used to go downtown every morning, and my mother did the housework'
Saat dörttü ve vapur kalkmıştı	'It was four o'clock, and the steamer had left'
Çocuk ağaçtan düşecekti	'The child was about to fall from the tree'
O işi ben yapardım	'I would have done that job'
Mehmedin karısı Ankaraya gitmişti, onun için burada yoktu	'Mehmet's wife had gone to Ankara; therefore, she was not here'
Yaşar Kemal'in ikinci eseri, birincisi kadar iyi değildi	'Yasar Kemal's second work was not as good as the first'
Bize haberi söylemiyecek miydiniz?	'Weren't you going to tell us the news?'
Saat ikiyi çeyrek geçiyordu	'It was quarter after two'

1. The past auxiliary

The action of any sentence may be placed in the past with the addition of the suffix -DI, or -yDI after vowels. The suffix -DI follows the predicate, or the tense in verbal sentences, and precedes the personal ending; it is followed by the same personal endings that are used with the definite past tense -DI.

Yalnızım	'I am alone'
Yalnızdım	'I was alone'
Bugün evdeyim	'I am at home today'
Bugün evdeydim	'I was at home today'
Çay su gibi	'The tea is like water'
Çay su gibiydi	'The tea was like water'
O kalem benim	'That pen is mine'
O kalem benimdi	'That pen was mine'
Yaşar Kemal'in yeni eserini okuyorum	'I am reading Yasar Kemal's new work'
Bu sabah Yaşar Kemal'in yeni eserini okuyordum	'This morning I was reading Yasar Kemal's new work'
Bende para var	'I have money on me'
Bende para vardı; şimdi kalmadı	'I had money on me; now there is none left'
Ahmet bizimle gelecek	'Ahmet will come with us'
Ahmet bizimle gelecekti	'Ahmet was going to come with us'
Arabistanda at eti yerler	'In the Arab countries they eat horsemeat'
On sekizinci asırda at eti yerlerdi	'In the eighteenth century they used to eat horsemeat'
Halil sigara içmez	'Halil doesn't smoke'
Halil sigara içmezdi	'Halil didn't use to smoke'
Size yemek getiririm	'I'll bring you food'
Size yemek getirirdim	'I would have brought (was going to bring) you food'

Orhan İzmire gitmiş (gitti) — 'Orhan went to Izmir'

Orhan İzmire gitmişti (gittiydi) — 'Orhan had gone to Izmir'

1.1. Forms of the past auxiliary

The suffix -*DI* may be added directly to the predicate, as in all of the examples just cited. In that case, it alternates according to consonant and vowel harmony. It may also be added to a stem *i*-; in that case, the combination *idi*- follows the predicate as a separate word and does not change. Thus we have:

Yorgundu	'He was tired'
Yorgun idi	
Meşguldük	'We were busy'
Meşgul idik	
Söyliyecekti	'He was going to tell'
Söyliyecek idi	
Yatmıştı	'He had gone to bed'
Yatmış idi	
Bakıyordum	'I was looking'
Bakıyor idim	

The choice between these two forms is almost entirely a matter of style. The suffixed form (*yorgundu*) is almost invariably found in the spoken language, except when the speaker wishes to place special emphasis on the past: *Yorgun idi*, *şimdi değil* 'He *was* tired; now he's not'. In the written language, the form that is found depends on the inclination of the individual writer.

When -*DI* is attached to a predicate ending in a vowel, a *y* appears between the predicate and the suffix; this *y* is a remnant of the stem *i*-. Thus we have:

Hastaydı Hasta idi	'He was sick'
Ankaradaydım Ankarada idim	'I was in Ankara'

When -DI appears in the suffixed form, it is unaccented; accent therefore falls on the preceding syllable:

çalışkándım	'I was industrious'
evdéydim	'I was at home'
koyacáktım	'I was going to put'
içérdim	'I used to drink (smoke)'

The suffix -DI follows the interrogative mI or the negative değil if they are present:

Ahmet o kadar çalışkan değildi	'Ahmet didn't used to be so industrious'
Dün hasta mıydınız?	'Were you sick yesterday?'
O adam müdür değil miydi?	'Wasn't that man the director?'
Bu sabah çalışıyor muydun?	'Were you working this morning?'

When -DI follows mI after the definite past -DI, the personal ending may be attached to either the first -DI or the second:

Geldiniz miydi Geldi miydiniz	'Had you come?'
Gelmedim miydi Gelmedi miydim	'Hadn't I come?'

Some speakers will accept mI following the whole construction, thus geldiydiniz mi, gelmediydim mi.

As an additional irregularity, the third person plural -lEr tends to precede, rather than follow, -DI when the predicate is a verb:

Geliyorlardı	'They were coming'
Geleceklerdi	'They were going to come'
Gelirlerdi	'They would have come'

However, -lEr tends to follow when the predicate is nonverbal:

İyiydiler	'They were good'
Evdeydiler	'They were at home'

1.2. Meaning of the past auxiliary

For nonverbal predicates, -DI forms a simple past tense; the difference between Evdeyim and Evdeydim is the same as that between English 'I am at home' and 'I was at home'.

For verbal predicates, -DI forms compound (or "periphrastic") tenses, some of which have special meanings. The combination -Ir+DI (gelirdi) can mean either 'used to', with the "aorist" sense of the present tense, or 'would have', with the "voluntative" sense. The combination -(y)EcEk+DI (gelecekti) means 'he was going to come'; that is, at some time in the past he was about to come. The combination normally corresponding to the traditional "pluperfect" is -mIş+DI (gelmişti 'he had come'); forms like geldiydi are relatively rare.

1.3. Auxiliaries

From the discussion in Lessons 3 and 5, you will remember that a sentence in Turkish consists of subject, predicate, and auxiliary. The predicate may be nonverbal (iyi, evde) or verbal (gidiyor, verdi). The auxiliary consists of the personal endings, sometimes preceded by the interrogative -mI. The suffix -DI, in the use that has been presented in this lesson, is also part of the auxiliary. A sentence such as Siz geliyordunuz 'You were coming' may therefore be represented graphically, as in Figure 5.

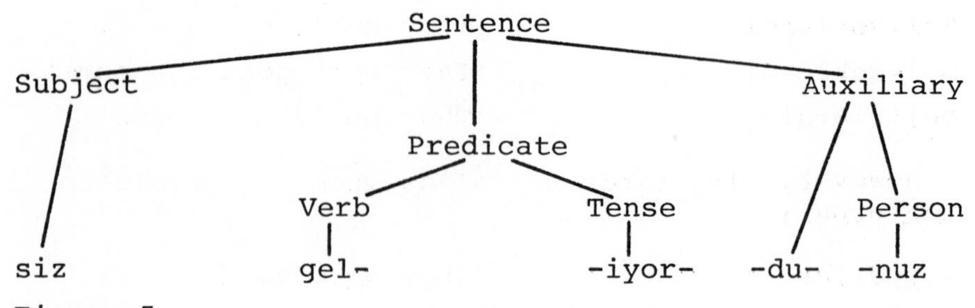

Figure 5

It is especially important to distinguish the use of *-DI* as the definite past tense from the use of this suffix as the past auxiliary. Notice in particular the following:

A. As tense, *-DI* is attached only to verb stems; in the auxiliary, it may be added to all predicates, verbal or nonverbal. With verbal predicates, it follows the tense suffix on the verb (which may also be *-DI*).
B. The interrogative *mI* is normally placed after the predicate, at the beginning of the auxiliary; thus *Tembel misiniz?* 'Are you lazy?' and *Geliyor musunuz?* 'Are you coming?' The interrogative therefore follows the tense *-DI* but precedes the auxiliary *-DI*:

Geldi mi?	'Did he come?'
Geliyor muydu?	'Was he coming?'

C. As pointed out in Lesson 3, suffixes that are part of the auxiliary (with certain exceptions) are unaccented. Accent therefore falls on the last syllable of the predicate:

tembélsiniz	'you are lazy'
gelecéksiniz	'you will come'

Therefore *-DI* in the auxiliary is unaccented, although the tense *-DI*, part of the predicate, is accented normally:

tembéldiniz	'you were lazy'
gelecéktiniz	'you were going to come'
geldiniz	'you came'

tembéldi	'he was lazy'
geldí	'he came'

Notice that the rule for the accent of compounds, presented in Lesson 11, will explain why the auxiliary is unaccented. A form like *Tembeldi* 'He was lazy' can be interpreted as a shortened form of *Tembel idi* and therefore as a compound. Notice also:

vardí	'he arrived'
várdı	'it existed'

D. Auxiliary -*DI* must be preceded by *y* after a vowel, while tense -*DI* is not:

bekledi	'he waited'
evdeydi	'he was at home'

2. Numerical expressions: ordinals

Ordinal numerals are made in Turkish with the suffix -*IncI*. In addition, there is a special adjective *ilk* 'first'.

birinci, ilk	'first'
ikinci	'second'
üçüncü	'third'
altıncı	'sixth'
on dokuzuncu	'nineteenth'
otuz yedinci	'thirty-seventh'
Halilin ilk kitabı bu sene çıkacak	'Halil's first book will come out this year'
Orhanın evi, soldan beşinci	'Orhan's house is the fifth on the left (fifth by way of the left'
Halilin yeni karısı dördüncüsü	'Halil's new wife is the fourth (of them)'
Mehmet, ikinci şişe içkisini içiyor	'Mehmet is drinking his second bottle of liquor'

Notice that page numbers are always expressed with ordinals in Turkish:

Ellinci sayfaya kadar okudum	'I read as far as page fifty'
Bu gazetenin onuncu sayfasında Halilin bir yazısı var	'Halil has an article on page ten of this newspaper'

Turkish, like English, uses ordinals for the numbers of centuries and rulers; these numbers may also be expressed with Roman numerals. But because the ordinal adjective precedes the noun in Turkish, the Roman numeral also precedes in writing: XIX asır, II Selim.

Yirminci asırda (XX asırda) kaç harp oldu?	'How many wars have there been in the twentieth century?'

Ordinals are normally abbreviated—for example: 5inci or 5ci, 4üncü or 4cü.

Kaçıncı is the interrogative ordinal; it is used when the speaker expects the answer to be an ordinal number. It does not translate well into English; something like 'which' usually reads best, although 'how-many-eth' would be most accurate:

II Mehmet kaçıncı asırda yaşamış?	'Which century did Mehmet II live in?'
Yaşar Kemal kaçıncı kitabını yazıyor?	'Yasar Kemal is writing which (the how-many-eth) of his books?'
Halilin yeni karısı kaçıncısı (karısı)?	'Halil's new wife is the how-many-eth (wife)?'
Halil kaçıncı şişe içkisini içiyor?	'Halil is drinking his how-many-eth bottle of liquor?'

3. Usage

Defa and kere mean 'time' in the sense of 'occasion'. The rule of thumb is to use defa with ordinals, kere with cardinal numerals.

Evine beş kere gittim	'I went to his house five times'
Evine beşinci defa gittim	'I went to his house for the fifth time'
Bunu bir kere gördüm	'I saw this once'
Bunu ilk defa görüyorum	'I am seeing this for the first time'

Recently kez has become common, replacing defa: ilk kez 'the first time'. Sefer is used mainly in the expression bu sefer (bu defa, bu kez) 'this time':

Bu sefer parayı doğru sayacağım	'This time I'll count the money right'

The difference between talebe and öğrenci is the same as that between hoca and öğretmen, or mektep and okul: öğrenci is a primary school student or a 'pupil'; talebe is a student at any level, from grammar school to university.

Yatmak means 'lie down' or 'lie'; in various derived meanings, it can correspond to English 'go to bed', 'be in bed', and so on.

Köpek yere yattı	'The dog lay down on the floor'
Köpek yerde yatıyordu	'The dog was lying on the floor'

Yalnız as an adjective (/yalníz/) means 'alone'; as an adverb (/yálnız/), it means 'only' or 'however'.

Sana gelecektim; yalnız, param kalmadı	'I was going to come to (visit) you; only I had no money left'

VOCABULARY

Arabistan		Arabia, Arab countries
Arap	/arab/	Arab
asır	/asr/	century

defa	/defā/	time (see "Usage")
eser		work (of art)
ilk		first
karı		wife
kere		time (see "Usage")
kez		time (see "Usage")
öğrenci		pupil
sayfa, sahife		page
sefer		time (see "Usage")
talebe		student
yalnız (adj)		alone
yalnız (adv)	/yálnız/	only, however
yaşamak		live
yatak		bed
yatmak		lie, lie down
yüzyıl		century

EXERCISES

A. Compose an answer to the following questions:

1. Eskiden sabahları kaçta kalkardınız?
2. Dün sabah saat 10:00 da neredeydiniz?
3. Dün akşam odanızda ne yapıyordunuz?
4. Bu kitabı kaçıncı sayfaya kadar okudunuz?
5. Türkler onuncu asırda nerede yaşamışlardı?
6. Dün gece yorgun muydunuz?

B. Translate into English:

1. Ayşe bu sene ilk defa üniversiteye giriyor.
2. Karabaş adında bir köpeğim vardı, şimdi yok oldu.
3. Gazeteyi size verirdim, ama okumamıştım.
4. Saatim neredeydi? Bilmem; burada yok muydu?
5. Meyva isterdim ama iyi bir çeşit arıyordum.

6. Halil bize saat ikide gelecekti; saat üç oldu da hâlâ gelmemişti.
7. Türkler 11. asırda Anadolu'ya gelmişlerdi, 1453'te İstanbul'u aldılar.
8. Yalnız ben yalnız oturuyorum; öbür öğrenciler anne ile babalarının evlerinde kalıyorlar.
9. Bu sefer işimi erken bitirecektim; yalnız, gece 12:00ye kadar sürdü.
10. Gazeteyi ben getirirdim, ama sen istememiştin.

C. Add the past auxiliary to each sentence. Then make each of the resulting sentences interrogative if it is not already a question.

Example:

Köpek yerde yatıyor

Answers:

Köpek yerde yatıyordu

Köpek yerde yatıyor muydu?

1. Ben günde üç paket sigara içerim.
2. Ahmet saat sekizde gelecek.
3. Arapların el yazısı güzel.
4. Siz Hasan'ın odasında ne yapıyorsunuz?
5. Mehmedin eski odası o evde.
6. Siz bizimle gelmiyeceksiniz.
7. Ahmet'in parası yok.
8. Fatma İstanbulda her sabah erken kalkar, denize bakar.
9. Sizin yazınız kaç sayfa tutacak?
10. Biz bir çay içeriz.
11. Orhan o gece bizi bir saat beklemiş.
12. Türkiyeye kaç kere gittiniz?
13. Ayşe'nin çocukları pek hoş.
14. Gazete masamda duruyor.

D. Translate into Turkish:

1. I was tired.
2. Their house was white.
3. Fatma was a student.
4. We were friends.
5. The chair was made of stone.
6. Mehmet was in bed.
7. The picture was on page eight.
8. How was Orhan?
9. Orhan was like a horse.
10. Orhan was like this.
11. The room was suitable for them.
12. The house was her husband's.
13. It was five o'clock.
14. It was ten-thirty.
15. It was ten minutes after two.
16. It was quarter of three.
17. He did not have a wife.
18. There used to be a good restaurant downtown.
19. He was living on (by) bread and water.
20. We were waiting for four hours.
21. I was going to read your book.
22. I didn't have time.
23. I would have liked coffee too.
24. At that time I didn't like his works very much.
25. His mother had written him a letter.
26. Didn't he have any students?
27. Weren't we going to go?
28. What were we going to do?

E. Translate into Turkish:

1. On Monday evenings he used to go to bed early.
2. On Tuesday nights he used to drink.
3. We didn't use to work on Saturdays.
4. On Sundays he remained alone.
5. Our door is the sixth on the right.
6. The fourth house from the corner is Orhan's.
7. Mahmut Makal's third book has just come out. There is a picture of his village on page forty-three. But the book is not as good as his second.

LESSON 18: THE DUBITATIVE AUXILIARY

Study the following sentences:

Ankaranın havası çok temizmiş	'The air of Ankara is said to be very clean'
Paketler ikişer üçer gelecekmiş	'The packages will supposedly arrive in twos and threes'
Amerikada her ailenin ikişer arabası varmış	'In America every family supposedly has two cars each'
Talebeler dersi iki kere okumuş, hâlâ anlamıyormuş	'The students have read the lesson twice, and still it seems they don't understand it'
İnsanın hayatı doksan sene sürermiş	'Man's life is said to last ninety years'
Dünyanın sonu bu sene olacakmış	'The end of the world will supposedly be this year'
Yurtsever ailesi, bizimle aynı apartmanda otururmuş. Dairesi bizden uzak değilmiş	'It turns out the Yurtsever family lives in the same apartment building as we. Their apartment is not far from us'

1. The dubitative auxiliary

The speaker may disassociate himself from the truth of any sentence, or cast doubt upon the statement, by the addition of the suffix -mIş, or -ymIş after vowels. The suffix -mIş follows the predicate, or the tense in verbal sentences, and precedes the personal ending; it is followed by the same personal endings that are used with the narrative past tense -mIş, except that -DIr may not be used.

Hastayım	'I am sick'
Hastaymışım	'They say I am sick'
İyi değilsin	'You are not well'
İyi değilmişsin	'You are supposedly not well'
Ailesi çok zengin	'His family is very rich'
Ailesi çok zenginmiş	'His family is said to be very rich'

O beyin ismi Raif	'That gentleman's name is Raif'
O beyin ismi Raifmiş	'Supposedly that gentleman's name is Raif'
Müdür dairesinde	'The director is in his office'
Müdür dairesindeymiş	'The director is supposedly in his office'
Odasında bir tek iskemle yok	'There is not a single chair in his room'
Odasında bir tek iskemle yokmuş	'They say there is not a single chair in his room'
Bize gülüyor	'He is laughing at us'
Bize gülüyormuş	'It appears he is laughing at us'
Dünya değişiyor	'The world is changing'
Dünya değişiyormuş	'It seems the world is changing'
Ali bey içki içmez	'Ali Bey doesn't drink'
Ali bey içki içmezmiş	'They say Ali Bey doesn't drink'
Yarın hava güzel olacak	'Tomorrow the weather will be beautiful'
Yarın hava güzel olacakmış	'Tomorrow the weather is supposed to be beautiful'

1.1. Forms of the dubitative auxiliary

The forms of the dubitative auxiliary parallel closely those of the past auxiliary. In particular, notice the following points:

A. The suffix -mIş is added directly either to the predicate or to a stem i-; the combination imiş follows the predicate as a separate word and does not alternate according to vowel harmony.

İyi değilmişsin	'You are supposedly not well'
İyi değil imişsin	
Evi büyükmüş	'His house is supposedly big'
Evi büyük imiş	
Yatacakmış	'He says he is going to go to bed'
Yatacak imiş	

B. When -mIş is attached to a predicate ending in a vowel, a y must appear between the predicate and the suffix:

Dairesindeymiş	'He is supposedly in his office'
Dairesinde imiş	
Kitap fenaymış	'The book is said to be bad'
Kitap fena imiş	
O hanım, Raif bey'in karısıymış	'That lady is supposedly Raif Bey's wife'
O hanım, Raif bey'in karısı imiş	

C. In the suffixed form, -mIş is unaccented:

hastáymışım	'I am supposedly sick'
ölecékmiş	'They say he is going to die'
Burada yer yókmuş	'It seems there is no room here'

D. The suffix -mIş follows mI or değil:

Hasta mıymışsınız?	'Is it true that they say you are sick?'
O adam müdür müymüş?	'Is that man (supposedly) the director?'
—Hayır, değilmiş	'—No, it seems he isn't'

D. The third person plural -lEr tends to precede -mIş

when the predicate is a verb:

Bize gülüyorlarmış	'It appears they are laughing at us'

If the predicate is nonverbal, -lEr may either precede or follow:

Açmışlar	'They seem to be hungry'
Açlarmış	

F. The suffix -mIş may be added to any nonverbal predicate or to any tense. This means that grammatically it could be added to the definite past -DI or the narrative past -mIş.

geldiymiş or geldi imiş

gelmişmiş or gelmiş imiş

Both of these forms, however, would be rare. In the first case, the definite past -DI indicates that the speaker saw the action personally, and he cannot state both the definiteness and doubtfulness of the action at once. In the second case, the two -mIş would be unnecessary because the second would not add much to the meaning of the first.

1.2. Meaning of the dubitative auxiliary

The dubitative auxiliary -mIş must be distinguished from the narrative past tense -mIş for a number of formal reasons. These are the same as the reasons for distinguishing the past auxiliary -DI from the definite past tense -DI and were discussed in Section 1.2 of Lesson 17. But in this case, there is an additional important reason for making this distinction: the dubitative auxiliary and the narrative past do not mean the same thing.

The narrative past -mIş is a past tense: Gelmiş 'He came' describes an event in the past. It also describes an event that the speaker does not claim to have observed personally. Geldi 'He came', on the other hand, describes an event that the speaker does claim to have witnessed personally. As far as the distinction between the two past tenses is concerned, it is -DI that has an extra component of meaning; it contains the claim of personal observation that -mIş lacks.

The dubitative auxiliary -mIş has no past meaning; the time of the event must be given by other elements in the sentence. Thus Gençmis 'He is supposedly young' is present, Geliyormuş 'He is supposedly coming' is present progressive, Gelirmiş 'He supposedly comes' is habitual, Gelecekmiş 'He supposedly will come' is future.

But the auxiliary -mIş does contain a particular component of meaning: it indicates that the speaker wishes to disassociate himself from the statement or does not wish to affirm the truth of the statement; he indicates instead that he is merely repeating what he has heard or recently found out.

Notice that there are cases where the speaker may know that the statement he is making is true but uses -mIş to show that the information comes as a surprise or was not part of his knowledge previously. Thus the meaning of the dubitative auxiliary may sometimes be captured with the translation 'seemingly'.

Burası meşgulmüş	'This place seems to be occupied'
Ne çok kitabım varmış!	'How many books I have!'
	'How many books I seem to have!'

2. Numerical expressions: distributive

Distributive adjectives are made with the suffix -(ş)Er added to numerals:

birer	'one each'
ikişer	'two each'
üçer	'three each'
altışar	'six each'
kırkar	'forty each'
elli yedişer	'fifty-seven each'
iki yüzer, ikişer yüz	'two hundred each'

O portakalları elli kuruşa aldım	'I bought those oranges for fifty kurus'
O portakalları ellişer kuruşa aldım	'I bought those oranges for fifty kuruş each'
Üç şişe elma suyu aldık	'We bought three bottles of apple juice'
Üçer şişe elma suyu aldık	'We bought three bottles of apple juice each'
Her odada ikişer büyük masa var	'There are two large tables in each room'

The distributive of yarım is yarımşar; and for numbers containing buçuk, -(ş)Er is attached to the numeral preceding buçuk.

Yarımşar bardak su içtik	'We drank a half glass of water each'
Üçer buçuk bardak su içtik	'We drank three and a half glasses of water each'

The distributive suffix may also be added to tek 'single', to produce teker 'singly, one by one', and to az to produce azar 'little by little, in small quantities'. These forms, like the distributive numerals, may be used adverbially and in this use are normally reduplicated (doubled):

Hayvanlar vápura ikişer ikişer bindi	'The animals got on the steamboat two by two (in groups of two each)'
Hayvanlar vapura birer birer bindi	'The animals got on the steamboat singly, one by one (in groups of one each)'
Hayvanlar vapura teker teker bindi	'The animals got on the steamboat singly, one by one'
Ekmeği azar azar yedi	'He ate the bread little by little (in small pieces)'

The distributive interrogative is kaçar:

Bunlar için kaçar lira verdiniz?	'How many liras each did you give for these?'

3. Names

There is an old way and a new way of forming personal names in Turkish. Of these, the old way is still the most frequently used. By this method, the person's first name is followed by bey 'gentleman' or hanım 'lady'.

Ahmet bey burada mı oturuyor?	'Does Mr. Ahmet live here?'
Fatma hanım yarın gelecek	'Mrs. Fatma will come tomorrow'

English-speaking students should be reassured that it is not impolite or overly familiar to use a person's first name in Turkish, if bey or hanım are also used. Bey and hanım may also be used simply as nouns.

The new way is to use Bay 'Mr.' or Bayan 'Mrs.' preceding the last name or both names. Sayın is another form of address, more formal and used mainly for men:

Bay Yurtsever burada oturuyor	'Mr. Yurtsever lives here'
Bayan Nevra Bozkurt yarın gelecek	'Mrs. Nevra Bozkurt will come tomorrow'
Sayın Güneş yarın Ankaraya dönecek	'Mr. Güneş will return to Ankara tomorrow'

Terms like Bay and Bayan, as well as the use of last names, were introduced by the Language Reform movement, in this case to make the language look more European. These terms are used in official and formal documents and in styles of the language designed for public consumption—for example, in newspapers and on television. In summary, address a man as Bay Halil Ürkmez on the envelope but as Halil bey on the letter inside.

In English, the plural suffix may be added to a last name to denote a person and his family: 'the Smiths'. In Turkish, the plural may be added to either first or last names to denote a person and his family or a person and his group of associates and friends. The plural may also be added to certain kinship terms.

Ekmekçioğluların dairesi bu apartmanda	'The Ekmekçioğlu's apartment is in this building'

Fatmalar bugün gelecekti	'Fatma and her family (or Fatma and her friends) were going to come today'
Teyzemler şimdi New York'ta oturuyorlar	'My aunt and her family are now living in New York' (teyze 'maternal aunt')

Efendi following the first name (Mustafa efendi) is used for male tradesmen or servants (women in this class are referred to with hanım).

The form efendim is used as a form of address for people of all classes; it is somewhat weaker than English 'Sir'. It may be used for men or women, but there is also the form hanımefendi 'Madam'. Efendim is also a favorite hesitation word, used in the middle of a sentence whenever the speaker cannot think of anything else to say.

4. Usage

Aile 'family' can be used as a euphemism for 'wife', especially in older speech.

Apartman does not mean 'apartment' but means 'apartment building'; an individual apartment ('flat') is a daire or apartman dairesi, although some speakers who know English may use apartman as an abbreviation for apartman dairesi. Daire is also, and more frequently, the word for 'office', in both the physical and institutional senses: Mehmedin dairesi geniş 'Mehmet's office is large'; Kültür Dairesi 'Cultural Office'. Yazıhane means 'office' in the physical sense only, while the English word ofis is coming into use in both senses.

Ömür means 'life' in the sense of 'life-span': Ömrü bitti 'His life ended'. Hayat means 'life' not only in the sense 'life-span', but also in the sense 'act of living' or 'conditions of life': talebe hayatı 'the life of a student, student life'.

Son means 'end' as a noun; it means 'last' as an adjective:

Hayatının son senesinde	'In the last year of his life'

The adjective tek means 'only', 'the only', or 'single' and corresponds to a variety of expressions in English:

Otobüste bir tek kişi var	'There is only one person on the bus'
Odada tek kişi kaldım	'I remained (as) the only person in the room'
Bir tek sigaram yok	'I don't have a single cigarette'

VOCABULARY

aile	/aīle/	family
Amerika		place name
apartman		apartment building (see "Usage")
Bay		Mr.
Bayan		Mrs.
bey		gentleman
daire		office, apartment (see "Usage")
değişmek		change (intrans)
dünya	/dünyā/	world, Earth
efendi		(see Section 3)
gülmek (dat)		laugh, smile; laugh (at)
hanım		lady
hava		weather, air
hayat	/hayāt/	life
ofis		office (see "Usage")
ömür	/ömr/	life
son		end (n); last (adj)
tek		single
yazıhane		office (see "Usage")
zengin		rich

EXERCISES

A. Answer the following questions:

1. Dünyada kaç insan yaşıyormuş?
2. "Hamlet"in sonunda kaç kişi ölüyor?
3. İstanbul Üniversitesi nasılmış, biliyor musun?
4. Her işin bir sonu varmış, değil mi?
5. Sizin işlerinizin sonu ne zaman gelecekmiş?

B. Translate into English:

1. Üçüncü Dünya Harbi bu sene çıkacakmış.
2. Halil bey her kitabını sonuna kadar okurmuş.
3. İçkiler beşer lira tutacakmış.
4. Bir gün Nasrettin Hoca bir ağaca çıkmış; ağaç düşmüş, Hoca havada kalmış.
5. Amerikada öyle şey olurmuş, ama burada olmaz.
6. Bu evin yerinde koca bir apartman yapacaklarmış. Her dairenin dörder odası olacakmış. Yalnız zenginler orada oturacakmış.
7. Her köyde üçer saat kaldık; onun için eve vaktinde varmıyacakmışız.
8. Mahmut bey kahve ister mi? —İstemezmiş.
9. Bize yalnız birer buçuk bardak su kalmış.
10. Bu köy son iki yılda çok değişmiş; eskiden burada sokak yokmuş.
11. Amerika'da hâlâ kovboylar varmış.
12. Ben New York'u görmedim ama orada çok büyük evler, geniş yollar ve geniş dükkânlar varmış.

C. Add the dubitative auxiliary suffix to each sentence. Then make each of the resulting sentences interrogative.

1. Bu ders zor.
2. Bu apartman Mehmet beyin değil.
3. Amerika'da hayat çok pahalı.
4. Orhan havayı beğenmiyor.
5. Beş liram var.
6. Müdür dairesinde.

7. Paket benim için.
8. Fatma hanım tayyareye binmez.
9. Ahmet beyin dersleri pek iyi değil.
10. Bekir bey, yeni lokantasını yarın açacak.

D. Translate into Turkish:

1. The place is said to be large.
2. The news is supposedly good.
3. This is supposed to be his last year in school.
4. Isn't he supposed to be rich?
5. Where is his office supposed to be?
6. This apartment is supposedly Ali Bey's.
7. The Korkmaz family is supposedly living in the same apartment building.
8. They say the weather will change tomorrow.
9. Mehmet's young son is supposed to be like his father.
10. The Arabs supposedly write from right to left.
11. They say the main road does not pass through here.

LESSON 19: USES OF -DIR AND THE RELATIVE -KI

Study the following sentences:

Dün akşam Şiledeki Büyük Otel yanmıştır	'Yesterday evening the Grand Hotel at Şile burned down'
Yarınki toplantıda Başbakan Demirel konuşacaktır	'Prime Minister Demirel will speak at tomorrow's meeting'
Ahmet herhalde dairesindedir; evde yok	'Ahmet presumably is in his office; he isn't at home'
Bu adam buraya yeni gelmiştir; şimdiye kadar onu görmedim	'This man must have come here recently; I haven't seen him until now'
Muhakkak hastayımdır; başım dönüyor	'I must certainly be sick; my head is turning around'
O memleketlerdekiler pek çalışmaz	'The people in those countries don't work very much'
Öbür masalarda yer yok; köşedeki masada otururuz	'There is no room at the other tables; we'll sit at the table in the corner'
Öbür masalarda yer yok; köşedekinde otururuz	'There is no room at the other tables; we'll sit at the one in the corner'
O eşyalar sizin değil; sizinkini rafa koydum	'Those things aren't yours; I put yours on the shelf'
Dün akşam arkadaşımın odasında değildim; kardeşiminkindeydim	'Yesterday evening I was not in my friends's room; I was in my brother's'

1. The suffix -DIr

The function of -DIr is to emphasize the truth of the statement being made. It is added after the personal ending; it is most frequently, and in the written language almost invariably, used with the third person. Since the third person ending is otherwise zero, -DIr becomes attached to the predicate (or tense). One use, as we have seen already, is for statements of general validity:

İstanbul şehrinde iki milyon kişi vardır	'There are two million people in the city of Istanbul'

It may also be used with the narrative past -mIş to remove the connotations of doubtfulness from this tense. That is, the speaker affirms the truth of the statement although he did not witness it personally. The construction -mIştIr is therefore the favorite past tense in newspaper and written Turkish, along with the corresponding future -(y)EcEktIr.

Başbakan Demirel, dün saat 8.30'ta uçakla Irak'a gitmiştir	'Prime Minister Demirel went to Iraq by air at 8:30 yesterday'
Başbakan, 24 Ekim'de Türkiyeye dönecektir	'The prime minister will return to Turkey on October 24'

There are thus essentially three past tenses in Turkish:

gitti	'he went' (and the speaker saw him)
gitmiş	'he went' (supposedly)
gitmiştir	'he definitely went' (although the speaker didn't see him)

In the spoken language, the meaning of -DIr is normally somewhat different: gitmiştir means 'he must have gone'. That is, the speaker assumes, from the evidence, that the statement is true although he does not know it definitely. For example:

Öğretmen bugün gelmedi; herhalde hastadır	'The teacher didn't come today; presumably he is sick'
Yorgunsundur	'You must be tired'
Beş saat güneşte durdum; muhakkak yanmışımdır	'I stood in the sun five hours; I must certainly be burned'
Bir şey söylemedi ama muhakkak biliyordur	'He hasn't said a thing, but he must certainly know'
Ahmet şimdi işten çıkmıştır; saat beşi çeyrek geçiyor	'Ahmet must have left work by now; it is quarter after five'

The suffix -DIr may also be placed within the sentence, normally after an adverb of time; it then places emphasis on the element to which it is attached:

Ahmet üç haftadır hasta	'Ahmet has been sick for all of three weeks (It is three weeks that Ahmet is sick)'
Bir senedir bunu kullanıyorum	'I have been using this for a whole year (It is a year that I am using this)'

2. The "relative" suffix -ki

In Turkish we have the sentence:

Sokak geniş	'The street is wide'

And we have the corresponding noun phrase:

geniş sokak	'the wide street'

Almost any sentence with a nonverbal predicate can be "turned around" to produce a noun phrase in which the predicate serves as a modifier of the subject. To put it another way, almost any construction that can serve as a nonverbal predicate can also function as a modifier of a noun. The same principle applies in the following examples:

Ev taştan	'The house is of stone'
taştan bir ev	'a stone house'
Ahmet dostum(dur)	'Ahmet is my friend'
dostum Ahmet	'my friend Ahmet'
Demirel Başbakan(dır)	'Demirel is Prime Minister'
Başbakan Demirel	'Prime Minister Demirel'
İş tam bana göre	'The job is exactly suitable for me'
tam bana göre bir iş	'a job exactly suitable for me'

When a noun in the locative or genitive is used to

modify another noun, however, there is a complication: the so-called "relative" suffix -ki must be added. Thus, corresponding to the sentence Kitap masada 'The book is on the table', we get the noun phrase masadaki kitap 'the book on the table'. Similarly, we have:

Ankaradaki yeni binalar çok büyük	'The new buildings in Ankara are very big'
Babamın evindeki eşyaları istemiyorum; güzel değil	'I don't want the things (furniture) in my father's house; they aren't attractive'

Sometimes the noun that is modified is omitted, and the noun in the locative with -ki stands alone. In such a case, 'person' (or 'people') should normally be understood, as in the case of adjectives used alone, such as gençler 'the young (people)'. Sometimes 'one' (for a thing) may be understood, if the thing in question has been mentioned previously:

O kutuda eşyam var, ama buradaki kutu boş	'My things are in that box, but the box here is empty'
O kutuda eşyam var, ama buradaki boş	'My things are in that box, but the one here is empty'
Bu bardak temiz değil; raftaki bardağı kullanırım	'This glass is not clean; I'll use the glass on the shelf'
Bu bardak temiz değil; raftakini kullanırım	'This glass is not clean; I'll use the one on the shelf'
O köydekiler çok tembel	'The people in that village are very lazy'

The suffix -ki is also added to a noun in the genitive to produce, for example, benimki 'that which is mine' or simply 'mine'. A construction of this sort is not normally used to modify another noun (benimki kitap would mean the same thing as benim kitabım) but is usually used alone:

Bu araba iyi değil, Halilinki ama güzel	'This car is not good, but Halil's is nice'
Bu kalem benim; seninki rafta	'This pen is mine; your's is on the shelf'

Sizin sigaralarınızı almadım; onunkini içiyorum 'I didn't take your cigarettes; I am smoking *his*'

Because the decision when or when not to use -*ki* usually causes difficulty, some additional discussion may be useful. If a noun in the locative is the predicate of a sentence, or if it functions as an adverb indicating the place where the action occurred, then it is simply in the locative. But if it modifies a noun, indicating the place where the object was located, then -*ki* must be used. Thus, consider the following example:

Masadaki kitabı okudum 'I read the book on the table'

This means 'I read the book that was on the table' or 'The book was on the table, and I read it'. But compare this sentence:

Masada kitabı okudum 'I read the book on the table'

This means 'I read the book while on the table' or 'Sitting on the table, I read the book'. Compare also:

Köşedeki kadını gördüm 'I saw the woman on the corner (I saw the woman, who was on the corner)'

Köşede kadını gördüm 'I saw the woman on the corner (While I was on the corner, I saw the woman)'

Compare finally:

Odada ne var? 'What is in the room?'

Odadaki ne? 'What is the thing in the room?'

In the first of the preceding sentences, *odada* is an adverb and goes with *var*; the subject of the sentence is *ne*. In the second sentence, *odadaki* is a noun and is the subject of the sentence; *ne* is the predicate.

If a noun in the genitive is the predicate of a

sentence, it is simply in the genitive. But if it is functioning as a noun, then -ki must be used.

Masadaki kalem Orhanın	'The pen on the table is Orhan's'
Bu kalem benim; Orhanınki masada	'This pen is mine; Orhan's is on the table'
Bu kalem benim; Orhanınki, masadaki kalem	'This pen is mine; Orhan's is the pen on the table'

The suffix -ki may also be attached to certain nouns indicating days (dün, bugün, yarın, gün) or parts of days (sabah, akşam, gece) or to şimdi:

Dünkü gazetede Halilin yazısı çıkmış	'Halil's article came out in yesterday's newspaper'
Dün akşamki yemeği kardeşimin evinde yedim	'I ate yesterday evening's dinner in my brother's house'
Perşembe günkü toplantıya bakan gelmedi	'The minister did not come to Thursday's meetıng'
Memleketin şimdiki hali çok fena	'The present condition of the country is very bad'

You will have noticed from several of the preceding examples that the suffix -ki uses an "oblique stem" -kin-, with the same -n- that appears in the declension of several of the pronouns, before any case suffix, but not before the plural (compare köydekiler).

In the written language, -ki is normally invariable: the vowel i does not change according to vowel harmony; thus we have onunkinden 'from that which is his'. But in expressions such as dünkü, bugünkü, we usually find a rounded ü instead of i, both in pronunciation and spelling. Furthermore, in conversation (but never in writing), it is possible to hear this suffix alternate according to front-back harmony as well; thus we find Ankaradakı instead of Ankaradaki.

3. Adjectives as adverbs

Many adjectives in Turkish may also be used as adverbs, with only minor modification in meaning. For example, iyi means 'good' as an adjective, 'well' as an adverb;

Kullanmak - drive

kötü and fena mean 'bad' as adjectives, 'badly' as adverbs.

Bu işi iyi yaptınız	'You did this job well'
O adam çok kötü yazı yazar	'That man writes very badly'
Mehmet fena araba kullanıyor	'Mehmet drives (a car) badly'

Other adjectives that are frequently used as adverbs are the following:

güzel	'well, nicely'
yeni	'recently' (or English 'just' in the meaning 'recently')
doğru	'straight, right, truthfully'
Mehmet arabayı güzel kullandı	'Mehmet drove the car well'
Doktor yeni geldi	'The doctor came recently'
Doğru yürüdü	'He walked straight'
Doğru konuştu	'He spoke truthfully; he spoke the truth'
İşi doğru yaptı	'He did the job right'

Similarly, uzun means 'long' as an adjective, 'at length' as an adverb; kısa means 'short' as an adjective, 'briefly' as an adverb.

Bakan uzun konuştu	'The minister spoke at length'
Kısa bir zaman için geldim	'I came for a short time'
Kısa konuşurum	'I'll speak briefly'

In a different sense, adjectives may serve as adverbs indicating, not the manner in which the action was performed, but the condition of the subject. For example, the English sentence 'He came home tired' does not mean 'He came home in a tired manner' but 'He came home in a tired condition'. Similarly, in Turkish, note the following example:

Eve yorgun geldi	'He came home tired'

This is equivalent to

Eve yorgun bir halde geldi	'He came home in a tired condition'

Similarly:

Çocuk doğru oturdu	'The child sat up straight'

The verbs durmak and kalmak are expecially popular in this type of construction and lose most of their meaning; they should be translated by English 'be':

Pencere temiz durdu	'The window was clean'
Köpekler aç kaldı	'The dogs are (have remained) hungry'
Attila geç kaldı	'Attila is (has remained) late'

4. Usage

Think twice before using eşya to translate English 'thing'; it means 'thing' only in the sense of 'movable property' and can refer to furniture, clothes, and similar objects. It does not have the extended meanings of şey.

Hal is the most general word for 'condition' or 'state':

Ali ne halde?	'What condition is Ali in?'

It is used in a number of quasi-idiomatic expressions—for example, o halde 'in that case'. Herhalde, which you might translate literally as 'in any case', does not have that meaning but means 'presumably'.

A dost is a closer friend than an arkadaş. Colloquially, dost can also be 'mistress' or 'lover'.

Konuşmak means 'speak' or 'speak with'; the person spoken with is indicated by ile:

O adamla kim konuşacak?	'Who will speak with that man?'

Kullanmak means 'use'; but with the noun araba, it means 'drive' (sürmek may also be used, in a more technical sense, for 'drive'). In such constructions, araba sometimes has the status of an "obligatory object" and is not needed in the translation.

Arabayı kim kullanacak?	'Who will drive the car?'
	'Who will drive?'

VOCABULARY

bakan		minister (governmental)
başbakan		prime minister
bina	/binā/	building
dost		friend
eşya	/eşyā/	thing, things, property (see "Usage")
hal	/hāl̂/	state, condition (see "Usage")
herhalde	/hérhal̂de/	presumably
kısa		short, briefly
konuşmak		speak, talk
kullanmak		use; drive (see "Usage")
memleket		country
muhakkak		certainly
raf		shelf
toplantı		meeting
Türkiye	/türkíye/	Turkey
uzun		long
vekil		minister (governmental)
yanmak		burn (intrans)

EXERCISES

A. Answer the following questions:

daire - office, apartment

1. Kaç senedir mektebe gidiyorsunuz?
2. Penceredeki kadın kimdir?
3. Dünkü toplantıya kimler geldi?
4. Mustafa fena mı araba kullanıyor, iyi mi?
5. Hasan benim sigaralarımı mı içiyor, seninkini mi?
6. Odanızdaki eşyalar kimin?
7. Ömrünüzde traktör kullandınız mı?

B. Translate into English:

1. Elinizde ne var?
2. Elinizdeki ne?
3. Elinizde ne tutuyorsunuz?
4. Elinizdekini neden tutuyorsunuz?
5. Attilanın dairesi bu binada.
6. Bu binadaki daire Attilanın.
7. Benim dairem, Attilanınkine yakın.
8. Attilanınki, bu binadaki daireye yakın.
9. Bizim bakkal dükkânımızda ekmek yoktu; Ankara Sokağındaki bakkal dükkânına gittim.
10. Bizim bakkal dükkânımızda ekmek yoktu; Ankara Sokağındakine gittim.
11. Benim kâgıdım yoktu, sizinkini kullandım.
12. Halilin arabası çok küçük, bizimkiyle gideriz.

C. Change the sentences in parentheses into relatives with -ki.

Example:

(Kitap pencerede) kitabı sana verdim.

Answer:

Penceredeki kitabı sana verdim.

1. (Adam köşede) adam Ahmet'in babasıdır.
2. (Adam ayda) adam bize gülüyor.
3. (Su bardakta) suyu köpeğe verdim.

4. (Resim gazetede) resim çok güzel çıkmış.
5. Eşyalarınızı (kutu odanızda) kutuya koydum.

D. Change the sentences in parentheses into relatives with -ki, and delete any repeated nouns.

Example:

(Kahve rafta) kahve iyi değil, (kahve masada)-i kullanacağım.

Answer:

Raftaki kahve iyi değil, masadakini kullanacağım.

1. Kitabımı Orhan'a verdim, ben (kitap Ayşe'nin)-i kullanırım.
2. (Daireler Orhan beyin apartmanında) daireler küçük, ama (daireler bu binada) kadar pahalı.
3. (Kitap yerde) kitabı (çocuk köşede) çocuğa verdim, (kitap masada)-i (çocuk kapıda)-e verdim.
4. Orhan'ın evini biliyorum; (ev Mehmed'in) ama hangisidir?
5. Kâtiplerin ofisinde boş bir masa var; (ofis benim) -de ama yer yok.

E. Translate into Turkish:

1. What is in the shop at the end of that street?
2. What is in the university building?
3. What is on that shelf?
4. What is on the shelf over there?
5. Who is in the prime minister's office?
6. How many students are in that class (lesson)?
7. Who are the students in that class?
8. I didn't go to yesterday morning's meeting; I'll go to today's meeting.
9. I didn't go to yesterday's meeting; I'll go to today's.
10. I didn't use that glass; I used the glass on the shelf.

11. I didn't use that glass; I used the one on the shelf.
12. Mehmet was not in this hotel; he was in the hotel on the corner.
13. Mehmet was not in this hotel; he was in the one on the corner.
14. I didn't speak with that woman; I spoke with the woman over there.
15. I didn't speak with that woman; I spoke with the one over there.
16. My book is Bizim Köy; his is Ince Memed.
17. My book is Bizim Köy; what is his?
18. My name is Raif; what is yours?
19. I have looked at my friend's letter; now I am starting yours.
20. Their country is like ours.
21. Did he find your things or mine?
22. I always use this box for cigarettes, the one over there for fruit.
23. Tonight's meeting is in the old building at the corner of Ankara Street. Presumably it won't be long.
24. According to the article in yesterday's Akşam newspaper, the prime minister will be occupied with these matters until Saturday. I didn't understand the article, but it must certainly be right.
25. What is the animal holding in his mouth? The thing in his mouth is a piece of wood.

LESSON 20: POSTPOSITIONS WITH THE ABLATIVE

Study the following sentences:

Tren kalktı, amma yarım saat sonra başka bir tren var	'The train left, but half an hour later there is another train'
"İnce Memed" ten başka, Yaşar Kemal'in eserlerini pek beğenmiyorum	'Except for Ince Memed, I don't like Yasar Kemal's works very much'
Arkadaşınız Ekimden beri derse gelmedi	'Your friend hasn't come to class since October'
Cevabınızı iki haftadan beri bekliyorum	'I have been waiting for your answer for two weeks'
Attila dertlerinden dolayı işe gitmiyor	'Because of Attila's troubles, he hasn't been going to work'
Güneşten gözlerim görmüyor	'Because of the sun, my eyes don't see (I can't see)'
Bursadan sonra yol daha fena oluyor	'After Bursa the road gets worse'
Yarından evvel daha iyi bir yer bulurum	'I'll find a better place before tomorrow'
İki gün evvel işe başladı, daha bitirmedi	'He began the work two days ago and hasn't finished yet'
Kitabın en iyi yeri, bundan sonraki sayfadadır	'The best part of the book is on the page after this'
Bu yemekten biraz yedim, ama beğenmedim; öbüründen fena	'I ate some of this food, but I didn't like it; it is worse than the other'
Buralarda en güzel ev bizim	'The nicest house around here is ours'

1. Postpositions with the ablative

Some of the most common postpositions with the ablative are the following:

A. başka
This is most frequently used as an adjective meaning 'other' or 'another', either in the sense of 'different' or 'additional'. A noun phrase containing başka is always indefinite.

Orada Halil değil, başka bir adam oturuyor	'Not Halil, (but) another man is sitting there'
Bu cins meyva sevmiyorum; başka cins yok mu?	'I don't like this kind of fruit; isn't there another kind?'
Başka bir çay ister misiniz?	'Would you like another (glass of) tea?'
Başka çay ister misiniz?	'Would you like more tea?'

As a postposition, başka means basically 'other than'; it may be translated with a variety of English expressions, such as 'apart from, besides, in addition to, except for'.

Hasan'dan başka kim gelecek?	'Who will come besides Hasan?'
Bundan başka ne aldınız?	'What did you buy besides this?'
Etten başka, bu lokantada her çeşit yemek var	'In addition to meat, there is every kind of food at this restaurant'

B. beri

This postposition corresponds to English 'since', and to some uses of English 'for', in expressions of time:

Dün akşamdan beri hastayım	'I have been sick since yesterday evening'
O zamandan beri dertlerim bitmedi	'Since that time my troubles have not ended'

Notice that Turkish uses the progressive tense where English uses the past progressive ('have been'), to describe an action that began at some indicated time and is still continuing at the time of the utterance:

Saat ikiden beri sizi bekliyorum	'I have been waiting for you since two o'clock'
Perşembeden beri çok çalışıyorum	'I have been working hard since Thursday'

The use of the past auxiliary in a sentence with beri gives a construction corresponding to the English past perfect:

O zaman kitabını iki seneden beri yazıyordu	'At that time he had been writing his book for two years'

English uses 'for' instead of 'since' in expressions of this sort, if the preceding noun phrase denotes a period of time rather than a particular point. Turkish uses beri in these cases also, if the action is still continuing:

İki saatten beri yürüyorum	'I have been walking for two hours'
Bu bina iki asırdan beri burada duruyor	'This building has been standing here for two centuries'

But beri is not used if the action is not still continuing; remember that English 'for' in most expressions of time is translated simply with the expression of time itself.

Bugün iki saat yürüdüm	'Today I walked for two hours'
Seyahatim üç ay sürdü	'My trip lasted for three months'

C. dolayı

This postposition and the considerably more rare ötürü mean 'because of'.

Sözünden dolayı, Attilayla bir daha konuşmıyacağım	'Because of his words (what he said), I am not going to talk to Attila again'
İşimden dolayı başka vaktim kalmadı	'Because of my work, I have no other time left'

Dolayı may be omitted from these constructions, leaving the noun phrase in the ablative to indicate the reason for which the action was performed. This produces a construction that may be called the "ablative of cause," although it amounts simply to the omission of dolayı. When dolayı is omitted, the construction is considered to be emphasized and is placed immediately in front of the verb:

Bundan dolayı onunla konuşmıyacağım	'Because of this I will not talk to him'
Onunla bundan dolayı konuşmıyacağım	
Onunla bundan konuşmıyacağım	

Notice that the interrogative neden 'why' is thus simply a reduction of neden dolayı 'because of what'; similarly, ondan may be used to mean 'therefore':

Gözlerimi ondan dolayı kapadım	'I closed my eyes because of that'
Gözlerimi ondan kapadım	'Therefore I closed my eyes'

D. evvel, önce, sonra
As postpositions with the ablative, evvel and önce mean 'before', and sonra (/sóra/ in Istanbul) means 'after':

Hasan benden evvel vardı	'Hasan arrived before me'
Toplantıdan sonra bir lokantaya gittik	'After the meeting we went to a restaurant'
Bunu Perşembeden evvel bitiririm	'I'll finish this before Thursday'
Bu haftadan sonra daha çok vaktim olacak	'After this week I'll have more time'
Bundan evvel nerede oturuyordunuz?	'Where were you living before this?'
Bundan sonra sabahları daha erken kalkacağım	'From now on (after this) I will get up earlier in the mornings'

These words may also be used as quasi postpositions with the nominative to mean 'earlier' (or 'ago') and 'later':

Bir hafta evvel gelecektiniz	'You were going to come a week ago'

Eski mektep binası iki sene evvel yanmıştı	'The old school building had burned down two years ago'
Beş gün sonra aynı adam yine geldi	'Five days later the same man came again'

Be sure to distinguish between:

bu haftadan evvel	'before this week'
bir hafta evvel	'a week earlier, a week ago'
bugünden sonra	'after today'
bir gün sonra	'a day later'

Evvel and *sonra* can be combined with *-ki* to produce *evvelki* 'the preceding' and *sonraki* 'the following'. Except in certain idioms, these forms must still be preceded by a noun phrase in the ablative.

Bundan sonraki otobüse bineceğiz	'We will take the bus after this (one)'
Bundan evvelki otobüse binecektik	'We were going to take the bus before this (one)'
Bu otobüsten sonrakine bineceğiz	'We will take the one after this (bus)'
Bu otobüsten evvelkine binecektik	'We were going to take the one before this (bus)'

The two idioms in question are *evvelki sene* 'the previous year' and *evvelki gün* 'the previous day'. The first can be used for 'last year', as a reduction of *bundan evvelki sene*, 'the year before this'. The second can be used for 'the day before yesterday', as a reduction of *dün değil, evvelki gün* 'not yesterday, the day before'; the latter expression is sometimes used in its full form.

We shall have to wait a while to learn how to say 'next year', because **sonraki sene* is impossible. 'The day after tomorrow' is *öbür gün*, a reduction of *yarın değil, öbür gün*, 'not tomorrow, the day after'; this latter expression is sometimes used in its full form.

Finally, the three words *evvel*, *önce*, and *sonra*, and forms derived from them, are frequently used as simple adverbs:

evvelki sene 'last year'
evvelki gün 'not yesterday, the day before'

sonra	'then, afterward'
ondan sonra	'after that, afterward'
evvelâ	'first'
ilkönce	'first of all'
en sonunda	'at last, finally'
Evvelâ senin işini bitiririz, sonra benimkini	'First we'll finish your work, then mine'
İlkönce kapıyı kapadı, sonra masaya oturdu	'First of all he closed the door; then he sat down at the table'

2. Comparative and superlative of adjectives

2.1. Comparative

The comparative of adjectives is made basically with the word daha, preceding the adjective: daha ucuz 'cheaper', daha pahalı 'more expensive'. Daha may be preceded in turn by the noun indicating the object of comparison, expressed in the ablative:

Hasan, Halil'den daha hoş bir insandır	'Hasan is a more pleasant person than Halil'
Benim arabam, senin arabandan daha yeni	'My car is newer than your car'
Benim arabam, senin-kinden daha yeni	'My car is newer than yours'
Bu oda çok küçük; daha büyük bir oda isterim	'This room is too small; I would like a larger room'
Daha güzel bir odanız yok mu?	'Don't you have a nicer room?'
Yeni yol, eski yoldan daha uzun	'The new road is longer than the old road'

In addition, various combinations of daha with az, çok, and biraz 'a little' are possible, with the indicated meanings:

daha tembel	'lazier'

daha çok tembel	'more lazy' (slightly intensified)
çok daha tembel	'much more lazy'
daha az tembel	'less lazy'
az daha tembel biraz daha tembel	'slightly lazier, a little bit lazier'
biraz daha az tembel	'slightly less lazy'
çok daha az tembel	'much less lazy'
biraz daha çok tembel	'slightly more lazy'

When the object of comparison is present, <u>daha</u> may be omitted; we can have <u>Hasan, Halil'den tembel</u> 'Hasan is lazier than Halil' as a short form of <u>Hasan, Halil'den daha tembel</u>. This produces a construction that may be called the "ablative of comparison," although it amounts simply to the omission of <u>daha</u>.

Kardeşim benden büyük	'My brother is bigger than I'
Babasından zengin oldu	'He became richer than his father'

The comparative of adjectives used as adverbs is made in the same way:

Hasan benden daha çok çalışır Hasan benden çok çalışır	'Hasan works harder than I do'
Çaydan daha çok kahve içer	'He drinks more coffee than tea; he drinks coffee rather than tea'
Hasan, Halil'den daha fena araba kullanır Hasan, Halil'den fena araba kullanır	'Hasan drives a car worse than Halil'

2.2. Superlative

The superlative is made with en, preceding the adjective: en ucuz 'cheapest', en pahalı 'most expensive'. The resulting phrase is pronounced as one word, with the accent on en; the final n of en tends to assimilate to any following consonant:

en büyük	/émbüyük/	'biggest'
en güzel	/éŋgüzel/	'prettiest'

Either the genitive or the locative may be used in superlative constructions:

Bu şehrin en güzel yeri Bebek'tir	'The most beautiful place of this city is Bebek'
Bu şehirde en güzel yer Bebek'tir	'The most beautiful place in this city is Bebek'
Dünyanın en büyük binaları nerede?	'Where are the biggest buildings in (of) the world?'
Bu evde en çok Halil çalışır	'Halil works the hardest in this house'
Bu işi en kısa zamanda bitiririm	'I'll finish this job in the shortest (possible) time'

3. Partitive ablative

Compare the following:

Ekmek yedim	'I ate bread'
Ekmeği yedim	'I ate the bread'
Ekmekten yedim	'I ate some bread; I ate some of the bread'

In Turkish, the ablative case may be used instead of the objective to show that only a portion of the indicated object is involved in the action. Thus, in Ekmeği yedim, some specific quantity is involved, all of which was eaten; in Ekmek yedim, the quantity is not indicated; in Ekmekten yedim, only a portion of some stated or implied larger quantity was eaten. This is called a "partitive construction" and has parallels in some European languages—for example, French:

J'ai mangé le pain	'I ate the bread'
J'ai mangé du pain	'I ate some bread'

Some other examples:

Biraz bundan yedi, ondan yemedi	'He ate a little of this, none of that'
Bu büyük elmalardan alırım	'I'll get some of these big apples'
Kitaplarından en çok "İnce Memed"i beğeniyorum	'Of his books, I like Ince Memed the most'

4. Usage

In addition to its use in the comparative, daha as an adverb has a number of meanings:
A. 'still', synonymous with hâlâ:

Onu daha bekliyor musunuz?	'Are you still waiting for him?'

B. 'more', usually with a number:

Bir kişi daha geldi	'One more person came'

C. 'yet', in negative sentences:

Orhan daha gelmedi	'Orhan hasn't come yet'

D. Bir daha means 'again'; it is probably best treated as a reduced form of bir kere daha 'one more time' (see meaning B):

Dersi bir daha okurum	'I'll read the lesson again'
Evine bir daha gitmem	'I won't go to his house again'

Dert has a number of meanings: 'trouble, care, pain, illness, problem', and so on. An example is Derdin ne? 'What's your problem?'

The adjective diğer has the features both of başka and öbür; it means 'other, the other, another' and can be definite or indefinite.

Gözlerim görmüyor is the idiomatic way of saying 'I can't see'.

Öğle 'noon' is not normally used by itself but appears in a number of idiomatic constructions, notably öğleden sonra 'afternoon' and öğleyin 'at noontime'.

Yarın öğleden sonra denize gideceğiz	'Tomorrow afternoon we will go to the seashore'
Hasan, öğleden sonraları hep yatağa yatar	'Hasan always goes to bed in the afternoons'
Öğleyin nerelere gidiyorsunuz?	'Where do you go at noontime?'

Söz means 'word, utterance, thing spoken, speech, promise, what (someone) said'.

VOCABULARY

başka (abl)		other, other than
beri (abl)		since
biraz	/bíraz/	a little
bitirmek		finish (trans)
bitmek		finish (intrans)
daha	/dáha/	more (see "Usage")
dert	/derd/	trouble, illness, problem
diğer		other (see "Usage")
dolayı (abl)		because (of)
evvel (abl)		before, earlier, ago
evvelâ	/évvelā/	first
gene, gine, yine	/géne, gíne, yíne/	again
göz		eye
Hasan		man's name
kapamak		close
öğle		noon (see "Usage")
önce (abl)		before

sonra (abl) /sónra/ after, later

söz word (see "Usage")

tekrar /têkrar/ again

EXERCISES

A. Answer the following questions:

1. Dün öğleden sonra neredeydiniz?
2. Buraya kaç sene evvel geldiniz?
3. Kahveden başka bir şey istiyor musunuz?
4. Dünyanın şehirlerinden en çok hangisini seviyorsunuz?
5. Derdiniz nedir?

B. Translate into English:

1. Benim gözlerim seninkilerden daha iyi görür.
2. Annesinin halinden dolayı, Fatma ailesinin evinde kalacak.
3. Bugünkü dersi bitirdim; şimdi başka bir derse başlıyacağım.
4. Saat önce beşi vurdu, sonra altıyı vurdu.
5. Benim senden başka kimim var?
6. Hasan trafikten dolayı bugün biraz geç kaldı, ama işlerini öğleden evvel bitirecek.
7. Tekrar söylüyorum: memleketin dertleri her şeyden önce gelir.
8. Söz gider, yazı kalır.
9. Ahmet'ten başka bir adam bu işi çok daha iyi yapardı. Bir aydan beri hâlâ bitirmedin.
10. Bundan büyüğü yok; en büyüğü bu.

C. Supply the correct case suffixes:

1. Şubat Ocak___ sonra mı gelir, önce mi?
2. Bu___ gibi ders görmedim.
3. Fatma Ayşe___ daha çalışkan.
4. Halil biz___ için dükkânını erken açtı.

5. Sen___ önce Ahmedi gördüm.
6. Beş lira___ başka param kalmadı.
7. Saat sekiz___ beş___ kadar burası boş kalır.
8. Siz___ göre bu işlerin sonu gelecek mi?
9. Hasan sabahları on bir___ evvel kalkmaz.
10. Bir hafta___ beri derse gelmiyorsunuz, bu___ dolayı anlamıyorsunuz.
11. Akşam___ doğru siz___ ile yemeğe gideriz.
12. Mustafanın eski arkadaşları o___ karşı döndü.
13. Yeni arabam, Halilinki___ kadar büyük olacak.
14. Deniz___ doğru beş saat___ beri yürüyoruz.

D. Translate into Turkish:

1. Süleyman Demirel became Prime Minister after Inönü.
2. He closed one eye and looked at us with the other.
3. According to what Hasan says, his new car is worse than ours.
4. Our job will finish before theirs.
5. He walked as far as the door but didn't enter.
6. Apart from the two men, what do you see in the picture?
7. He always says bad things against us.
8. His face is as black as an Arab's face.
9. Because of the weather, the children stayed in the house again today.
10. This world is like an enormous airplane.
11. His trip was for business.
12. He came toward the window.

E. Translate into Turkish:

1. Ali told me his troubles for four hours.
2. Hasan Bey has been director since January.
3. He has been speaking for forty-five minutes.
4. Fatma's family has been living in Izmir since the seventeenth century.

5. We made a big meal for Saturday.
6. That package has been on the floor for three days.
7. I looked for my pen for two hours this morning; finally I took yours.

F. Translate into Turkish:

1. Oranges were less expensive a week ago.
2. After the month of February, there will be three more people here.
3. Ahmet Bey's article came out in June, but he had finished it four months earlier.
4. Our work in Erzurum will finish before September, God willing.
5. Five weeks later the tree fell for the second time.

G. Translate into Turkish:

1. The prime minister before this one was much more hardworking.
2. Ahmet's picture is on the page after page thirty.
3. We were on the train before Ahmet's.
4. The two buses after this will go by the old road.

çıkmak - go out, leave
atmak - throw
throw away

LESSON 21: POSTPOSITIONAL CONSTRUCTIONS

Study the following sentences:

Bir adam, vapurun arkasından suyun içine düştü	'A man fell from the back of the ship into the water'
Onlarla bizim aramızda, bahçe üzerine kavga çıktı	'A fight arose between them and us over the garden'
Büyük bir ağacın altında yere yattı	'He lay on the ground under a big tree'
Her şeyim el altında	'Everything of mine is at hand'
Dükkânın arkasında büyük elma ağaçları var	'There are big apple trees behind the store'
Halil her akşam içki içer, gece ortasında eve gelir	'Halil drinks every evening and comes home in the middle of the night'
Size bir paket getirdim, eşyalarınızın arasına attım	'I brought you a package and threw it among your things'
Bu kış, sizinkinin karşısındaki evde oturacağız	'This winter we will live in the house opposite yours'
Paketin içindekilerini bize gösterir misiniz?	'Will you show us the contents of the package?'
Evin dış kısmına baktık, içine ama girmedik	'We looked at the outside part of the house, but we didn't go inside'
Yunus Emre'nin Ahmedin üstündeki tesiri çok büyüktür	'Yunus Emre's influence on Ahmet is very great'
Askerler, şehrin önüne duvar yaptılar	'The soldiers made a wall in front of the city'
Ahmet daima o kızın peşinden gider	'Ahmet always follows that girl'
Senin koca ayaklarının yanında yer kalmadı	'There is no room left beside your enormous feet'

Kısım ⇒ part

1. Postpositional constructions

Postpositional constructions in Turkish are not postpositions; they are simple genitive-possessive constructions of the type that was considered in Lesson 9. But they normally correspond to prepositional phrases in English; furthermore, some of them have acquired idiomatic meanings.

The basis of a postpositional construction is a noun such as iç 'inside' or 'interior'. With this, we can form a possessive construction like evin içi 'the inside of the house'. If the dative, locative, or ablative suffix is then added, we have:

evin içine	'into the house' ('to the inside of the house')
evin içinde	'in the house' ('at the inside of the house')
evin içinden	'from within the house' ('from the inside of the house')

Consider the following examples:

Otobüsün içinde yer buldu, oturdu	'He found a place in the bus and sat down'
Bu kutuda ne var? —Bilmem; içine bakmadım	'What is in this box? —I don't know; I haven't looked inside'
Odanın içinden bir ses geliyordu	'A voice was coming from inside the room'
Bu odanın içindekiler çok içki içiyor	'The people in this room are drinking too much'

In many cases the genitive suffix may be omitted from the first noun, so that the result is not a genitive construction but a possessive compound. Sometimes there is very little difference in meaning between the two possiblities:

İstanbulun içinde çok insan var	'There are too many people in (within) Istanbul'
İstanbul içinde çok insan var	

But in other cases the two constructions are clearly distinct. Frequently the distinction is one of definiteness: if the first noun is in the genitive, it is definite and refers to some specific object known to the speaker. But if it is without the genitive, it is indefinite and often used in a general sense:

Bu hayvanlar ağacın içinde yaşar	'These animals live inside the tree'
Bu hayvanlar ağaç içinde yaşar	'These animals live inside trees'
Eşyalarımı kutu içine koydum	'I put my things into a box/boxes'
Eşyalarımı kutunun içine koydum	'I put my things into the box'

Sometimes the Turkish possessive compound corresponds to an idiomatic expression in English:

Dairesi, şehrin içinde	'His office is within the city'
Dairesi, şehir içinde	'His office is downtown'

Several other cases will be pointed out in the course of this lesson.

Furthermore, when a postpositional construction is used in a metaphorical rather than a strictly physical sense, the genitive is normally omitted:

Bir hafta içinde kitabını bitirecek	'He will finish his book within a week'

When the first noun is definite, it must have the genitive suffix—for example, if it is preceded by a demonstrative pronoun:

Bu şehrin içinde çok insan var	'There are too many people in this city'

1.1. Nouns used in postpositional constructions

Some of the other nouns that are frequently used in postpositional constructions are the following:

A. <u>dış</u> 'outside, exterior'

Evin dışına çıktı	'He went out of the house (to the outside of the house)'
Kapının dışında bir adam bekliyordu	'A man was waiting outside the door'
Evin dışından arabalar geçiyor	'Cars are passing outside the house (by way of the outside of the house)'

Compare the use of <u>dış</u> in possessive compounds:

Kış zamanında kapı dışında beklemez	'In wintertime he doesn't wait outdoors (outside of doors)'

B. <u>üst</u>, <u>üzer-</u> 'top'
The stem <u>üzer-</u> is used only in postpositional constructions, while <u>üst</u> is also used as a noun.

Kitabı masanın üstüne koydu	'He put the book on top of the table'
Kapının üzerinde büyük bir taş vardı	'There was a big stone over (on top of) the door'
Bozkurtların üstündeki dairede oturuyorlar	'They live in the apartment over the Bozkurts'

Since the last example just given is more or less metaphorical, the genitive could be omitted with no significant change in meaning. Note also:

Uçak Bulgaristan üzerinden geldi	'The plane came over (by way of) Bulgaria' (Compare German 'über')
Uçak Bulgaristanın üzerinden geldi	'The plane came over (physically) Bulgaria'
V Mehmet üstüne kitap yazıyor	'He is writing a book on Mehmet V'

But remember that if the noun is definite, it must be in the genitive, even if the use is metaphorical:

Bu sözün üzerine çok kızdım	'Upon these words I became very angry'

Bunun üzerine çok kızdım	'Upon this I became very angry'

C. alt 'bottom'

Köpek yatağın altına girdi, orada yatıyor	'The dog went under the bed (entered underneath the bed) and is lying there'
Köpek yatağın altında yatıyor	'The dog is lying under the bed'

In possessive compounds or metaphorical use:

Ahmet, Yunus Emre'nin tesiri altında	'Ahmet is under the influence of Yunus Emre'
Bu köpek hep ayak altında	'This dog is always underfoot'

D. ön 'front'

Otobüs, tam bizim apartmanımızın önünde durur	'The bus stops just in front of our apartment building'
Bahçenin önündeki duvarda oturduk	'We sat on the wall in front of the garden'

E. arka 'back'
Besides arka, there is the considerably more rare art (/ard/):

Evimizin arkasında büyük bir bahçe var	'There is a big garden behind our house'
İskemlenin arkasına baktınız mı?	'Did you look behind the chair?'

F. peş 'back'
Peş has this meaning only in a certain sense: 'back of a moving object'. It is used primarily with verbs of motion and usually in the form peşinden, which is best translated 'after'. It is used when something (or someone) moves after something else that is also in motion.

Otobüsün peşinden gittik	'We went after the bus (we followed the bus)'

It may be used metaphorically:

Bu kitabın peşindeyim	'I am on the track of this book (I am looking for this book)'

Notice the verbs peşine düşmek (or takılmak) 'follow', and peşini bırakmak (bırakmak 'leave') 'cease following'.

G. orta 'middle'

Yemeğin ortasında geldi	'He arrived in the middle of dinner (the meal)'
Sokağın tam ortasında yürüyor	'He is walking exactly in the middle of the street'
Tam sokağın ortasında yürüyor	
Tam sokağın ortasından yürüyor	'He is walking exactly down the middle of the street'
Ahmedin kitabının ortasına kadar okudum	'I read as far as the middle of Ahmet's book'

Compare the use of orta in possessive compounds:

Hep yemek ortasında gelir	'He always comes in the middle of dinner'
Buraya kış ortasında vardı	'He arrived here in mid-winter'
Buraya kışın ortasında vardı	'He arrived here in the middle of the winter'

H. ara 'interval'

This word refers to the space between two or more things; it is used in postpositional constructions in the meaning 'between' or 'among' and is preceded either by a plural noun or several nouns connected by ile:

Evlerimizin arasında büyük bir bahçe var	'There is a big garden between our houses'
Bu insanların arasında üç tane ihtiyar var	'Among these people there are three old people'

Türkiye ile Yunanistanın arasında Ege Denizi var	'The Aegean Sea is between Turkey and Greece'
İkisinin arasında kavga çıktı	'A fight arose between the two of them'

I. yan 'side'

Fatma, Orhanın yanına oturdu	'Fatma sat down next to Orhan'
Fatma, Orhanın yanında oturdu	'Fatma sat next to Orhan'
Kitabı, yatağın yanındaki masanın üstüne attı	'He threw the book on top of the table beside the bed'
Yunus Emre'nin kitabı yanında, Halilinki o kadar iyi değil	'Beside Yunus Emre's book, Halil's is not so good'

J. karşı 'place opposite'

Lokanta, evimizin karşısında	'The restaurant is opposite our house (across from our house)'
Hocanın karşısına oturdu	'He sat down facing (opposite, across from) the teacher'
Bir köpek karşıma çıktı	'A dog appeared in front of me'

1.2. Use of possessive suffixes

Remember that when the genitive member of the construction is first or second person, or plural, the possessive suffix must change accordingly; önümüzde 'in front of us', from bizim önümüzde 'at our front'. Similarly:

Üstüme bir elma düştü	'An apple fell on top of me'
Peşlerinden yürüdü	'He walked after them'
Aramızda kavga çıktı	'A fight arose between us'

2. Usage

Most of the words that are used in postpositional constructions may also be used freely as nouns:

Kapı arkada	'The door is at the back'
Kutunun içi boş	'The inside of the box is empty'
Binanın dışı beyaz	'The outside of the building is white'
Hafta içi çok meşguldüm	'I was very busy in the middle of the week'
Ekmeğin ortasını yedi	'He ate the middle of the piece of bread'

Many of them may also be used as adjectives:

gazetenin iç sayfaları	'the inside pages of the newspaper'
ön kapı, arka kapı	'front door, back door'
Bınanın alt kısmında dükkân var, üst kısmında insanlar oturuyor	'In the bottom part of the building there are stores; in the top part people are living'

These nouns are used in a large number of idiomatic expressions, which it would be impossible to list here. Notice, however, the expressions iç işleri (içişleri) 'internal affairs', dışisleri (dış işleri) 'external affairs', yanyana 'side by side' (adverb) , and also the verb ortaya çıkmak 'come forth'. Ara as a noun may mean 'intermission'; ara vermek means 'call a halt'.

VOCABULARY

alt	bottom
ara	interval
arka	back
asker	soldier
atmak	throw, throw away
ayak	foot

bahçe		garden
Bulgaristan		Bulgaria
dış		outside
duvar		wall
Ege Denizi		Aegean Sea
elbise		clothes, clothing, dress
göstermek		show
iç		inside, interior
karşı		place opposite
kavga		fight, quarrel
kısım	/kısm/	part
kış		winter
kızmak (dat)		become angry (at)
orta		middle
ön		front
peş		back (of a moving object)
ses		voice, sound, noise
tesir	/tēsir/	influence
üst		top
üzer-		top
yan		side

EXERCISES

A. Answer each questions with a Turkish sentence, in the process repeating the Turkish expression corresponding to each English preposition:

1. What is outside the window?
2. What is on top of the table?
3. What is under the table?
4. What is in front of you?
5. What is behind you?

6. What is between the table and the door?
7. What is in the middle of the room?
8. What is beside the table?
9. What is opposite you?

B. Translate into English:

1. Mektuplarınızı masanızın üstüne attım.
2. Eşyalarınızın arasında elbise yoktu.
3. Otobüsün arka kısmında çok yer var.
4. Üniversitenin bahçe duvarının önünde iki adam bekliyor.
5. Yolun ortasında yürüyorduk: iki yanımda birer asker, önümde yaşlı bir adam, peşimde de iki küçük çocuk vardı.
6. Klasik müziğin dışında başka neler seviyorsunuz?
7. Karşıdaki odadan geceleri ayak sesleri geliyor.
8. İki ders arasında size müdürün kapının karşısındaki odasını göstereceğim.
9. Vapurun içinden hayvanlar ikişer ikişer çıktı.
10. Fatma, arka odada yatıyor.

C. Supply the correct possessive and case endings:

1. Uçak evin üzer___ geçti.
2. Köpek masanın alt___ yatıyor.
3. Otobüs evimizin ön___ duruyor.
4. Fatma odanın orta___ kadar yürüdü.
5. Bizim evimizin yan___ yol geçiyor.
6. Kitabı rafın alt___ aldım, pencerenin iç___ koydum.
7. Kadın, benim üst__ su attı.
8. Orhan Bey hep karısının peş___ gidiyor.
9. Bizim arka___ iki adam var.
10. Sizin ara___ neden kavga çıktı?
11. Senin karşı___ oturururum.

D. Translate into Turkish:

1. My pen is under your foot.
2. He is standing in front of the grocery.
3. I put your money on top of the table.
4. Water is coming out from under the door.
5. He threw Hasan into the sea.
6. He pulled the dog out from behind the bed.
7. Is there a doctor among you?
8. People were passing in front of us.
9. The school is across from the store.
10. He showed us the front part of the house.
11. These animals live under stones.
12. The inside of the apple was bad.
13. The soldier stood beside the tree.
14. Halil went in front; we came after him.
15. There is a chair in the middle of the garden.
16. I put your clothes beside mine.
17. The villages outside the city are very small.

D. Translate into Turkish:

1. The minister of external affairs is writing an article on the Second World War.
2. One dog sat down on one side of me, the other on the other side.
3. This morning there was a fight between two men outside our back door.
4. Children's voices are coming from behind us.
5. There is always more room in the back part of the bus.
6. In midwinter the weather here is beautiful.

LESSON 22: COMPOUND VERBS

Study the following sentences:

Bu sabah Ali size iki kere telefon etti	'This morning Ali called you twice'
Yeni başbakanın hareketlerine çok dikkat etmedim	'I haven't paid much attention to the actions of the new prime minister'
Müdürümüz pek yavaş hareket eder	'Our director acts very slowly'
Bu genç çocuk yolunu kaybetmiştir; ona yardım eder misiniz?	'This young child seems to have lost his way; will you help him?'
Onun bu mesele hakkındaki hislerini bilmiyorum	'I don't know his feelings about this problem'
Hayvanlar bizim gibi hisseder mi?	'Do animals feel like us? (have feelings like us?)'
İstasyonun etrafında her çeşit ucuz otel var	'There are all kinds of cheap hotels around the station'
Türkler askerlerini Viyanadan geri çekti	'The Turks pulled their soldiers back from Vienna'
Hava yüzünden geriye döndük	'We turned back because of the weather'
İçki Orhana çok tesir etmiştir; lokantadan dışarı çıktı, tekrar içeri gelmedi	'The liquor must have had too much effect on Orhan; he went out of the restaurant and didn't come in again'
Orhanın yardımıyla paketlerin yarısını yukarıya getirdik; aşağıda daha üç tane kaldı	'With Orhan's assistance we brought half of the packages upstairs; three more remain downstairs'
Sandalyenizi biraz ileri çeker misiniz?	'Will you pull your chair a little bit forward?'
Dersi aşağı yukarı anladım	'I more or less understood the lesson'

1. Variation in stems: double final consonants

We have seen already that no Turkish word may be pronounced with two final consonants; thus when a stem ends basically in two consonants, the vowel I must be inserted between them, unless a suffix beginning with a vowel is added; thus /resm/ 'picture' becomes resim, but the possessive is resmi 'picture of it'. There are also stems ending basically in a double consonant—for example, /hakk/ 'right'. In this case, the final consonant simply drops if the word stands alone, or if a suffix beginning with a consonant is added; the result is therefore hak 'right', haklar 'rights'. But if a suffix beginning with a vowel is added, the final consonant does not need to be dropped, and it therefore remains: hakkım 'my right'.

Similarly af 'pardon', 'amnesty' is basically /aff/; compare affı 'his pardon'; his 'feeling' is /hiss/; compare hissi 'his feeling'.

2. Compound verbs

Many verbs in Turkish are compounds, formed by a noun indicating an action, followed by the auxiliary verb etmek (stem /ed-/). The noun is usually, although not always, of Arabic, Persian, or European origin; Turkish has borrowed many nouns from other languages but rarely borrows verbs. Thus, with the word telefon 'telephone', we get the verb telefon etmek 'to telephone'; the noun remains invariable, and the verb is conjugated as any other verb:

telefon ettim	'I telephoned'
telefon edecektik	'we were going to telephone'
telefon etmedi	'he did not telephone'

Similarly:

dikkat	'attention'	dikkat etmek	'pay attention'
yardım	'help, assistance'	yardım etmek	'help'
kavga	'fight, quarrel'	kavga etmek	'fight, quarrel'

tesir	'influence'	tesir etmek	'influence'
hareket	'motion, action'	hareket etmek	'move, act'
seyahat	'journey'	seyahat etmek	'travel'

Yunus Emre Halil'e çok tesir etti	'Yunus Emre influenced Halil greatly'
Sözüme dikkat ettin mi?	'Did you pay attention to what I said?'
Sokağın ortasında iki erkek kavga ediyordu	'Two men were fighting in the middle of the street'
Bugün öğleden sonra sana yardım ederim	'I'll help you this afternoon'
En sonunda tren istasyondan hareket etti	'Finally the train moved out of the station'

The construction is normally pronounced as a single compound word, with accent on the last syllable of the first member, although the noun and verb are written separately:

dikkat ettim [dikkátettim] 'I paid attention'

However, if the noun is one that changes its form if followed by a vowel, the noun and etmek are written as one word, with the noun in its prevocalic form; thus we have affetmek 'to pardon', with the noun /aff/ 'pardon', which would have to be af if written separately. Similarly, we have hissetmek 'feel' from his, and kaybetmek 'lose' from kayıp 'loss', basically /kayb/.

Remember that many of the nouns that are used in compound verbs may also be used simply as nouns—for example, kavga and tesir in the preceding lesson; also:

Fatma, kocasından yardım istedi	'Fatma asked for help from her husband'
Bu yazı dikkatimi çekti	'This article drew my attention'

Orhan, başka insanların hislerine dikkat etmez	'Orhan doesn't pay attention to the feelings of other people'

Dikkat 'Attention!' is commonly found at the beginning of notices and announcements. Notice also the expression Affedersiniz 'Pardon me', literally 'You will pardon'.

3. Additional postpositional constructions

Some nouns, when used in postpositional constructions, have acquired an idiomatic meaning that is quite different from their normal meaning when used as nouns. For example, yüzünden 'from his face' means 'because of him' as a postpositional construction.

Bu çocuk yüzünden eve döndük	'Because of this child we returned home'

Because these constructions are metaphorical in meaning, the first member almost always appears without the genitive suffix, as shown. If the first member is genitive, then we no longer have a postpositional construction but have simply a noun phrase; bu çocuğun yüzünden 'from this child's face'.

The nouns to be considered are the following:

A. Hak 'right', in the construction hakkında means 'about' or 'concerning':

Bakan, af meselesi hakkında konuşacak	'The minister will speak about the amnesty problem'
Yunanistan hakkındaki haberleri dikkatle okudum	'I read the news about Greece with attention'

B. Taraf 'side' is used in the construction tarafından, which means 'by' or 'by means of'. This construction is normally used with passive verbs and will be discussed again later. Taraf is also simply the noun for 'side' and in this use is more common than yan.

Sokağın karşı tarafına geçti	'He crossed to the opposite side of the street'

C. The Arabic plural of the preceding word, etraf, is used in postpositional constructions either with or without the genitive in the meaning 'around':

Evin etrafında bahçe ve ağaç var	'There are gardens and trees around the house'

It may also be used simply as a noun, meaning 'surroundings':

Evin etrafı çok güzel	'The surroundings of the house are very attractive'

D. Baş 'head' is used in constructions meaning 'near' or 'at'; it is most frequent in certain idiomatic expressions, such as iş başında 'at work'.

Doktor, hasta başında	'The doctor is beside the patient'
Masa başında oturduk	'We sat at the table'
Adam başına beşer lira aldık	'We got five liras apiece'

E. Other constructions are:

yerine	'in place of, instead of'
bakımından	'from the point of view of'
yüzünden	'because of'

Remember that a pronoun used with these constructions, as with any postpositional constructions, must be in the genitive, and the possessive suffix must still agree with the pronoun:

Muhakkak benim hakkımda konuşuyorlar	'They are certainly talking about me'
Sizin yüzünüzden eve döndük	'Because of you we returned home'

4. Directional adverbs

içeri	'inward' or 'inside'
dışarı	'outward' or 'outside'
aşağı	'downward' or 'down'
yukarı	'upward' or 'up'
ileri	'forward'
geri	'backward'
beri	'here'

When these words are used with no suffix, they have an inherently dative meaning and indicate the direction toward which something moves:

Köpek dışarı gitti, etrafa baktı, yine içeri geldi	'The dog went outside, looked around, and came in again'
Tayyare yavaş yavaş aşağı indi	'The airplane descented slowly'
Masayı ileri çekti	'He pulled the table forward'
Yukarı çıktım	'I went upstairs'

They may also be used as noun stems, and like bura-, şura-, ora-, they require some suffix, either possessive or case. There are two additional stems, öte- 'there' and karşı- 'across', which must be used with a suffix.

If the dative suffix is added, there is no change in meaning: dışarıya gitti, içeriye girdi, aşağıya baktı 'he looked down'. The locative or ablative suffixes may also be used, and in that case the final vowel may drop from içeri, dışarı, yukarı, or ileri: içeride or içerde.

Orhan içerde oturuyor	'Orhan is sitting inside'
Evleri karşıda	'Their house is on the other side'
Annesi yukarda yatıyor	'His mother is lying down upstairs'
Yemeği aşağıdan getirdi	'He brought the food from downstairs'

With a possessive suffix, we get simple nouns:

Evin içerisi çok güzel	'The inside of the house is very beautiful'
Şişenin yarısını ben içerim, gerisini size veririm	'I'll drink half of the bottle and give you the rest'

These words may also be used, without suffix, as adjectives:

Bu saat geri	'This watch is slow (backward)'
Türkiye, Arap memleketlerinden daha ileri	'Turkey is more advanced than the Arab countries'

The expression aşağı yukarı means 'more or less'.

The difference between a directional adverb and a postpositional construction is that a directional adverb indicates a location only, while a postpositional construction always contains explicit or implied reference to a genitive. Thus, while İçeri gitti means 'He went inside', İçine gitti means 'He went to the inside of it': the possessive suffix in içine has to refer to something, like Onun içine gitti or Evin içine gitti.

5. Usage

Besides hakkında, için can also be used for 'about' if the sentence refers to the actual things spoken:

Senin için neler söylüyorlar, biliyor musun?	'Do you know what (things) they are saying about you?'

Hareket etmek and hissetmek are both intransitive. As an exception, however, hissetmek may take the reflexive pronoun (to be discussed later) as an object:

Yorgun hissediyorum	'I feel tired'
Kendimi yorgun hissediyorum	'I feel (myself) tired'

His is 'feeling' or 'sense': altıncı his 'sixth sense'.

Tesir etmek is 'influence', 'affect', or 'move' in an emotional sense:

Bu kitap bana çok tesir etti	'This book moved me greatly (had a great effect on me)'

VOCABULARY

af	/aff/	pardon, amnesty
affetmek		pardon
aşağı		down, downward
beri		here, hither
dışarı		outside, outward
dikkat	(-i)	attention, care
dikkat etmek (dat)		pay attention (to)
etraf		surroundings
geri		back, backward
hak	/hakk/	right (legal)
hareket		motion, action
hareket etmek		move, act
his	/hiss/	feeling, sense
hissetmek		feel
içeri		inside, inward
ileri		forward
istasyon		station
karşı-		opposite
kavga etmek		fight, quarrel
kaybetmek		lose
mesele		problem
öte-		there, thither
seyahat etmek		travel
taraf		side
telefon		telephone

telefon etmek	telephone, call
tesir etmek (dat)	influence
yardım	help, assistance
yardım etmek (dat)	help, assist
yavaş	slow
yukarı	up, upward

EXERCISES

A. Answer the following questions:

1. Size hayatta en çok kim tesir etmiştir?
2. Bu gün etrafınızda nelere dikkat ettiniz?
3. Hasan bu gün istasyondan saat kaçta hareket ediyor?
4. Bizimle ne hakkında konuşacaktınız?
5. Evinizde telefon var mı? Numaranız kaç?

B. Translate into English:

1. Hasan bey, eski müdürün yerine geçti.
2. Et yerine ekmek yiyeceğim.
3. Halil, başbakanın her hareketine kızar.
4. Dün Mehmet derse dikkat etmedi; ondan dolayı öğretmen onunla kavga etti.
5. Bu adamın af meselesi hakkındaki yazısı dikkatimi çekti.
6. Senin tarafındanım.
7. Telefonumuzu beş yüz liraya kasaptan aldık.
8. Bu kitabın ikinci kısmında Bulgaristan hakkında bir yazı var.
9. Para istemiyoruz; hakkımızı istiyoruz.
10. Kavgada kimin tarafını tuttunuz?

C. Supply the correct case suffix:

1. Kim___ telefon edeceksiniz?

2. Sözlerimiz onlar___ tesir etmedi.
3. Telefon___ cevap verdiniz mi?
4. Bakkal yukarı___ mı oturuyor, aşağı___ mı?
5. Hareketlerim___ neden kızıyorsunuz?

D. Supply the correct directional adverb:

1. Çocuklar ağaçtan ___ indiler.
2. Hava çok fena: evden ___ çıkmıyacağım.
3. Başbakan Ankaradan dün geldi, bugün ___ gidecek.
4. Benim saatim hep ___ gidiyor.
5. Bakkal ___da oturuyor, dükkânı ___da.
6. Köpek, sokağın öbür tarafında ağaç gördü, ___ya geçti.

E. Translate into Turkish:

1. The dining room is downstairs.
2. I won't go outside in this weather.
3. Ahmet brought the bottle from upstairs.
4. Orhan walked more slowly than us and got (remained) behind.
5. A house was burning on the opposite side of the village. We went upstairs and looked across.
6. The car moved forward slowly, then stopped again.
7. We'll eat inside today because of the weather.
8. He lives over that way.
9. Orhan lives in the downstairs room.

F. Translate into Turkish:

1. The Turks always act this way.
2. I feel hungry.
3. What will the director speak about?
4. I would like help with this. We will open the box outside and bring the pieces inside one by one.
5. Halil had a fight with his friend.

6. Fatma lost five kilos this week.
7. I hadn't paid much attention to this problem.
8. The earth turns around the sun.

LESSON 23: INDEFINITE AND NEGATIVE EXPRESSIONS

Study the following sentences:

Sen bir şey söyliyecektin	'You were going to say something'
Kâtibin biri kâğıtlarımızı kaybetmiştir	'Some clerk must have lost our papers'
Mühim birisi üniversiteye geliyor	'Someone important is coming to the university'
Kalemimi ya sen, ya bir başkası bozdu	'Either you or someone else ruined my pen'
Başka bir şey yok mu?	'Isn't there anything else?'
Bu mesele hakkında bazı önemli fikirleri var	'He has some important ideas about this problem'
Bu mesele hakkındaki fikirlerinin bazısı önemli	'Some of his ideas about this problem are important'
Bazı zamanlar çalışır, amma çoğu zaman hiç bir şey yapmaz	'Sometimes he works, but most of the time he does nothing'
Herkes seni bekliyor	'Everyone is waiting for you'
Her mektubundan yeni bir şey öğreniyorum	'I learn something new from every one of his letters'
Bütün kitaplarımı evde bıraktım	'I left all my books at home'
Orhan Beyin oğullarının hepsi tembel	'All of Orhan Bey's sons are lazy'
İstanbuldakilerin çoğu, yaz aylarında denize gider	'Most of the people of Istanbul go to the seashore in the summer months'
Bu yaz bir yere gitmiyecek misiniz? Kimimiz denize gidecek, kimimiz çalışacak	'Aren't you going anywhere this summer? Some of us are going to the seashore; some of us will work'

1. Indefinite expressions

Before discussing Turkish indefinite expressions, we should point out that most of these are normal combinations of adjectives, articles, and nouns. Although some of these expressions have particular idiomatic status in Turkish, others are included here only because they correspond to idiomatic expressions in English.

A. 'some'

The basis of many Turkish indefinite expressions is the article bir used in an indefinite sense, that is, as 'some'. Expressions corresponding to English 'someone', 'somewhere', and so forth are made with bir and a small set of nouns:

biri, birisi	'someone'
bir şey	'something'
bir yer	'somewhere'
bir zaman, bir vakit, bir ara	'sometime'
Bunu bana birisi verdi	'Someone gave me this'
Senden bir sey istiyorum	'I want something from you'
Şapkamı bir yerde bırakmışımdır	'I must have left my hat somewhere'
Bunu bir zaman yaparım	'I'll do this sometime'

Any of these expressions may be used with an appropriate adjective, after the pattern yeni bir şey 'something new':

Çalışkan birisini arıyoruz	'We are looking for someone industrious'
Şehre yakın bir yerde yaşıyor	'He lives somewhere near the city'
Ondan daha iyi bir şey istiyorum	'I want something better than that'

In addition, an indefinite expression may be made with any noun in the language, by placing the noun in the genitive before biri:

günün birinde	'one day'
adamın biri	'one man, a certain man'

B. 'other'

Among the "appropriate adjectives" that can be added to the indefinite expressions with *bir* is *başka*, which produces expressions that are translated with English 'other' or 'else':

başka birisi, başka biri, bir başkası, başkası	'someone else'
başka bir şey	'something else'
başka bir yer	'somewhere else'
başka bir zaman, başka bir vakit	'some other time'

Halilin yerine bir başkası geldi	'Someone else came instead of Halil'
Orhan burada yok, başka bir yerdedir	'Orhan is not here; he must be somewhere else'
Bunu başka bir zaman yaparım	'I'll do this some other time'

Başka may be combined with other adjectives:

Başka mühim bir şey öğrendim	'I learned something else important'

Notice also:

Başka ne çeşit var?	'What other kinds are there?'

C. 'some' (pl)

'Some' in the plural sense ('some people' as opposed to 'someone') involves constructions with the adjective *bazı* (/bâzı/). The important thing to remember about *bazı* is that the noun with it must always be plural. In addition, the pronoun *kim*, otherwise familiar as the interrogative 'who', is used here.

bazı insanlar, bazıları, bazısı, kimisi	'some people'

Bazı insanlar bu gazeteyi sever	'Some people like this newspaper'

The form kimi may be used for 'some people' but only in sentences where 'some' is opposed to 'others'—that is, where there are two kimi in the sentence:

Kimi bu gazeteyi okur, kimi öbürünü	'Some read this newspaper, some (others) the other'

Otherwise, bazı is used and may appear not only with şeyler, zamanlar, and yerler but with any plural. There are two possibilities, depending on whether the noun with bazı is definite or indefinite. If it is indefinite, bazı precedes as an adjective: bazı şeyler 'some things'. If it is definite, the noun precedes and is placed in the genitive: şeylerin bazısı 'some of the things'.

Bazı Türk sigaralarını seviyorum	'I like some Turkish cigarettes'
Bu dükkânda bazı güzel şeyler var	'There are some nice things in this store'
Bu sokaktaki bazı evler güzel	'Some houses on this street are nice'
Bu sokaktaki evlerin bazısı güzel	'Some of the houses on this street are nice'

In addition to the expression bazı zamanlar 'some times', there is the adverb bazen, bazan 'sometimes'.

D. 'every'
Here we deal with the adjective her. 'Everyone' is herkes; otherwise, her is used simply as an adjective.

Bunun hakkında herkesin bir fikri var	'Everyone has an idea about this'
Her yere baktım	'I looked everywhere'
Her tarafa baktım	'I looked on every side (everywhere)'
Hasan her zaman meşgul	'Hasan is always (every time) busy'
Hasan her an meşgul	'Hasan is busy every moment'

E. 'all'

Here we deal with the adjective bütün, the noun hepsi,

and tüm, which can be either adjective or noun. Bütün functions like any other adjective:

Bütün bu bardaklar temiz	'All these glasses are clean'
Bütün bu insanlar talebe	'All these people are students'
Bütün kutulara baktım	'I looked in all the boxes'
Bütün kitabı okudum	'I read the whole book (all of the book)'
Bütün yaz çalıştım	'I worked all summer'

Hepsi (presumably from *hepisi, like birisi) is a noun; the noun that it goes with is placed before it, in the genitive. Compare the English expression 'all of . . .':

Bu bardakların hepsi temiz	'All of these glasses are clean'
Bu insanların hepsi talebe	'All of these people are students'
Kutuların hepsine baktım	'I looked in all of the boxes'
Kitabın hepsini okudum	'I read all of the book'

Tüm, like bazı, may precede the noun as an adjective, or the possessive form (tümü) follows the noun in the genitive:

Tüm gözler başbakanın üstünde	'All eyes are on the prime minister'
Mustafa, paranın tümünü istiyor	'Mustafa wants all the money'

The expressions *bütün zaman (*tüm zaman) or *zamanların hepsi (*zamanın tümü) do not exist; instead, her zaman may be used (as noted earlier) or the adverbs hep or daima 'always'.

Hasan hep meşgul	'Hasan is always busy'

F. 'most'

çoğu insanlar, çoğu	'most people'
Çoğu bu gazeteyi okur	'Most (people) read this newspaper'

More generally, çoğu (the possessive of çok) means 'most' or 'most of'; like bazı, it can be used in two ways, depending on whether the noun with çoğu is definite or indefinite. If it is indefinite, çoğu precedes as an adjective: çoğu kitaplar 'most books'. If it is definite, the noun precedes and is placed in the genitive: kitapların çoğu 'most of the books'.

Türkiyedeki arabaların çoğu çok eski	'Most of the cars in Turkey are very old'
Çoğu Türk sigaralarını seviyorum	'I like most Turkish cigarettes'
Çoğu günler ya yatakta yatar, yahut ta bahçede oturur	'Most days he either lies in bed or sits in the garden'

The expression çoğu zaman 'most of the time' is standardized, and zamanın çoğu is not used. 'Most things' can be çoğu şeyler or birçok şeyler. Birçok more generally means 'a lot of' or 'many' and belongs to a set of words including birkaç 'several' and biraz. Thus:

Biraz kitabı var	'He has a few books'
Birkaç kitabı (kitapları) var	'He has several books (a moderate number)'
Birçok kitabı (kitapları) var	'He has a lot of books'

2. Negative expressions

We should start this section by pointing out that Turkish has no negative expressions as such, that is, expressions like English 'no one' and 'never'; there are, instead, expressions that are negative by being in a negative sentence or by being used with a negative verb.

For example, the English word 'any', which is used in negatives and questions, is simply a variant of 'some' in these constructions:

He saw something

He did not see anything

Did he see anything?

(The question 'Did he see something?' is also possible but normally means something different; it means that the speaker has some particular object in mind.)

Turkish, on the other hand, uses the expressions corresponding to 'some' (given in item A of the list in Section 1) in all cases:

Bir şey gördü

Bir şey görmedi

Bir şey gördü mü?

Similarly:

Bu akşam bakan önemli bir şey söyledi	'The minister said something important this evening'
Bakan önemli bir şey söyledi mi?	'Did the minister say anything important?'
Bakan önemli bir şey söylemedi	'The minister didn't say anything important'

It should be clear that Turkish is completely regular on this point; and although <u>bir şey</u> has to be translated as 'something' in some sentences and 'anything' in others, this is a problem of English, not of Turkish.

(In another sense, 'any-' words in English are equivalent to '-ever' constructions. Thus, 'Give it to anyone you want' is equivalent to 'Give it to whoever you want'. These constructions in Turkish are somewhat complex, involve the use of the conditional auxiliary, and will be considered much later.)

Some more examples of the use of <u>bir</u> as 'any' follow:

Bugün bir yere gitmedim 'Today I didn't go anywhere'

Bu dükkânda iyi bir şey yok	'There isn't anything good in this store'

The exception here is that *birisi* may not be used in a negative sentence with the meaning 'anyone' or 'no one'; it retains the meaning 'someone'. Thus if someone says *Bugün birisi gelmedi* 'Today someone did not come', it means that the speaker has someone particular in mind but is not giving the name. Normally, *birisi* must be replaced by *kimse* (see the next paragraph) in negative sentences:

Bugün kimse gelmedi	'Today no one came'
Ofiste kimseyi görmedim	'I didn't see anyone in the office'

A. *kimse*

In positive sentences, *kimse* means 'person' and is more or less equal to *insan*. It may be used in most of the expressions on the preceding pages, wherever *insan* may be used:

Bir kimse geldi	'Someone came'
Başka bir kimse geldi	'Someone else came'
Bazı kimseler bu gazeteyi sever	'Some people like this newspaper'
Çoğu kimseler bu gazeteyi okur	'Most people read this newspaper'

In negative sentences, as we saw earlier, *kimse* is negative and should be translated 'anyone' or 'no one' according to the requirements of English:

Bize bu işte kimse yardım etmedi	'No one helped us with this job'
Biz de kimseye yardım etmedik	'We didn't help anyone either'

B. *hiç*

In positive sentences, *hiç* is used in questions, in the meaning 'ever' or 'at all':

Öyle bir şey hiç gördünüz mü?	'Did you ever see such a thing (a thing like that)?'

Halil hiç çalışır mı? — 'Does Halil work at all? (Does Halil ever work?)'

It is used in the same way in negative sentences but has to be translated 'never' or 'not at all':

Ömrümde öyle bir şey hiç görmedim — 'I never saw such a thing in my life'

Halil hiç çalışmaz — 'Halil doesn't work at all (never works)'

Talebeler bunu hiç anlamıyacak — 'The students won't understand this at all'

The most common use of *hiç* in negative sentences is as an adjective, preceding any noun, in order to intensify the negative meaning:

Buna hiç kimse yardım etmedi — 'No one at all helped with this'

Hiç bir yere gitmedim, hiç bir şey yapmadım — 'I went nowhere and did nothing'

O dükkânda hiç iyi bir şey yok — 'There is nothing good in that store'

1957den beri hiç kitap yazmadı — 'He hasn't written a single book (has written no book) since 1957'

3. Possessive suffixes

Many of the expressions that we have seen in this lesson may appear with *plural possessive suffixes*. In particular, suffixes may be added to the following:

A. the indefinites *bazı*, *hep*, *çoğu*, and *kimi*, subject to the same restrictions that were given for *kimi* earlier:

bazımız, bazılarımız — 'some of us'

bazıları — 'some of them'

hepiniz — 'all of you'

çoğumuz — 'most of us'

kimimiz...kimimiz — 'some of us . . . others (some) of us'

B. numerals:

birimiz	'one of us'
ikiniz	'two of you, the two of you, you two'
üçümüz	'three of us, the three of us, us three'
dördü	'four of them, the four of them'

C. the interrogatives hangi and kaç:

hanginiz?	'which of you?'
kaçımız, kaç tanemiz?	'how many of us?'

When one of these forms is the subject of a sentence, the verb may be third person, or it may agree with the person of the possessive suffix. The rule governing which personal ending is to be used is subject to a great deal of individual variation and considerable difference between written and spoken forms. As a general rule, however, when the pronoun refers to the entire group of people involved, the verb agrees with the possessive suffix in person, while if the pronoun refers only to a portion of the group, the verb is third person.

Hepimız gideceğiz	'All of us will go'
Çoğumuz gidecek	'Most of us will go'
İkiniz gideceksiniz	'Both of you will go'
İkiniz gidecek	'Two of you will go'

There is still, however, much variation and uncertainty for example, with pronouns such as bazımız or hangimiz either form of the verb may be used, while with kaçımız the verb must be third person. Notice also that in Hiç birimiz gitmiyeceğiz 'Not one of us will go' the verb is first person, since the entire group of 'us' is involved in 'not going'.

4. Usage

An 'moment' is used in a large number of idioms and standard expressions, including:

bir an evvel	'as soon as possible, at once'
bir anda	'in a moment, in an instant'
o an, o anda	'at that moment, then'

'He changed his mind' is *fikri değişti*, literally 'his opinion changed'.

The words for 'or' are *veya*, *yahut*, or *veyahut*. 'Either-or' constructions are made in the following manner: 'either' is *ya*; 'or' may be *ya*, *ya da*, *yahut*, *yahut ta*, or *veya*.

O beyin ismi ya Nüshet, ya Nusret	'That gentleman's name is either Nüshet or Nusret'
Ya evvelâ yemek yiyeceğiz de sonra şehre ineceğiz, yahut ta evvelâ şehre ineceğiz, sonra yemek yiyeceğiz	'Either we will eat first and then go downtown, or we will go downtown first and then eat'

'Neither-nor' constructions are made with *ne* for 'neither', *ne* or *ne de* for 'nor'. The important thing to remember about this construction is that it requires a *positive* verb. Notice also that the personal ending has to agree with the subject; it is not third person as in English.

Ne ben ne sen cevabı biliyoruz	'Neither you nor I know the answer'
Ne çay ne de kahve içer	'He drinks neither tea nor coffee'

Kışın and *yazın* mean 'in the winter' and 'in the summer', respectively.

Yazın herkes denize gider, kışın Ankaraya döner	'In summer everyone goes to the seashore and returns to Ankara in the winter'

göre - according to
suitable for

VOCABULARY

an		moment (see "Usage")
bazan, bazen	/bázan, bāzen/	sometimes
bazı	/bázı/	some
bırakmak		leave
bozmak		spoil, ruin, break
bütün		all
fikir	/fikr/	idea, opinion
herkes	/hérkes/	everyone
hiç		ever, never, not at all
kimse		no one
mühim		important
ne . . . ne		neither . . . nor
öğrenmek		learn
önemli		important
şapka		hat
tüm		all
veyahut, veya, yahut		or
ya . . . ya, yahut		either . . . or
yaz		summer

EXERCISES

A. Answer the following questions:

1. Bugün yeni bir şey öğrendiniz mi?
2. Bütün insanları sever misiniz?
3. Bu dersi sizden başka kim anlıyor?
4. Size göre Mao'nun fikirleri önemli midir?
5. Dersten sonra talebelerin çoğu nereye gidecek?

B. Translate into English:

1. Başka bir fikriniz var mı?
2. Yaz ortasında Ankaradaki herkes bir yere gider.
3. Aynı odada üçümüz beraber çalıştık.
4. Hiç kimse doğru cevap vermiyecek mi?
5. Orhana hiç bir şey tesir etmez.
6. Daha herkese kahve vermedin; bir kişi daha kaldı.
7. Bakkalda ekmek vardı, ama sizden önce birisi geldi ve hepsini aldı.
8. Bu dersi sizden başka kimse anlamadı.
9. Hiç kimsenin tesiri altında değilim.
10. Fatma ne annesini seviyor ne babasını.

C. Combine the following pairs of sentences with ne . . . ne. Remember that ne . . . ne constructions require a positive verb.

Example:

Ali okula gitmiyor.

Ali işe gitmiyor.

Answer:

Ali ne okula gidiyor ne işe (gidiyor).

1. Ben sizi beğenmiyorum.
   Ayşe sizi beğenmiyor.
2. Ben Hasan'ı görmedim.
   Ben başka birisini görmedim.
3. Bu lokantada sigara yok.
   Bu lokantada içki yok.
4. Orhan kitap okumuyor.
   Orhan ders çalışmıyor.
5. Hasan'ın işi mühim değil.
   Hasan'ın işi uzun değil.

D. Turn the following sentences into ya . . . ya constructions.

Example:

Fatma Yunanistana veya İtalyaya gidecek

Answer:

Fatma ya Yunanistana, ya İtalyaya gidecek

1. Paramı evde veya otobüste bıraktım.
2. Bu işi ben yapacağım veya Ayşe yapacak.
3. Bu elmalardan bazısını veya hepsini alacağım.
4. İnsan doğru söyler veya hiç bir şey söylemez.
5. Bardaklar bu rafta veya öbür rafta.

E. Translate into Turkish:

1. I have read a lot of books.
2. I have read all of the books on that shelf.
3. I have read no books since January.
4. I have read no books besides Ince Memed.
5. I have read several books.
6. I have read some books, but not many.
7. I have read all the new books this year.
8. Ahmet reads every kind of book.
9. Ahmet is always reading books.

F. Translate into Turkish:

1. Where did you go? —Out. —What did you do? —Nothing.
2. I counted all of the papers and threw most of them away.
3. Some of his works are more important than (the) others.
4. No one is afraid of that animal.
5. Orhan ruined our whole trip.
6. There is no one here but us.
7. Which of you is the oldest?
8. He neither read my book nor gave it back.
9. He is looking for his hat everywhere.

10. Doesn't anyone like tea?
11. Some people don't ever get up before noon.
12. Hasan's opinion about this has changed.
13. All of us will be here until midsummer.
14. He did not go outside the building at any time.
15. Somebody seems to have left something on the shelf.
16. They don't learn anything important at the university.
17. In August most people go either to the seashore or somewhere else.

LESSON 24: RELATIVE CONSTRUCTIONS AND SUBJECT PARTICIPLES

Study the following sentences:

Yemeğe gelen adam Mehmedin arkadaşıydı	'The man who came to dinner was Mehmet's friend'
Bahçede oynayan oğlanlara taş attı	'He threw stones at the boys playing in the garden'
Bu sınıfta çalışmayan yok	'There is no one who does not work in this class'
Pencereyi kıranlar kimlerdi?	'Who were the ones who broke the window?'
Yeni Türk yazarlarına en çok tesir eden kitap "İnce Memed" tir	'The book that has had the most influence on modern Turkish writers is Ince Memed'
Yanmış eti köpeğe verdim	'I gave the burned meat to the dog'
"Bizim Köy" ü okumamış olan insan var mı?	'Is there anyone who has not read Bizim Köy?'
Şimdi parçayı çalacak olan adam odaya girdi	'Now the man who will play the piece has entered the room'
Oturacak bir yer buldum	'I found a place to sit down'
Gülecek ne var?	'What is there to laugh at?'

1. The nature of relative constructions

Constructions with participles in Turkish correspond to constructions with relative clauses in English. It will be considerably easier to explain these constructions in Turkish if we start by examining the way in which relative clauses are made in English.

Consider an example such as the following:

The man who came to dinner was John's friend.

This sentence is composed of two simple sentences: 'The man was John's friend', which is the main statement, and 'The man came to dinner', which is included within the main sentence in order to modify the noun 'man'. We therefore have:

Main sentence: The man was John's friend

Included sentence: The man came to dinner

We might show how these sentences are combined by writing them this way:

The man—the man came to dinner—was John's friend

But this is not a grammatical sentence in English, so the included sentence is transformed into a relative clause by replacing 'the man', which we may call the "head noun" of the construction, by the relative pronoun 'who'.

Every relative clause corresponds to a simple sentence, and the form of the relative can often be understood by comparing it with the corresponding sentence. Consider some additional examples:

The people who are in this room (all speak two languages)

= The people are in this room

The boy who is bringing the newspaper (should be given a tip)

= The boy is bringing the newspaper

(I didn't see) the person who broke the window

= The person broke the window

(John threw stones at) the children who were playing in the garden

= The children were playing in the garden

In these examples, the head noun in each case is the subject of the included sentence, although it may be subject, object, or object of a preposition in the main sentence. Consequently the relative pronoun 'who' is used. But the relative pronoun may also be 'whom' or 'whose':

The man whom I saw last night was drunk

This is composed of the following:

Main sentence: The man was drunk

Included sentence: I saw the man

In this case, the head noun ('the man') is the object of the included sentence. Other examples:

The old man whom John ran over (is in the hospital)

= John ran over the old man

(John gave money to) the child whom George sent with the newspaper

= George sent the child with the newspaper

Finally, consider these examples:

The man whose son is at the university came to dinner

Main sentence: The man came to dinner

Included sentence: The man's son is at the university

They found the man whose dog John ran over

Main sentence: They found the man

Included sentence: John ran over the man's dog

In these examples, the head noun ('the man' again, in each case) is the possessor of one of the nouns in the included sentences.

Thus the choice between the relative pronouns 'who', 'whom', and 'whose' in English depends on the grammatical function of the head noun in the included sentence (its position in the main sentence makes no difference). The rule is as follows:

'who': when the head noun is subject of the included sentence

'whom': when the head noun is object of the included sentence (or object of a preposition in it)

'whose': when the head noun is the possessor of some other noun in the included sentence

(These rules work only if the head noun is human.

If it is nonhuman, 'which' may be used in all cases, and 'that' may also be used in most cases: 'the stone which (that) fell from the roof', 'the stone which (that) John threw', 'the stone which (that) I sat on'. This information, included for the sake of completeness, does not affect the point made here.)

In Turkish, as in English, the form of the relative clause is determined by the grammatical role of the head noun in the included sentence; in particular, this determines the choice between subject and object participles. In this lesson, we will consider the subject participles, which are used when the head noun is the subject of the included sentence.

2. Subject participles

In English, a relative clause is formed from a simple sentence in the following steps:
1. Move the head noun to the beginning of the sentence.
2. Insert the appropriate relative pronoun, according to the rule given in the preceding section.
Observe the following derivation:

Simple sentence:	I saw the man last night
Step 1:	the man —— I saw last night
Step 2:	the man whom I saw last night

In Turkish, a relative clause is formed by the following steps:
1. Move the head noun to the end of the sentence (in Turkish, a modifying phrase must precede the word it modifies).
2. Select the appropriate form of participle: if the head noun was the subject of the sentence, a subject participle is used.
3. Replace the tense suffix of the verb with a participle suffix. The most common subject participle is *-(y)En*, the "present participle."

For example, given *Adam yemeğe geldi*, 'The man came to dinner', we (1) move *adam* to the end, and (2-3) replace the tense -*di* with the participle -*en*, to produce:

yemeğe gelen adam 'the man who came to dinner'

Other examples:

Taş pencereyi kırdı	'The stone broke the window'
pencereyi kıran taş	'the stone which (that) broke the window'
Çocuklar bahçede oynıyordu	'The children were playing in the garden'
bahçede oynayan çocuklar	'the children who were playing in the garden'

A special problem arises when the predicate of the simple sentence is nonverbal—for example, Adamlar bu odada, 'The men are in this room'. Participles are strictly verbal suffixes and may be attached only to verb stems, never to nouns or adjectives. In this situation, the stem ol- is supplied; if the sentence is negative, we get olma-:

Adamlar bu odada	'The men are in this room'
bu odada olan adamlar	'the men who are in this room'
O kadın üniversitede hocadır	'That woman is a teacher at the university'
Üniversitede hoca olan o kadın	'that woman, who is a teacher at the university'
Su pek sıcak değil	'The water is not very hot'
pek sıcak olmayan su	'the water, which is not very hot'

The most important thing to remember about participle constructions is that a participle phrase always has exactly the same word order as the corresponding simple sentence, the only difference being that the head noun is removed.

Meydan, Ankara Sokağının sol tarafında	'The square is on the left side of Ankara Street'
Ankara Sokağının sol tarafında olan meydan	'the square which (that) is on the left side of Ankara Street'
Mektep binası, üç asırdan beri aynı yerde duruyor	'The school building has stood in the same place for three centuries'

üç asırdan beri aynı yerde duran mektep binası	'the school building, which has stood in the same place for three centuries'
Her sözümüzü kapının dışından bir adam dinliyor	'A man is listening to everything we say from behind the door'
her sözümüzü kapının dışından dinleyen bir adam	'a man who is listening to everything we say from behind the door'

A participle construction, like an adjective, is part of the noun phrase. The noun that it modifies may be used in any grammatical function in the main sentence; this grammatical function has no effect on the internal organization of the participle phrase.

A participial phrase normally precedes all other modifiers of the noun; a demonstrative, however, may precede the participial phrase only if there are no other modifiers.

gazeteyi getiren iki küçük oğlan	'the two small boys who brought the newspaper'
bu, gazeteyi getiren oğlan	'this boy who brought the newspaper'
gazeteyi getiren bu oğlan	
gazeteyi getiren bu iki küçük oğlan	'these two small boys who brought the newspaper'

A participle, like any other adjective, may be used with no noun following; the nouns 'person' or 'people' should be supplied (remember gençler, 'young people').

O dairede oturanlar her gece içki içer	'The people living in that apartment drink every night'
Daha kahve istiyen var mı?	'Does anyone want more coffee?' ('Does one exist who wants...')

3. The present participle

The suffix of the present participle is -*(y)En*. As shown earlier (see Lesson 11), *y*-conditioning takes place in pronunciation when this suffix is added to a low vowel but is not always indicated in writing; thus 'one who wants' is pronounced [istiyen] but may be written *istiyen* or *isteyen*; similarly, we have *olmıyan* or *olmayan*, pronounced [olmıyan], 'one who is not'.

This suffix is by far the most common subject participle. Although it is usually called the "present participle," it actually does not denote action in the present but denotes action more or less at the same time as the main verb. Thus, in the following sentence, the action of the participle is past:

Kapıyı çalan kimdi?	'Who (was it who) knocked at the door?'

However, in this sentence, the action is future:

Bundan sonra gelen mektupları bu kutuya koyarız	'We'll put the letters that come from now on in this box'

Some words formed with this suffix have acquired the status of simple nouns:

bakan	'minister' (one who looks after)
işveren	'employer' (one who gives work)

4. The past participle

The suffix of the past participle is -*mIş*, and forms of this participle are identical with those of the narrative past tense.

This participle is used for actions that took place before the time of the main verb:

Yolda düşmüş bir ağaç vardı	'There was a fallen tree in the road'

In normal usage, this participle is usually followed by *olan*. Although the rules are not fixed, it appears that *olan* is required if the head noun is either definite or human and is optional otherwise.

İstasyona gelmiş olan trenden insanlar iniyordu	'People were getting off the train, which had come into the station'
Masada oturmuş olan Ahmet gazeteyi okuyordu	'Ahmet, who was seated at the table, was reading the newspaper'
Masada oturmuş olanlar gazeteyi okuyordu	'The people seated at the table were reading the newspaper'
O kitabı okumamış olan insan yok	'There is no one who hasn't read that book'

The combination of past participle and future tense of *olmak* gives expressions corresponding to what has been called the "future perfect" tense in some descriptions of European languages:

Gelecek sene bu apartmanlar bitmiş olacak	'Next year these apartment buildings will be finished'

Note the expressions *geçmiş zaman* 'past time' and *geçmişte* 'in the past'.

5. The future participle

The suffix of the future participle is -(y)EcEg, and forms of this participle are identical with those of the future tense.

This participle is used for actions that will take place in the future, with respect to the time of the main verb and normally also with respect to the time of utterance.

Yarın kalkacak vapurla gideceğim	'I will go by the boat that will leave tomorrow'

The use of *olan* after this participle is usually possible, but not as strictly required as in the case of the past participle, except in some cases:

Gazeteyi getirecek (olan) çocuğa para vereceğim	'I will give money to the child who is going to bring the newspaper'
Bu yazıyı okuyacak olan sen . . .	'You who will read this (writing) . . . '

An idiomatic use of the future participle is illustrated by the following:

Evde yiyecek bir şey var mı?	'Is there anything to eat in the house?'
Giyecek bir şeyim yok	'I have nothing to wear'
Bu içecek su değil	'This is not water to drink'

Note the expressions *gelecek zaman* 'future time' and *gelecekte* 'in the future'. *Gelecek* also corresponds to English 'next' in expressions of time: *gelecek sene* 'next year'.

6. The aorist participle

The forms of the aorist participle, for all verbs, are identical with those of the present tense.

This participle is used to express conditions that are habitually, permanently, or inherently properties of the head noun. For this reason the term "aorist" is appropriate for this participle, although not for the corresponding tense.

Ata benzer bir yüzü var	'He has a face resembling a horse'

This participle is not productive (except possibly in the passive: *okunur bir kitap* 'a readable book' from *okunmak* 'to be read'), and most aorist participles are treated as simple nouns or adjectives.

sözünde durur bir erkek	'a man who keeps his word'
okur yazar bir insan	'a moderately educated person (one who can read and write)'
bilir kişi	'wise man, expert'
çalar saat	'alarm clock'
yazar	'writer'

gelir	'income'
çıkmaz	'dead-end street'

The aorist participle can be used productively, however, in certain expressions of the following sort, using <u>olmak</u>:

Sabahları erken kalkar oldum	'I began to make a habit of getting up early in the morning (I became one who gets up early)'
Toplantılara gelmez oldun	'You stopped coming to the meetings (You became one who does not come)'

7. Usage

The meanings of <u>çalmak</u> seem to begin with 'strike', in the sense of striking on a bell or a musical instrument; it may correspond to English 'knock' (on a door), 'play' (on any musical instrument), and, in the colloquial language, 'steal'.

<u>Dinlemek</u> is transitive in Turkish, although 'listen' is intransitive in English:

Parçayı dinledim	'I listened to the piece'

<u>Giymek</u> 'wear' or 'put on' is also transitive.

Babasının elbisesini giymiş bir oğlan gördüm	'I saw a child who had put on his father's clothes'

<u>Meydan</u> means 'square' in the geographical, not the geometrical, sense. The idiom <u>meydana çıkmak</u> means 'appear' or 'come forth'.

The meanings of <u>oynamak</u> begin with 'play', in the sense of 'play games' or 'The children are playing'; it may correspond to English 'fiddle' or, used intransitively, to 'oscillate' or 'vibrate'. An important meaning is 'dance', but it is used only of (Turkish) folk dancing. The corresponding noun is <u>oyun</u>, meaning 'game' or '(folk) dance'. A European-style dance is <u>dans</u> and the corresponding verb is <u>dans etmek</u>.

gelecek sene - next year
kardeş - brother, sister
çıkmak - leave, go out, go up
aramak - search, look for

VOCABULARY

benzemek (dat)	resemble
çalmak	strike, knock, play (see "Usage") steal
dinlemek	listen
giymek	wear, put on
kırmak	break
meydan	square
oğlan	boy
oynamak	play, dance (see "Usage")
oyun	game, dance (see "Usage")
sıcak (adj)	hot
sıcak (n)	heat, hot weather
sınıf	class, classroom
soğuk (adj)	cold
soğuk (n)	cold, cold weather

EXERCISES

A. Answer the following questions:

1. Dün Beethoven'in beşinci senfonisini çalan kimdi?
2. Meydanın ortasında oynayan oğlan sizin mi?
3. Sınıfın arkasında oturan çocuk en çok kime benziyor?
4. İtalya'dan yeni gelen profesörü dinleyecek misiniz?
5. Norman Mailer'in yeni çıkan kitabını okudunuz mu?

B. Translate into English:

1. Yapacak bir şeyiniz var mı? birisi ⇒ someone
2. O apartmanda oturacak olanlar daha yoklar.
3. Bahçemize bakacak birisini buldum.
4. İstasyonda bekliyenlerin arasında kardeşinizi aradım, fakat ona benziyen biri yoktu.

Do you have anything to do? Is there any of your thing that is to do?
Those who will live in that apartment have not moved in yet.

5. Bu sınıfta benden başka çalışan yok.

6. Hep soğuk yerlerde yaşayan Eskimolar, sıcakta hasta olurlarmış.

7. Derslerine hiç çalışmayan, sabahtan akşama kadar sokakta oynayan bir çocuğu ne annesi babası sever ne de öğretmenleri.

8. Harbe gitmek isteyen gençler asker elbisesi giydiler ve meydana çıktılar.

9. Bugün bize kızan ve bizi istemeyenler bir gün bizi anlayacaklardır.

10. Hiç çalışmayan bir saat günde iki defa doğru zamanı gösterir.

C. Identify, in English, the main sentences and included sentences that make up each of the following examples:

1. The train that is coming from Ankara will be two hours late.

2. The theory that George explained to me was not particularly convincing.

3. I don't know the name of the man with whom I spoke.

4. The statue that George resembles is in the Louvre.

5. The statue that you are looking for is in the museum that has the glass flowers in it.

6. This is the same picture as the one that was in the book that I showed you yesterday.

7. At the time when we began this project, there was no one to advise us.

8. They attacked the man whom they believed to be their enemy.

9. There was a pool of water in the place where I was sitting.

D. Correct the following sentences by making the sentence included within parentheses into a relative clause:

1. (Genç denize girdi) genç bir daha çıkmadı.

2. (Adam üstümüzde oturuyor) adam başbakan olmuş.

göstermek - show

3. (Kız evin penceresinden bakıyor) kız Ayşe'nin kardeşi.
4. (Küçük çocuk bize yol gösterecek) küçük çocuğa para vereceğiz.
5. (İnsanlar meydanda bekliyor) insanlar için otobüste yer yok.
6. Oradaki (adam Araba benziyor) adam kimdir?
7. Orhan hep (lokanta Atatürk Sokağın köşesinde duruyor) lokantada öğle yemeği yer.
8. (Hasan Bey yeni müdürümüz) Hasan Bey bugün ilk defa ofise geldi.
9. (Köyümüz on sene içinde çok değişmişti) köyümüze geçen yaz gittik.
10. Üniversite, (talebeler zengin değil) talebelere para verecek.

E. Translate into Turkish:

1. The man is wearing a white hat.
2. The man who is wearing a white hat
3. The trip will take exactly two years.
4. The trip, which will take exactly two years
5. The restaurant is next to Atatürk Square.
6. The restaurant, which is next to Atatürk Square
7. The man hit the boy twice.
8. The man who hit the boy twice
9. His daughters are not very pretty.
10. His daughters, who are not very pretty
11. This hot weather affects everyone.
12. This hot weather, which affects everyone
13. A child has been playing in front of the apartment building all morning.
14. A child who has been playing in front of the apartment building all morning

Eskimos who always live in cold places, may get sick in heat.

F. Translate into Turkish:

1. We'll get on the first bus that comes.
2. Orhan, who is our classmate, knows more than anyone.
3. This is the man who will watch the store.
4. Is there anyone who is going to take more of the meat?
5. By tomorrow he will have reached Istanbul, hopefully.
6. There is a dead animal in the middle of the road.

binmek - mount, get on
yerine - instead
Korkmak - fear

kalmak - remain
yanmak - burn
kısım - part

LESSON 25: OBJECT PARTICIPLES

Study the following sentences:

Bindiğim otobüs Bebek yerine Ortaköye gitti	'The bus that I got on went to Ortaköy instead of Bebek'
En korktuğunuz şeyler hep oldu	'The things that you were most afraid of all happened'
Hasan Bey'in öğrenmediği dil kalmadı	'There is no language that Hasan Bey has not learned'
Yemekten sonra, Orhan uyuduğu odaya doğru gitti	'After dinner, Orhan went straight to the room where he sleeps'
Tam o sırada baktığımız evin içinde bir ışık yandı	'Exactly at that moment a light went on in the house we were looking at'
Talebenin çaldığı parçayı dinledik: ama en çok beğendiğimiz kısımlarını iyi çalmadı	'We listened to the piece that the student played; but he didn't play well the parts that we like most'
En çok istediğim şey, yeni bir radyodur. Babamın gönderdiği eski radyo artık çalışmıyor	'The thing that I want the most is a new radio. The old radio that my father sent doesn't work any more'
Gideceğimiz yer, o tepelerin karşi tarafında	'The place where we are going is on the opposite side of those hills'
Sana yazacağım son mektup budur	'This is the last letter I will write you'
Tekrar baktığımız zaman, komşumuz yok olmuştu	'When we looked again, our neighbor had disappeared'
Trenin kalkacağı zamanı biliyor musunuz?	'Do you know when the train will leave?'
Kedi hâlâ olduğu yerde duruyor	'The cat is still in the place where he was'

1. Object participles

We should point out at once that the term "object participle" is misleading, since these participles are used not only when the head noun is the object in the included sentence but when it is serving in any grammatical function other than subject. In practice, however, the head noun is most frequently the object, and the term is therefore adequate.

The relative clause is formed by the following steps:
1. Move the head noun to the end of the sentence.
2. Replace the tense suffix of the verb with an object participle. The object participle that is almost always used is -DIg-.
3. Add a genitive suffix to the subject of the included sentence, and add the corresponding possessive to the participle.

Thus, given Ahmet kitabı istiyor 'Ahmet wants the book', we can derive Ahmedin istediği kitap 'The book that Ahmet wants'.

If the subject is a first or second person pronoun, the possessive suffix on the participle must, of course, change accordingly:

(benim) istediğim kitap	'The book that I want'

Similarly:

istediğin kitap	'the book that you (sg) want'
istediği kitap	'the book that he (she, it) wants'
istediğimız kitap	'the book that we want'
istediğiniz kitap	'the book that you (pl) want'
istedikleri kitap	'the book that they want'

A verb in Turkish must indicate the person of the subject. In the case of a subject participle, it is clear that the subject must be the noun that the participle modifies. In the case of an object participle, however, the subject of the verb is somewhere in the relative clause or may not be expressed at all (if it is a pronoun). Therefore, the possessive personal ending and the corresponding genitive must be attached.

2. Examples of head nouns

The head noun of an object participle may be not only the object but almost any noun in the simple sentence—for example:

A. a dative with a verb that takes the dative:

Bugün başladığımız yirmi dördüncü ders (= Bugün 24cü derse başlıyoruz)	'Lesson 24, which we start today'
bastığınız ayak (= Ayağa bastınız)	'the foot that you stepped on'

B. an ablative with a verb that takes the ablative:

Fatma'nın en çok korktuğu dert (= Fatma en çok bu dertten korkar)	'the trouble that Fatma fears most'

C. a dative indicating motion toward a place:

bu sabah çıktığım tepe (= Bu sabah tepeye çıktım)	'the hill that I climbed this morning'
Türkiye'nin her girdiği harp (= Türkiye harbe girdi)	'every war that Turkey has entered'

D. an ablative indicating motion away from a place:

çocuğun düştüğü ağaç (= Çocuk ağaçtan düştü)	'the tree that the child fell out of'
kedinin kaçtığı köpek (= Kedi köpekten kaçtı)	'the dog that the cat ran away from'

E. a dative indirect object:

Ahmedin arabasını sattığı hanım (= Ahmet arabasını hanıma sattı)	'the lady to whom Ahmet sold his car'
haberleri söylediğim insan (= İnsana haberleri söyledim)	'the person to whom I told the news'

F. a locative:

kedinin uyuduğu köşe (= Kedi köşede uyuyor)	'the corner that the cat is sleeping in'

bakkalın olduğu sokak (= Bakkal sokaktadır)	'the street where the grocery is'

G. a noun with *ile*, if the verb is one that regularly calls for a noun with *ile* (that is, if *ile* does not mean 'and'):

her hafta kavga ettiğimiz komşumuz (= Her hafta komşumuzla kavga ederiz)	'our neighbor, whom we fight with every week'
dün konuştuğum adam (= Dün adamla konuştum)	'the man with whom I spoke yesterday'

H. a noun with a transitive adjective, that is, an adjective that regularly is accompanied by a noun in the dative or ablative, or with *ile*:

hükümetin meşgul olduğu meseleler (= Hükümet meselelerle meşguldü)	'the problems with which the government has been occupied'
yakın olduğumuz lokanta (= Lokantaya yakınız)	'the restaurant that we are close to'

Note that in several of the preceding cases, the predicate of the simple sentence is not a verb but an adjective, and therefore the participle is formed on the verb *ol-*.

3. The future participle

There are two object participles, *-DIg-*, and *-(y)EcEg-*, which also functions as a subject participle and as the future tense. The future participle is used when the tense of the included sentence is future, the participle *-DIg-* is used in all other cases. Thus, consider the following:

Mehmedin ailesine göndereceği mektup	'the letter that Mehmet will send to his family'

This corresponds to:

Mehmet mektubu ailesine gönderecek	'Mehmet will send the letter to his family'

But *Mehmedin ailesine gönderdiği mektup* may be present, progressive, or past; in translating, the context, and frequently the tense of the main verb, must be considered in deciding what tense should be used.

4. 'When'

An object participle construction may be used with *zaman* or *vakit*, corresponding to English constructions with 'when':

Radyoyu açtığım zaman başbakan konuşuyordu	'When I turned on the radio, the prime minister was speaking' ('At the time when I turned on...')
Pencereyi kapadığımız vakit oda çok sıcak olur	'When we close the window, the room gets too hot'

The noun *sıra* 'time' or 'occasion' and the locative *sırada* may also be used in this way:

Toplantının başlıyacağı sıra (sırada) Hasan içeriye koştu	'When the meeting was about to begin, Hasan ran in (At the time when the meeting was going to begin...)'

Notice that these constructions are simply special cases of the general principle that a noun indicating a moment or period of time, or functioning in any other adverbial use in a simple sentence, may be made the head noun of a relative construction:

Işığı açtığım anda köpek yatağın altına kaçtı	'At the moment when I turned on the light, the dog fled under the bed'
Hasan, annesinin öldüğü sene, üniversitede talebeydi	'In the year when Hasan's mother died, he was a student at the university'
Çalışacağımız yer, şehirden çok uzaktır	'The place where we will work is very far from the city'

5. A translation procedure

Because constructions involving object participles are

kullanmak - drive, use

often considerably more complicated than those in this lesson, it may be useful to set forth a practical procedure for translating them.

Consider an example:

Attila'nın eşyaları için kullandığı kutu

The translation should be carried out in the following steps:

1. Translate the head noun of the relative clause, with its modifiers, if any: 'the box'.
2. Insert the word 'which' or 'that'.
3. Translate the subject of the included sentence with its modifiers, if any. Look first at the personal ending on the participle; if it is third person, look toward the beginning of the relative clause for a genitive: 'Attila'.
4. Translate the verb of the included sentence: 'used'.
5. Translate the rest of the included sentence, going backward (leftward) from the verb: 'for his things'.

The result, then, is 'the box which (that) Attila used for his things', which is fully accurate. In some cases it may be necessary to insert a preposition in the English, or to replace 'which' by 'whom' or 'when', in a second pass over the translation.

Let us take a more complicated example:

Bu asırdan sonraki Türk dilinde gördüğümüz bir çok yeni sözler

Here the procedure gives us the following:

1. 'several new words'
2. 'which'
3. 'we'
4. 'see'
5. 'in the Turkish language after this century'

6. Usage

Artık as an adverb means 'henceforth' or 'in the future', as opposed to 'in the past'.

Yahya Kemal'in eserlerini artık seviyorum	'I like Yahya Kemal's works now (I didn't like them before)'

It is usually used in negative sentences, where it means 'no more':

Onun eserlerini artık sevmiyorum	'I don't like his works any more'

Basmak has two distinct uses. Used with the dative, it means 'press' or 'step on':

Ayağıma bastınız	'You stepped on my foot'

Used as a transitive verb with the objective, it means 'print':

Hükümet para basar	'The government prints money'

Sıra has a large number of meanings:

A. 'row' ('line', 'series', etc.):

Ön sırada oturuyor	'He is sitting in the front row'
Herkes sırada bekliyor	'Everyone is waiting in line'

B. 'occasion' ('time'):

O sırada evde hiç kimse yoktu	'At that time (moment) there was no one at home'
Şimdi sırası değil	'It's not the (appropriate) time for it now'
Her şeyin bir sırası var	'There is a time for everything'

C. 'turn' in a game:

Sıra sende (senin)	'It's your turn'

Açmak and kapamak mean 'open' and 'close', respectively, but when used of electrical appliances (lights, radios, etc.), they mean 'turn on' and 'turn off'. For lights, yanmak is not only 'burn' but also 'go on' ('start burning').

VOCABULARY

artık		henceforth, no more (see "Usage")
basmak (dat)		step (on); press (see "Usage")
dil		tongue, language
göndermek		send
hükümet		government
ışık		light
kaçmak		flee, escape
kedi		cat
komşu		neighbor
koşmak		run
radyo	/rádyo/	radio
sıra		time, occasion, row (see "Usage")
tepe		hill, top
uyumak		sleep

EXERCISES

A. Answer the following questions:

1. Işığı açtığınız zaman odada ne gördünüz?
2. Sizin oturduğunuz apartmanda başka kimler oturuyor?
3. Size söylediğim şeyleri anladınız mı?
4. Okul, oturduğunuz yerden ne kadar uzak?
5. En sevdiğiniz oyun nedir?

B. Translate into English:

1. Açtığınız pencereden soğuk hava giriyor.
2. En kızdığım şey, olduğum yerde durmıyan otobüslerdir.
3. Yazısında kimsenin anlamadığı bazı şeyler vardı.
4. Sana söyliyeceğim başka bir şey var.

5. Yeni hükümetin bastığı paralarda Atatürk'ün resmi var.

6. Komşumuz yeni aldığı radyosunu sonuna kadar açıyor.

7. Sırası geldiği zaman, dünkü toplantıda başbakanın söylediklerini size birer birer söyliyeceğim.

8. Gönderdiğim mektuplara hiç cevap vermediniz; artık size bir şey göndermiyeceğim.

9. Işığın geldiği eve doğru kaçtığımız zaman orada oturanlar hâlâ uyuyorlardı.

10. Marko Polo Çin'e gittiği zaman insan yiyen ağaçlar görmüş.

C. Correct the following sentences by making the sentence included within parentheses into a relative clause:

1. (Dün lokantaya gittik) lokantayı ben hiç sevmedim.
2. (Sen cevaplar yazdın) cevapların hepsi doğru.
3. (Adam her gün sokağın köşesinde duruyor ve bizim eve bakıyor) adam herhalde askermiş.
4. Orhan (karısı ona şapka veriyor) şapkaları hep kaybeder.
5. (Çocuklar bir oyun oynuyor) oyun nedir?
6. (Adam bize telefon edecek) adamın ismi nedir?
7. Ahmet beyin evi, (istasyon sokakta) sokakta.
8. Ahmet, her (kadını görür) kadının peşinden koşar.
9. (Sınıfta bir talebe en çok çalışır) talebe Orhan'dır.
10. (Kitabı bugün okuyacağız) kitap İnce Memed'dir.
11. (Hasan sırada oturuyor) sırada daha yer var.
12. (Siz paketi göndereceksiniz) paketi kime göndereceksiniz?

D. Translate into Turkish:

1. I am holding the orange in my hand.
2. The orange which I am holding in my hand
3. We descended from the hill.

4. The hill from which we descended
5. Our neighbor drinks in that restaurant every night.
6. The restaurant in which our neighbor drinks every night
7. You are stepping on the board.
8. The board on which you are stepping
9. The cat is sleeping beside the chair.
10. The cat which is sleeping beside the chair
11. The teacher helped the students with their lesson.
12. The students whom the teacher helped with their lesson
13. My brother sent his article to the newspaper.
14. The newspaper to which my brother sent his article
15. We are not far from the hotel.
16. The hotel which we are not far from
17. A light is burning in that office.
18. The light which is burning in that office

E. Translate into Turkish:

1. Where did the ten liras which I gave you go?
2. I don't understand the language which they speak in this country.
3. The book is about the years when the author lived in Istanbul.
4. When Ahmet arrived at the meeting, he found room in the last row.
5. The hotel we went to in Konya was expensive but not clean at all.
6. When Fatma lived alone, she used to listen to the radio every evening.

LESSON 26: PARTICIPLES FROM POSSESSIVES

Study the following sentences:

Arabası yolumuzu kesen adama çok kızdık	'We got very angry at the man whose car blocked our way'
Arabamızın yolunu kestiği adam bize çok kızdı	'The man whose way our car blocked got very angry at us'
İşi biten herkes şarap içecek	'Everyone whose work is finished will drink wine'
Merkezi Tegucigalpa olan memleket hangisidir?	'Which is the country whose capital is Tegucigalpa?'
Üstü beyaz, altı sarı olan bir araba gördüm	'I saw a car whose top was white and whose bottom was yellow'
Hasan'ın çok daha fazla işi olan yeni bir vazifesi var	'Hasan has a new position with much more work'
Fatma'nın yeni kocası, beş parası olmıyan bir adamdır	'Fatma's new husband is a man without five cents to his name'
Etrafında büyük bir bahçe olan bina Ankara Bankası'dır	'The building with a big garden around it is the Bank of Ankara'
Bütün korktuklarım oldu	'Everything that I was afraid of happened'
Dediğim gibi, pek çalışkan değilsin, doğrusu da bu	'As I said, you are not very hardworking; that is the truth'

1. Participles from possessives

The only type of relative construction that remains to be discussed is that in which the head noun is in the genitive in the underlying simple sentence. In English, such relative clauses use the pronoun 'whose', or sometimes 'of which':

the man whose house is on the square
= The man's house is on the square

the man whose car I bought
= I bought the man's car

In Turkish, these constructions can be divided into two groups: if the noun that is possessed by the head noun is the subject of the sentence, a subject participle is used; if it is not, an object participle is used.

Consider, for example, the expression:

the butcher whose son sells us meat

In Turkish, this is:

oğlu bize et satan kasap

And the corresponding simple sentence is:

Kasabın oğlu bize et satar	'The butcher's son sells us meat'

The subject of this simple sentence is the noun phrase kasabın oğlu, and the head noun (kasap) is picked out of this noun phrase. Therefore a subject participle is used, even though kasap itself is not, strictly speaking, the subject. Note that oğlu (which is the subject) is left behind in the relative clause, with its possessive suffix.

On the other hand, consider:

the butcher whose son we buy meat from

In Turkish, this is:

oğlundan et aldığımız kasap

It corresponds to the following simple sentence:

(Biz) kasabın oğlundan et alırız	'We buy meat from the butcher's son'

Here kasap is in a noun phrase (kasabın oğlundan) that is not the subject, and therefore an object participle is used.

Compare also the following pair of expressions:

ısırmak - to bite
yüksek - high
kullanmak - use, drive

köpeği kedimizi ısıran oğlan (= oğlanın köpeği kedimizi ısırdı)	'the boy whose dog bit our cat'
kedimizin köpeğini ısırdığı oğlan (= kedimiz oğlanın köpeğini ısırdı)	'the boy whose dog our cat bit'

Constructions of this sort, in which a subject participle is used with a head noun that is the possessor of the subject, are particularly common where the verb is intransitive:

kocası Merkez Bankasında çalışan hanım	'the lady whose husband works at the Central Bank'
babası askere gitmiş olan çocuk	'the child whose father has gone into the army'
evleri yananlar	'people whose house burned down'

Notice the use of this construction with nonverbal predicates:

tepesi çok yüksek olan ağaç (= ağacın tepesi çok yüksek)	'the tree whose top is very high'
Niye içi temiz olmayan bir şişe kullanıyorsun?	'Why are you using a bottle whose inside isn't clean?'
kocası doktor olan hanım	'the lady whose husband is a doctor'

1.1. Cases involving *var* and *yok*

Relative clauses formed from sentences with *var* and *yok* follow the same pattern. Consider the formation of the expression:

a room which has a beautiful view

The corresponding simple sentence in Turkish is:

Bir odanın güzel manzarası var	'A room has a beautiful view'

The subject of this sentence is the entire noun phrase *bir odanın güzel manzarası* (and the predicate is *var*). The genitive *bir odanın* is removed and made the head noun, while *güzel manzarası* remains. Since *oda* is the possessor of the subject, a subject participle is called for. The stem *ol-* must be supplied, to replace *var*; *olma-* replaces *yok*. The result is therefore:

güzel manzarası olan bir oda

Some additional examples:

İstanbulda en ucuz fiatları olan lokanta	'the restaurant which has the cheapest prices in Istanbul'
bir tek hoş tarafı olmıyan bir insan	'a person without a single pleasant side (aspect)'

1.2. Cases involving postpositional constructions

We should discuss one more set of constructions in which a subject participle is used. Most of these cases involve a postpositional construction; more importantly, they normally involve an indefinite subject. Consider:

içinde Mehmedin eşyaları olan paket	'the package which has Mehmet's things in it'

The simple sentence corresponding to this is:

Paketin içinde Mehmedin eşyaları var

In this sentence *paket* is neither the subject nor part of the subject noun phrase. We would therefore expect an object participle, and in fact an object participle is also possible here:

içinde Mehmedin eşyalarının olduğu paket

In some cases the choice between a subject or object participle corresponds to a distinction between an indefinite or definite subject in the basic simple sentence:

şarap - wine   yaşamak - live

üstünde şarap olan masa — 'the table with wine on it'

üstünde şarabın olduğu masa — 'the table with the wine on it'

içinde kuşlar yaşayan ağaç — 'the tree with birds living in it'

içinde kuşların yaşadığı ağaç — 'the tree with the birds living in it'

There are still other cases involving, not a postpositional construction, but some other kind of locative expression:

odasında ışık yanan adam — 'the man in whose room a light is burning'

evinden köpek sesleri gelen adam — 'the man from whose house the sounds of dogs are coming'

We may now make a formal definition of the conditions under which a subject participle is used. Remember that an indefinite subject is placed next to the verb (Lesson 7, Section 4); when this happens, some adverbial element, such as a locative expression, may precede the subject. Then note that wherever a subject participle is used in a relative construction, the head noun is the first word in the basic simple sentence: either as subject of the sentence, as possessor of the subject, or as genitive member of a locative expression at the beginning of the sentence. Study the parallelism among the following examples:

yemeğe gelen adam (= adam yemeğe geldi) — 'the man who came to dinner'

oğlu yemeğe gelen adam (= adamın oğlu yemeğe geldi) — 'the man whose son came to dinner'

köpeği olan adam (= adamın köpeği var) — 'the man who has a dog'

evinde köpek olan adam (= adamın evinde köpek var) — 'the man in whose house there is a dog'

2. Adjectives with possessive suffix

We have seen several times that an adjective may be used without a following noun, with 'person' or 'people' understood: gençler 'young people', evleri yananlar 'people whose house burned down'.

When the noun to be understood is not 'person' but 'thing', it is customary to add the third person possessive suffix to the adjective. That is, a word such as iyisi, with no noun following, should be interpreted as 'the good one' or 'the good thing'.

Bunların hangisini istiyorsunuz? —Sarısını	'Which of these do you want? —The yellow one'
Aynısını ben de istiyorum	'I want the same (one)'
Saatimi kaybettim; bir yenisini alırım	'I lost my watch; I'll buy a new one'
En büyüğünü aldınız	'You bought the biggest one'

Some more or less standard expressions are formed on this model:

En iyisi, ekmeği yarıya keseceğiz	'The best (thing to do is) we'll cut the bread in half'
İşin kötüsü, hem Halil hem de Hasan burada yok	'The bad part of the business (is that) both Halil and Hasan are absent from here'
Doğrusu, Attila'nın yeni vazifesi çok az para getirir	'The truth (is that) Attila's new position brings very little money'

3. Additional uses of object participles

Under some conditions, object participle constructions may also be used without a noun following. The meaning to be understood is something like 'that which' or 'the things which', normally in an abstract sense:

Halil'in yaptıklarına çok kızdım	'I got very angry at the things that Halil did'
Bütün bildiğim, işi bugün bitirmediler; neden ama bilmiyorum	'All that I know is that they didn't finish the work today, but I don't know why'

Kısa - short, brief

Her dediğin doğru	'Everything you say is true'

This use is particularly common with certain postpositions, especially gibi, göre, and kadar in its nominative/genitive use:

müdürün dediğine göre	'according to what the director said'
Her şey istediğim gibi çıktı	'Everything came out as I wanted'
İstediğiniz kadar yemek alırsınız	'You may take as much food as you want'

4. Usage

'Both-and' constructions are made with hem for 'both', hem or hem de for 'and'.

Hem Rumlar hem Araplar Türk yemekleri yapar	'Both the Greeks and Arabs make Turkish foods'
Hem yol uzun, hem de hava sıcak	'(Both) the trip is long, and the weather is hot'

The basic meaning of kesmek is 'cut', but it has a number of related meanings, which seem to fall into two groups: (1) meanings centering around 'discontinue', such as 'stop, cease, break off'; (2) meanings related to 'kill', such as 'slaughter' or 'massacre'.

Otobüs yolumuzu kesti	'The bus blocked our way'
Sözümü kesti	'He interrupted me'
Sözümü kısa keserim	'I'll be brief'

In addition, this verb is used in a large number of idiomatic expressions.

The number of pieces into which something is cut is expressed in the dative:

Elmayı ikiye kestik	'We cut the apple in two'
Elmayı üç parçaya kestik	'We cut the apple in three pieces'

Merkez is the 'center' of a circle or the principal

place of a geographical area, such as the capital of a country or the business district of a city.

The meanings of vazife fall into two groups: (1) 'position' or 'job'; in this sense, it is slightly more elegant than iş; (2) 'duty' or 'function'. Note this example:

O asker vazifesini yapmıyor	'That soldier is not doing his duty'

VOCABULARY

banka		bank
demek		say
hem . . . hem		both . . . and
ısırmak		bite
kesmek		cut (see "Usage")
kuş		bird
manzara		view
merkez		center (see "Usage")
sarı		yellow
şarap	/şarab/	wine
vazife	/vazīfe/	position, duty (see "Usage")
yüksek		high

EXERCISES

A. Answer the following questions:

1. Amerika'da hiç parası olmıyan insan var mı?
2. Yazısı sağdan sola giden bir dil biliyor musunuz?
3. Odasından sesler gelen talebe kim?
4. Hasan'ın vazifesinin olduğu banka nerede?
5. Hiç kitabını okumadığınız yazar var mı?

B. Convert each of the following simple sentences into a relative clause modifying the noun ev ('the house which . . .'). Give the resulting clauses in Turkish and translate them into English.

1. Eve baktık.
2. Ev köyün ortasında duruyor.
3. Hasan üç gün evde oturdu.
4. Bankanın yanında ev var.
5. Hasan bu köşede ev yapacak.
6. Hasan evin kapısını kapadı.
7. Evin bahçesi geniş.
8. Evin etrafında yüksek ağaçlar var.

C. Correct the following sentences by making the sentence included within parentheses into a relative clause. Then translate the result into English.

1. (Komşunun radyosu sabaha kadar çalıyor) komşuyla bir gün kavga edeceğim.
2. (Siz adamın arabasını kullanıyorsunuz) adam onu geri istiyor.
3. (Yatağın üstünde kedi var) yatak sizin.
4. (Köpek Ayşe'yi ısırdı) köpek Fatma'yı da ısırdı.
5. Bir kaç (adamları beğenmiyoruz) adam bakan oluyor.
6. (Kadının elbisesi beyaz) kadına herkes bakıyor.
7. (Odadan sesler geliyor) odanın kapısını kapayacağım.
8. (İskemlenin arkasında isminiz var) iskemle sizin.
9. (Başbakan kitap yazdı) kitabın içinde hiç önemli bir şey yok.
10. Çocuklar (meydanın ortasında bahçe var) bahçede bir oyun oynuyor.
11. (Siz adamın mektuplarını açtınız) adam size çok kızdı.
12. (Bahçemizin etrafına duvar yapacağız) duvar taştan olacak.
13. (Köpek kuşu ağzında tutuyor) köpek kaçtı.
14. Hasan, (şarabın çoğunu içti) şarabın gerisini nereye koydu?
15. (Kedinin hiç yemeği kalmadı) kedi başka bir eve gitti.

D. Translate into Turkish:

1. The doctor's office is near the center of the city.
2. The doctor whose office is near the center of the city
3. You are looking at a picture of Ahmet Bey.
4. Ahmet Bey, whose picture you are looking at
5. A wine glass is standing on the shelf.
6. That shelf on which a wine glass is standing
7. That child's dog bit me.
8. The child whose dog bit me
9. Hasan has not had a good position since January.
10. Hasan, who has not had a good position since January
11. The director of the bank will come to our office tomorrow.
12. The bank whose director will come to our office tomorrow
13. Both that woman's father and her husband are soldiers.
14. The woman (both) whose father and husband are soldiers
15. There is a bird in the dog's mouth.
16. The dog in whose mouth there is a bird
17. Hasan is using someone's car.
18. The person whose car Hasan is using

E. Translate into Turkish:

1. The man whose car you bought still wants his money.
2. Ahmet doesn't pay attention to what his wife says.
3. Ahmet's wife gets angry at everything he does.
4. We'll find a store which doesn't have such high prices.
5. Which is the cheapest of these?
6. The youngest of her sons is Mehmet.

LESSON 27: VERBAL NOUNS AND INFINITIVES

Study the following sentences:

Yaşamak, çalışmaktır	'To live is to work'
En istediğim şey, Ahmedin bana araba kullanmağı göstermesi	'What I want the most is for Ahmet to show me how to drive a car'
Bu sabah alışveriş etmek için şehre inmeği düşünüyordum	'This morning I was thinking of going downtown to do some shopping'
Bu lokantayı denemek fikri kimindi?	'Whose idea was it to try this restaurant?'
Yemek yemekten başka işin yok mu?	'Don't you have anything to do besides eat? (Don't you have another job besides eating?)'
Hasanın eşyalarımı çalmasını affettim	'I forgave Hasan's stealing my things'
Bu işi görmemiz için bize kaç para verecekler?	'How much will they pay for us to do this job?'
Ay doğuşundan, insan yürüyüşünden belli olur (Proverb)	'The moon becomes clear from its rising, the man from his walking' (doğmak 'be born', belli 'clear')
Her gidişimde oranın havasına yeniden alışmam lâzım	'Every time I go I have to get used to the weather there anew'
Başkalarının işine karışmaman lâzım	'You mustn't interfere in other people's business'
Çocuğun o kadar çok ağlamasına lüzum yok	'There is no need for the child to cry so much'

1. Verbal noun constructions

Verbal noun constructions, in Turkish as in English, are devices by means of which one sentence may be included within another to fill the grammatical role of "noun phrase" within the main sentence. Consider the following English example:

I got angry at Orhan's being late

Here the main sentence is 'I got angry at (something)' where the 'something' is the sequence 'Orhan's being late'. This sequence is a nominal expression and functions as the object of the main sentence; but at the same time it is related to the simple sentence 'Orhan was late', and its meaning is the action of that simple sentence. We may say, therefore, that 'Orhan was late' becomes converted into the verbal noun construction 'Orhan's being late' in order to serve as a noun phrase in some other sentence.

Thus, in the Turkish equivalent, *Orhan'ın geç kalmasına kızdım*, the object is *Orhan'ın geç kalmasına*, which functions like any other noun phrase; compare *Orhan'ın dostuna kızdım* 'I got angry at Orhan's friend'. But it is formed from the simple sentence *Orhan geç kaldı* by the use of a "verbal noun" suffix, in this case *-mE* (we shall explain the rest of the grammar later).

Verbal noun constructions in English may be of the '-ing' type, as already shown, or the 'for-to' type:

I am waiting for you to go

For the students to learn this is very difficult

Here the simple included sentences are 'you go' and 'the students learn this', respectively. Turkish does not make this elusive distinction.

English also has constructions of the simple 'to' type, which indicate only the action but not the subject of the action:

I am waiting to go

To learn this is very difficult

In the second of these examples, we have to assume that the included sentence is something like '(Someone) learns this', because the subject is not overtly expressed. In the first example, the included sentence might be '(Someone) goes', but it is clear that it is actually 'I go' and that 'I am waiting to go' is a reduction of 'I am waiting for me to go', on the model of 'I am waiting for you to go'.

Turkish also has this construction and normally uses the suffix *-mEg*:

Gitmeği bekliyorum

Bunu öğrenmek çok zor

2. Turkish verbal nouns

Turkish has three verbal noun suffixes: -mEg, -mE, and -(y)Iş. We shall discuss the differences between these suffixes later. There are a number of general points to be made about these constructions.

Verbal noun suffixes, like participles, replace the tense suffix of the verb. The subject of the included sentence, if it is expressed, is in the genitive, and the corresponding possessive suffix is added to the verbal noun; the result is a normal possessive construction, as in English:

Mehmed'in gelmesi	'Mehmet's coming'

Similarly, we have benim gelmem or gelmem 'my coming', gelmeniz 'your coming', and so forth. If there is no subject, there is no possessive: gelmek 'to come'.

The verbal noun has whatever case suffix is required by its function in the main sentence; see the examples that follow.

Verbal nouns, like participles, are strictly verbal suffixes and may be attached only to verb stems. If the simple sentence is nonverbal, the stem ol- must be supplied for the verbal noun:

Mehmet yorgun	'Mehmet is tired'
Mehmed'in yorgun olması	'Mehmet's being tired'
yorgun olmamak	'not to be tired'

The most important thing to remember about verbal noun constructions is that they always have exactly the same word order as the corresponding simple sentence:

Halil her dakika işime karışır	'Halil constantly (every minute) interferes with my business'
Halil'in her dakika işime karışması	'Halil's constantly interfering with my business'

(Birisi) Rumların kullandıkları harfleri öğrenir	'(Someone) learns the letters which the Greeks use'
Rumların kullandıkları harfleri öğrenmek (herhalde zordur)	'To learn the letters which the Greeks use (is presumably difficult)'

2.1. The infinitive

We are already familiar with the use of the suffix -mEg to form the "citation forms" of verbs: gitmek 'to go'. In addition, -mEg is used in verbal noun constructions where only the action of the given verb, or verb phrase, is indicated.

Çocuk ağlamağa başladı	'The child began to cry'
Hazır olmağa çalışırım	'I'll try to be ready'

When an infinitive is the object of a transitive verb, the objective suffix is normally optional. As a general rule, the suffix is omitted if the main verb is one that is frequently used in this construction (sevmek, istemek, bilmek), but retained if the main verb is less common.

Gelecek ay denize gitmeği düşünüyorduk	'We were thinking of going to the seashore next month'
Fatma zengin ve meşhur olmak istiyor	'Fatma wants to be rich and famous'
Küçük oğlu şimdi yürümeği öğreniyor	'Her small son is now learning to walk'

An infinitive construction may function not only as the object of a main verb but also as subject or predicate of a sentence, or it may appear in any construction where a noun phrase can be used.

En sevmediğim şey, ders çalışmaktır	'The thing which I dislike the most is studying'
Evlerini bulmak kolay olacak	'It will be easy to find their house'
Şimdi eve dönmek vakti geldi	'Now it is time to go home'

Çok uyumaktan dolayı tembel oldun	'You became lazy from sleeping too much'

The postposition için with an infinitive means 'in order to':

Yemekleri denemek için Bebekteki yeni lokantaya gittik	'We went to the new restaurant in Bebek in order to try the food'

Another way of expressing purpose is simply to put the infinitive in the dative. This is normally done, however, only with short or colloquial constructions, many of them idiomatic:

Hasan biraz yürümeğe çıktı	'Hasan went out for a little walk'

2.2. The "short infinitive"

The suffix -mE, sometimes called the "short infinitive," is theoretically interchangeable with -mEg. It could grammatically substitute for -mEg in all the examples in Section 2.1; in practice, however, it is common only in the objective and dative cases:

Ahmet kızmamayı öğreniyor	'Ahmet is learning not to get angry'
Ahmet erken yatmaya (yatmağa) alışıyor	'Ahmet is getting used to going to bed early'

In practice, -mE is the form of the infinitive used when a possessive suffix follows, that is, when the subject is explicitly expressed:

Ahmedin erken yatmasına alışıyoruz	'We are getting used to Ahmet's going to bed early'
Ahmedin hasta olması herkes için zor oldu	'Ahmet's being sick was difficult for everyone'
Böyle hareket etmenin mânası nedir?	'What is the meaning of your acting like this?'

The suffix -mE is the one used for so-called indirect commands, that is, commands that are not stated directly as imperatives but included within other sentences as the objects of verbs like 'tell' or 'request':

Doktorun hemen gelmesini istedik	'We wanted the doctor to come at once' 'We asked the doctor to come at once'
Fatmanın yedide hazır olmasını söyledim	'I told Fatma to be ready at seven'

İçin with a construction using -mE still means 'in order to':

Hasan'ın mektebine devam etmesi için, bu yaz çalışması lâzım	'In order for Hasan to continue at school, he has to work this summer'

Frequently constructions formed with -mE serve simply as nouns or adjectives. Dolma, formed from the verb dol- 'fill', is the name of a type of food made by stuffing vegetables with a mixture of rice and meat—for example, yaprak dolması 'stuffed grape leaves'. Similarly, we have the following examples:

konuşma	'speech'
deneme	'test, experiment'
okuma kitabı	'reader'
dolma kalem	'fountain pen (filling-pen)'
bekleme odası	'waiting room'

2.3. The suffix -(y)Iş

The suffix -(y)Iş is used to make verbal nouns that refer not only to the action but to the manner of performing the action involved. Thus yaşayış means 'style of living' or 'manner of living', as in Ahmedin yaşayışı 'the way in which Ahmet lives'.

Words formed with this suffix normally serve simply as nouns:

alışveriş	'shopping'
anlayış	'understanding'

çıkış	'exit' (as in çıkış kapısı 'exit (door)')
dönüş	'return'
gidiş	'going'
giriş	'entrance' (as in giriş kapısı 'entrance (door)')
gösteriş	'display, ostentation'
satış	'selling' (as in satış fiatı 'selling price')
yürüyüş	'walk; way of walking'
Bu adam bize karşı çok anlayış gösterdi	'This man showed great understanding toward us'
Dönüşümüzde hemen işe başlıyacağım	'Upon our return I will start work at once'
Bugün kısa bir yürüyüş yaptım	'Today I took a short walk'
O adamın çok tuhaf bir yürüyüşü var	'That man has a very strange way of walking'

3. The suffix -mEktEdIr

We saw in Lesson 19 that in some styles of written Turkish—for example, newspapers and scholarly works—the normal past tense is neither -DI nor -mIş but the combination -mIştIr (-mIş+DIr). The future, similarly, is not -(y)EcEk but -(y)EcEktIr. In the same written style, the normal progressive tense is not -Iyor but the construction -mEktEdIr, which is made up of the infinitive -mEg, the locative -DE, and -DIr. Thus a sentence like Hükümet, bu mesele üzerine çalışmaktadır 'The government is working on this problem' means literally 'The government is at working on this problem'.

This construction is normally used in the third person but also appears less frequently in the first or second person:

On üçüncü asrın Türk dilinde birçok yeni sözlerin meydana çıkmasını görmekteyiz	'In the Turkish language of the thirteenth century, we see the appearance of a number of new expressions'

It is important to remember that when the locative suffix is added to an infinitive like çalışmak to form çalışmakta, the result is simply a nonverbal predicate like evde 'at home' and functions in exactly the same way in participle and verbal noun constructions. Compare the following sentences:

Bakan evdedir	'The minister is at home'
Bakan, bu mesele üzerine çalışmaktadır	'The minister is working on this problem'
şimdi evde olan bakan	'the minister, who is now at home'
şimdi bu mesele üzerine çalışmakta olan bakan	'the minister, who is now working on this problem'
bakanın evde olması	'the minister's being at home'
bakanın bu mesele üzerine çalışmakta olması	'the minister's working on this problem'

We can sum up the systems of tenses in "journalistic" and "normal" (for want of a better term) styles in the accompanying table.

Tense	Normal	Journalistic
Present	-Ir	-Ir
Progressive	-Iyor	-mEktEdIr
Future	-(y)EcEk	-(y)EcEktIr
Definite past	-DI	-mIştIr
Narrative past	-mIş	

4. The adjective lâzım

The adjective lâzım is used as a predicate meaning 'necessary'; its subject is the thing that is necessary while the thing for which something is needed is in the dative:

Bu odaya sandalye lâzım	'This room needs a chair (A chair is necessary for this room)'

Bana para lâzım	'I need money (Money is necessary for me)'

The subject of lâzım may be a verbal noun construction:

Bu işi bitirmek için çalışmak lâzım	'To finish this job, it is necessary to work (One must work to finish this job)'
Bu meseleyi biraz düşünmemiz lâzım	'We must think about this problem a little (Our thinking about this problem a little is necessary)'
Orhanın ne zaman gitmesi lâzım?	'When does Orhan have to go?'

It is worth noting that in the colloquial language an expression like Evde olması lâzım means 'He must be at home' in the two senses that this expression has in English, namely (1) 'It is necessary for him to be at home', and (2)'The evidence indicates that he is at home', and also has a third sense, 'He is supposed to be at home'.

We might expect the negative of lâzım to be lâzım değil. But in practice the noun lüzum 'necessity', from the same Arabic root, is used with yok; thus we have lüzum yok 'there is no need', preceded by a verbal noun construction in the dative. Compare:

Gitmemiz lâzım	'We have to go'
Gitmemize lüzum yok	'We do not have to go (There is no need for us to go)'

Note the expressions lâzım gelmek 'be necessary' or 'become necessary' and lüzum görmek 'consider something necessary'.

5. Usage

Denemek means 'try' in the sense of 'test' and takes the objective; çalışmak means 'try' in the sense of 'make an effort' and takes the dative:

Çocuk uyumağa çalışıyor	'The child is trying to sleep'

Yahya Kemal'i okumayı denedim, fakat dili çok zordu	'I tried reading Yahya Kemal, but his language was too difficult'

The verb düşünmek 'think' is transitive, and the thing thought about is in the objective case:

Bu meseleyi düşündük	'We thought about this problem'
Mehmedi düşündük	'We thought about Mehmet'

It is also possible, but less common, to use hakkında with this verb:

Bu mesele hakkında düşündük	'We thought about this problem'

Harf means 'letter' of a writing system.

Hemen means 'at once', but hemen hemen means 'almost'.

Karışmak is basically intransitive: İşler karıştı 'Things got mixed up'. But it can also be used with the dative: Halil konuşmalarımıza karıştı 'Halil interfered with (got mixed up in) our conversation'.

Kolay 'easy' takes the dative for the person for whom something is easy:

Bu iş bana kolay	'This job is easy for me'

Alışmak 'become accustomed', devam etmek 'continue', and hazır 'ready' all take the dative:

Hasan okumağa alıştı	'Hasan got used to reading'
Hasan okumağa devam etti	'Hasan continued reading'
Hasan gitmeğe hazır	'Hasan is ready to go'

VOCABULARY

acayip	/acāyip/	strange
ağlamak		cry
alışmak (dat)		become accustomed, get used (to)

denemek		try (see "Usage")
devam	/devām/	continuation
devam etmek (dat)		continue
düşünmek		think (see "Usage")
harf	(-i)	letter
hazır (dat)		ready (to, for)
hemen	/hémen/	immediately
karışmak (dat)		get mixed up (in), interfere (with) (see "Usage")
kolay		easy
lâzım	/lāzım/	necessary
lüzum		necessity, need
mâna	/mānā/	meaning
meşhur		famous
tuhaf		strange
ünlü		famous
z[illegible]		difficult

EXE[illegible]

A. Answ[illegible]ollowing questions:

1. Türk [illegible]i öğrenmek için ne lâzım?
2. Gelece[illegible] ıl için neler düşünüyorsunuz?
3. İstanbul'da yaşamağa alıştınız mı?
4. Derse başlamağa hazır mısınız?
5. Bu akşam saat kaça kadar çalışmağa devam edeceksiniz?

B. Translate into English:

1. Meyvamız hemen hemen bitti.
2. Bunu söylemeniz kolay.
3. Buna ne lüzum var?

yürümek - walk, march
gibi - like

4. Mehmedin yürüyüşü, kardeşininki gibi.
5. Talebeler, bu dersi bir haftadan beri anlamağa çalışıyor.
6. Ahmet, parasını saymaktan başka bir sey yapmıyor.
7. Kavga etmemek için, adama istediği fiatı verdim.
8. Hasanın araba kullanmayı bilmemesinden dolayı, otobüsle gitmemiz lâzım gelecek.

C. Correct the following sentences by making the sentence included within parentheses into a verbal noun construction. Be sure to add the correct case suffix required by the main sentence. Then translate the result into English.

1. (Mehmet hep bilmediği işlere karışıyor) çok kızdım.
2. (Böyle hareket ediyorsun) ne lüzum var?
3. Çocuk, (çocuk ağladı) devam etti.
4. (Kuşlar günde bir kaç defa yemek yer) lâzım.
5. (Köyde hayat pek ucuz) alıştık.
6. Halil, (siz mektuplarını açtınız) affetmiyecek.
7. (Müdür bize iş veriyor) kolay, (biz yapıyoruz) ama zor.
8. (Uçakların geliş zamanları değişti) [illegible] beklemedik.
9. (Orhan o kadar tembel değil) istedi[illegible]

D. Translate into Turkish:

1. Halil understands the meaning of thi[illegible]ook.
2. To understand the meaning of this boo[illegible]
3. It is difficult to understand the meaning of this book.
4. Attila reads Greek letters.
5. To read Greek letters
6. Attila is learning to read Greek letters.
7. Hasan waits for Fatma every morning.
8. To wait for Fatma every morning.
9. Hasan is getting used to waiting for Fatma every morning.

10. You smoke too much.
11. To smoke too much
12. You'll get sick from smoking too much.
13. Your father is drinking his coffee.
14. To drink his coffee
15. Your father is occupied with drinking his coffee.
16. I am finishing my work.
17. To finish my work
18. I will stay here in order to finish my work.
19. You are acting strangely.
20. To act strangely
21. There is no need to act so strangely.
22. From now on we will go to bed earlier.
23. To go to bed earlier
24. It is necessary to go to bed earlier from now on.
25. Mehmet answers Fatma's letters.
26. For Mehmet to answer Fatma's letters
27. What Fatma wants the most is for Mehmet to answer her letters.
28. This child cries every minute.
29. This child's crying every minute
30. I don't like this child's crying every minute.
31. Hasan was not ready on time.
32. Hasan's not being ready on time
33. Fatma got angry at Hasan's not being ready on time.
34. A man laughed.
35. A man's laughing
36. The sound of a man's laughing came from across the street.
37. Halil was tired.
38. Halil's being tired
39. Halil did not come with us because of his being tired.

40. You tried Arab food once.
41. You must try Arab food once.
42. Ahmet is lazy.
43. Ahmet's being lazy
44. How long will Ahmet's being lazy continue?
45. To be lazy
46. How long will Ahmet continue to be lazy?

D. Translate into Turkish:

I'll read you this piece which I saw in the newspaper: a famous Turkish writer, who is now working on his fourth book, yesterday spoke at a meeting of university students. The writer, whose name we do not know, is thinking of living in our city.

LESSON 28: NOMINALIZATIONS

Study the following sentences:

Mehmedin o kadar değiştiğini bilmiyordum	'I didn't know Mehmet had changed so much'
Her yazar, en yeni eserinin öbürlerinden daha iyi olduğunu sanıyor	'Every writer thinks his latest work is better than the others'
Her yazar, eserlerini iyi sanıyor	'Every writer thinks his works good'
Kıbrısın Türk olduğu fikri 1960 senelerinde ortaya çıktı	'The idea that Cyprus is Turkish arose in the 1960s'
Hasta olduğunuz yüzünüzden belli	'It is clear from your face that you are ill'
O adamın kim olduğunu unuttum, amma meşhur olduğundan eminim	'I forgot who that man is, but I am sure he is famous'
Ankaraya vardığı zaman, nereye gideceğini, hangi otelde kalacağını bilmiyor	'He doesn't know where he will go, or which hotel he will stay in, when he gets to Ankara'

1. Nominalizations

Nominalizations, like verbal noun constructions, are devices by which one sentence may be included within another to fill the grammatical role of "noun phrase" within the main sentence. The difference between them is that a verbal noun construction refers to a certain action, while a nominalization refers to a certain fact. Compare these English examples:

I heard that Halil came

I heard Halil's coming (= I heard Halil come)

The sequences 'that Halil came' and 'Halil's coming' both function as noun phrases and as the object of the main verb; compare 'I heard the radio'. But in the former case, the speaker heard a certain fact; while in the latter case, the speaker heard a certain action (in particular, here, the sound of the action).

In the following Turkish sentence, the speaker has heard a certain fact, not the action itself:

Halil'in geldiğini duydum	'I heard that Halil came'

Another difference is that while verbal noun constructions contain no indication of tense, nominalizations distinguish between future and nonfuture actions. The suffix -(y)EcEg is used when the tense of the corresponding simple sentence is future; the suffix -DIg is used in all other cases. (These are, of course, identical with the object participle suffixes.)

Halil'in geleceğini biliyorum	'I know that Halil will come'
Halil'in geldiğini biliyorum	'I know that Halil came/comes/ is coming'

Nominalizations are formed in the same way as object participle phrases. The suffix -DIg or -(y)EcEg replaces the tense suffix of the verb; the subject of the sentence is placed in the genitive, and the corresponding possessive suffix is added to the verb. Thus we have:

Halil geldi	'Halil came'
Halil'in geldiği	'(the fact) that Halil came'
Oynıyorsunuz	'You are playing'
oynadığınız	'(the fact) that you are playing'

The nominalization then has whatever case suffix is required by its function in the main sentence:

Bu oğlanın babasına benzediği belli	'It is clear that this boy resembles his father'
Şimdi şapkamı evde unuttuğumu hatırlıyorum	'Now I remember that I forgot my hat at home'
Bu dersi anlamıyacağınızdan korkuyorum	'I am afraid you will not understand this lesson'
Kıbrıs üstüne harp çıkmadığına memnunuz	'We are glad that war did not break out over Cyprus'

If the predicate is nonverbal, the stem ol- must be supplied, as usual:

Buradaki kışların pek soğuk olduğu malûm	'It is well known that the winters here are very cold'
Tayyarede hâlâ yer olduğunu işittim	'I heard that there is still room on the airplane'

It is important to remember about nominalizations that, like participle phrases and verbal noun constructions, they have exactly the same word order as the corresponding simple sentence:

Bu mesele hakkında bir kaç gün sonra daha iyi hissedeceksiniz	'You will feel better about this problem in a few days'
Bu mesele hakkında bir kaç gün sonra daha iyi hissedeceğinizden eminim	'I am sure that you will feel better about this problem in a few days'

2. The difference between nominalizations and verbal nouns

Study the following pairs of sentences carefully. The first member of each pair includes a nominalization, and it should be clear from the translation that a certain fact is under discussion; the second member includes a verbal noun, and it should be clear that a certain action is under discussion.

Orhan'ın deli olduğuna karar verdik	'We decided that Orhan was crazy'
Orhan'ın doktora gitmesine karar verdik	'We decided for Orhan to go to the doctor'
Ahmet Bey, kızının saat ondan evvel eve döndüğünü söyledi	'Ahmet Bey said that his daughter returned home before ten o'clock'
Ahmet Bey, kızının saat ondan evvel eve dönmesini söyledi	'Ahmet Bey told his daughter to return home before ten o'clock'
En iyi kitapları seçeceğinizi biliyorum	'I know that you will choose the best books'

En iyi kitapları seçmeyi biliyorum	'I know how to choose the best books'
Kediye yemek vermediğiniz doğru mu?	'Is it true that you did not give food to the cat?'
Kediye yemek vermemeniz doğru mu?	'Is it right for you not to give food to the cat?'
Türkiye'nin harbe girdiği haberi	'the news that Turkey entered the war'
Türkiye'nin harbe girmesinin sebebi	'the reason for Turkey's entering the war'

It may be helpful to remember that verbal nouns usually appear with main verbs and predicate adjectives that deal with actions, while nominalizations appear with main verbs and predicate adjectives that deal with facts. Thus we should expect to find a verbal noun construction as the object of such verbs as başlamak, beklemek, çalışmak, denemek, istemek, kızmak, and so on, or as the subject of such predicate adjectives as kolay or zor, while we should expect to find a nominalization as the object of such verbs as hissetmek or emin olmak, or as the subject of such predicate adjectives as belli or malûm.

The preceding examples show that there are many verbs and adjectives, such as bilmek, doğru, öğrenmek, söylemek, and yazmak, that may be used with both types of construction, but that mean different things (or at least the entire sentences mean different things) depending on the type of construction. There is another small class of verbs, including sevinmek and memnun olmak, that seem to appear with either type of construction without difference:

Köpeğini evde bıraktığına memnun oldum	'I was pleased that you left your dog at home'
Köpeğini evde bırakmana memnun oldum	'I was pleased at your leaving your dog at home'

3. Nominalizations with postpositions

We saw in Lesson 26 the use of object participle constructions with the postpositions gibi, göre, and kadar. Nominalizations are also frequently used with certain other postpositions:

Buraya geldiğimizden beri güneşi görmedik
'We haven't seen the sun since we came here'

Mehmedin babası çalışmaz olduğundan beri paraları kalmadı
'Since Mehmet's father stopped working (became not working), they have no money left'

İçin in this use means 'because of'; dolayı is also used, less frequently:

İçki Orhan'a çok tesir ettiği için, hemen yattı
'Because the liquor affected Orhan too much, he went to bed at once'

Halde, literally 'in the state', is used idiomatically with nominalizations to mean 'although' (and in such constructions, gene (de) or yine (de) mean 'still'):

Orhan çok içki içtiği halde, yine de hasta olmadı
'Although Orhan drank a lot, he still didn't get sick'

Notice that the subject of a nominalization is always in the nominative, not the genitive, when the nominalization is used with a postposition: Ahmet geldiği için 'because Ahmet came', not *Ahmedin geldiği için.

The use of nominalizations with evvel, önce, and sonra will be discussed later.

4. Indirect questions

Interrogative words may be contained within nominalizations; the result is an expression similar to the traditional "indirect questions":

Kalemimi nereye koyduğumu hatırlamıyorum
'I don't remember where I put my pen'

Bunun kimin arabası olduğunu biliyor musunuz?
'Do you know whose car this is?'

Ne kadar zengin olduğumu sanıyorsun?	'How rich do you think I am?'
Beni ne kadar zengin sanıyorsun?	
Ahmedin ne yaptığını sordum	'I asked what Ahmet was doing'

Beware of a difficulty that arises here because English 'what' can be either interrogative or relative. That is, some English sentences involving 'what' correspond to Turkish sentences involving a nominalization containing ne:

Ahmedin ne yaptığını biliyorum	'I know what Ahmet is doing'

Others correspond to Turkish sentences involving an object participle construction, without ne:

Ahmedin yaptığını beğenmiyorum	'I don't like what Ahmet is doing'

In the latter case, English 'what' actually stands for 'that which' or 'the things which', and the Turkish object participle is simply being used without a noun following (see Lesson 26, Section 3). It would be possible to insert some actual noun, like şey or iş:

Ahmedin yaptığı işi beğenmiyorum	'I don't like the things which Ahmet is doing'

But in the cases of genuine questions, such a noun cannot be inserted; we cannot have:

*Ahmedin ne yaptığı işi biliyorum

5. Usage

Malûm 'well known' is used only of facts; for people, use meşhur or ünlü 'famous'.

Sanmak and zannetmek mean 'think' (or 'consider') in the sense 'think that a given fact is true', and are used with nominalizations; düşünmek means 'think' in the sense 'think about a given action' and is normally used with verbal noun constructions.

Halil'i tembel sanıyorum	'I consider Halil lazy'
Halil'in tembel olduğunu sanıyorum	'I think Halil is lazy'

In English, the object of the verb 'ask' is the person to whom the question is directed, while the person or thing asked about is indicated with a preposition, usually 'about'. In Turkish, the object of sormak is the person or thing asked about, while the person to whom the question is directed is expressed in the dative. Compare:

Ahmede sizi sordum	'I asked Ahmet about you'
Size Ahmedi sordum	'I asked you about Ahmet'
O adama vapurun ne zaman geleceğini sorarım	'I'll ask that man when the boat will come'

Sormak is an obligatory object verb (Lesson 5, Section 5); in the preceding examples, sizi, Ahmedi, and the nominalization ending in geleceğini are the objects. If there is no other object, either of the nouns soru or sual 'question' must be included:

Ahmet hakkında soru sordum	'I asked (questions) about Ahmet'

VOCABULARY

belli		clear, obvious
deli		crazy, insane
duymak		hear
emin (abl)	/emīn/	sure (of)
hatırlamak		remember
işitmek		hear
karar		decision
karar vermek (dat)		decide (on)
Kıbrıs		Cyprus

malûm	/mālum/	well known
memnun (dat)		please (at), satisfied (at)
sanmak		think, consider (see "Usage")
sebep	/sebeb/	reason, cause
sebep olmak (dat)		cause
seçmek		choose; elect
sevinmek (dat)		be pleased (at)
sormak		ask (see "Usage")
soru		question
sual	/sual/	question
unutmak		forget
zannetmek		think, consider (see "Usage")

EXERCISES

A. Answer the following questions:

1. Attila'nın nasıl bir adam olduğunu zannediyorsunuz?
2. Bu yıl yazın nereye gideceğiniz hakkındaki kararı ne zaman vereceksiniz?
3. Ders çalışmanızdan memnun musunuz?
4. İlk defa ne zaman sigara içtiğinizi hatırlıyor musunuz?
5. Mehmedin bugün sınıfa gelmemesine sebep nedir?

B. Translate into English:

1. Üniversiteyi bitirdiğinizi duyduğum zaman memnun oldum.
2. Bu haberi birisi söyledi, ama kim olduğunu hatırlamıyorum.
3. Bu köşede yeni bir apartman yapacakları doğru mu?
4. İstanbul Üniversitesindeki derslerin kolay olduğu malûm.

5. Orhan'ın geç kalmasına sebep ben oldum.
6. Bu iskemle boş olduğu için oturdum; sizin olduğunu bilmiyordum.
7. Türkiyede oturmanın ne kadar ucuz olduğunu unutmuştum.
8. Bu kitabı okumamız lâzım geldiğini söylemeniz kolay.
9. Kıbrıs hakkındaki haberi hâlâ okumadığım için, ne yapacağım hakkında daha bir karar vermedim.
10. Memleketi bu hale getiren ekonomik sebeplerin hâlâ ortada olduğunu unutmamamız lâzım.

C. Correct the following sentences by making the sentence included within parentheses into a nominalization. Be sure to add the correct case suffix required by the main sentence. Then translate the result into English.

1. Birisi, (bugün Hasan gelmiyecek) söyledi.
2. (Tepe yüksek) için, üstünden çok güzel bir manzara var.
3. (Fatma hanım nerede oturuyor) pek emin değilim.
4. (Kediler hep aç) herkes biliyor.
5. (Hiç sözüme dinlemiyorsun) belli.
6. (Halil beyin yeni yazdığı kitap pek önemli değil) karar verdim.
7. (Ahmed'in sualine nasıl cevap vereceğim) daha bilmiyorum.
8. (Harp yakında bitecek) haberi, herkesin sevinmesine sebep oldu.
9. (Üniversiteye girdiniz) beri hiç çalışmıyorsunuz.
10. (Odamda masa yok) için oturma odasında çalışıyorum.

D. Translate into Turkish:

1. Your friend is a very nice man.
2. It is obvious that your friend is a very nice man.
3. There is someone behind that door.
4. I am sure that there is someone behind that door.

5. The fruit juice was very bad.
6. Although the fruit juice was very bad, Orhan drank all of it.
7. Her son became rich.
8. Mehmet's mother was pleased that her son became rich.
9. War will break out.
10. The idea that war will break out
11. I heard the idea that war will break out from Ahmet Bey.
12. How much will you sell your house for?
13. Someone asked how much you will sell your house for.
14. Which page was that picture on?
15. I don't remember which page that picture was on.

E. Translate into Turkish:

1. It is not true that I consider Ahmet insane.
2. It is not right for you to consider Ahmet insane.
3. I don't want Ahmet to be late.
4. I forgot that Ahmet will be late.
5. We decided that Orhan will choose the best table.
6. We decided for Orhan to choose the best table.
7. Ahmet showed us how to open the box.
8. Ahmet showed us that the box was empty.
9. I don't understand the news that the prime minister is going to Cyprus.
10. I don't understand the reason for the prime minister's going to Cyprus.

LESSON 29: THE PASSIVE

Study the following sentences:

Yeni alınan masa yukarıdaki odada kurulacak	'The newly bought table will be set up in the upstairs room'
Tamamen beklenmeyen bir hâdise oldu	'A completely unexpected event occurred'
Balkanlardan Türkiyede yaşamağa gelen insanlara Göçmen adı verilir	'The name "Göçmen" is given to people who come from the Balkans to live in Turkey'
Ahmed'in arabası, bir genç tarafından çalındı	'Ahmet's car was stolen by a young man'
İstanbul'un Türkler tarafından alınması 1453 senesinde oldu	'The taking of Istanbul by the Turks happened in the year 1453'
Cevap yazmak için kâğıtla kalem kullanılır	'Paper and pencil may be used to write the answer'
Buraya Girilmez	'Do Not Enter' 'One does not enter here' 'To here is not entered'
Öbür arabalara dikkat edilmesi lâzım	'It is necessary to pay attention to the other cars' 'It is necessary that attention be paid to the other cars'
Bu yoldan geçilir mi?	'Can one pass by (way of) this road?'

1. The passive verb

The passive suffix is normally -<u>Il</u>, except that after a verb stem ending in a vowel or the consonant <u>l</u>, it is -<u>In</u>.

aramak	'search'	aranmak	'be sought'
demek	'say'	denmek	'be said'
okumak	'read'	okunmak	'be read'
çalmak	'strike'	çalınmak	'be struck'
bilmek	'know'	bilinmek	'be known'
vermek	'give'	verilmek	'be given'
kullanmak	'use'	kullanılmak	'be used'
yormak	'tire'	yorulmak	'be tired'
kaybetmek	'lose'	kaybedilmek	'be lost'
tamir etmek	'repair'	tamir edil-mek	'be repaired'

Whenever the passive suffix is -In, it is homophonous with the reflexive suffix -In. For this reason, Turkish can avoid ambiguity by using a double passive, the first suffix -In, the second -Il after the n of -In:

demek	'say'	denmek or denilmek
istemek	'want'	istenmek or istenilmek

The passive suffix precedes all the other verb suffixes that we have seen so far, including: negative; tense, participle, or infinitive; and person.

bekleyen	'(one) who waits'
beklenen	'(one) who is awaited'
bitirdi	'he finished'
bitirildi	'it was finished'
yapmadı	'he did not do'
yapılmadı	'it was not done'
içmez	'he does not drink'
içilmez	'it is not drunk'

2. The passive of transitive verbs

In the case of transitive verbs, the Turkish passive

is very much like that of English: any noun that can be the object of a transitive verb can be the subject of the corresponding passive.

Bu iş akşama kadar bitirilmiyecek	'This job will not be finished until evening'
Dün gece alınan habere göre . . .	'According to the news received last night . . .'
Paket açıldığı zaman, içinde bir şey yoktu	'When the package was opened, there was nothing in it'
Yaşar Kemal, en büyük yeni Türk yazarlarından sayılır	'Yaşar Kemal is considered one of the greatest modern Turkish writers'

The "agent" of a passive sentence is the noun which would be the subject if the sentence were active. Thus, consider the following English sentence:

The window was opened by John

Here the agent is 'John', since it would be the subject of the active sentence:

John opened the window

In Turkish, the agent of a passive sentence is most frequently expressed by tarafından (see Lesson 22).

Pencere Hasan tarafından açıldı	'The window was opened by Hasan'
Halk Partisi, 1923 senesinde Atatürk tarafından kuruldu	'The People's Party was founded by Ataturk in 1923'

The agent in a passive sentence may also be indicated by the use of various adverbs. Adverbs formed from some nouns by the suffix -CE (see Section 5) may be used in passive constructions:

Eski bakanlar hükümetçe affedildi	'The former ministers were pardoned by the government (governmentally)'
Mini elbiselerin yasak edileceği halkça bilinir	'It is known by the people (popularly) that miniskirts will be forbidden'

In addition, adverbs such as resmen 'officially' may be used.

Mini elbise giymek resmen yasak edildi	'Wearing miniskirts was officially forbidden'

Notice sentences such as this one:

Pencere bir taş ile kırıldı	'The window was broken with a stone'

Here the word taş is not the agent, but the instrument, since we can have:

Hasan pencereyi bir taş ile kırdı	'Hasan broke the window with a stone'

The instrument in a passive sentence may be expressed with vasıtasıyle (or vasıtasıyla) 'by means of' from vasıta 'means' or 'instrument'; or with tarafından.

Pencere bir taş vasıtasıyle kırıldı

3. The "impersonal" passive

Another use of the passive is in so-called "impersonal" sentences:

Sigara İçilmez	'No Smoking'
	'One does not smoke'
	'Cigarettes are not smoked'
Şoförle Konuşulmaz	'No Talking with the Driver'
	'One does not talk with the driver'
	'It is not talked with the driver'

In such sentences the agent is left indefinite. If the verb is transitive, the object of the corresponding active sentence is the subject of the passive: Sigara içilmez is the passive of something like Birisi sigara içmez. For transitive verbs, then, the impersonal passive does not differ from the passive constructions that we discussed in Section 2.

For intransitive verbs, which have no object, the impersonal passive has no subject. For example, Sola Sapılmaz 'No Left Turn' means, more literally, "To the left is not turned' or 'One does not turn to the left'. Similarly:

Bu saatte çalışılır mı?	'Does one work at this hour?'
Ankaraya bu yol ile gidilir	'One goes to Ankara by this road'
Ankaraya gidildi	'There was a trip to Ankara (One went to Ankara)'

This construction is used only with the present or definite past tenses.

Remember, from Lesson 7, that there is a class of verbs that are intransitive in Turkish but whose normal English translations are transitive. These are the verbs that are sometimes said to "take the dative" (or the ablative). For example, English 'begin' is transitive: 'We began the lesson'. But Turkish başlamak is intransitive: in Derse başladık, the noun ders is not the object (since it is not in the objective case) but is in an adverbial relation like any other dative. Therefore, ders may not be the subject of the passive verb başlanmak. Instead, Derse başladı 'He began the lesson' is exactly parallel to Sola saptı 'He turned to the left': the only possible passive is an impersonal construction, Derse başlandı 'There was beginning of the lesson', which may be translated 'The lesson was begun' in English.

Similarly:

Hocanın dediklerine pek dikkat edilmedi	'Not much attention was paid to what the teacher said (There was not much attention-paying to . . .)'
Hayvandan çok korkulurdu	'The animal was much feared (There was much fearing of the animal)'

The rule is that a noun may be the subject of a passive verb only if it may be the object of the corresponding active verb. Thus we can have Burada portakal satılır 'Oranges are sold here' with portakal as the subject of satılmak, only because portakal can be the (indefinite) object of satmak in:

Burada birisi portakal satar	'Someone sells oranges here'

4. Transitive and intransitive pairs

Sometimes the passive suffix serves simply to derive intransitive verbs from transitive ones. For example, *yormak* 'tire', *yorulmak* 'be tired' ('of': ablative).

Bu iş beni yordu	'This job tired me'
Bu işten yoruldum	'I got tired of this job'

Similarly, *kırmak* 'break' (transitive), *kırılmak* 'break' (intransitive):

İskemleye oturduğum zaman kırıldı	'When I sat down on the chair, it broke'

In some cases the derived intransitive verbs do not have exactly the same meaning as the active verb from which they come:

atılmak	('be thrown')	'attack' (with dative)
bozulmak	('be spoiled')	'become angry' ('at': dative)
çekilmek	('be pulled')	'withdraw, get out of the way; resign, retire' (with ablative)
sarılmak	('be wrapped')	'embrace' (with dative)

In addition, each of these passives may be used in its literal meaning, 'be thrown', and so forth.

There are pairs of transitive and intransitive verbs that are historically related by means of the passive suffix—for example, *ayırmak* 'put (something) aside', *ayrılmak* 'separate':

Orhan Bey karısından ayrıldı	'Orhan Bey separated from his wife'
Gazeteler geldiği zaman, bir tanesini size ayıracağım	'When the newspapers come, I will put one aside for you'

Similarly, *kurtulmak* 'be saved' obviously resembles

kurtarmak 'save', although in the modern language there is no way we can say one is directly derived from the other.

The passive of compound verbs formed with etmek uses edilmek:

Araba tamir edildi	'The car was repaired'

In addition, there are a number of intransitive compound verbs, formed with olmak, side by side with the transitive verbs with etmek—for example, memnun olmak 'be pleased', memnun etmek 'please'. Similarly, there are the verbs kaybetmek 'lose', kaybolmak 'get lost'. Kaybolmak is much more common than the passive kaybedilmek; as a general rule, use kaybedilmek only when an agent is explicitly expressed.

In the written language, the passive of compound verbs may be made with olunmak as well as edilmek.

5. Derivation: -CE

The suffix -CE serves to make adverbs of various sorts. In this use, it is unaccented: hálkça, iyíce, bénce, İngilizce. Its uses are the following:

A. Added to nouns, it makes adverbs that may serve as agent of a passive construction (see Section 2): hükümetçe, halkça, dünyaca.

More generally, -CE added to nouns means 'like': çocukça 'childishly' or 'like a child'.

Askerce yürüyor	'He walks in a soldierly fashion'
Öğretmence konuşuyor	'He talks like a teacher'
Onunla erkekçe kavga etmen lâzım	'You must fight him like a man'

B. Added to adjectives, it forms adverbs and at the same time tends to intensify the meaning of the adjective:

Doğruca eve geldim	'I came directly home'
Her şeyi iyice bozdunuz	'You spoiled everything thoroughly (well)'
Seninle açıkça konuşurum	'I'll talk openly with you'

Similarly, there are the forms çokça 'in quantity', güzelce 'well'.

C. It may be added to pronouns: bence 'on my part' or 'in my opinion'.

Sizce dedikleri doğru mu?	'In your opinion, are the things he says right?'

D. It may be added to names of nationality to produce names of languages: Türkçe konuşuyor 'He is speaking like a Turk' or 'He is speaking Turkish', Kitap Yunanca yazılmış 'The book is written in Greek (like a Greek)'. These constructions, originally adverbs, have come to be used as nouns and may take noun suffixes:

İngilizcemi biraz unuttum	'I forgot my English a little'
Türkçede böyle bir söz yoktur	'There is no such expression in Turkish'

Notice also nece 'what language':

Nece konuştuklarını bilmiyorum	'I don't know what (language) they are speaking'

Warning: these constructions are names of languages only, not adjectives of nationality. In place of adjectives of nationality, Turkish uses the corresponding noun in a possessive compound: Rum yemeği 'Greek food', bir Türk vapuru 'a Turkish boat'. Compare: bir İngilizce kitap 'an English book (in the English language)' bir İngiliz kitabı 'an English book (published in England)'.

E. It may be added to certain nouns of time or measure, or to numbers:

Buna senelerce çalışıyorum	'I have been working on this for years'
Yüzlerce kitabı var	'He has hundreds of books (books by the hundred)'

6. Usage

Turkish parti has a mixture of the English and French

meanings of the word: (1) political party, (2) social gathering, (3) game, as in Bir parti satranç oynadık 'We played a game of chess'.

Sayılmak 'be counted', the passive of saymak, is extremely common in the sense 'be considered' and may be considered synonymous with sanılmak and zannedilmek, both of which are rare.

Halil tembel sayılır	'Halil is considered lazy'

Because vurmak 'hit' or 'strike' takes the dative, it is an intransitive verb and cannot be made passive (except in the impersonal construction). Vurmak 'shoot' or 'stab' is a transitive verb and may be passivized:

Mustafa bir şoför tarafından vuruldu	'Mustafa was stabbed (shot) by a driver'

Yasak, in addition to its use in the compound verb yasak etmek 'forbid', may also be used as an adjective, 'forbidden':

Buraya girmek yasak	'It is forbidden to enter here'

VOCABULARY

açık		open (adj)
atılmak		be thrown (out); attach (with dat)
ayırmak		set aside
ayrı		separate
ayrılmak		separate (intrans); depart
bozulmak		be ruined; be angry (at: dat)
çekilmek		be pulled; withdraw (with abl)
hâdise	/hādise/	event
halk		people, populace
İngiliz		Englishman

kapalı		closed
kurmak		set up, found, establish
kurtarmak		save
kurtulmak		be saved
olay		event
parti		party
resmen		officially
sapmak		turn
sarmak		wrap
sarılmak		be wrapped; embrace (with dat)
şoför		driver
tamamen	/tamāmen/	completely
tamir	/tāmir/	repair (n)
tamir etmek		repair (v)
vasıtá	/vāsıta/	means, instrument; vehicle; motor vehicle
yasak		forbidden
yasak etmek		forbid
yormak		tire (trans)
yorulmak		tire, be tired (of: abl)

EXERCISES

A. Answer the following questions:

1. Geldiğiniz memlekette, insanlar hangi dili konuşuyor?
2. Türkçe sınıfında sigara içilir mi?
3. Amerika resmen ne zaman kuruldu?
4. Ahmet Türkiyeden ne zaman ayrılacak?
5. Sorulara cevap vermekten yoruldunuz mu?

B. Translate into English:

1. Kedi sevilmek ister.
2. Fatma'nın dertlerini dinlemekten yoruldum.
3. Geçen haftanın olayları sorulacak.
4. İstanbul Üniversitesinin kuruluşu on dokuzuncu asırda oldu.
5. Demokrat Parti, Halk Partisinden ayrılan üç meşhur adam tarafından kuruldu.
6. Devalüasyon meselesi radyoda kısaca konuşulacak.
7. Kediyle köpek ayrı odalara kapandı.
8. Kalemimin kimin tarafından kaybedildiğini bilmek istiyorum.
9. Parti içindeki olaylar, başbakanın çekilmesine sebep oldu.
10. Bakan, halkın meydandan ayrılmasını resmen istedi.

C. Put the following sentences into the passive:

1. Biz sandalyeyi ileri çektik.
2. Şoför arabayı tamir etti.
3. Bir köpek elimi ısırdı.
4. Bir oğlan Halil'e bir mektup gönderdi.
5. Halil, şişenin yarısını içti.
6. Pencereyi kim kırdı?
7. Bütün komşular, partinin sesini duydu.
8. Herkes seni sordu.

The following sentences are made up of two simple sentences each; put both in the passive:

9. Herkes, hükümetin yeni bir şey yapmıyacağını biliyor.
10. Biz, senin arabamızı bozduğunu unutmıyacağız.

D. Translate into Turkish:

1. The stone was thrown outside.

2. The job was begun.
3. The article in the newspaper was not paid attention to.
4. Such an event was feared.
5. These problems were asked about.
5. Yahya Kemal was greatly influenced.
7. The Turks on Cyprus were helped.
8. A new school was founded.
9. The package was brought to Hasan.
10. The pen was put on the table.

E. Translate into Turkish:

1. No Right Turn.
2. In this grocery apples are sold for five kuruş each.
3. Turkish is easily forgotten.
4. This work was written in the thirteenth century by a man whose name is not known.
5. Is this book written in Arabic? —No, it's written in Turkish with Arabic letters.
6. Because the watch was completely broken, Orhan did not try to repair it.
7. The bird was saved from being eaten by the cat.

LESSON 30: THE CAUSATIVE

Study the following sentences:

Bu yemek beni doyurdu; sen doymadın mı?	'This meal filled me up (satisfied me); aren't you satisfied?'
Kadın eti pişiriyor; piştiği zaman yeriz	'The woman is cooking the meat; when it is cooked, we'll eat'
Kış bizim için yavaş geçti; siz kışı nasıl geçirdiniz?	'The winter passed slowly for us; how did you pass the winter?'
Polis Hasana bütün paketlerini açtırdı	'The police made Hasan open all his packages'
Hükümet yeni para bastıracak	'The government will have new money printed'
Kediyi kim çıkardı?	'Who let the cat out?'
Köpeğe kuşları uçurtacağım	'I'll have the dog make the birds fly away'
Harp sırasında gemi batırılmıştı	'The ship was sunk during the war'
Komşular, partiyi gece yarısından sonra devam ettirmiyecekler	'The neighbors will not let the party continue after midnight'

1. The causative verb

A. The most general form of the causative, used when none of the suffixes listed here are called for, is -DIr.

yemek	'eat'	yedirmek	'feed'
ölmek	'die'	öldürmek	'kill'
bilmek	'know'	bildirmek	'announce'
kızmak	'get angry'	kızdırmak	'anger'
sevinmek	'be pleased'	sevindirmek	'please'

B. After stems of more than one syllable, which end in a vowel or in the consonants r or l, the causative is -t.

anlamak	'understand'	anlatmak	'explain'
hatırlamak	'remember'	hatırlatmak	'remind'
okumak	'read, study'	okutmak	'teach'
oturmak	'sit'	oturtmak	'seat, make sit'

C. The causative is -Ir after a certain number of stems. The more common of these are:

batmak	'sink (intrans)'	batırmak	'sink (trans)'
bitmek	'finish (intrans)'	bitirmek	'finish (trans)'
doğmak	'be born'	doğurmak	'bear, give birth to'
doymak	'be satiated'	doyurmak	'satiate'
duymak	'hear'	duyurmak	'make hear'
düşmek	'fall'	düşürmek	'drop'
geçmek	'pass (intrans)'	geçirmek	'pass (trans)'
içmek	'drink'	içirmek	'make drink'
kaçmak	'escape'	kaçırmak	'miss'
pişmek	'cook (intrans)'	pişirmek	'cook (trans)'
uçmak	'fly (intrans)'	uçurmak	'fly (trans)'
yatmak	'lie'	yatırmak	'make lie'

Some of the others which may be encountered are:

aşmak	'pass over'	aşırmak	'make pass over'
taşmak	'overflow'	taşırmak	'make overflow'
göçmek	'die; move'	göçürmek	'kill; make move

Artmak 'increase' or 'be left over' has either artırmak or the more regular arttırmak as causatives.

D. The causative is -*It* after a smaller number of stems. The more common of these are:

akmak	'flow'	akıtmak	'pour'
korkmak	'fear'	korkutmak	'frighten'

Sapmak has the causative *sapıtmak*, but in the colloquial language *saptırmak* is also found. Some of the other stems with this suffix are:

azmak	'go wild'	azıtmak, azdirmak	
sarkmak	'hang (intrans)'	sarkıtmak	'hang (trans)'
sürçmek	'stumble'	sürçütmek	'make stumble'
ürkmek	'fear'	ürkütmek	'frighten'

E. The causative is -*Er* after a few stems. These are:

çıkmak	'come out'	çıkarmak	'bring out'
kopmak	'break off (intrans)'	koparmak	'break off (trans)'

The verb *gidermek* is related to *gitmek* but is used only in the meaning 'get rid of', not in the more general causative meanings of 'make go' or 'let go'. Notice, however, that *göndermek* 'send' is the causative of *gitmek* in the sense 'make go'.

F. Certain verbs have irregular causative forms:

kalkmak	'get up (intrans)'	kaldırmak	'get up (trans)'
gelmek	'come'	getirmek	'bring'

Görmek 'see' corresponds to *göstermek* 'show', but there is also the regular *gördürmek* 'make see'. *Emmek* 'suck' has the causative *emzirmek* 'suckle' but also the regular *emdirmek* 'make suck'.

2. Meanings of the causative

There are two principal meanings of the causative construction: either (1) the subject caused the indicated action to take place, or (2) the subject permitted the action to take place. The first of these meanings is considerably more common. Compare the following sentences:

Hasan öldü	'Hasan died'
Mehmet Hasan'ı öldürdü	'Mehmet killed Hasan (caused Hasan to die)'
Yusuf dişini çekti	'Yusuf pulled his tooth'
Yusuf dişini çektirdi	'Yusuf had his tooth pulled'
Yusuf doktora dişini çektirdi	'Yusuf had the doctor pull his tooth (caused the doctor to pull his tooth)'
Yüzü bana bir atı hatırlatıyor	'His face reminds me of a horse (His face causes me to remember a horse)'

In the second meaning, the subject does not cause but permits the action to take place:

Yusuf treni kaçırdı	'Yusuf missed the train (permitted the train to escape)'
Yusuf bardağı düşürdü	'Yusuf dropped the glass (let the glass fall)'

This meaning is especially common in the negative:

Kuşlar beni uyutmadı	'The birds kept me awake (did not let me sleep)'
Hasan'ın geleceğini bana unutturmamanız lâzım	'You must not let me forget that Hasan is coming'

In many cases a given Turkish causative verb usually corresponds to a particular English idiomatic translation. In such cases, the usual English translation is given in the preceding section: for example, *anlatmak* 'explain', *kaçırmak* 'miss'.

It is important to remember, however, that *akıtmak* does *not* simply mean 'pour'; it is, instead, the causative of *akmak* and may be used in any of the senses of which the causative is capable: sometimes 'pour', sometimes the more literal 'make flow', sometimes 'let flow' Thus *Suyu bardaktan akıttı* could be translated 'He made the water flow out of the glass', 'He let the water flow out of the glass', or 'He poured the water out of the glass', depending on the context (that is, depending on what he did).

Similarly:

Orhan otobüsü kaçırdı	'Orhan missed the bus'
Orhan kuşu kaçırdı	'Orhan let the bird escape'
Orhan kediyi kaçırdı	'Orhan made the cat flee'

3. Grammar of the causative

Causative constructions are made by the addition of a new subject to a basic sentence. This new subject is the person (or thing) that caused or permitted the action described in the basic sentence. Thus, consider the following sentence:

Ahmet Bey, herkesi masaya oturttu	'Ahmet Bey sat everyone down (had everyone sit down) at the table'

This is formed by adding the subject *Ahmet Bey* to the basic sentence:

Herkes masaya oturdu	'Everyone sat down at the table'

Similarly, note this sentence:

Yusuf kasaba eti kestirdi	'Yusuf had the butcher cut the meat'

It is formed by adding the subject *Yusuf* to the basic sentence:

Kasap eti kesti	'The butcher cut the meat'

If the basic sentence is intransitive—that is, if it has no object—then the subject of the basic sentence becomes the object of the causative construction; and is put into the objective case:

Kalkmak - arise

İş bitti	'The job finished'
Hasan işi bitirdi	'Hasan finished the job'
Gemi battı	'The ship sank'
Düşman gemiyi batırdı	'The enemy sank the ship'
Erken kalktım	'I got up early'
Kuşlar beni erken kaldırdı	'The birds got me up early'

These examples show that sometimes the causative suffix serves simply to derive transitive verbs from intransitive ones.

If the basic sentence is transitive and has an object, then the subject of the basic sentence is put into the dative, and the object of the basic sentence remains as the object of the causative:

Bir işçi arabayı tamir etti	'A workman repaired the car'
Ali bir işçiye arabayı tamir ettirdi	'Ali had a workman repair the car'
Talebeler İngilizce okuyorlar	'The students are studying (reading) English'
Öğretmen talebelere İngilizce okutuyor	'The teacher teaches the students English'
Biz Halilin yeni ofisini gördük	'We saw Halil's new office'
Halil bize yeni ofisini gösterdi	'Halil showed us his new office'

Frequently the subject of the basic sentence is simply omitted:

Birisi bir kutu yaptı	'Someone made a box'
Yusuf birisine bir kutu yaptırdı	'Yusuf had someone make a box'
Yusuf bir kutu yaptırdı	'Yusuf had a box made'
Orhan yeni fikirlerini anlattı	'Orhan explained (made someone understand) his new ideas

Polis gazeteyi kapattı	'The police closed (made someone close) the newspaper'

4. Causative and passive

The causative suffix precedes all the other verb suffixes that we have seen so far, including, in particular, the passive. This means that the passive suffix may be added to the causative; in other words, that causative sentences may be made passive.

Hasan öldü	'Hasan died'
Mehmet Hasan'ı öldürdü	'Mehmet killed Hasan'
Hasan, Mehmet tarafından öldürüldü	'Hasan was killed by Mehmet'
Gazete polis tarafından kapatıldı	'The newspaper was closed (was caused to be closed) by the police'
Bardak düşürüldü	'The glass was dropped'

Since the causative suffix cannot follow the passive, passive sentences may not be made causative.

5. Multiple causatives

It is possible to repeat the causative suffix—that is, to make a causative sentence doubly causative. The sentence is treated like any other transitive sentence: its subject is put into the dative, and its object remains as the object of the new sentence. The form of the causative suffix after itself is either -DIr or -t depending on what precedes (see Section 1, A and B).

Mehmet Hasan'ı öldürdü	'Mahmet killed Hasan'
Polis Mehmede Hasanı öldürttü	'The police made Mehmet kill Hasan'
Her sabah gazeteyi bir oğlana getirtir	'Every morning he has a boy bring the newspaper'
Orhana kedileri bahçeye çıkartacağım	'I will have Orhan let the cats out to the garden'

6. Derivation: -CI

The suffix -CI, attached to a noun, forms a noun denoting a person professionally, occupationally, or habitually associated with the indicated object:

denizci	'sailor'
dişçi	'dentist'
dükkâncı	'shopkeeper'
ekmekçi	'baker'
gazeteci	'journalist'
haberci	'reporter'
işçi	'workman'
kahveci	'coffeehouse keeper'
kapıcı	'doorman, concierge'
lokantacı	'restauranteur'
sözcü	'spokesman'
sucu	'water seller'
yardımcı	'assistant'
yolcu	'traveler'

Nouns formed with -CI may denote a person who is a partisan of, or a lover of, the indicated object, after the pattern gerici 'reactionary' from geri 'backward'.

halkçı	'populist, democrat'
kavgacı	'quarrelsome (person)'
sağcı	'rightist'

Similarly, in the colloquial language, içkici 'lover of liquor', güneşçi 'sun lover', and so forth.

The suffix -CI may not be added directly to verbs, but it may be added to nouns formed from verbs with the suffix -(y)I. (This suffix forms, for example, yapı 'activity' from yapmak.) In other words, the combined suffix -(y)ICI is added to verbs:

satıcı	'seller'
dinleyici	'listener, auditor'

geçici	'transitory'
yazıcı	'clerk, scribe'
hastabakıcı	'nurse'
yorucu	'tiresome'

7. Usage

Artmak has two distinct meanings: 'increase', given in most dictionaries, and 'be surplus' or 'be left over':

Biraz çay arttı; onu kim ister?	'There is a little tea left; who wants it?'

Benzetmek, the causative of benzemek 'resemble', is used in the meaning 'see a resemblance' or 'compare'.

Orhan babasına benzer	'Orhan resembles his father'
Orhanı babasına benzettiler	'They compared Orhan with his father (said that he resembled his father)'
Orhan babasına benzetildi	'Orhan was compared with his father (was found similar to his father)'

Benzetmek may also be used literally as 'make resemble', as a statue or a picture.

Çıkarmak has a wide range of meanings, related to 'put out' or 'let out': 'remove', 'expel', 'produce', and so on.

The verbs doğmak and batmak, which normally mean 'be born' and 'sink', mean 'rise' and 'set' when used with words like 'sun' and 'moon'.

The verb yemek 'eat' has two causatives, both normally meaning 'feed'. In one case, the noun that does the eating is placed in the dative, the thing eaten is in the objective; this is a completely regular formation:

Kediye et yedirdim	'I fed meat to the cat (made/let the cat eat meat)'

Otherwise, the thing eaten may be left out, and the thing that does the eating is then put into the objective:

duymak - hear
satmak - sell

Kısım - part
parça - piece

~~öldü~~
ölmek - die
satıcı - salesman

Kediyi yedirdim 'I fed the cat'

This construction, therefore, is formed as though <u>yemek</u> were intransitive.

VOCABULARY

akmak	flow
artmak	increase; be left over
batmak	sink, set (see "Usage")
diş	tooth
doğmak	be born, rise (see "Usage")
doymak	be satisfied, be satiated
düşman	enemy
gemi	ship
kopmak	break off (intrans)
pişmek	cook (intrans)
polis	police, policeman
uçmak	fly
Yusuf	man's name

EXERCISES

A. Answer the following questions:

1. Sokaktaki adam ne satıcısı?
2. Hangi memlekette doğdunuz?
3. Dişlerinizi kime baktırırsınız?
4. Halil bey, gazetesini her gün kime aldırıyor?
5. Orhanı kime benzetiyorsunuz?
6. Abraham Lincoln'un kimin tarafından öldürüldüğünü hatırlıyor musunuz?

B. Translate into English:

1. Evin ön tarafında yeni bir kapı yaptırdık.
2. Parçanın en güzel kısmını kaçırdınız.
3. Hasan, üniversiteye girmek için ismini yazdırdı.

4. Who takes Halil bey's newspaper everyday?

4. Yunan askerlerinin Kıbrıstan çekileceği bildiriliyor.
5. Bizi iki saat beklettiniz, çok kızdırdınız.

C. Make the following sentences causative by adding the new subject given in parentheses. Then translate the result into English.

Example:

Hasan öldü. (Mehmet)

Answer:

Mehmet Hasanı öldürdü 'Mehmet killed Hasan'

1. Kahve şimdi pişiyor. (Fatma)
2. Herkes otobüse bindi. (şoför)
3. Çocuk denizci elbisesi giydi. (biz)
4. Kedi bir kâğıt parçasıyla oynıyordu. (ben)
5. Atatürk, 1881 senesinde doğdu. (annesi)
6. Fatma çok korkmadı. (köpek)
7. Yeni bir mesele çıktı. (müdür)
8. Doktor Mehmedin dişine baktı. (Mehmet)
9. Yarın saat sekizde kalkar mıyım? (siz)
10. Çocuklar binanın içinde koşmadı. (polis)

D. Make the following sentences doubly causative by adding the two new subjects given in parentheses in the indicated order. Drop any occurrence of <u>birisi</u> from the result. Then translate the result into English.

Examples:

Hasan öldü. (Mehmet) (polis)

Yol kapadı. (birisi) (polis)

Answers:

Polis Mehmede Hasanı öldürttü	'The police made Mehmet kill Hasan'
Polis yolu kapattırdı	'The police had the road closed'

1. Her sabah gazete gelir. (birisi) (Halil)

2. Uçak Viyanaya uçtu. (birisi) (Türkiyeden kaçan bakanlar)
3. Şarap şişeden aktı. (Orhan) (ben)
4. Askerleri düşmana doğru yürüdü. (birisi) (Atatürk)
5. Tahtanın bir parçası koptu. (işçi) (Ahmet)

E. Translate into Turkish:

1. Ali dropped a bottle on his foot.
2. They are trying to get the sailors off the sinking ship.
3. The moon will not rise before midnight.
4. Orhan was going to speak at a meeting of leftists last night, but the police, who are all war lovers, did not let him speak.
5. Tomorrow you must certainly get me up at nine o'clock.
6. In the old days they used to make the coachmen sleep with their horses, and the travelers slept upstairs.
7. Ahmet is a receiver of stolen goods.
8. The quantity of water under the house has increased since yesterday.
9. Three people got on the plane and made it fly to Havana.
10. Children born outside the country will henceforth be considered Turkish.
11. It was announced by a government spokesman that children born outside the country will henceforth be considered Turkish.

LESSON 31: THE REFLEXIVE

Study the following sentences:

Ahmet Bey, kendine daha geniş bir daire buldu	'Ahmet Bey found himself a more spacious apartment'
Oraya bugün taşınacak	'He will move there today'
Eşyaları çok ağır olduğu için, kendi taşımıyacak	'Because his things are very heavy, he will not carry them himself'
Hem kendi ailesi, hem de kardeşinin ailesi orada oturacak	'Both his own family and his brother's family will live there'
Kardeşi, Ahmed'in kendine yer bulduğuna sevinmesi lâzım	'His brother should be pleased that Ahmet found a place for himself (Ahmet)'
Kardeşi, Ahmed'in kendisine yer bulduğuna sevinmesi lâzım	'His brother should be pleased that Ahmet found room for him (the brother)'
Biz kendimiz (biz şahsen) öyle bir vaziyeti beğenmezdik	'We ourselves (we personally) would not like such a situation'
Kendi fikirlerimiz biraz başka	'Our own ideas are somewhat different'
Kendinize çok zorluk çıkarıyorsunuz	'You are causing yourself a lot of trouble'
Orhan, fena bir vaziyette bulunuyor	'Orhan is (finds himself) in a bad situation'
Oda, sekiz metre uzunluğunda, üç metre 75 santim genişliğinde	'The room is eight meters in length, three meters 75 centimeters in width'

1. The reflexive pronoun

The reflexive pronoun stem kendi- means 'self'; like the corresponding English pronoun, it refers to the subject of the sentence, and a possessive suffix is attached to indicate the person and number of the subject:

kendim	'myself'
kendin	'yourself'

kendi or kendisi	'himself, herself, itself'
kendimiz	'ourselves'
kendiniz	'yourselves, yourself (polite)'
kendileri	'themselves'

These pronouns may be used in any grammatical position in the sentence:

Kendime yeni bir palto alacağım	'I will buy myself a new coat'
Oğlunuz, kendinizden büyük	'Your son is bigger than you yourself'

There are two third person singular forms, kendisi with the suffix and kendi without it; kendi, however, has a "pronominal n" (see Lesson 9) before any case suffix. The difference between them is that kendi is more strictly reflexive ('himself') than kendisi, which frequently simply reinforces a third person pronoun ('he himself'). In simple sentences, kendi is normally preferred:

Orhan kendine yeni bir palto alacak	'Orhan will buy himself a new coat'
Orhan kendini aynada gördü	'Orhan saw himself in the mirror'
Orhanın oğlu, kendinden daha büyük	'Orhan's son is bigger than (he) himself'
Orhanın oğlu, kendisinden daha büyük	

In subordinate clauses, kendi refers to the subject of the subordinate clause, while kendisi may refer to the subject of the clause or of the main sentence:

Orhan, Mehmedin kendine palto almasına sevindi	'Orhan was pleased that Mehmet bought a coat for himself (Mehmet)'
Orhan, Mehmedin kendisine palto almasına sevindi	'Orhan was pleased that Mehmet bought a coat for himself (Orhan or Mehmet)'

These pronouns may be used as subjects of sentences, meaning 'I myself', 'he himself', and so forth:

Kendisi kâtiptir, amma oğlu bankacı olmak istiyor	'He himself is a clerk, but his son wants to be a banker'
Odayı ben kendim ölçmedim, yardımcı ölçtü	'I didn't measure the room myself; the helper measured it'

The stem may also, although infrequently, be reduplicated: kendi kendi-. The expressions kendi kendine (kendi kendisine), kendi başına, and tek başına all mean 'by oneself'. Remember that the possessive suffix must change if the expression refers to the first or second person:

Bunu kendi kendime yaptım	'I did this by myself'
Çocuk kendi kendine giyinir	'The child gets dressed by himself'

As an adjective, kendi means 'own': kendi kitabım 'my own book'. If the noun phrase containing kendi is not itself the subject of the sentence, kendi must refer to the subject.

Kendi sigaralarımı içiyorum, seninkini değil	'I'm smoking my own cigarettes, not yours'
Kendi sigaralarım öbür odada	'My own cigarettes are in the other room'

2. The reflexive verb

The causative and passive suffixes are "productive": given any verb in the Turkish language, it is possible to make this verb causative or passive. The reflexive suffix, on the other hand, is not productive; there are only a certain number of reflexive verbs, each related in meaning in some way to the corresponding simple verb. The reflexive suffix is -In.

The most readily definable use of the reflexive is to form verbs in which the subject acts upon himself rather than upon some other object (or person). For example, yıkanmak 'wash oneself' is formed from yıkamak 'wash'.

Ahmet yıkandı	'Ahmet washed himself'
Ahmet kendini yıkadı	

Similarly, there are the verbs <u>aranmak</u> 'search oneself', <u>süslenmek</u> 'decorate oneself'.

Other reflexives have a similar meaning:

bulunmak	'be' (literally: 'find oneself'; compare French <u>se trouver</u>)
övünmek	'boast, be proud' (literally: 'praise oneself')
taşınmak	'move (from one living place to another)' (literally: 'carry oneself')

Still other reflexives are related in meaning to the corresponding simple verb in less predictable ways. The verbs listed here, however, are all common:

bakınmak	'look around'	(bakmak 'look')
çekinmek	'be shy'	(çekmek 'pull')
dinlenmek	'rest'	(dinlemek 'listen')
edinmek	'acquire; get for oneself'	(etmek 'do')
geçinmek	'get along'	(geçmek 'pass')
gezinmek	'stroll'	(gezmek 'tour, walk')
giyinmek	'get dressed'	(giymek 'wear')
görünmek	'seem'	(görmek 'see')
sevinmek	'be pleased'	(sevmek 'love')
söylenmek	'talk to oneself'	(söylemek 'speak')

3. Reflexive, causative, and passive

The reflexive suffix precedes all the other verb suffixes that we have seen so far, including in particular the causative and passive. It follows that reflexive verbs may be made causative or passive or both:

Çocuk giyindi	'The child got dressed'
Ben çocuğu giyindirdim	'I caused (enabled) the child to dress'
Çocuk giyindirildi	'The child was dressed (by someone)'
Bu suda yıkanılmaz; çok pistir	'One does not wash in this water; it's too dirty'
Talebelerin dersi öğrenmesi öğretmeni sevindirdi	'The students' learning the lesson pleased the teacher'

Since the causative and passive suffixes follow the reflexive, causative and passive sentences may not be made reflexive.

4. Nominal derivation: -lIk

The suffix *-lIk* (/-lIg/) is added to adjectives to form abstract nouns denoting the indicated quality, as *güzellik* 'beauty' from *güzel*, or denoting persons, things, or actions possessing the indicated quality, as *gençlik* 'youth (young people)' from *genç*. A noun formed in this manner may have both meanings: thus *iyilik* means either 'goodness' or 'good deed'. This suffix may be added to almost any adjective, although some such constructions are more common than others. We give a few examples:

açlık	'hunger'
ağırlık	'weight'
birlik	'unity'
boşluk	'emptiness; void, vacuum'
delilik	'madness, insane action'
genişlik	'width'
hastalık	'sickness'
pislik	'filth'
şimdilik	'at present'
zorluk	'difficulty'

It may also be added to common nouns to form abstract

nouns, for example:

aralık	'interval'
askerlik	'military service'
bakanlık	'ministry' (there are also the older word vekâlet and the hybrid vekillik)
çocukluk	'childishness'
dişçlik	'dentistry'
hocalık	'profession of teaching' (and other nouns denoting profession, such as işçilik, denizcilik)
insanlık	'humanity'
karşılık	'reciprocity; equivalent, something given in exchange'
yolculuk	'travel'

It may also form nouns indicating an object intended for or associated with the noun to which the suffix is attached: thus başlık 'headgear', 'helmet', that is, 'something for the head'. Similarly, there are the following:

gözlük	'eyeglasses'
kitaplık	'library' (there is also the older word kütüphane)
kışlık	as in kışlık elbise 'winter clothes')
önlük	'apron'
sözlük	'dictionary'

Finally, it may be added to numerical expressions or expressions of measure to form adjectives:

Beş saatlik yol	'five hours' journey'
Otuz kilometrelik bir mesafe	'a distance of thirty kilometers'
Beş liralık et	'five liras worth of meat'

Elli kuruşluk pul 'fifty-kurus stamp'

Notice that -*CI* and -*lIk* may be added to each other: *dişçilik* 'dentistry', *milliyetçilik*, 'nationalism' (from *milliyet* 'nationality' via *milliyetçi* 'nationalist') versus *gözlükçü* 'seller of eyeglasses'.

5. Usage

Gezmek with the objective means 'tour', with the locative 'take a walk'. *Gezinmek*, with the locative, means 'stroll', and the causative *gezdirmek* means 'take someone on a tour' or 'show'.

Şehri gezdik	'We toured the city'
Şehirde gezdik	'We walked around the city'
Şehirde gezindik	'We strolled in the city'
Ahmet bize şehri gezdirdi	'Ahmet took us on a tour of the city'

Övünmek 'boast (about)' or 'be proud (of)' takes *ile*:

Ahmet artık yeni vazifesiyle çok övünüyor	'Ahmet boasts too much about his new position'

(The meaning of *artık* here is 'I'm tired of his boasting'.)

VOCABULARY

ağır		heavy
ayna		mirror
durum		situation
gezmek		walk, tour (see "Usage")
kilometre		kilometer
mesafe	/mesāfe/	distance
metre		meter
ölçmek		measure
övmek		praise

palto		coat (overcoat)
pis		dirty, filthy
pul		stamp
santim, santimetre		centimeter
şahsen	/şáhsen/	personally
taşımak		carry
vaziyet		situation
yıkamak		wash

EXERCISES

A. Answer the following questions:

1. Eviniz buraya kaç kilometre mesafede?
2. Bir kilo taş mı daha ağırdır, bir kilo kâğıt mı?
3. Türkiyeye mektup göndermek için kaç kuruşluk pul lâzım?
4. Egzersizleri kendiniz mi yapıyorsunuz, bir başkasına mı yaptırıyorsunuz?
5. Mehmet en son ne zaman yıkandı?

B. Translate into English:

1. Bunu tek başınıza mı yaptınız?
2. İhtiyar kendi kendine konuşuyor.
3. Meydanın genişliği ile uzunluğu aynıdır.
4. Ahmedin çok konuşmasına karşılık, ağzını kapattık.
5. Müdürün bize karşı düşmanlığını anlamıyorum.
6. Kendi vaziyetinizde övünecek bir şey yok.
7. On beş kuruşluk pul istedim, fakat on tane beş kuruşluk pul verdiler.
8. Bankada bin lira bozdurdum: beş tane yüzlük, altı tane ellilik, beş tane yirmilik, beş tane onluk, on tane beşlik verdiler.
9. Ali'nin karısı hep kendisini yalnız hissediyor.
10. Başbakanı gördüğüm zaman, memleketin durumundan memnun olmadığımı kendisine şahsen söyliyeceğim.

birisi - someone yüksek - high

C. Using the verb taşımak, compose one grammatical Turkish sentence illustrating each of the reflexive, causative, and passive forms of this verb, and all possible combinations of these forms, for a total of seven sentences; and translate each sentence into English.

D. Translate into Turkish:

1. The package is five hundred grams in weight.
2. The tree is fifteen meters in height.
3. I need two one-lira stamps.
4. I lost my cigarette case.
5. The coldness that he showed us seems a little strange.
6. Today Fatma got out her summer clothes and put some of them on.
7. In the villages everyone must show his masculinity by killing an animal.
8. He carried the box with ease. (Note: not 'easily')
9. Hasan passed his two years' military service in Ankara.

E. Translate into Turkish:

1. Someone stole my overcoat and left his own overcoat in its place.
2. Someone who breaks a mirror brings seven years' trouble on himself.
3. You talk about Orhan, but you yourself are in the same situation.
4. I personally don't think Hasan measured that distance himself.
5. I don't know who is going on this journey besides myself.
6. Mr. Ekmekçioğlu himself gave us a tour of his new apartment buildings.

hazır (ready to/for)
çarpmak · strike

LESSON 32: THE RECIPROCAL

Study the following sentences:

İki hayvan birbirini parçalamağa hazırlanıyorlar	'The two animals are getting ready to tear each other apart'
Birbirimize her hafta mektup yazarız, tamam mı?	'We'll write each other a letter every week, OK?'
Mehmedin arabası bir otobüse çarptı	'Mehmet's car struck a bus'
Mehmedin arabası bir otobüsle çarpıştı	'Mehmet's car collided with a bus'
Tam evimizin önünde iki araba çarpıştı	'Two cars collided exactly in front of our house'
Partide herkes içki içmiş, gülüyordu	'At the party everyone had drunk (something) and was laughing'
Hasan ile kız arkadaşı bahçede oturmuş, gülüşüyorlardı	'Hasan and his girl friend were seated in the garden and joking together'

1. The reciprocal pronoun

The reciprocal pronoun stem birbiri or biribiri means 'each other'. It refers to the subject of the sentence, which must be plural, and a possessive suffix is attached to indicate the person of the subject:

birbirimiz (biribirimiz)	'each other of us'
birbiriniz (biribiriniz)	'each other of you'
birbiri, birbirleri (biribiri, biribirleri)	'each other of them'

Notice by comparing birbiri and birbirleri that the final -i of this pronoun is a third person possessive suffix; thus it has a pronominal n before any case suffix. These pronouns may be used in any grammatical position in the sentence, except as subject:

Çocuklar birbirine taş attılar	'The children threw stones at each other'
Birbirimize yardım etmemiz lâzım	'We must help each other'
Hepsi birbirinden güzel	'They are all prettier than each other (Each is prettier than the other)'

2. The reciprocal verb

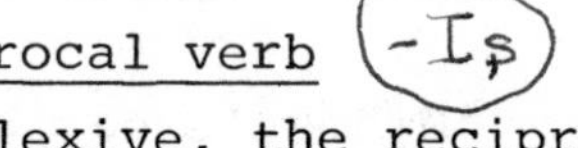

Like the reflexive, the reciprocal suffix is only partially productive; there are a certain number of reciprocal verbs, and while it is possible to make some general statements about the meaning of many of these verbs, there are still many exceptions. The reciprocal suffix is -Iş.

One of the more readily definable uses of the reciprocal is to form verbs in which the (plural) subjects act upon one another. For example, anlaşmak 'reach an understanding' means literally 'understand one another' from anlamak.

Türkler ile Rumlar anlaştılar	'The Turks and the Greeks reached an understanding'
Bunun hakkında anlaşmamız lâzım	'We must reach an agreement about this'

Because a reciprocal verb involves mutual action, the actors must be plural. The subject of a reciprocal verb may be either a plural pronoun or two nouns (or pronouns) joined by ile. If ile comes between the two nouns, then the two together are considered to be the grammatical subjects of the verb, which therefore has a plural personal ending. If ile follows the second noun, then only the first noun is the grammatical subject of the verb, which therefore has a singular personal ending (if the first noun is singular). Study the following examples:

Ayşe ile Hasan anlaştılar	'Ayse and Hasan reached an understanding'
Ayşe, Hasan ile anlaştı	'Ayse reached an understanding with Hasan'

Hasanla ben anlaştık	'Hasan and I made an agreement'
Ben Hasanla anlaştım	'I made an agreement with Hasan'
Hasan benimle anlaştı	'Hasan made an agreement with me'

The addition of the short infinitive to this verb produces the noun <u>anlaşma</u> 'understanding' or 'agreement'. Study the following additional examples:

Türkler ile Rumlar arasında bir anlaşma var	'There is an agreement between the Turks and the Greeks'
Türklerin Rumlar ile bir anlaşması var	'The Turks have an agreement with the Greeks'

Some other reasonably common reciprocal verbs with the meaning 'act on one another' are the following:

çarpışmak	'collide' from <u>çarpmak</u> 'strike'
dövüşmek	'fight' from <u>dövmek</u> 'beat'
sevişmek	'make love' from <u>sevmek</u> 'love'
tanışmak	'be acquainted (with)' from <u>tanımak</u> 'recognize, know'
vuruşmak	'fight' from <u>vurmak</u> 'hit' (this verb is less common than <u>dövüşmek</u>)

Some verbs have the meaning 'act on one another' and are reciprocal in form although, in the modern language, there is no surviving simple verb from which they are derived:

konuşmak	'talk, converse'
mektuplaşmak	'correspond' (compare <u>mektup</u> 'letter', and see Section 4)
sözleşmek	'converse'

Some reciprocal verbs have acquired special meanings:

görüşmek	'have a conference' from görmek 'see'
çekişmek	'argue' from çekmek 'pull'

A second readily definable use of the reciprocal is to form verbs in which the (plural) subjects act separately but with a common goal or purpose—that is, in which a number of separate actions are in some way related. If the subjects act jointly or together, the action is not reciprocal. For example, Kuşlar uçtular means 'The birds flew' and implies that they all flew together in a flock; thus there was, so to speak, only a single action of flying. But Kuşlar uçuştular implies that although each bird flew in a different direction, the actions were related: either they flew toward or away from a common point, or flew for a common reason, or simply flew simultaneously. For example, the following sentence implies that the action was carried on by a single flock of birds:

Kuşlar denize doğru uçuyordu	'The birds were flying toward the sea'

But compare:

Onlara taş attığım zaman kuşlar uçuştu	'When I threw stones at them, the birds flew'
Yere ekmek parçaları attığım zaman kuşlar uçuştu	'When I threw pieces of bread on the ground, the birds flew'

In each case each bird flew separately and in a different direction; but in the first sentence they flew away from a common point, and in the second sentence they flew toward a common point, and furthermore the various acts of flying were related by a common motivation. Similarly, the following sentence means that although each bird went about his own business, the various acts of flying took place simultaneously:

Kuşlar ağaçlarda uçuşuyordu	'The birds were flying about in the trees'

Compare also:

Çocuk ağaçtan düştüğü zaman insanlar koştu	'When the child fell from the tree, the people ran'
Çocuk ağaçtan düştüğü zaman insanlar koşuştu	

In Figure 6, * indicates the point at which the child fell, x indicates the locations of the people prior to the fall, and arrows indicate the directions in which they ran.

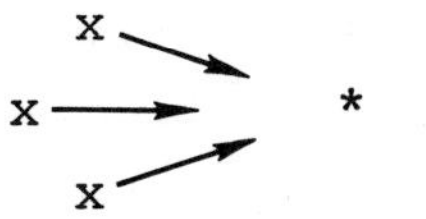

insanlar koştu insanlar koşuştu

Figure 6

It might be convenient to remember *uçuşmak* and *koşuşmak* as 'fly (mutually)' and 'run (mutually)' (not 'together'!). Some of the other common verbs in the meaning 'act mutually' are:

duruşmak	'confront (stand mutually)' from *durmak* 'stand'
gülüşmek	'joke (together)'
kaçışmak	'flee (mutually)'
oynaşmak	'play (mutually)'

Finally, there are some verbs that appear to be formed with the suffix *-Iş*, but there is no particular reason, in the modern language, to analyze them as reciprocals. For example, there is only a faint relationship in meaning between *gelişmek* 'grow up' or 'mature' and *gelmek* 'come' or *dolaşmak* 'wander' and *dolamak* 'wind'

3. Reciprocal and other suffixes

The reciprocal and reflexive suffixes are mutually exclusive; that is, it is not possible to add both at the same time to the same stem. The reciprocal suffix precedes all the other verb suffixes that we have seen so far, including in particular the causative and passive. It follows that reciprocal verbs may be made causative or passive or both:

Polis, şoförleri sokağın ortasında dövüştürmedi	'The police did not let the drivers fight in the middle of the street'
Sokağın ortasında dövüşülür mü?	'Does one have a fistfight in the middle of the street?'

Tanışmak behaves somewhat strangely in these constructions. Its causative is *tanıştırmak* 'introduce', and regular causative and passive constructions are possible:

Hasan beni Ahmetle tanıştırdı	'Hasan introduced me to Ahmet'
Ben Ahmetle tanıştırıldım	'I was introduced to Ahmet'

But more common are constructions in which the "object" (person to whom one is introduced) is marked not by *ile* but by the dative:

Hasan beni Ahmede tanıştırdı

Ben Ahmede tanıştırıldım

Since the causative and passive suffixes follow the reciprocal, causative and passive sentences may not be made reciprocal.

4. Derivation: *-lE*

The suffix *-lE*, alone or in combination with other suffixes, makes verbs from nouns and adjectives. There are a very large number of verbs formed with this suffix. Some examples are:

bağlamak	'tie' (*bağ* 'bond')
ellemek	'handle, touch'
gecelemek	'spend the night'
hatırlamak	'remember' (compare *hatır* 'memory')
hazırlamak	'prepare'

ilerlemek 'advance'
işlemek 'operate, work' (of a machine)
karşılamak 'meet'
kurulamak 'dry' (*kuru* 'dry')
parçalamak 'break into pieces'
sulamak 'water'
tamamlamak 'complete' (*tamam* 'complete')
temizlemek 'clean'
yenilemek 'renew'
yollamak 'send'

The suffix -*lE* may also be combined with the reflexive -*In*, which, however, has no reflexive meaning here and simply serves as an extension of the suffix. Most verbs formed with -*lEn* involve the meaning 'become'. While most verbs formed with -*lE* are transitive, those with -*lEn* are all intransitive:

canlanmak 'come to life, become cheerful' (*can* 'soul, life')
evlenmek 'marry' (*ev* 'house')
hastalanmak 'become sick'
seslenmek 'make a noise'

Verbs in -*lE* can also have regular passives and reflexives, formed with the suffix -*In*: *hazırlanmak* 'prepare oneself', *yollanmak* 'be sent'.

The suffix -*lE* may also be combined with the reciprocal -*Iş*, which, however, has no reciprocal meaning here and simply serves to form a combined suffix -*lEş*. Unlike -*lE* and -*lEn*, which are used only in certain verbs, -*lEş* is fully productive: it may be added freely to nouns and adjectives to form verbs meaning 'become' the indicated object or attribute:

birleşmek 'unite'
güzelleşmek 'become beautiful'
iyileşmek 'improve, get better, become well'

Türkleşmek	'be Turkicized, become a Turk'
yerleşmek	'settle down'
uzaklaşmak	'become far, go away'
yaklaşmak	'approach' (from the same stem as yakın 'near')

All verbs formed with this suffix are intransitive; the corresponding transitive verbs are made by adding the causative:

birleştirmek	'unify'
güzelleştirmek	'beautify'
Türkleştirmek	'Turkicize'
yerleştirmek	'settle (trans); cause to settle'

5. Usage

Most verbs formed with -lE are transitive. Two exceptions among the verbs given in this lesson are ilerlemek and işlemek, which are intransitive but can be made transitive with the causative suffix.

Telefonumuz sabahtan beri işlemiyor	'Our telephone hasn't been working since morning'
Bu çeşit arabayı işletmesini biliyor musun?	'Do you know how to operate this kind of car?'

Can 'soul' or 'life' is used in a large number of idiomatic and metaphorical expressions, such as (birisinin) canını kurtarmak 'to save (someone's) life', canım 'my dear', canım istemez 'I don't want (it)', literally 'my soul does not want it'.

Çarpmak 'strike' takes the dative.

Dolaşmak 'wander' may be transitive or intransitive.

Şehri dolaştım	'I wandered the city'
Şehirde dolaştım	'I wandered in the city'

In addition to 'have a conference', görüşmek has a

a number of related meanings: 'meet', 'discuss', 'have relations', or simply 'see one another'.

In addition to gecelemek 'spend the night', there are kışlamak 'spend the winter' and yazlamak 'spend the summer', both intransitive.

Karşılamak means 'meet intentionally', while the reciprocal karşılaşmak means 'meet unintentionally' or 'run into':

Hasan beni istasyonda karşıladı	'Hasan met me at the station'
Sokakta Hasanla karşılaştım	'On the street I met Hasan'

Tamam 'complete' is one of the most common words in Turkish, since it is the expression corresponding to English 'OK'.

VOCABULARY

bağ		tie, bond
can		soul, life
çarpmak		strike
dolaşmak		wander
dövmek		beat
gelişmek		develop
kuru		dry
tamam	/tamām/	complete
tanımak		recognize, know
yaklaşmak (dat)		approach

EXERCISES

A. Answer the following questions:

1. Ahmet karısıyla haftada kaç kere dövüşüyor?
2. Türkiyede kimlerle tanışıyorsunuz?
3. Mustafa ile kız arkadaşı birbirine ne verdi?
4. Gelişmiş memleketlerden hangilerine seyahat ettiniz?
5. Kitabın sonuna yaklaştığımıza göre, senenin sonuna da mı yaklaşıyoruz?

B. Translate into English:

1. Şoförle Konuşulmaz.
2. Mehmedin kızının beş sene içinde ne kadar geliştiğini bilmiyordum.
3. Orhan radyoyu işletmeği denedi, fakat nasıl işlediğini hatırlamadı.
4. Köpek, hiç kimseyi eve yaklaştırmıyor.
5. Mehmet bey, ihtiyarlığında çocuklaşıyor.
6. Tayyare göründüğü zaman sokaktakiler her tarafa kaçıştı.
7. Partiyi canlandırmak için Attila'yı getirdik.
8. Bay Bozkurt, Bebek'te yeni bir otel açmak için hazırlıklarını tamamlıyor.
9. Hayat zorlaşıyor.

C. Using the verb <u>sevmek</u>, compose one grammatical Turkish sentence illustrating each of the reflexive, reciprocal, causative, and passive forms of this verb, and each of all possible combinations of these forms, for a total of eleven sentences; and translate each sentence into English.

D. Translate into Turkish:

1. The dogs sat down opposite each other.
2. The two brothers did not recognize each other.
3. The girls were holding each other by the hand.
4. The boys were running about in the garden and playing together.
5. Two buses collided in the square.
6. Why are those men fighting in the middle of the street?
7. Orhan's wife has been sick for weeks, and she is getting worse.
8. Halil had his room cleaned.
9. At the conference among the teachers, a new agreement was completed.

10. Hasan has been exchanging letters with Fatma for two years

11. Mehmet was tired at first, but when he had some drinks, he came to life.

12. Attila has wandered the whole world.

LESSON 33: ADVERBIAL CONSTRUCTIONS AND SUFFIXES

Study the following sentences:

Erkekler köyden İstanbula gelip amele olarak çalışır, sonra köylerine dönüp toprak alır	'Men come from the villages to Istanbul and work as laborers; then they return to their villages and buy land'
Halilin üniversiteden atılıp başka bir yere gittiğini sandım	'I thought Halil was thrown out of the university and went somewhere else'
Padişah, büyük bir ordu toplayarak, İstanbul üzerine yürüdü	'The Sultan, gathering a large army, marched on Constantinople'
Köpeği bir eliyle tutarak, öbürüyle ona üç kere vurdu	'Holding the dog with one hand, he hit it three times with the other'
Dost olarak mı geliyorsunuz, düşman olarak mı?	'Do you come as a friend or an enemy?'
Aşağıya baka baka başım dönmeye başladı	'Looking (protractedly) downward, my head began to turn'
Buraya alışınca seveceksin	'You'll like this place as soon as you get used to it'
Güneş batınca eve dönmeniz lâzım	'As soon as the sun goes down, you must return home'
Tren kalkıncaya kadar istasyonda bekledik	'We waited at the station until the train left'
Mustafa doğdu doğalı hiç köyünden çıkmamış	'Since Mustafa was born, he has never gone out of his village'

1. Adverbial constructions

Adverbial constructions are devices by which one sentence or verb phrase may be subordinated to another. Thus consider these English examples:

When he comes, I will go

As soon as he comes, I will go

Because he came, I will go

Here the subordinated sentence ('he comes' or 'he came'), with the addition of a subordinating conjunction, functions as an adverb within the main sentence ('I will go').

In Turkish, this subordination is accomplished by adverbial suffixes. For example, take these two sentences:

Ankaraya gideceğim	'I will go to Ankara'
Ankaradan döneceğim	'I will return from Ankara'

They may be combined in the following manner:

Ankaraya gidip döneceğim	'I will go to Ankara and return'

The main verb of this sentence is döneceğim; gideceğim has been replaced by gidip, where the auxiliary -im has been dropped, and the adverbial suffix -ip has replaced the tense suffix of the subordinated verb. A similar example follows:

Orhan gelince yemeğe başlarız	'As soon as Orhan comes, we'll start eating'

Here the adverbial expression is Orhan gelince, with the adverbial suffix -ince occupying the position of tense. Notice that although the subject of the subordinated sentence, Orhan, is expressed, there is no personal ending; adverbial suffixes are never followed by personal endings or by any of the suffixes that can be in the auxiliary.

Adverbial suffixes, like participles and verbal nouns are strictly verbal suffixes and may be attached only to verb stems. If the subordinated sentence is basically nonverbal, ol- must be supplied for the suffix:

Ahmet mühendis olarak çalışacak	'Ahmet will work as an engineer (Ahmet will work being an engineer)'

Remember that because adverbial constructions are subordinated sentences, they have exactly the same word order as simple sentences:

Köpek kuşu ağzında tuttu	'The dog held the bird in his mouth'
Köpek, kuşu ağzında tutarak sahibine götürdü	'Holding the bird in his mouth, the dog took it to his master'

2. Adverbial suffixes

A. -(y)Ip

This suffix has little meaning of its own; essentially the tense and person suffixes of the main verb, whatever they are, apply also to the subordinated verb. Thus consider the following sentence:

Bu akşam kitap okuyup dinlenecektim	'This evening I was going to read a book and rest'

This is equivalent to:

Bu akşam kitap okuyacaktım

Bu akşam dinlenecektim

The two actions are either performed simultaneously, as in the preceding example, or, more frequently, performed in sequence:

Gidip bize sigara alır mısın?	'Will you go and buy us cigarettes?'

Notice that the subject of a verb with -(y)Ip must be the same as that of the main verb.

In practice, the use of -(y)Ip is the standard method of compounding verb phrases. Thus, although the two sentences that follow are equivalent, the first would be much more common:

Mehmet gelip gitti	'Mehmet came and went'
Mehmet geldi ve gitti	

B. -(y)ErEk

This suffix and the next both normally correspond to English '-ing'. It is used for a single action, or one that is described as a single action, which takes place at the same time as the main verb or immediately preceding.

Kapıya vurarak onlara açtırdı	'Pounding on the door, he made them open (it)'
Yunanistandan geçerek Istanbula geldik	'Passing through Greece, we came to Istanbul'
Ahmedi istasyonda karşılıyarak eve getirdik	'Meeting Ahmet at the station, we brought him home'
Bilmiyerek kediyi dışarı kaçırdım	'Not knowing (unknowingly), I let the cat escape outside'

This suffix is frequently used to indicate the manner in which the action of the main verb is performed:

Küçük küş ağaçtan düşerek öldü	'The little bird died falling from a tree'
Bütün gün çalışarak işi bitirdiler	'Working all day, they finished the job'

The work olarak deserves special attention because of its high frequency and the necessity of idiomatic constructions to translate it into English. It is normally used with nouns and is best translated 'as'; but it may also be used to emphasize adverbs:

Yusuf askerliğini öğretmen olarak geçirecek	'Yusuf will pass his military service as a teacher'
Masa olarak büyük bir kutu kullandık	'As a table, we used a big box'
Buraya üçüncü defa olarak geliyorum	'I am coming (have come) here for the third time (it being the third time)'
İsmini tam olarak bilmiyorum	'I don't know his name exactly'

C. -(y)E

Although this suffix also corresponds to English '-ing' it differs from -(y)ErEk in a number of ways. The most important of these is that -(y)E emphasizes the repeated or continuous nature of the action. For example:

Kapıya vura vura onlara açtırdı — 'Pounding (repeatedly, or for a long time) on the door, he made them open (it)'

In addition, -(y)E constructions indicate the manner in which the action of the main verb is performed. In the modern language, verbs with this suffix must always be reduplicated.

Koşa koşa içeri geldi — 'He came running inside'

Birbirimize yardım ede ede işi bitirdik — 'Helping each other, we finished the job'

Because -(y)E constructions indicate the manner of an action, and because they are normally short, they are frequently most elegantly translated into English with a single adverb:

Düşüne düşüne oturuyordu — 'He was sitting thoughtfully (in thought)'

Similar examples are seve seve 'gladly', çekine çekine 'shyly', The standard Turkish expression of farewell, güle güle, is presumably a reduction of something like güle güle gidiniz 'go laughingly'.

D. -(y)IncE

This suffix means 'as soon as', or, with less urgency, 'when'. The subject of a -(y)IncE construction need not be the same as the subject of the main verb.

Çocuk doktoru görünce hemen ağlamağa başladı — 'As soon as the child saw the doctor, he at once began to cry'

Sayfayı çevirince acaip bir resim gördü — 'When he turned the page, he saw a strange picture'

Sultan Mehmet ölünce oğlu II. Bayezit padişah oldu — 'When Sultan Mehmet died, his son Bayezit II became sultan'

The suffix -(y)IncE with the dative suffix and followed by kadar means 'until':

Hasan gelinceye kadar burada bekleriz — 'We'll wait here until Hasan comes'

ondan - therefore

In the colloquial language, however, 'until' is normally expressed, not by -(y)IncE, but by the participle -(y)En with the dative suffix and followed by kadar:

Hasan gelene kadar burada bekleriz	
Bunu yapana kadar ne kadar olacak?	'How much (long) will it be until you do (or he does) this?'

E. -(y)ElI

This suffix means 'since'; it is considerably less common than the others, since there are more common ways of saying 'since' (with beri).

Biz geleli üç hafta oldu	'It has been three weeks since we came'
Harp başlıyalı Orhan'dan haber almadık	'We have not had news from Orhan since the war begun'

There are a number of variants of this construction; in addition to Orhan gideli 'since Orhan went' we can have:

Orhan gitti gideli

Orhan gideliden beri

Orhan gideli beri

Orhan gitti gideli ondan haber almadık	'Since Orhan left, we have not had news from him'

3. Variation in stems: glottal stops

Some words borrowed into Turkish from Arabic end in a vowel in Turkish but end with a glottal stop or ain in Arabic. These include cami 'mosque', mevzu 'topic', and others. Especially in the usage of learned speakers these words are sometimes treated as though they ended in a consonant; that is, they take postconsonantal, rather than postvocalic, variants of suffixes. Thus 'his mosque' may be camii or camisi; the latter is increasingly common.

In transcriptions, we shall mark these words with a final apostrophe: /cāmi'/, /mevzū'/.

Other originally Arabic words, like sanat 'art' or Kuran 'Koran', had a glottal stop or ain after the middle consonant: /san'at/, /kur'an/. While the glottal stop is not pronounced in these words, it may affect the syllable structure: [san-at] instead of the normal [sa-nat]. This too is found more in the pronunciation of learned speakers. The words may also be written with an apostrophe in place of the glottal stop: san'at, Kur'an, sun'î 'artificial'.

4. Usage

Götürmek means 'take' in the sense 'carry something to a place'.

Padişah is the ordinary noun for 'sultan'. Sultan (or padişah) may be used preceding the name as a title: II Sultan Mehmet 'Sultan Mehmet II'. Sultan may also be used as a title following the name of a close female relative of the sultan: Ayşe Sultan is the sultan's wife or daughter. We shall not go further into the complexities of Ottoman titles.

Sahip primarily means 'owner' in the modern language (or 'master' of an animal), but it may turn up in expressions meaning 'possessor' (of an abstract quality) or 'protector'.

Toplamak means 'collect' or 'gather'; 'gather up', 'gather together'; also 'tidy up' in reference to a room or house.

Toprak has two basic meanings: (1) 'land' or 'territory'; (2) 'earth' or 'ground', 'dirt'.

VOCABULARY

amele		workman
cami	/cāmi'/	mosque
çevirmek		turn over (trans)
götürmek		take (see "Usage")
mevzu	/mevzū'/	topic
mühendis		engineer
ordu		army
padişah	/pādişah/	sultan (see "Usage")
sahip	/sāhib/	owner (see "Usage")

sanat	/san'at/	art
sultan		sultan (title)
toplamak		gather, collect (see "Usage")
toprak		land, earth

EXERCISES

A. Answer the following questions:

1. Hayatınızda hiç cami gördünüz mü?
2. Ahmet, Mehmed'i görünce ne yaptı?
3. Yazı masası olarak ne kullanacaksınız?
4. Fatma, o sandalyede oturup ne düşünüyor?
5. Sene başlıyalı Mustafa kaç ders kaçırdı?

B. Translate into English:

1. Halilin Ankaraya gidip dönmiyeceğini sandım.
2. Çocuk, eşyalarını toplayana kadar odasında kalacak.
3. Padişah, hazırlıklarını tamamlayarak harbe girdi.
4. En sonunda Ahmet mühendis olarak iş buldu.
5. Bunu bitirene kadar sabah olur.
6. Haberi işitince, Orhan odasına gidip kapıyı kapadı.
7. Bunu sana son defa olarak söylüyorum.
8. Güneş batıncaya kadar tepede oturup manzaraya baktık.
9. Sayfaları çevire çevire kendi resmini arıyor.
10. Sen bu mektubu Ahmede götürünce, onun sana cevap vermesi lâzım.
11. Bozkurtlar İzmire taşınalı onlarla pek görüşmüyoruz

C. Combine the following sentences by making the first sentence in each pair into an adverbial construction using the indicated suffix. Delete any repeated noun from the result.

Example:

Mustafa köye gidecek — Mustafa toprak alacak (-(y)Ip)

Answer:

Mustafa köye gidip toprak alacak

1. Mühendis amele tuttu — Mühendis işe başladı. (-(y)ErEk)
2. Çocuk pencereye vurdu — Çocuk pencereyi kırdı. (-(y)E)
3. Turistler camiye girdi — Turistler etrafa bakmağa başladı. (-(y)IncE)
4. Kapıyı açar mısın? — Kediyi içeri getirir misin? (-(y)Ip)
5. Hasan İstanbula geldi — Hasan hiç bir şey yapmamış. (-(y)ElI)
6. Bütün şehri dolaşıyoruz — Ev arıyoruz. (-(y)E)
7. Kalkmamız lâzım — Çalışmamız lâzım. (-(y)Ip)
8. Halil gülüyordu — Halil odaya girdi. (-(y)ErEk)
9. Fatma otobüse bindi — Fatma şehre indi. (-(y)Ip)
10. Gazeteciler bu mevzu hakkında sordu — Vekil odadan çıktı. (-(y)IncE)

D. Translate into Turkish:

1. Who will go to the grocery and buy fruit?
2. Mehmet Bey will not change his mind until he dies.
3. I got tired walking all day.
4. Orhan entered the room smiling.
5. How long has it been since Ali returned?
6. Meeting us at the door in friendly fashion, he took us inside.
7. As soon as Hasan finds the owner of that car, he will telephone us.
8. The workmen, collecting big stones, made a wall around the garden.
9. As soon as the sultan's army was seen, the enemy fled in every direction.
10. The director turned over the paper and wrote something on the back of it.

11. Until the new building is completed, Orhan Bey will use his house as an office.
12. I will take my radio to the shop and have it repaired.

LESSON 34: COMPOUND ADVERBIAL CONSTRUCTIONS

Study the following sentences:

Kar yağdıkça etraf beyazlaşıyor	'As the snow falls, the surroundings become white'
Halil komşularla karşılaştıkça kavga eder	'Whenever Halil meets with the neighbors, he has a fight'
İşlerimi bitirmedikçe burada kalmam lâzım	'As long as I have not finished my work, I must stay here'
Hükümetin durumu gittikçe fenalaşıyor	'The situatıon of the government is gradually getting worse'
Bu meseleyi fark ettikten sonra, onunla devamlı meşgul olmağa başladık	'After noticing this problem, we began to be constantly occupied with it'
Üniversiteden eve gelmeden evvel, Mustafa saçını kestirdi	'Before coming home from the university, Mustafa had his hair cut'
Trenler durmadan Bursadan geçiyor	'The trains pass through Bursa without stopping'
Hazırlanmamıza vakit bırakmadan hepimizi arabasına bindirdi	'Without leaving time for us to get ready, he made us all get into his car'
Vapur kalkar kalkmaz, Hasan hastalanmağa başladı	'As soon as the steamship departed, Hasan began to get sick'

1. Compound adverbial suffixes

There are several adverbial suffixes that behave very much like those introduced in the last lesson but that are not single units; rather they are combinations of other suffixes, most of which are already familiar.

A. -DIkçE
This is a combination of the nominal -DIg and the adverbial -CE (Lesson 29). Remember that -CE is unaccented; thus the combination is accented on the first syllable: -DÍkçE.

yaklaşmak - approach yorulmak - tire
yürülmek - walk, march

-DIkçE

When it describes a noncontinuous but repeated action, it means 'whenever':

Memleketini düşündükçe ağlar	'Whenever he thinks of his country, he weeps'
Eve geldikçe bir şey getirir	'Whenever he comes to the house, he brings something'

The suffix is more frequently, however, used to describe a continuous action; then it means 'as' or 'as long as':

Eve yaklaştıkça etrafı güzelleşir	'As one approaches the house, its surroundings become more attractive'
Eseri okudukça daha az beğeniyorum	'The more I read the work, the less I like it (As I read the work, I like it less)'
Yürüdükçe yoruluyordum	'As I walked, I became tired'
Çocuk büyüdükçe yeni şeyler öğreniyor	'As the child grows, he learns new things'
Öğrenciler çalışmadıkça hiç bir şey öğrenmiyecek	'As long as the students don't work, they won't learn anything'

Notice the expressions gittikçe 'gradually', literally 'as one goes' (also gitgide), and oldukça 'somewhat, rather, fairly'.

B. -DIktEn (sonra) "after"

We saw in earlier lessons that verbal noun and nominalization constructions may be used with postpositions—for example, with sonra:

Halil'in gelmesinden iki hafta sonra hastalandı	'Two weeks after Halil's coming, he got sick'
Halil geldiğinden iki hafta sonra hastalandı	'Two weeks after Halil came, he got sick'

In the case of a nominalization, the possessive suffix is usually dropped, and the ablative case is added directly to -DIg. The possessive must be dropped if there is no expression of time before sonra, that is, if sonra follows the sequence -DIktEn directly:

Halil geldikten iki hafta sonra hastalandı

Halil geldikten sonra hastalandı

The following examples are similar:

Ateşi yaktıktan sonra, üstüne eti koydu	'After lighting the fire, he put the meat on it'
Yağmur durduktan sonra dışarı çıktık	'After the rain stopped, we went outside'

C. -mEdEn 'without'
The last part of this suffix looks like the ablative; because the ablative is added to nouns, the -mE preceding ought to be a verbal noun. But this suffix is unaccented, so that we get the stress pattern characteristic of the negative:

dúrmadan	'without stopping'

Examples follow:

Arkaya bakmadan devam etti	'He proceeded without looking back'
Evde birisi olmadan evden çıkmak istemiyorum	'I don't want to leave the house without someone being at home'

Perhaps the most common construction with this sequence is durmadan, 'without stopping, constantly, ceaselessly':

Yağmur durmadan yağıyordu	'It was raining continuously'
Mektupları durmadan geliyor	'His letters keep coming (come without stopping)'

When -mEdEn is used with the postpositions evvel and önce it means 'before'. While sonra is normally used with the nominalization -DIg, evvel and önce are normally used with the verbal noun -mE. If there is an expression of time between the verbal noun construction and the postposition, the genitive and possessive suffixes within the verbal noun construction are optionally dropped:

Halil'in gelmesinden iki hafta önce ondan bir mektup aldık	'Two weeks before Halil came, we got a letter from him'
Halil gelmeden iki hafta önce ondan bir mektup aldık	

If there is no time expression, that is, if evvel or önce follow the verbal noun directly, the genitive and possessive are usually, but not necessarily, omitted. Thus the first of these two examples would be much more common:

Halil gelmeden evvel ondan bir mektup aldık

Halil'in gelmesinden evvel ondan bir mektup aldık

The following sentences also illustrate this usage:

Gitmeden evvel Hasan'a haber vermemiz lâzım	'Before we go (before going), we must inform Hasan'
Ankaradan gitmeden evvel başbakanla görüşmek istiyordu	'Before leaving Ankara, he wanted to have an interview with the prime minister'

Evvel or önce may sometimes simply be dropped from this construction, giving what appears to be a suffix -mEdEn 'before', when there is no danger of confusion with -mEdEn 'without':

Gitmeden Hasan'a haber vermemiz lâzım	'Before going we must inform Hasan'
Güneş doğmadan kalktı	'He got up before sunrise'

D. -mEksIzIn 'without'
This suffix, which we will not attempt to analyze here, is somewhat rare, since -mEdEn is normally used in the meaning 'without'.

E. -Ir-mEz
This "suffix" is, in fact, the juxtaposition of the positive and negative present tense forms of the verb.

hep - always

It means 'as soon as' and differs from -(y)IncE in the previous lesson in that -(y)IncE may also mean 'when', while -Ir-mEz always indicates that the action of the main verb follow immediately upon the action of the adverbial. In the colloquial language, -Ir-mEz is somewhat more common than -(y)IncE.

Hasan gelir gelmez, hep beraber çıktık	'As soon as Hasan came, we all left together'
Ev biter bitmez içine taşınacağız	'As soon as the house is finished, we will move in'

2. Nominal derivation: -lI and -sIz

The suffix -lI is added to nouns to form adjectives meaning 'having' or 'with' the indicated property. Some examples:

akıllı	'intelligent'
ateşli	'fiery'
atlı	'having a horse' (atlı araba 'horse-drawn cart')
dikkatli	'attentive, careful'
etraflı	'detailed (considering all sides)'
evli	'married' (compare evlenmek 'marry')
farklı	'different'
hızlı	'fast'
kuvvetli	'strong'
renkli	'colored, colorful'
resimli	'illustrated'
yağmurlu	'rainy'
yaşlı	'old'
yazılı	'written, in writing'

Although many of the preceding examples have idiomatic meanings, constructions with -lI are normally quite literal in meaning. They may be formed freely not only from nouns but also from short noun phrases, such as sequences of number and noun, or adjective and noun:

Şu beyaz şapkalı adam kim?	'Who is that man in the white hat?'
Bahçeli bir ev bulduk	'We found a house with a garden'
İki yataklı bir oda var mı?	'Is there a room with two beds?'
Ne istediğim mektupta yazılı	'What I want is written in the letter'

Notice also uzun boylu 'tall' ('having a long stature') and kısa boylu 'short'.

The suffix -lI is added to names of places to form nouns indicating 'inhabitant of' the place: köylü 'villager' or 'peasant', yerli 'native', Amerikalı 'American', Londralı 'Londoner', İstanbullu, Ankaralı, İzmirli. Notice also Nerelisiniz? 'Where do you come from?'

When -lI is added to a possessive compound, the possessive suffix is dropped: kahve renkli 'brown', literally 'coffee-colored'; compare kahve rengi 'coffee color'.

The suffix -sIz is the opposite of -lI; it is added to nouns to form adjectives meaning 'without' the indicated property.

akılsız	'foolish, unintelligent'
dikkatsiz	'inattentive'
haksız	'unjust, wrong'
manasız	'meaningless'
renksiz	'colorless'
sonsuz	'endless, endlessly'
susuz	'dry, arid; thirsty'

Constructions with -sIz are normally quite literal in meaning and may be formed freely:

Arabasız nasıl oraya gideceğim?	'How will I go there without a car?'

Şurası havasız	'This place is airless (The air here is stuffy)'
Ev geniş, ama bahçesiz	'The house is spacious, but without a garden'
Parasız kaldım	'I ended up without money'
Fatma ile kocası kavgasız iki hafta geçirmiş	'Fatma and her husband have spent two weeks without a quarrel'

The suffixes -lI and -sIz may be added to nouns formed with -lIk, and -lIk may be added to adjectives formed with -lI and -sIz to form abstract nouns:

yağmurluklu	'having a raincoat'
gözlüksüz	'lacking eyeglasses'
akıllılık	'intelligence'
haksızlık	'injustice'
evlilik	'marriage'

3. Usage

Ateş is a small fire or fire from a weapon; a large fire, such as the kind that burns down a house, is yangın. Some verbs are used idiomatically with ateş:

Ateşi yaktı	'He lit the fire' (also ışığı yaktı or açtı 'he turned on the light')
Polis ateş açtı	'The police opened fire'
Polis ateş kesti	'The police ceased fire'

Ateş also means 'fever' or 'temperature':

Çocuğun 38 ateşi var	'The child has a fever of 38'
Çocuğun ateşini ölçtün mü?	'Did you take the child's temperature?'

The postpositional construction boyunca means 'along' with reference to space, 'throughout' or 'during the course of' with reference to time:

Yol boyunca yürüdük	'We walked along the road'
14cü asır boyunca padişahlar durmadan Bizanslılarla harp ediyordu	'Throughout the fourteenth century the sultans were constantly waging war with the Byzantines'

Fark means 'difference':

Bunların arasındaki farkı görmüyor musunuz?	'Don't you see the difference between these?'

Fark etmek means (1) 'make a difference'; (2) 'perceive' or 'notice'. There are also the idioms farkında olmak 'be aware of' or 'notice' and farkına varmak 'realize'.

Ahmedin burada olduğunu fark etmemiştim	'I hadn't noticed that Ahmet was here'
Ahmedin burada olduğunun farkında olmamıştım	

Many languages have some sort of idiomatic expression for weather, like English 'It is raining' or 'It is snowing' (what is 'it'?). In Turkish, the verb yağmak, meaning something like 'precipitate', is used with the subjects yağmur 'rain', kar 'snow', dolu 'hail', and kırağı 'frost':

Yağmur yağıyor	'It is raining' or 'Rain is falling'
Kar yağıyor	'It is snowing' or 'Snow is falling'

VOCABULARY

akıl	/akl/	mind, intelligence
ateş		fire (see "Usage")
boy		stature, height
büyümek		grow
fark		difference (see "Usage")
hız		speed

kar		snow
kuvvet		strength, force
renk	/reng/	color
saç		hair
yağmak		see "Usage"
yağmur		rain
yakmak		burn (trans)
yaş		age

EXERCISES

A. Answer the following questions:

1. Nerelisiniz?
2. Mustafa ile Orhan arasındaki kavgada sence kim haklı?
3. Derse gelmeden evvel ne yapıyordunuz?
4. Türkçeyi öğrendikten sonra ne yapacaksınız?
5. Titanik battıktan sonra kimse kurtarıldı mı?

B. Translate into English:

1. Seneler geçtikçe ihtiyarlıyoruz.
2. Tren hızlandıkça bazı yolcular korkmağa başladı.
3. Halil kızar kızmaz yüzünün rengi değişti.
4. Mozart, otuz yaşına gelmeden önce, birçok büyük eserler yazmıştı.
5. Bunun üzerine iki ay durup dinlenmeden çalıştım.
6. Nereye gittiğimizi sormadan peşimizden koştu.
7. Ara vermeden toplantı sekiz saat sürdü.
8. Ağaç büyüdükten sonra boyu aşağı yukarı on metre olacak.
9. Çocuğun ateşi olduğunu fark eder etmez onu doktora götürdüm.

C. Translate into English:

1. Böyle lüzumsuz bir şey görmedim.

haraket - movement, motion
hal - state, condition

2. Çocuk sessiz oturup kitaba bakıyor.
3. Ne hareketli çocuk!
4. Yaptıkların tamamen sebepsizdi.
5. Evlilik ne gibi bir hal?

D. Correct the following sentences by making the sentence included within parentheses into an adverbial construction, using the indicated suffix. Tense and person suffixes have been omitted from the included sentences.

Example:

(Sabah kalk___) pencereyi açtım. (-Ir-mEz)

Answer:

Sabah kalkar kalkmaz pencereyi açtım.

1. (Yağmur yağ___) havayı temizler. (-DIkçE)
2. (Ahmet tahtaya bas___) kırıldı. (-Ir-mEz)
3. Fatma, (ışığı aç___) bir odaya girmez. (-mEdEn)
4. (Gemiler çarpış___) battılar. (-Ir-mEz)
5. Attila, (karısının dediğini dinle___) odasına girip kapıyı kapadı. (-mEdEn)
6. Şoför, (sağa sola bak___) vasıtayı hareket ettirdi. (-mEdEn)
7. (İnsanlar birbirini sevme___) dünya değişmiyecek. (-DIkçE)
8. (Kar dur___) çocuklar dışarı koştu. (-Ir-mEz)
9. (Gözlerimi kapat___) acaip sesler duyuyorum. (-DIkçE)

E. Correct the following sentences by making the sentence included within parentheses into an adverbial construction, using the suffix called for by the postposition.

1. (Arkadaşlarımız gel___) evvel burasını toplamamız lâzım.
2. Ayşe, (mektubu oku___) sonra hemen attı.
3. Mustafa, (üniversiteye gir___) sonra saçını kesmez oldu.

4. (Siz evden çık___) iki dakika sonra birisi telefonda aradı.
5. (Ders başla___) bir saat evvel, Fatma hazırlanmağa başladı.

F. Translate into Turkish:

1. Whose is the room with four windows?
2. The two women are very different from each other.
3. Hasan is without a chair; will you bring him one?
4. Tuesday was sunny and hot.
5. Both boys have yellow hair.
6. The boys are both intelligent and hardworking.
7. The quarrel between the neighbors continued endlessly.
8. There is no car more powerful than mine.
9. This morning he came to work without a hat.
10. We want a hotel with a restaurant.

G. Translate into Turkish:

1. The police searched the whole house without finding anything.
2. As soon as it started to rain, he came running back.
3. Mehmet Bey worked without stopping throughout his whole life.
4. As soon as Hasan entered the army, they cut his hair.
5. As long as you stay in bed, you won't get better.
6. Mustafa listened without saying anything.
7. As soon as the prime minister arrived at the station, he was met by several hundred natives of Bolu. After speaking with them briefly, he went to his hotel. The following morning, before returning to Ankara, he toured the city.

LESSON 35: THE ADVERBIAL AUXILIARY AND POSSIBILITY

Study the following sentences:

Elimi uzatırken şarap bardağımı devirdim	'While stretching out my hand, I knocked over my wine-glass'
Demokrat Parti memleketi idare ederken, birçok yeni ana yollar yapıldı	'When the Democrat Party was administering the country, a number of new highways were made'
Fatma'nın babası dinlenirken, belki onun partiye gitmesini kabul edecek	'While Fatma's father is resting, perhaps he will agree to her going to the party'
Biz evde yokken birisi içeri girmiş	'While we were not at home, someone entered'
Bütün hazırlıklarımız tamamlanmışken, yola çıkabiliriz	'Now that all our preparations are complete, we can set out'
Halil yorgunken, bir şeyler unutabilir	'When Halil is tired, he may forget things'
Banka kapanmadan gitmek istedik, ama yetişemedik	'We wanted to go to the bank before it closed, but we couldn't make it'
Ahmet oyunu oynaya oynaya en sonunda kazanabildi	'Playing the game over and over, Ahmet was finally able to win'

1. The adverbial auxiliary -ken

The adverbial suffixes considered in Lessons 33 and 34 occupy the position of tense in a verb form. The adverbial suffix -ken, however, is part of the auxiliary, like the past -DI and dubitative -mIş. (Review, if necessary, the discussion of the auxiliary in Lesson 17.) This means that -ken differs from the other adverbial suffixes in several important respects.

A. The other adverbial suffixes are added only to verbs and are attached to the verb stem: gelip, gelerek. The suffix -ken, however, is added to predicates and may be attached to any type of predicate:

yorgunken	'while being tired'
askerken	'while (being) a soldier'
Ankaradayken	'while (being) in Ankara'
yokken	'while not existing'

If the predicate is verbal, -ken must be preceded by a tense suffix, since all verbal predicates must include a tense. The tense that is usually used with -ken is the present.

gelirken	'while coming'
yardım ederken	'while helping'
bilmezken	'while not knowing'

B. The suffix -ken may either be added directly to the predicate as a suffix or be attached to a stem i-, in which case the combination iken follows the predicate as a separate word. We can thus have the following variants of the preceding examples:

yorgun iken

asker iken

Ankarada iken

gelir iken

bilmez iken

The choice between these two forms is almost entirely a matter of style; the suffixed forms (askerken) are much more common in the spoken language, and -ken is almost always suffixed if the predicate is a verb.

C. If the predicate ends in a vowel, -ken must be preceded by a y, which is a remnant of the stem i-:

hastayken	'while (being) sick'
evdeyken	'while (being) at home'
böyleyken	'while (being) thus'

D. The suffix -ken is unaccented, since no suffix that is part of the auxiliary may be accented. Accent therefore falls on the preceding syllable:

Çalmak - strike, knock, play, steal
artık - henceforth, no more

askérken

hastáyken

gelírken

bilmézken

2. Uses of -ken

This suffix normally corresponds to English 'while', but it need not always be translated 'while'; sometimes 'when' or simply '-ing' is more appropriate.

Ben evdeyken, birisi kapıyı çaldı	'While I was at home, someone came to the door (rang the bell)'
Evde köpek varken, kedi girmez	'While there is a dog in the house, the cat (or cats) will not enter'
Portakallar o kadar pahalıyken onları almayız	'While oranges are so expensive, we won't buy them'
Çocukken, ailesi köyde oturuyordu	'When he was a child, his family lived in the village'
Bir sabah otobüsü beklerken, Halil'i gördüm	'Waiting for the bus one morning, I saw Halil'

As we saw earlier, when -ken is attached to a verbal predicate, the tense used with it is almost always the present. The reason for this is that -ken itself indicates the time of the action, so that from the point of view of meaning, a tense suffix is not strictly necessary; and the present is the tense that has the least specific meaning of its own.

Among the other tenses, the future and narrative past may be used with -ken with a reasonable degree of frequency. In this construction -mIş has very much the meaning of the past participle; that is, the sequence -mIş-ken means something like 'having done' the indicated action.

O kadar yapmışken, artık bitirmemiz lâzım	'Having done so much, we ought to finish'

	'Now that we have done this much, . . .'
	'Since we have done so much, . . .'
Hazır gelmişken, biraz oturup çay içeriz	'As long as we have come, we'll sit for a while and drink tea'

The sequence -(y)EcEk-ken means 'while being about to' do the indicated action:

Bir şey söyliyecekken, birdenbire sustu	'When he was about to say something, he suddenly became silent'
Hayvan Mustafayı öldürecekken, Mustafa onu öldürdü	'When (as) the animal was about to kill Mustafa, Mustafa killed it'

Remember from Lesson 17 that although most personal endings follow an auxiliary suffix, the third person plural -lEr tends to precede: gidiyorlardı 'they were going'. With -ken, as with any adverbial suffix, the personal endings that follow the position of the adverbial are dropped; but -lEr tends to remain with -ken, preceding it:

giderlerken	'while they were going'
yorgunlarken	'while they are tired'

Study the following examples, which illustrate the way in which Turkish distinguishes the two meanings of 'I saw Halil going downtown':

Şehre giderken Halil'i gördüm	'While (I was) going downtown, I saw Halil'
Halil'i şehre giderken gördüm	'I saw Halil while (he was) going downtown'

3. 'Impossible'

The suffix -(y)E preceding the negative—that is, the combination -(y)EmE—means that the subject is unable to perform the indicated action. The combination thus differs from the negative alone in that the negative merely states that the subject is not doing the action, without stating why. Study the following examples:

Kaleminizi her yerde aradım, ama bulamadım	'I looked for your pen everywhere but couldn't find it'
Bu dersi hiç anlayamıyorum	'I can't understand this lesson'
Bu fikri hiç kabul edemiyorum	'I can't accept this idea at all'
Bunun faydasını göremiyorum	'I can't see the use of this'
Büyüyene kadar araba kullanamazsın	'You can't drive a car until you grow up'
İngilizce konuşmuyorum	'I am not speaking English'
İngilizce konuşamıyorum	'I don't (can't) speak English'

Remember that the negative is unaccented, so the accent falls on -(y)E:

bulámadım

görémiyorum

4. 'Possible'

The suffix -(y)Ebil, added after the verb stem and before the tense, indicates that the subject is able to perform the indicated action or, more generally, that the action is possible. This suffix was originally a combination of the verb bilmek 'know' and the adverbial -(y)E. The tense that is almost always used with this suffix is the present.

Ahmet gelebilir	'Ahmet is able to come'
	'It is possible that Ahmet will come'
	'Ahmet may come'
	'Ahmet can come'

Bunu yapabilir misiniz?	'Can you do this?'
Tepenin üstünden belki denizi görebiliriz	'Perhaps we can see the sea from the top of the hill'
Köpekle çok oynamaman lâzım; ısırabilir	'You shouldn't play with the dog too much; he may bite'

Sometimes this suffix is used with tenses other than the present:

En sonunda kutuyu açabildim	'At last I was able to open the box'
Yarın inşallah denize girebileceğiz	'Tomorrow, hopefully, we will be able to go swimming'
Bunu yapabildiğinizi biliyorum	'I know that you can do this'

The negative suffix may not be added to -(y)Ebil, since the sequence *gelebilmez would be equal to Gelemez, 'He cannot come'. But -(y)Ebil may be added to verb stems ending in the negative; that is, the negative may precede but not follow this suffix. The meaning then is almost always the 'It is possible that . . .' type.

Ahmet gelmeyebilir	'It is possible that Ahmet will not come (Ahmet may not come)'
Bakanı göremiyebilirim	'It is possible that I will be unable to see the minister (I may be unable to see the minister)'
Çocuk uyumayabilir	'The child may not be asleep'

Notice the common expression Olabilir 'It is possible':

Hasan evde mi? —Olabilir.	'Is Hasan at home? —It is possible.'

5. Other periphrastic constructions

The suffix -(y)Ebil was made by the addition of a verb stem (bil-) to an adverbial form of the main verb. The original meaning of the verb bilmek is largely lost in this construction. There are other constructions made in the same way, all of them much less common than -(y)Ebil.

A. The suffix -(y)Iver, composed of vermek added to an archaic adverbial suffix -(y)I, indicates that the action is performed quickly or suddenly:

Hasan mektubu yazdı	'Hasan wrote the letter'
Hasan mektubu yazıverdi	'Hasan dashed off the letter'
İhtiyar hanım bir gün ölüverdi	'One day the old lady (suddenly) died'

B. The suffix -(E)dur, composed of durmak added to -(y)E, indicates that the action is performed continuously, or begins and continues. The main verb may also have the -(y)Ip suffix, followed by durmak:

Sen yemeği yiyedur, ben bakkala gidip ekmek alırım	'You start eating; I'll go to the grocery and buy bread'
Çocuk iki saattir ağlayıp duruyor	'The child has been crying continuously for two hours'

(For the imperative see Lesson 37.)

The periphrastic constructions involving gelmek and kalmak are not common enough to be worth learning here.

6. Usage

Kabul etmek with a nominalization or a word denoting an idea means 'accept'; with a verbal noun or a word denoting an action it means 'agree (to)':

Senin dediğini kabul ediyorum, ama benim dediğim de doğru	'I accept what you say, but what I say is also true'
Bizim partiye gitmemizi kabul etti	'He has agreed to our going to the party'

It also means 'receive' in the sense of receiving a visitor.

Kazanmak normally means 'win' but also 'earn':

Doktorlar iyi para kazanıyor	'Doctors earn good money'

Uzamak (intransitive) and uzatmak (transitive) cover a range of meanings related to 'stretch, extend, stretch out', both in the spacial and temporal senses:

Bu iş çok uzadı	'This business has lasted too long'

Notice also uzanmak 'lie down' ('stretch oneself out').

Yetişmek is sometimes synonymous with yetmek 'be sufficient', and has two additional meanings: (1) 'develop'; (2) 'reach' a place at a given time:

Kapıyı açmağa kuvvetim yetmedi (yetişmedi)	'I wasn't strong enough (My strength was not sufficient) to open the door'
Trene yetişmen için erken kalkman lâzım	'You have to get up early to get to the train'

VOCABULARY

belki	/bélki/	perhaps
devirmek		overturn, overthrow
devrilmek		be overturned; fall over
fayda		use
faydalı		useful
faydasız		useless
idare	/idāre/	administration, management
idare etmek		administer, manage
kabul	/kabūl/	acceptance, agreement; reception
kabul etmek		accept, agree (to); receive (see "Usage")
kazanmak		win; earn
susmak		be quiet; stop talking
uzamak		stretch (intrans)

uzatmak	stretch (trans)
yetmek	be sufficient
yetişmek	develop; reach, arrive (see "Usage")

EXERCISES

A. Answer the following questions:

1. Köpek neden seslenip duruyor?
2. Gözlüksüz okuyabilir misiniz?
3. İşinizden istediğiniz kadar para kazanabiliyor musunuz?
4. Hayatta en faydalı şeyler nelerdir?
5. Hiç durmadan kaç saat konuşabilirsiniz?

B. Translate into English:

1. Biraz paramız artmışken, renkli bir televizyon almak isteriz.
2. Yusuf beyler bizim fikirlerimizi kabul etmedikçe onlarla anlaşamayacağız.
3. Otobüse yetişemeyebilirsin.
4. Hükümeti devirdikten sonra askerler memleketi kendi kendilerine idare ettiler.
5. Yaptığınız işlerin ne kadar faydasız olduğunu gördükten sonra, belki benim size söylediklerimi kabul edeceksiniz.
6. İnsan hayatının sonuna yaklaştıkça bazı şeylerin gençken yapılabileceğini daha iyi anlıyor.
7. Son olaylardan sonra çok dikkatli olmamız lâzım. Polisler bizi görür görmez tanıyabilir.
8. Aramızdaki mesafe gittikçe uzuyor ve onlarla artık görüşemiyoruz.
9. Baba uyurken çocukların susması lâzım.
10. Radyomuz yokken, haberleri duyamıyoruz.

C. Combine the following sentences by making the first sentence in each pair into an adverbial construction with -ken. If the included sentence is verbal, change the tense to the present; remove the auxiliary (if any) and the personal ending, and replace them with -<u>ken</u>; delete any repeated nouns from the result.

Example:

Halil gözlüğünü arıyordu — Halil kalemini buldu.

Answer:

Halil gözlüğünü ararken kalemini buldu

1. Çocuk evde yok — Çocuğun odasını temizliyeceğiz.
2. Çocuk iskemlenin üstünde duruyordu — İskemle devrildi.
3. Televizyona bakıyordum — Aklıma bir fikir geldi.
4. Yemek sıcak — Yemek yeriz.
5. Çocuk kücük — Rafa yetişemedi.
6. Kazanıyorum — Oyunu bırakmak istemiyorum.
7. Araban burada — Belki (arabanın) bir faydası olabilir.
8. Masayı tamir ediyorsun — İskemleye de bakar mısın?

In the following sentences, do not change the tense of the included sentence:

9. Halil hazır susmuş — Ben de bir şey söylemek istiyorum.
10. Orhan tam bardağa elini uzatacak — Bardağı aldılar.

D. Translate into Turkish:

1. While Orhan is like this, no one goes near him.
2. While the dog is beside her, she is not afraid.
3. While you were buying oranges, I was looking at the apples.
4. While they were waiting on the corner, they read the newspaper.
5. While Hasan is not working, he is not earning any money.
6. While Menderes was prime minister, the army overthrew the government.
7. While collecting Orhan's things, I found some useful books.

8. When I was young, I could do such things.
9. When Mehmet was a student, he could find work only as a laborer.
10. When Ahmet was small, his family was always hungry.
11. While your wife's mother is here, you must manage the situation carefully.
12. When Attila is working, he can't remember anything.

herkes - everyone

uyumak - sleep

uymak - suit, fit

dinlenmek - rest

LESSON 36: THE CONDITIONAL

Study the following sentences:

Yaptıklarını doğru olarak anlatabilirse, ona inanırız	'If he can explain truthfully what he did, we will believe him'
Ahmet bey evini satmıyacaksa, neden herkese gösteriyor?	'If Ahmet Bey is not going to sell his house, why is he showing it to everyone?'
Benim dairem serbest değilse, seninkini kullanırız	'If my office is not free, we will use yours'
Elbise size uymazsa, onu değiştirebilirsiniz	'If the dress doesn't suit you, you can have it changed'
Eğer Halil o gün evdeydiyse (evde idiyse), polis bulacak	'If Halil was at home on that day, the police will find it out'
Sen olsan, ne yapardın?	'If it were you, what would you do?'
Biraz dinlensek olur mu?	'Will it be all right if we rest a little?'
Her şeyde anlaşamasak bile, hiç olmazsa bu noktada anlaşabiliriz	'Even if we can't agree on everything, at least we can agree on this point'
Sözümü dinleseydin, şimdi bu derdin olmazdı	'If you have listened to me (my words), you wouldn't have this problem now'
Eğer şartları uygun olmasaydı, kabul etmezdik	'If his conditions had not been favorable, we would not have accepted'
Keşki gözlüğümü kırmasaydım!	'If only I hadn't broken my glasses!'
Keşki Ahmet bunu duyabilse!	'If only Ahmet could hear this!'

1. The conditional

1.1. The conditional tense

The conditional suffix is -sE. It may be used as either a tense or an auxiliary; in either case, it is used with the same personal endings as the definite past -DI. The paradigm for the conditional tense is therefore as follows:

gelsem	'if I come'
gelsen	'if you (sg) come'
gelse	'if he comes'
gelsek	'if we come'
gelseniz	'if you (pl) come'
gelseler	'if they come'

1.2. The conditional auxiliary

As an auxiliary, the conditional suffix is attached to the predicate or to the tense in a verbal sentence. If the predicate ends in the negative değil, -sE follows değil.

hazırsan	'if you are ready'
bu oda serbestse	'if this room is free'
otobüste yer varsa	'if there is room on the bus'
kapı açıksa	'if the door is open'
Ahmet gelecekse	'if Ahmet is going to come'
siz isterseniz	'if you wish'
bize inanmazsa	'if he doesn't believe us'
işini bitirmişse	'if he has finished his work'
yeri bulabilirsek	'if we are able to find the place'
palto senin değilse	'if the coat is not yours'
işiniz mühim değilse	'if your business is not important'

Like the other auxiliaries, this suffix may be added to the predicate directly, in which case it is subject to vowel harmony, or it may be added to the stem i-, in which case the combination ise is written as a separate word and is not subject to vowel harmony. If -sE is added directly to a predicate ending in a vowel, a y must appear between the predicate and the suffix.

tamamen memnunsanız	'if you are completely pleased'
tamamen memnun iseniz	
para kaybolmuşsa	'if the money is lost'
para kaybolmuş ise	
Mehmet Ankaradaysa	'if Mehmet is in Ankara'
Mehmet Ankarada ise	
Ahmet dediğin gibiyse	'if Ahmet is as you say'
Ahmet dediğin gibi ise	
para kaybolduysa	'if the money was lost'
öğleden sonraysa	'if it is afternoon'

The conditional auxiliary may also follow (but not precede) the past or dubitative auxiliary suffixes:

evdeydiyse (idiyse)	'if he was at home'
zenginmişsem	'if I am said to be rich'

Remember that all suffixes that are part of the auxiliary are unaccented, and accent falls on the last syllable of the predicate:

evdéyse	'if he is at home'
evde değílse	'if he is not at home'
gelírse	'if he comes'
gelmézse	'if he does not come'

The plural suffix -lEr regularly precedes the conditional auxiliary:

gelirlérse	'if they come'
geleceklérse	'if they will come'

1.3. Uses of the conditional

The auxiliary form of the conditional is used for cases where it is likely that the condition is true, or where there is no presupposition about whether it is true or not. Although this auxiliary may be added to any tense, in practice the tense that usually precedes it is the present.

Herkes hazırsa, sınıf başlayabilir	'If everyone is ready, the class may begin'
Yeni kanun kabul edilirse, Halil'in Türkiye'ye dönmesi lâzım gelecek	'If the new law is passed, Halil will have to return to Turkey'
Bunu sen istemezsen, bir başkasına veririm	'If you don't want this, I'll give it to someone else'

The conditional phrase may optionally be preceded by the particle eğer 'if', which is normally used in more formal styles or if the phrase is long.

Eğer Türkiyedeki yaşama şartları yakında iyileşmezse, hükümetin durumu zorlaşacak	'If living conditions in Turkey do not improve soon, the government's position will become difficult'

The conditional tense occupies the position of a tense suffix in a verbal construction, but its meaning is more that of a mood than a tense. It is used in cases where the possibility is more remote; thus while gelirsem means 'if I come', gelsem usually means 'if I were to come'.

Sizin yerinizde olsam, başka bir şekilde hareket ederim	'If I were in your place, I would act differently'
Parçayı yüz defa dinlesem, yine bıkmam	'If I listened to the piece a hundred times, I still wouldn't tire of it'
Fiatını indirse, o malını alırız	'If he were to lower his price, we would buy his good (those goods of his)'

Notice the difference between the last example of the preceding group and this one:

Fiatını indirirse, o malını alırız	'If he lowers his price, we will buy his goods'

The difference is in the degree of probability: *indirirse* 'if he lowers' either presupposes that the seller is likely to lower his price or makes no presupposition; *indirse* 'if he were to lower' presupposes that the lowering is unlikely. The verb in the main clause, *alırız*, is in the present tense in both examples; it is translated 'would buy' in one case and 'will buy' in the other because of English requirements on the sequence of tenses in conditional clauses.

The conditional tense with *de* or *bile* 'even' is used in a "concessive" sense: 'even if . . .'.

Çoğu zaman toplantılara gelmez, gelse de bir şey söylemez — 'Most of the time he doesn't come to the meetings, and even if he comes, he doesn't say anything'

Bize yüz lira verse de, istediğini yapmayız

Bize yüz lira verse bile, istediğini yapmayız — 'Even if he gives us a hundred liras, we won't do what he wants'

Orhan'ı sevmesen bile, onunla kavga etmene lüzum yok — 'Even if you don't like Orhan, you don't have to fight with him'

The combination of the conditional tense and past aspect is used for "contrary-to-fact" conditions, where it is known that the condition is unfulfilled: *gelseydi* 'if he had come'. The main verb is then in either the present or future tense, followed by the past auxiliary: *gelirdim* or *gelecektim* 'I would have come'.

Bilseydim, ben de sizinle gelirdim — 'If I had known, I too would have come with you'

Yapabileceğimiz bir şey olsaydı, yapardık — 'If there had been anything we could do, we would have done it'

Çocuğun yanından ayrılmasaydın, suya düşmezdi — 'If you hadn't left the child's side, he wouldn't have fallen in the water'

Although the conditional phrases in the preceding examples are translated with the past tense, the combination -*sEydI* may often be either past or present:

Tembel olmasaydın, şimdiye kadar bitirirdin	'If you were not lazy, you would have finished by now' 'If you had not been lazy, you would have finished by now'

If the main verb has the -(y)EcEktI combination, however, the phrase can only be past:

Hava soğuk olmasaydı, dışarı otururduk	'If the weather were not cold, we would sit outside' 'If the weather had not been cold, we would have sat outside'
Hava soğuk olmasaydı, dışarı oturacaktık	'If the weather had not been cold, we were going to sit outside'

Yet another use of the conditional tense is in the expression of wishes: paramız olsa or paramız olsaydı 'if we (only) had money!' In this use, the phrase may be preceded by keşki (keşke):

Bu akşam yemek güzeldi; keşki yeseydin	'The food was good this evening; you should have eaten'
Keşki gitseler!	'If they would only go!'
Keşki daha erken gitselerdi	'If they had only gone earlier'

2. Usage

A number of idioms are formed with the conditional, like yoksa 'or' (literally 'if not') and zannedersem 'in my opinion' (literally 'if I think'). Hiç olmazsa means 'at least'; its literal interpretation is left as an exercise to the reader.

The particle ise is used as a particle meaning 'as for', to direct attention to the preceding word:

Mehmet babasına, kardeşi ise annesine benzer	'Mehmet resembles his father, and as for his brother, he resembles his mother'

Polis adamların birini götürdü, diğerini ise serbest bıraktı	'The police took one man away, and let the other go (as for the other, they let him go)'

The particle bile 'even' is also used as an enclitic:

Bunu ben bile anlaya-mıyorum	'Even I can't understand this'
Yemeğinizi bitirmediniz bile	'You didn't even finish your meal'

Bıkmak means 'be tired' of something, with pejorative implications: 'be sick of'.

Mal means (1) 'property, wealth'; (2) 'goods, merchandise'. It is also used in indicating the origin of merchandise: Amerikan malı 'American made'.

Serbest means 'free' in two senses: (1) 'at liberty'; (2) 'unoccupied'. The third sense of English 'free, without cost', is parasız. Notice serbest bırakmak 'release, let free', serbest kalmak 'have free time', and serbest konuşmak 'speak freely'.

Şart 'condition' may be used as a predicate indicating strong necessity, with a verbal noun construction as subject:

Bunu bugün bitirmeniz şart	'It is absolutely necessary that you finish this today'

The basic meaning of şekil is 'shape' or 'form':

Bu binanın şekli, etraftaki binalara uymuyor	'The shape of this building doesn't fit the surrounding buildings'

It also means 'manner' or 'way', especially in standard expressions like bu şekilde or ne şekilde:

Bu şekilde oyunu kazandık	'In this way we won the game'

In addition, it can mean 'diagram'. There is also the postpositional construction şeklinde 'in the form of'.

VOCABULARY

bıkmak (abl)		be tired (of), be sick (of) (see "Usage")
bile		even (see "Usage")
eğer		if (see Section 1.3)
inanmak (dat)		believe
ise		as for (see "Usage")
kanun	/kānun/	law
keşki	/kéşki/	if only, would that (see Section 1.3)
mal		property, goods, merchandise (see "Usage")
nokta		point; dot, period
serbest		free (see "Usage")
şart		condition (see "Usage")
şekil	/şekl/	shape, form; manner (see "Usage")
uygun (dat)		fitting, suitable
uymak (dat)		suit, fit; adapt (to); be in harmony (with)

EXERCISES

A. Answer the following questions:

1. Türkçe öğrenmeseydiniz ne olurdu?
2. İstesek her işi yapabilir miyiz?
3. Bir sigara istesem verir misiniz?
4. Çok paranız olsa idi ne yapmak isterdiniz?
5. O kutuya bakarsam ne bulurum?

B. Translate into English:

1. Paketi şimdi gönderirsen, Cumartesi günü oraya varır.
2. Yeni kanuna göre, Orhan bey bu sene Türkiye'den dışarı seyahat etmişse, bir daha çıkamaz.

3. Oğlunuz mektebinden bıktıysa, neden hâlâ oraya gider?
4. Burada sigara içmek yasak ise, öbür odaya geçeriz.
5. Çalışsaydın, bunu yapabilirdin.
6. Cevabı bilseydim, size söylerdim.
7. Eğer bu işe karışmasaydın, her şeyi bozmazdın.
8. Keşki bunun yerine öbürünü seçseydim!
9. Mustafa bize inansaydı, belki şimdi yaşayabilirdi.
10. Fatma'nın babası o kadar zenginmişse, neden koca bulamıyor?

C. Add the conditional auxiliary to the following sentences. Then make up an appropriate conclusion for each sentence, and translate your sentence into English:

1. Bugün Salı.
2. Daha doymadın.
3. Yağmur yağar.
4. Kendi şapkamı bulamam.
5. Ekmek yok.
6. Bu oda serbest değil.
7. Ahmed'i otelde bulamayız.
8. O dükkân kasabın.
9. O araba çok pahalı.
10. Oturma odası toplanmış.

D. Translate into Turkish:

1. If the dog bit you, you must go to the doctor at once.
2. If I can't find a steamship, I'll go by plane.
3. If there is no meat, we'll eat bread.
4. If you're so smart, why aren't you rich?
5. If I understand the new law correctly, you can't leave Turkey this year.

6. If you can't work under these conditions, what else do you want?
7. If you continue in this manner, you will lose all your money.
8. If you tell this to Orhan, he won't believe you.
9. If you wait two minutes, I will be ready.

E. Translate into Turkish:

1. If Orhan didn't resemble his father so much, I would like him better.
2. If your prices weren't so high, you would sell more goods.
3. If I went to the university, I would soon get tired of it.
4. If Mustafa hadn't closed the door, we would have been able to hear his words.
5. Even if you finish the job by this evening, it will still be too late.

LESSON 37: IMPERATIVES, THE OPTATIVE, AND THE NECESSITATIVE + Ever Constructions

Study the following sentences:

Bil bakalım ben kimim	1.	'Let's see; guess who I am'
Biraz bekle de, eşyalarımı toplayım	2.	'Wait a little; let me collect my things'
Şoförle konuşmayınız	3.	'Don't talk with the driver' (Imp)
Lütfen geç kalmayınız	4.	'Please don't be late'
Lütfen meyvayı bana uzatsanıza	5.	'Please pass me the fruit'
Şu dükkânı deneyelim	6.	'Let's try this shop'
Hazır buradayken, Ahmetlere uğramıyalım mı?	7.	'As long as we're here, shouldn't we drop in on the Ahmets?'
Sevineyim mi üzüleyim mi bilemiyorum	8.	'I don't know whether to be happy or sad'
Çocuk böyle elbisesiz dolaşsın mı?	9.	'Should the child wander around without clothes that way?'
Bu apartmanın sahibi pek zengin olmalı	10.	'The owner of this apartment building ought to be very rich'
Bu hâdiseler sana bu kadar tesir etmemeli	11.	'These events shouldn't affect you so much'
Ofisi kim ziyaret ederse müdürle konuşmalı	12.	'Whoever visits the office should talk with the director'
Bu işi nasıl idare edersen et, yalnız çabuk olsun	13.	'Manage this matter however you want; only let it be quick'
Ne öğrendimse ondan öğrendim	14.	'Whatever I learned, I learned from him'

1. Imperatives

There are a number of ways of forming commands and requests in Turkish. The most straightforward is with the use of the imperative suffixes, which are:

zero: nonpolite, one person

-(y)In: nonpolite, two or more persons

-(y)InIz: polite, one or more persons

Thus -(y)InIz is used for anyone, either one person or several, to whom the speaker wishes to be polite; zero, that is, the bare stem of the verb, is used to a single person to whom the speaker does not wish to be polite, for example, a child, a servant, or an animal; -(y)In is used for several people to whom the speaker does not wish to be polite, for example, a group of children. These suffixes are added directly to the verb stem, without tense; they are unaccented, so that accent falls on the last syllable of the stem, except that in the case of a negative imperative, accent is on the syllable before the negative.

Ítiniz	'Push!'
Kediye básma	'Don't step on the cat'
Çekílin	'Get out of the way! (Withdraw!)'
Ben gelmeden başlámayınız	'Don't start before I come'

These are strictly verbal suffixes, and if they are to be added to a nonverbal predicate, the stem ol- must be supplied:

Sağ ol!	'Be well!'
Geldiği zaman burada olma	'Don't be here when he comes'

Another way of forming imperatives, very common in the spoken language but more rare in writing, is to use the second person of the conditional, either singular or plural, followed by a suffix -E. This gives two combinations:

-sEnE: nonpolite, one person

-sEnIzE: polite, one or more persons; or, nonpolite, two or more persons

Accent falls on the syllable before the -E, thus:

Çabuk gelséne	'Come quickly!'
İtmeseníze	'Don't push!'

There are two more polite ways of expressing requests. One is with the interrogative of the present tense: Gelir misiniz 'Will you come?' The other is with the verb rica etmek 'request':

Bu kâğıdı doldurmanızı rica ederim	'I should like you to fill out this paper (I request your filling out this paper)'

With all these constructions, the word for 'please' is lütfen:

Lütfen bağırmayınız	'Please don't shout'
Lütfen daha yavaş konuşmanızı rica ederim	'I should like you please to speak more slowly (Please, I request your speaking more slowly)'

2. The optative *let, let's, shall*

The suffix for this tense is -(y)E. The endings are irregular and are best given together with the tense sign:

'I'	-(y)EyIm	'we'	-(y)ElIm
'you (sg)'	-(y)EsIn	'you (pl)'	-(y)EsInIz
'he, she, it'	-sIn or -(y)E	'they'	-sInlEr or -(y)ElEr

By way of illustration, we give the full set of forms for two verbs, gitmek 'go' and bakmak 'look':

	'go'	'look'
(ben)	gideyim	bakayım
(sen)	gidesin	bakasın
(o)	gitsin or gide	baksın or baka

	'go'	'look'
(biz)	gidelim	bakalım
(siz)	gidesiniz	bakasınız
(onlar)	gitsinler or gideler	baksınlar or bakalar

The meanings of this tense are best explained for each person separately.

A. First person singular is gideyim 'let me go':

Parti böyle olacaksa, ben gideyim	'If the party is going to be like this, let me go'
Dur da biraz düşüneyim	'Stop and let me think a little'
Sizi Ahmetle tanıştırayım mı?	'Shall I introduce you to Ahmet?'

The sequence -EyIm is normally pronounced with a long /i/ vowel: gideyim [gidīm].

B. First person plural is gidelim 'let's go', like French allons or Italian andiamo:

Evvelâ denize girelim, sonra yemek yeriz	'First let's go swimming; then we'll eat'
Birbirimize düşman olmıyalım	'Let's not be enemies'
Ne yapalım?	'What shall we do? (Let us do what?)'
Biraz dinlenelim mi?	'Shall we rest for a while?'
Ne istediğini anlat bakalım	'Let's see, explain what you want'

C. Second person is gidesin, gidesiniz 'let you go, you should go'. These forms are not particularly common, since their primary functions are covered by the imperative and other constructions.

D. Third person forms with -E (gide, gideler) are archaic and rare; they are found only in a few formulaic utterances, such as Allah vere 'may God grant'.

Keşki - if only

The normal third person optative ending, also called third person imperative, is -sIn, plural -sInlEr.

Çocuk saat yedi buçukta yatsın	'Let the child go to bed at seven thirty'
Köpek yeni evine alışsın	'Let the dog get used to his new home'
Bu ay geçsin, gelecek ay daha çok vaktimiz olacak	'Let this month pass; next month we'll have more time'
Paket çok ağır olmasın	'The package shouldn't be too heavy (Let the package not be too heavy)'

Geçmiş olsun 'let it be past' is the standard expression for 'get well'.

The combination of -(y)E and -(y)DI, the past auxiliary, makes constructions synonymous with the combination of conditional tense and past auxiliary: bilseydim or bileydim 'if I had known'. This construction can be used in any person:

O resim daha ucuz olaydı, onu alırdım	'If that picture had been cheaper, I would have bought it'
Keşki meşhur olaydım	'I wish I were famous'

3. The necessitative

There is one more tense in Turkish: the "necessitative," -mElI, which is used with predicative endings:

gitmeliyim	'I have to go, I ought to go'
gitmelisin	'you (sg) have to go, you ought to go'
gitmeli	'he (she, it) has to go, he ought to go'
gitmeliyiz	'we have to go, we ought to go'
gitmelisiniz	'you (pl) have to go, you ought to go'

gitmeliler	'they have to go, they ought to go'

Gitmeliyim differs from *gitmem lâzım* in that *gitmeliyim* expresses a stronger degree of necessity or obligation than *gitmem lâzım*, while *gitmem şart* is stronger still. Under appropriate conditions, both the necessitative tense and the construction with *lâzım* are ambiguous:

Şu saatte Fatma hanım evde olmalı	'At this hour Fatma hanim ought to be at home' (She never goes out at this hour)
	'At this hour Fatma hanim has to be at home' (She is required to be at home)
Bu iki meseleyi ayırmalıyız	'We have to separate these two problems'
Böyle güzel evler pahalı olmalı	'Such beautiful houses must be expensive'
O mektubu dün yazmalıydınız	'You should have written that letter yesterday'

The third person singular of the necessitative tense can be used in a type of impersonal construction: 'someone ought to':

Şu duvarları yıkamalı	'Someone ought to wash these walls'
	'These walls ought to be washed'
İnsanın kulağına bağırmamalı	'One shouldn't shout in a person's ear'

Remember that *-lI* indicates possession and *-mE* is a verbal noun (infinitive) suffix; thus 'I have to go' is an exact, suffix-by-suffix translation of *gitmeliyim*

4. '-Ever' constructions

English expressions like 'whoever', 'whatever', and 'whenever' are expressed in Turkish by constructions combining an interrogative word in a phrase with the conditional auxiliary:

Kim gelirse kapıyı çalması lâzım	'Whoever comes has to knock on the door'

Literally this means 'If who comes, he has to knock on the door'. Similar examples follow:

Ne istersen yapabilirsin	'You can do whatever you want'
Hasan neye karar verirse, yapacağız	'Whatever Hasan decides on, we will do'
Hoca ne zaman gelirse, ders başlar	'Whenever the teacher comes, the class begins'

There is another type of '-ever' construction in which the conditional phrase is followed by a repetition of the verb, in the imperative for second person, the optative for first and third persons:

Kim gelirse gelsin, kapıyı açma	'Whoever comes, don't open the door'
Ne kadar bağırırsan bağır, ben dinlemem	'However much you shout, I won't listen'

Literally, these examples mean 'If who comes, let him come; don't open the door' and 'If you shout how much, shout; I won't listen'. These constructions have the sense 'No matter who comes . . .' or 'No matter how much you shout'.

Kaç kuruş olursa olsun, bunu almak istemiyorum	'Whatever it costs, I don't want to buy this'
İş ne kadar kolay olursa olsun, gine de yapamıyorsun	'However easy the job is, you still can't do it'
Ne kadar gülerseniz gülün, benim fikrim yine doğru	'However much you laugh, my idea is still right'

In the first person, the repetition of the verb is optional:

Ne kadar bağırsam, bir faydası yok	'However much I shout, it has no effect'
Ne kadar bağırırsam bağırayım, bir faydası yok	

When constructions of this type are used alone, there is a comma between the conditional and the repetition:

Ne olursa, olsun	'Whatever may be, let it be (Whatever happens, it doesn't matter)'
Orhan ne kadar kızarsa, kızsın	'However much Orhan is angry, let him be angry (It doesn't matter how angry he is)'

5. Usage

The normal place for lütfen is at the beginning. If it is at the end, the request is more insistent. The most insistent is to place lütfen after the first word:

Lütfen kapıyı kapayınız	'Please close the door'
Kapıyı kapayınız, lütfen	'Close the door, please'
Kapıyı lütfen kapayınız	'*Please* close the door'

VOCABULARY

bağırmak		shout
çabuk		quick
dolmak		fill (intrans)
doldurmak		fill (trans)
itmek		push
kulak		ear
lütfen	/lǘtfen/	please
rica	/ricā/	request (n)
rica etmek		request (v)
sağ		healthy
uğramak (dat)		visit (casually), drop in (on)

üzmek		grieve (trans)
üzülmek (abl)		grieve (intrans), be worried, be sorry (about)
ziyaret	/ziyāret/	visit (n)
ziyaret etmek		visit (v)

EXERCISES

A. Answer the following questions:

1. Türkiye'ye ziyaretimizde neler görelim?
2. Otobüsle mi gidelim, taksiyle mi?
3. Kapıcı, paketlerinizle ne yapsın?
4. Dün ne yaptığını lütfen anlat bize.
5. Neden üzüldüğünü söylesene.

B. Translate into English:

1. Şişeleri hangi rafa koyayım?
2. Ahmet hangi partiye gitse, partiyi canlandırır.
3. Bu oyunda sıra kimdeyse ona kadar sayması lâzım.
4. Mektup hangi dilde yazılmış olursa olsun, onu Türkçeye çevirebilirim.
5. Bu içki son olsun artık.
6. Ne rica ederseniz ediniz, yapmağa çalışırız.
7. Bugün geç kalmayım da, hoca kızmasın.
8. Benim şeylerimi bana sormadan almamalısın.
9. Bu saat, bu kadar kısa bir zamanda bozulmamalı.
10. Ayakta olanların öne doğru ilerlemesi rica olunur.

C. Translate into Turkish, and mark the position of accent on each verb:

1. Don't miss your train! (polite)
2. Don't be lazy! (nonpolite, several people)
3. Answer my question! (nonpolite, several people)
4. Open your mouth! (nonpolite, one person)

5. Either do something useful, or don't do anything. (nonpolite, several people)
6. Please don't step on that board. (polite)
7. Think a little before deciding. (polite)
8. Don't be sorry about this situation. (nonpolite, one person)
9. In my opinion, become an engineer. (polite)
10. Don't be like your brother! (nonpolite, one person

D. Translate into Turkish:

1. Let this job finish, and then let's rest.
2. Shall I fill your glass?
3. Shall we drop in on Fatma Hanim and drink tea?
4. Let them not interfere with my business.
5. Let the door remain closed.
6. Let your feelings not be obvious.
7. Let this table be closer to the light.
8. Let's not forget to send the package to Mehmet.
9. First let me learn to drive, then I'll buy a car.
10. Why shouldn't I be angry?

E. Translate into Turkish:

1. Whatever you do, just (only) don't shout.
2. Whoever comes to the party has to be pushed into the water.
3. Whatever language I speak, he still doesn't understand.
4. However much I try to close my ears, I still hear the noises in the street.
5. Whomever Mehmet visits, he can't find at home.
6. Wherever we travel, the people all seem the same.

LESSON 38: SUBORDINATING CONJUNCTIONS

Study the following sentences:

Profesör, "isminiz ne?" diye sordu	'The professor asked "What is your name?"'
Orada "Yol Kapalı" diye bir işaret var	'Over there is a sign saying "Road Closed"'
Manzarayı göresiniz diye yavaş gidiyorum	'I am going slow so that you can see the view'
Diyorlar ki son on sene içinde İstanbul çok değişmiş	'They say Istanbul has changed a lot in the last ten years'
Belli ki harp çıkarsa Türkiye'ye gidemiyeceğiz	'It is obvious that if war breaks out, we won't be able to go to Turkey'
Öyle şaşırdım ki ne yapacağımı bilemedim	'I was so surprised that I didn't know what to do'
Deniz o kadar pis oldu ki giremezsin	'The sea got so dirty that you can't go in'
Başbakanın dediğini anlamadım ki sana anlatayım	'I didn't understand what the prime minister said, that I should explain it to you'
Fatma hanım kaç yaşında? —Sormadım ki!	'How old is Fatma Hanim? —I didn't ask!'
Sen hâlâ küçük oğlansın gibi bana geliyor	'I have the feeling that you are still a small boy'
	'I have the feeling as though you were still a small boy'

1. Diye

When a direct quotation is followed by any verb other than demek, the particle diye must follow the quotation. Diye 'saying' is originally an adverbial form of demek with the suffix -(y)E.

Hasan, "hemen geliyorum" diye bağırdı	'Hasan shouted, "I'm coming at once"'
Fatma, "yemek hazır" diye çağırdı	'Fatma called, "Dinner is ready"'

Köpek, "hav! hav!" diye seslendi	'The dog went "Hav! Hav!"'

If the main verb is demek, diye is not necessary:

Polis memuru, "yol kapalı" dedi	'The policeman said, "The road is closed"'

Diye may also be used like a postposition, following entire sentences included within other sentences (without quotation marks). Sentences followed by diye are either literally or figuratively indirect quotations; they frequently indicate the reason for which the subject takes some action. Study the following examples:

Elbiseler kurusun diye güneşe koydum	'I put the clothes in the sun so that they would dry' (literally: 'Saying, let the clothes dry, I put them in the sun')
Su kesilebilir diye banyoları doldurdum	'I filled the bathtubs because the water may be cut off'

Ne diye is another way of saying 'why'.

1.1. Writing direct quotations

There is no standard way of writing direct quotations in Turkish; modern usage is a mixture of the various European ways of writing quotations. French quotation marks (« ») are normally used in print, but the English quotation marks are increasing in popularity because they are found on most typewriters. Quotation marks are normal in modern usage, but in older styles they were omitted:

"Evet" diye bağırdı	'He shouted "Yes"'
Evet diye bağırdı	

Another way is to introduce the quotation with a dash. Quotations treated in this way always begin a new paragraph, and whatever follows the quotation begins with a capital letter. Compare the following:

—Şöyle. Dedi.	'He said "Thus-and-such"'
"Şöyle" dedi.	

2. *Ki* complements

Another way of including a sentence as a noun phrase within another sentence is to use the relative conjunction *ki*. *Ki* 'that' is borrowed from Persian and is used with Indo-European syntax. The included sentence, which we shall call the "complement," follows *ki*, which in turn follows the main verb, just as in English.

İstiyorum ki herkes memnun olsun	'I want everyone to be happy'
Duydum ki Orhan askerliğini yapmıyacak	'I heard that Orhan will not do his military service'

Of course, it would also be possible to say the same things with more normal Turkish syntax, using verbal noun and nominalization constructions:

Herkesin memnun olmasını istiyorum

Orhan'ın askerliğini yapmıyacağını duydum

However, *ki* constructions are common in the modern colloquial language (especially in the speech of Americans trying to avoid Turkish syntax). *Ki* is likely to be used if the complement is complicated:

Umarım ki Fatma partiye gelmesinin lâzım geldiğini hatırlıyacak	'I hope Fatma will remember that she has to come to the party'

Ordinarily, where more traditional Turkish syntax would use a verbal noun construction, the *ki* complement comes out with the optative:

Parkın evlerle dolmamasını ümit ederiz	'We hope that the park won't be filled with houses'
Ümit ederiz ki park evlerle dolmasın	

Where the alternative is a nominalization, the *ki* complement has one of the declarative tenses:

Baba, bu yaz susuz kalacağımızı anlattı Baba anlattı ki bu yaz susuz kalacağız	'Father explained that we will be without water this summer'

Ki complements may be used not only as the objects of transitive verbs, as in the preceding examples, but also as the subjects of intransitive verbs. The main verb comes at the beginning and the complement follows:

Anlaşılır ki ziyaretçi istemiyor	'It is understood that (or it appears that) he doesn't want visitors'
Şüphesiz ki hükümetin asıl niyetini bilemeyiz	'Doubtlessly we can't know the government's real intentions (It is doubtless that . . .)'
Bu sebeptendir ki Kıbrısta harp çıktı	'It is for this reason that war broke out on Cyprus'

Another use of ki is to introduce complements for öyle and o kadar, 'so' or 'such':

Mustafa öyle değişmiş ki onu tanıyamadım	'Mustafa changed so much that I couldn't recognize him'
Türkçeyi o kadar iyi konuşur ki onu Türk sanırsın	'He speaks Turkish so well you would think he was a Turk'

As in English, the complement in such sentences may be left inexplicit: 'Today the weather was so hot!' But while in English the entire complement, including 'that', is omitted, in Turkish ki remains, followed by an exclamation point or a row of dots:

Bugün hava o kadar sıcaktı ki!	'Today the weather was so hot!'
O kitabı o kadar çok seviyorum ki . . .	'I like that book so much . . .'

We shall not attempt to cover all the many uses of ki here. One more that is worth mentioning is to introduce complements indicating the intention or purpose of an action. The verb in such complements is normally optative.

Pencereyi açtım ki oda havalansın	'I opened the window so the room would air'
Bende para yok ki sana vereyim	'I don't have any money, that I might give you'

Again, the complement may be left inexplicit, with only ki remaining at the end of the expression:

Hoca ne zaman gelecek? —Bilmiyorum ki!	'When will the teacher come? —I don't know (that I might tell you)'

Ki is unstressed and pronounced as a unit with the preceding word; the main stress thus falls on the last syllable of the preceding word:

anlaşılír ki

bilmiyorúm ki

3. Other subordinating conjunctions

A number of other conjunctions are formed with ki and used with Indo-European syntax; that is, they precede their complements. They include:

A. çünkü, çünki 'because'

Yarın erken kalkalım, çünkü çok işimiz var	'Let's get up early tomorrow, because we have a lot of work'

B. sanki 'as though'
Sanki is normally used with gibi, with sanki preceding the complement and gibi following. Sanki may be omitted from these constructions:

Kedi, sanki bütün gün bir şey yememiş gibi orada oturuyor	'The cat is sitting there as though it hasn't eaten anything all day'
Bir şey olmamış gibi hareket ediyorsun	'You are acting as though nothing happened'

C. halbuki 'although'

Sen altı yer tutmuşsun, halbuki biz sadece dört kişiyiz	'You reserved six places, although we are only four'

D. mademki (or madem) 'since, considering that (seeing as how)'

Mademki buraya gelmişiz, bir şey yapalım	'Since we have come here, let's do something'

E. keşki 'would that'
See Lesson 36.

4. Reduplication

We should finish with a discussion of a major grammatical and stylistic device in Turkish, the reduplication or repetition of words or parts of words. Reduplication is used throughout the language, in grammatical, syntactic, stylistic, and lexical areas. Some examples:

A. Adjectives may be reduplicated for emphasis.

Halil çok çok çalışkan bir adam	'Halil is a very hardworking person'
Sade sade bir elbise giydi	'She wore a very simple dress'

B. Adjectives used as adverbs are particularly prone to reduplication. The tendency toward the reduplication of adverbs has already been seen in constructions like güle güle.

Yavaş yavaş yürüdü	'He walked slowly'
Derin derin düşündü	'He thought deeply'

C. Certain adjectives have intensive forms, made by the reduplication of the first syllable. The meaning of the adjective is intensified with a connotation of completeness. Some examples:

açık	'open'	apaçık	'wide open'
temiz	'clean'	tertemiz	'spotless'

siyah	'black'	simsiyah	'jet black; black all over'
yalnız	'alone'	yapyalnız, yapayalnız	'completely alone'
boş	'empty'	bomboş	'completely empty'

Accent is on the syllable preceding the stem: bómboş, ápaçık, yápyalnız, yapáyalnız.

The reduplication is made by repeating the first consonant and vowel of the adjective, followed by a consonant that can be m, p, r, or s. The choice of consonant is fixed for each adjective; thus belli 'clear' uses s, as in besbelli 'obvious', while başka 'other' uses m, as in bambaşka 'completely different'. The consonant can be predicted to a very limited extent. All adjectives that begin in a vowel use p: apaçık, apayrı, upuzun. The reduplicating syllable may not end with the same consonant as either the first or the second consonant of the adjective. Thus, with mor 'purple', both m and r are excluded, and the reduplication must be with either p or s (the choice is s: mosmor 'purple all over').

Only certain adjectives, about fifty in all, have reduplicated forms of this sort. This process is not productive, and new formations cannot normally be made.

D. There is one other pattern of reduplication involving a prefix. Any word, usually a noun but sometimes a verb or an adjective, may be reduplicated, with m replacing the first consonant of the repetition (thus from kitap we get kitap mitap). The meaning is 'et cetera'. For example:

Odası, kitap mitap ile dolu	'His room is filled with books and stuff'
Attila Mattila İzmir'e gitti	'Attila and his friends (or his family) went to Izmir'
Çocuk ağladı mağladı	'The child cried and carried on'

This pattern cannot be used if the word to be reduplicated starts with m; thus from masa we cannot get *masa masa.

This pattern is fully productive, and constructions of this sort can be made at will.

E. There are a number of expressions in the language that look like reduplications, although they are not formed by any regular pattern. An example is çoluk çocuk 'household' (children and stuff).

Çoluk çocuğumu arabaya bindirip seyahatte gittim	'I loaded my family into the car and went on a trip'
Ahmet bağırdı, çağırdı	'Ahmet shouted and yelled'

New reduplicating expressions can be invented. For example, a cazlı sazlı nightclub is one that has both Turkish and European music (caz 'jazz'; saz a Turkish musical instrument).

5. Usage

Asıl is originally a noun meaning 'origin': Yunan asıllı Amerikalılar 'Americans of Greek origin'. It is now used sometimes as a noun in the form aslı 'the original of, the real' but more often as an adjective meaning 'real, true, essential'. Aslında is an adverb meaning 'really'.

While there is a verb niyet etmek 'intend', the postpositional construction niyetinde 'in the intention', used as a predicate preceded by a verbal noun, means the same thing and is more common:

Yarın erken kalkmak niyetindeyim	'Tomorrow I intend to get up early'

Şaşmak basically means 'be surprised, be amazed', as in şaşılacak şey 'amazing thing'. Şaşırmak means 'be confused'. However, the meanings of both verbs have been confused, so that now they can both be found in the general range of meanings 'be surprised, bewildered, confused'. When they mean 'be surprised', they take the dative; when they mean 'be confused', they take the objective:

Hasan'a şaştım	'I was surprised at Hasan'
Hasan'ın geldiğine şaşırdım/şaştım	'I was surprised that Hasan came'

Ne yapacağımı şaşırdım	'I was confused about what to do'
Yolumu şaşırdım	'I lost my way (got confused about my way)'

Şüphe means 'doubt' or 'suspicion'. A number of words are formed from şüphe, including şüphelenmek 'doubt' or 'suspect' (with the ablative), şüpheli 'doubtful' or 'suspicious', şüphesiz 'doubtless'. Kuşku basically means 'suspicion', with kuşkulanmak 'suspect'. But in the modern language the meaning of kuşku has widened to include all the meanings of şüphe, that is, 'doubt' as well as 'suspicion'.

Older forms ümit and ümit etmek 'hope' are being replaced by umut and ummak in the modern language. 'Give up hope' is ümidini kesmek (with the ablative).

Geleceğinden ümidimi kestim	'I gave up hope that he will come'

VOCABULARY

asıl	/asl/	real (see "Usage")
çağırmak		call; invite
çünkü	/çǘnkü/	because
derin		deep
halbuki	/hálbuki, halbúki/	although
işaret	/işāret/	sign, signal
kuşku		suspicion, doubt (see "Usage")
madem, mademki	/mādem, mādémki/	since
memur	/mēmur/	official, (police) officer
niyet		intention, resolve
niyet etmek		intend, resolve
sade	/sāde/	simple, plain
sadece	/sādece/	simply, merely, only

sanki	/sánki/	as though
şaşırmak		be confused, be surprised (see "Usage")
şaşmak		be surprised, be confused (see "Usage")
şüphe		doubt, suspicion (see "Usage")
ummak		hope, expect
umut	/umud/	hope, expectation
ümit	/ümid/	hope, expectation
ümit etmek		hope, expect

EXERCISES

A. Answer the following questions:

1. Kitabı bitirdik diye seviniyor musunuz?
2. Mademki Türkçeyi öğrendiniz, ne yapacaksınız?
3. "Mona Lisa" resminin aslı nerededir?
4. Yazın ne yapmak niyetindesiniz?
5. Fatma neden Hasan'a pis pis bakıyor?

B. Translate into English:

1. Oidipus'un karısı aslında annesidir.
2. Oraya yürüyerek kolay kolay gidersınız.
3. Bu şehirde asıl Türk yemekleri nerede bulunur?
4. Hocam diyor ki, Bartok'un en güzel parçaları en sadeleridir.
5. Polis memuru, bize "geç" diye işaret verdi.
6. Mehmet o kadar iyi niyetli ki senin için her şey yapar.
7. Orhan'ın öyle bir karakteri var ki her dediğini kabul etmen lâzım.
8. Benim fikrim, seninkinden bambaşka.
9. O güzel tepelerde apartman mapartman yapacaklar.
10. Yepyeni elbisemi giyiyim mi?

11. Mustafa, paltosuz maltosuz soğuğa çıktı.

C. The following sentences involve a verbal noun or nominalization construction. Change each to the corresponding sentence using ki.

Example:

Halil, kendi çocuğunun çok akıllı olduğunu zannediyor

Answer:

Halil zannediyor ki kendi çocuğu çok akıllıdır

1. Ayşe'nin vaktinde hazır olmıyacağı kuşkusuz.
2. Bu vaziyetin daha çok fenalaşmıyacağını ümit ediyorum.
3. Orhan beyin dükkânının kapandığını yeni öğrendim.
4. Yusuf beyin evimizi bulamadığından korkuyoruz.
5. On üçüncü asrın Türkçesinin bizim günümüzün Türkçesinden çok farklı olduğu görülüyor.
6. Yeni bakanın ne yapacağını bilmediği belli.
7. Hoca, herkesin bu kitabı yarına kadar okumasını istiyor.
8. Babası Ahmede arabayı gece yarısına kadar geri getirmesini söyledi.
9. Herkesin susmasını bekliyoruz.
10. Mustafa'nın yeni bir kız arkadaşı olduğundan şüpheleniyorum.

D. Translate into Turkish:

1. There were so many people on the boat that we couldn't sit down.
2. Mustafa always buys cheap clothes, although his father makes a lot of money.
3. His mother asked, "Where are you going?" He answered, "Out."
4. You seem as though you don't want to listen to us.
5. She is grieved because (diye) her sons don't write letters.
6. There are all kinds of packages and things in front of the door.

7. Doubtless you will be able to find a good job in Istanbul.
8. "I intend to become an official in the bank," he explained.
9. "Don't put your dirty feet on my spotless floor," she shouted.
10. We suspect that someone is stealing our coffee money.

GLOSSARY OF SUFFIXES

Numbers in parentheses refer to the lesson or lessons in which the suffix is introduced.

-CE	adverb derivation (29)
-CI	noun derivation (30)
DE	also (11)
-DE	locative (8)
-DEn	ablative (7)
-DI	definite past (5)
	past auxiliary (17)
-DIg	object participle (25)
	nominalization (28)
-DIkçE	adverbial (34)
-DIktEn	adverbial (34)
-DIr	causative (30)
-DIr	predicative (3, 19)
-Il	passive (29)
-Im	1 sg, possessive (5, 9)
-ImIz	1 pl, possessive (5, 9)
-In	2 sg, possessive (5, 9)
-In	reflexive (31)
-IncI	ordinal (17)
-InIz	2 pl, possessive (5, 9)
-Ir	present tense (14)
	aorist participle (24)
-Iş	reciprocal (32)
-Iyor	progressive (11)
-k	1 pl, possessive used with verb tenses (5)
-ken	adverbial auxiliary (35)
-ki	relative (19)
-lE	verb derivation (32)

-lEr — plural (3)
-lErI — 3 pI, possessive (9)
-lI — adjective derivation (34)
-lIg — noun derivation (31)
-mE — negative (6)
-mE — verbal noun (27)
-mEdEn — adverbial (34)
-mEg — verbal noun (5, 27)
-mElI — necessitative (37)
mI — question (6)
-mIş — dubitative auxiliary (18)
narrative past (16)
past participle (24)
-(n)In — genitive (9)
-rE — place (13)
-sE — conditional (36)
-sEnE — nonpolite imperative (37)
-sEnIzE — polite imperative (37)
-(s)I(n) — 3 sg, possessive (9)
-sIn — 2 sg, predicative (3)
-sIn — 3 sg, optative (37)
-sInIz — 2 pl, predicative (3)
-sIz — adjective derivation (34)
-(ş)Er — distributive (18)
-(y)E — adverbial (15, 33)
-(y)E — dative (7)
-(y)E — impossible (35)
-(y)E — optative (37)
-(y)Ebil — possible (35)
-(y)EcEg — future tense (13)
future participle (24, 25)

	nominalization (28)
-(y)Edur	durative (35)
-(y)ElI	adverbial (33)
-(y)En	present participle (24)
-(y)ErEk	adverbial (33)
-(y)I	objective (5)
-(y)IcI	noun derivation (30)
-(y)Im	1 sg, predicative (3)
-(y)In	nonpolite imperative (37)
-(y)IncE	adverbial (33)
-(y)InIz	polite imperative (37)
-(y)Ip	adverbial (33)
-(y)Iş	verbal noun (27)
-(y)Iver	momentaneous (35)
-(y)Iz	1 pl, predicative (3)

GLOSSARY

Numbers in parentheses indicate the lesson in which each word is introduced. Underlined numbers (for example, 17) indicate that the word is discussed in the "Usage" section of the indicated lesson.

Personal and place names are omitted.

acayip	/acāyip/	strange (27)
aç		hungry (3)
açık		open (29)
açmak		open (11); turn on (25)
ad		name (10)
adam		man (3)
aded		item (12)
af	/aff/	pardon, amnesty (22)
affetmek		pardon (22)
ağaç	/agac/	tree (4)
ağır		heavy (31)
ağız	/agz/	mouth (10)
ağlamak		cry (27)
Ağustos		August (14)
aile		family (18)
akıl	/akl/	mind, intelligence (34)
akmak		flow (30)
akşam		evening (13)
akşamleyin		in the evening (13)
alışmak (dat)		become accustomed, get used (to) (27)
almak		get, receive, take, buy (5)
alt		bottom (21)
ama, amma	/áma, ámma/	but (3)
amele		workman (33)

Temmuz (Pazartesi) 4
Mon., July 4

an		moment (23)
anlamak		understand (11)
anne, ana		mother; main (9)
apartman		apartment building (18)
ara 'between' 'among'		interval (21)
araba		car, cart, coach, carriage (8)
Arap	/arab/	Arab (17)
Aralık		December (14)
aramak		search, look for (12)
arka		back (21)
arkadaş		friend (10)
artık		henceforth, no more (25)
artmak		increase; be left over (30)
asıl	/asl/	real (38)
asır	/asr/	century (17)
asker		soldier (21)
aşağı		down, downward (22)
at		horse (3)
ateş		fire (34)
atılmak		be thrown; attack (29)
atmak		throw, throw away (21)
ay		moon, month (14)
ayak		foot (21)
ayırmak		set aside (29)
ayna		mirror (31)
aynı	/áynı/	same (14)
ayrı		separate (29)
ayrılmak		separate (intr); depart (29)

28 words

az		few (6, Section 5)
baba		father (9)
bağ		tie, bond (32)
bağırmak		shout (37)
bahçe		garden (21)
bakan		minister (governmental)(19)
bakkal		grocer, grocery (9)
bakmak (dat)		look (at), look after, watch (7)
banka		bank (26)
bardak		glass (12)
basmak		step (on), press (25)
baş		head; chief (9)
başbakan		prime minister (19)
başka (abl)		other (than)(20)
başlamak (dat)		begin (7)
batmak		sink; set (30)
Bay		Mr. (18, Section 3)
Bayan		Mrs. (18, Section 3)
bazan, bazen	/bázan, bázen/	sometimes (23)
bazı	/bā́zı/	some (23)
beğenmek		like (6)
beklemek		wait, watch, expect (16)
belki	/bélki/	perhaps (35)
belli		clear, obvious (28)
ben		I (3)
benzemek (dat)		resemble (24)
benzetmek		make resemble; compare (30)
beraber	/berāber/	together (15)

beri (adv)		here, hither (22)
beri (postp) (abl)		since (20)
bey		gentleman (18, Section 3)
beyaz		white (9)
bıkmak (abl)		be tired (of), be sick (of) (36)
bırakmak		leave (23)
bile		even (36)
bilmek		know (14)
bina	/binā/	building (19)
binmek (dat)		mount, get on (7)
biraz	/bíraz/	a little (20)
bitirmek		finish (trans) (20)
bitmek		finish (intrans) (20)
biz		we (3)
boş		empty (12)
boy		stature, height (34)
bozmak		spoil, ruin (23)
bozulmak		be ruined; be angry (29)
böyle		this way, like this, thus (15, Section 3)
buçuk		half (13, Section 3)
bugün	/búgün/	today (5)
bulmak		find (12)
bütün		all (23)
büyük		big (4)
büyümek		grow (34)
cami	/cāmi'/	mosque (33)
can		soul, life (32)
cevap	/cevāb/	answer (16)

cins		kind, sort (12)
Cuma	/cumā/	Friday (15)
Cumartesi		Saturday (15)
çabuk		quick (37)
çağırmak		call; invite (38)
çalışkan		hardworking, industrious (3)
çalışmak		work, work at, work on; try (6, 7, 27)
çalmak		strike, knock; play; steal (24)
çarpmak		strike (32)
Çarşamba		Wednesday (15)
çay		tea (11)
çekilmek		be pulled; withdraw (29)
çekmek		pull (16)
çeşit	/çeşid/	kind, sort (12)
çevirmek		turn over (trans)(33)
çeyrek		quarter (15)
çıkarmak		put out, let out; remove (30)
çıkmak		go out, leave, go up (7)
çocuk		child (4)
çok	/çog/	much (6, Section 5)
çoktan		a long time ago (7)
çünkü	/çǘnkü/	because (38)
daha	/dáha/	more (20)
daima	/dā́imā/	always (4, 14)
daire		office, apartment (18)
dakika	/dakīka/	minute (15)
defa	/defā/	time (17)

değişmek		change (intrans)(18)
deli		crazy, insane (28)
demek		say (26)
denemek		try (27)
deniz		sea, seashore (10)
derin		deep (38)
ders		lesson (7)
dert	/derd/	trouble, illness, problem (20)
devam	/devām/	continuation (27)
devam etmek (dat)		continue (27)
devirmek		overturn (35)
devrilmek		be overturned; fall over (35)
dış		outside (21)
dışarı		outside, outward (22)
diğer		other (20)
dikkat	(-i)	attention, care (22)
dikkat etmek (dat)		pay attention (to) (22)
dil		tongue, language (25)
dinlemek		listen (24)
diş		tooth (30)
doğmak		be born; rise (30)
doğru (adj)		straight, right, correct (16)
doğru (postp) (dat)		toward (16)
doktor		doctor (13)
dolaşmak		wander (32)
dolayı (abl)		because (of)(20)
doldurmak		fill (trans)(37)

dolmak		fill (intrans)(37)
dost		friend (19)
doymak		be satisfied, be satiated (30)
dönmek		turn, return (13)
dövmek		beat (32)
durmak		stand, stop (8)
durum		situation (31)
duvar		wall (21)
duymak		hear (28)
dükkân	/dükkan/	shop, store (9)
dün		yesterday (5)
dünya	/dünyā/	world, Earth (18)
düşman		enemy (30)
düşmek		fall (9)
düşünmek		think (27, 28)
efendi		(title)(18, Section 3)
eğer		if (36)
Ekim		October (14)
ekmek		bread, loaf of bread (5)
el		hand (9)
elbise		clothes, clothing, dress (21)
elma		apple (6)
emin (abl)	/emīn/	sure (of)(28)
erkek		man, male (11)
erken		early (7)
eser		work (of art)(17)
eski		old; former (4)
eskiden		formerly (7)
eşya	/eşyā/	thing, things, property (19)

et		meat (5)
etraf		surroundings (22)
ev		house, home (7)
evvel (abl)		before, earlier, ago (20)
evvelâ	/évvelā/	first (20)
Eylul	/eylul/	September (14)
fakat	/fákat/	but (4)
fark		difference (34)
fayda		use (35)
faydalı		useful (35)
faydasız		useless (35)
fena	/fenā/	bad, unwell (8)
fiat		price (16)
fikir	/fikr/	idea, opinion (23)
gazete	/gazéte/	newspaper (6)
gece		night (13)
geç		late (7, 8)
geçmek		pass (15)
gelişmek		develop (32)
gelmek		come (5)
gemi		ship (30)
genç	/genc/	young (4)
gene, gine	/géne, gíne/	again (20)
geniş		wide, spacious (10)
geri		back, backward (22)
getirmek		bring (12)
gezmek		walk, tour (31)
gibi (nom/gen)		like (15)
girmek (dat)		enter (7)
gitmek	/gid-/	go (5)

giymek		wear, put on (24)
göndermek		send (25)
göre (dat)		according (to), suitable (for) (16)
görmek		see (5)
görüşmek		see one another, meet, discuss, have a conference (32)
göstermek		show (21)
götürmek		take (33)
göz		eye (20)
gram		gram (13)
gülmek (dat)		laugh, smile; laugh (at) (18)
gün		day (13)
güneş		sun (16)
güzel		pretty, beautiful (6)
haber		news, piece of news; message (7)
hâdise	/hādise/	event (29)
hafta		week (15)
hak	/hakk/	(legal) right (22)
hal	/hal/	state, condition (19)
hala	/hālā/	still (11)
halbuki	/hálbuki, halbúki/	although (38)
halk		people, populace (29)
hangi	/hángi/	which (8)
hanım		lady (18)
hareket		motion, action (22)
hareket etmek		move, act (22)
harf	(-i)	letter (27)
harp	/harb/(-i)	war (16)

hasta		sick (3)
hatırlamak		remember (28)
hava		weather, air (18)
hayat	/hayāt/	life (18)
hayvan		animal (10)
hazır (dat)		ready (to, for) (27)
Haziran	/hazīran/	June (14)
hem . . . hem		both . . . and (26)
hemen	/hémen/	immediately (27)
hemen hemen		almost (27)
hep		always (14)
her		every (14)
herhalde	/hérhalde/	presumably (19)
herkes	/hérkes/	everyone (23)
hız		speed (34)
hiç		ever, never, not at all (23)
his	/hiss/	feeling, sense (22)
hissetmek		feel (22)
hoca		teacher (14)
hoş		pleasant, nice, agreeable (3)
hükümet		government (25)
ısırmak		bite (26)
ışık		light (25)
iç		inside, interior (21)
içeri		inside, inward (22)
için (nom/gen)		for; about (15, 22)
içki		(alcoholic) drink (11)
içmek		drink, smoke (11)
idare	/idāre/	administration, management (35)

idare etmek		administer, manage (35)
ihtiyar		old (4)
ile (nom/gen)		with (15)
ileri		forward (22)
ilk		first (17)
inanmak (dat)		believe (36)
inmek		descend, go down (7)
insan		person, human (12)
inşallah	/ínşallah/	God willing (13)
ise		as for (36)
isim	/ism/	name (10)
iskemle	/iskémle/	chair (10)
istasyon		station (22)
istemek		want (11)
iş		work, business, job (16)
işaret	/işāret/	sign, signal (38)
işitmek		hear (28)
itmek		push (37)
iyi		good, well (3)
kabul	/kabūl/	acceptance, agreement (35)
kabul etmek		accept, agree (to); receive (35)
kaç		how many? (12)
kaçmak		flee, escape (25)
kadar (nom/gen)		amount; as (much) as (15)
kadar (dat)		until, up to (16)
kadın		woman (8)
kâğıt	/kāgıd/	paper (12)
kahve		coffee, coffeehouse (11)

kalem		pen (12)
kalkmak		get up, arise, leave, depart (13)
kalmak		stay, remain, be left (8, 10)
kanun	/kānun/	law
kapalı		closed (29)
kapamak		close (20); turn off (25)
kapı		door (8)
kar		snow (34)
kara		black (10)
karar		decision (28)
karar vermek (dat)		decide (on) (28)
kardeş		brother, sister (11)
karı		wife (17)
karışmak (dat)		get mixed up (in), interfere (with) (27)
karşı (n)		place opposite (21)
karşı- (adv)		opposite (22)
karşı (postp) (dat)		against (16)
karşılamak		meet (32)
kasap	/kasab/	butcher (4)
Kasım		November (14)
kâtip	/kâtib/	clerk (4)
kavga		fight, quarrel (21)
kavga etmek		fight, quarrel (22)
kaybetmek		lose (22)
kazanmak		win; earn (35)
kedi		cat (25)
kere		time (17)

Begin 100% wds. (Study)

kesmek		cut (26)
keşki	/kéşki/	if only, would that (36)
kez		time (17)
kırmak		break (24)
kısa		short, briefly (19)
kısım	/kısm/	part (21)
kış		winter (21, 23)
kışın		in the winter (23)
kız		girl, daughter (3)
kızmak		become angry (at) (21)
kilo		kilogram (13)
kilometre		kilometer (31)
kim		who? (10)
kimse		no one (23)
kişi		person (12)
kitap	/kitab/	book (5)
koca (n)		husband (12)
koca (adj)		large, huge (12)
kolay		easy (27)
komşu		neighbor (25)
konuşmak		speak, talk (19)
kopmak		break off (intrans) (30)
korkmak (abl)		fear, be afraid (of) (7)
koşmak		run (25)
koymak		put, place (8)
köpek		dog (4)
köşe		corner (8)
kötü		bad (3)
fena · bad as in unwell		
köy		village (9)

kulak		ear (37)
kullanmak		use; drive (19)
kurmak		set up, found, establish (29)
kurtarmak		save (29)
kurtulmak		be saved (29)
kuru		dry (32)
kuruş		(unit of money) (16)
kuş		bird (26)
kuşku		suspicion, doubt (38)
kutu		box (11)
kuvvet		strength, force (34)
küçük		small (4)
lâzım	/lāzım/	necessary (27, Section 4)
lira	/líra/	unit of money (16)
lokanta	/lokánta/	restaurant (7)
lütfen	/lǘtfen/	please (37)
lüzum		necessity, need (27, Section 4)
madem, mademki	/mā́dem, mādémki/	since (38)
mal		property, goods, merchandise (36)
malûm	/mālum/	well known (28)
mâna	/mānā/	meaning (27)
manzara		view (26)
Mart		March (14)
masa	/mása/	table (8)
Mayıs		May (14)
mektep	/mekteb/	school (14)
mektup	/mektub/	letter (5)
memleket		country (19)

memnun (dat)		pleased (at), satisfied (at)(28)
memur	/mēmur/	official, (police) officer (38)
merkez		center (26)
mesafe	/mesāfe/	distance (31)
mesele		problem (22)
meşgul	/meşguḽ/	busy, occupied (6)
meşhur		famous (27)
metre		meter (31)
mevzu	/mevzū'/	topic (33)
meydan		square (24)
meyva		piece of fruit (6)
miktar		amount, quantity (13)
muhakkak		certainly (19)
müdür		director (4)
mühendis		engineer (33)
mühim		important (23)
nasıl	/násıl/	how? (15)
ne . . . ne		neither . . . nor (23)
neden		why? (15)
niçin	/níçin/	why? (15)
Nisan	/nīsan/	April (14)
niye		why? (15)
niyet		intention, resolve (38)
nokta		point; dot, period (36)
o		that; he, she, it (3)
Ocak		January (14)
oda		room (9)
ofis		office (18)

oğlan		boy (24)
oğul	/ogl/	son (10)
okul		school (14)
okumak		read (5)
olay		event (29)
olmak		be, become (14, Section 3)
onlar		they (3)
ordu		army (33)
orta		middle (21)
otel		hotel (9)
otobüs		bus (7)
otomobil		automobile (8)
oturmak		sit, live (8)
oynamak		play, dance (24)
oyun		game, dance (24)
öbür		the other (12)
öğle		noon (20)
öğleyin		at noontime (20)
öğrenci		pupil (17)
öğrenmek		learn (23)
öğretmen		teacher (14)
ölçmek		measure (31)
ölmek		die (14)
ömür	/ömr/	life (18)
ön		front (21)
önce (abl)		before (20)
önemli		important (23)
öte-		there, thither (22)
övmek		praise (31)
öyle		that way, like that (15, Section 3)

padişah	/pādişah/	sultan (33)
pahalı		expensive (16)
paket		pack, package (12)
palto		overcoat (31)
para		money (16)
parça		piece (12)
parti		party (29)
Pazar		Sunday (15)
Pazartesi		Monday (15)
pek		very (6, Section 5)
pencere		window (8)
Perşembe		Thursday (15)
peş		back (of a moving object)(21)
pis		dirty, filthy (31)
pişmek		cook (intrans)(30)
polis		police, policeman (30)
portakal		orange (12)
pul		stamp (31)
radyo	/rádyo/	radio (25)
raf		shelf (19)
renk	/reng/	color (34)
resim	/resm/	picture (10)
resmen		officially (29)
rica	/ricā/	request (37)
rica etmek		request (37)
Rum		Greek (16)
saat	(-i)	watch, clock, hour (15)
sabah		morning (13)
sabahleyin		in the morning (13)

saç		hair (34)
sade	/sāde/	simple, plain (38)
sadece	/sādece/	simply, merely, only (38)
sağ (n)		right (8)
sağ (adj)		healthy (37)
sahip	/sāhib/	owner (33)
Salı		Tuesday (15)
sanat	/san'at/	art (33)
sandalye	/sandálye/	chair (10)
sanki	/sánki/	as though (38)
sanmak		think, consider (28)
santim, santimetre		centimeter (31)
sapmak		turn (29)
sarı		yellow (26)
sarılmak		be wrapped; embrace (29)
sarmak		wrap (29)
satın almak		buy (5)
satmak		sell (14)
sayfa, sahife		page (17)
sayılmak		be considered (29)
saymak		count (12)
sebep	/sebeb/	reason, cause (28)
sebep olmak (dat)		cause (28)
seçmek		choose, elect (28)
sefer		time (17)
sen		you (sg)(3)
sene		year (14)
sepet 'basket'		
serbest		free (36)

ses		voice, sound, noise (21)
sevinmek (dat)		be pleased (at)(28)
sevmek		love, like (6)
seyahat	(-i)	journey (14)
seyahat etmek		travel (22)
sıcak (n)		heat, hot weather (24)
sıcak (adj)		hot (24)
sınıf		class, classroom (24)
sıra		time, occasion, row (25)
sigara	/sigára/	cigarette (9)
siyah		black (10)
siz		you (pl)(3)
soğuk (n)		cold, cold weather
soğuk (adj)		cold
sokak		street (7)
sol		left (8)
son (n)		end (18)
son (adj)		last (18)
sonra (abl)	/sónra/	after, later (20)
sormak		ask (28)
soru		question (28)
söylemek		tell; say, speak (7)
söz		word (20)
su		water; juice (10)
sual	/sual̂/	question (28)
sultan		sultan (33)
susmak		be quiet, stop talking (35)
sürmek		drive; last (14)
şahsen	/şáhsen/	personally (31)

şapka		hat (23)
şarap	/şarab/	wine (26)
şart		condition (36)
şaşırmak		be confused, be surprised (38)
şaşmak		be surprised, be confused (38)
şehir	/şehr/	city (10)
şekil	/şekl/	shape, form; manner (36)
şey		thing (14)
şişe		bottle (13)
şimdi	/şímdi/	now (6)
şimdiden		henceforth (7)
şoför		driver (29)
şöyle		that way, like that (15, Section 3)
Şubat		February (14)
şüphe		doubt, suspicion (38)
tahta		wood, board (8)
talebe		student (17)
tam		exactly (13)
tamam	/tamām/	complete (32)
tamamen	/tamāmen/	completely (29)
tamir	/tāmir/	repair (29)
tamir etmek		repair (29)
tane	/tāne/	grain (12, Section 2.2)
tanımak		recognize, know (32)
taraf		side (22)
taş		stone (8)
taşımak		carry (31)
tayyare	/tayyāre/	airplane (15)

tek		single (18)
tekrar	/tékrar/	again (20)
telefon		telephone (22)
telefon etmek		telephone, call (22)
tembel		lazy (3)
temiz		clean (12)
Temmuz		July (14)
tepe		hill, top (25)
tesir	/tēsir/	influence (21)
tesir etmek (dat)		influence (22)
toplamak		gather, collect (33)
toplantı		meeting (19)
toprak		land, earth (33)
tren		train (15)
tuhaf		strange (27)
tutmak		hold (9); amount to (16)
tüm		all (23)
Türk		Turk (4)
ucuz		cheap (16)
uçak		airplane (15)
uçmak		fly (30)
uğramak (dat)		visit (casually), drop in (on) (37)
ummak		hope, expect (38)
umut	/umud/	hope, expectation (38)
unutmak		forget (28)
uygun (dat)		fitting, suitable (36)
uymak (dat)		suit, fit; adapt (to); be in harmony (with) (36)
uyumak		sleep (25)

uzak (abl)		far (from) (7)
uzamak		stretch (intrans) (35)
uzatmak		stretch (trans) (35)
uzun		long (19)
ümit	/ümid/	hope, expectation (38)
üniversite		university (9)
ünlü		famous (27)
üst		top (21)
üzer-		top (21)
üzmek		grieve (trans) (37)
üzülmek (abl)		grieve (intrans), be worried, be sorry (about) (37)
vakit	/vakt/ (-i)	time (16)
vapur		steamship (15)
var		it exists (10)
varmak (dat)		arrive (at), reach (13)
vasıta	/vāsıta/	means, instrument; vehicle; motor vehicle (29)
vazife	/vazīfe/	position, duty (26)
vaziyet		situation (31)
vekil		minister (governmental) (19)
vermek		give (7)
veyahut, veya, yahut		or (23)
vurmak		shoot, stab (14)
vurmak (dat)		strike, hit (14)
ya . . . ya, yahut		either . . . or (23)
yağmak		rain, snow (34)
yağmur		rain (34)

yakın (dat)		near (to) (7)
yakında		soon (8)
yaklaşmak		approach (32)
yakmak		burn (trans) (34)
yalnız (adj)		alone (17)
yalnız (adv)	/yálnız/	only, however (17)
yan		side (21)
yanmak		burn (intrans) (19, 25)
yapmak		do, make (8)
yardım		help, assistance (22)
yardım etmek (dat)		help (22)
yarı		half (13, Section 3)
yarım		half (13, Section 3)
yarın		tomorrow (13)
yasak		forbidden (29)
yasak etmek		forbid (29)
yaş		age (34)
yaşamak		live (17)
yaşlı		old (4)
yatak		bed (17)
yatmak		lie, lie down (17)
yavaş		slow (22)
yaz		summer (23)
yazı		piece of writing, article (5)
yazıhane		office (18)
yazın		in the summer (23)
yazmak		write (5)
yemek (n)		meal, food, dish (of food) (5)
yemek (v)		eat (5, 30)

yeni		new (5)
yeniden		anew (7)
yer		place, ground, floor (6)
yetmek		be sufficient (35)
yetişmek		develop; reach, arrive (35)
yıkamak		wash (31)
yıl		year (14)
yine	/yíne/	again (20)
yok		it does not exist (10)
yoksa 'or'		
yol		road, path, way, journey (8)
yorgun		tired (3)
yormak		tire (trans)(29)
yorulmak		tire, be tired of (29)
yukarı		up, upward (22)
Yunanlı		Greek (16)
yüksek		high (26)
yürümek		walk, march (16)
yüz		face (16)
yüzyıl		century (17)
zaman	/zamān/	time (16)
zannetmek		think, consider (28)
zengin		rich (18)
ziyaret	/ziyāret/	visit (37)
ziyaret etmek		visit (37)
zor		difficult (27)
zannedsen	in my opinion	

INDEX

Ablative case, 68-69
for cause, 221-222
in comparative of adjectives, 224-225
for directions, 81
for materials, 80-81
partitive, 226-227
Accent, 18-19
preceding auxiliaries, 34, 184, 197, 400-401
in compounds, 117, 158, 226, 247, 435
in numbers, 124
in possessive compounds, 95
preceding predicative endings, 34, 115
on progressive tense, 113
on proper nouns, 61
unaccented suffixes, 34, 57, 82, 137, 337, 387, 389, 403, 422-423, 435
Adjectives
comparative and superlative, 224-226
position in noun phrase, 38
use without noun, 39, 302-303
Adverbial constructions, 377-382, 387-391, 399-402
Adverbs
adjectives used as, 212-214
derivation with -CE, 337-338
directional, 250-251
of place (bura, şura-, ora-), 136-139
Alphabet, table of, 19-21
Aorist tense. See Present tense
Auxiliary, 30-31, 49-50, 185-187
adverbial, 399-402
conditional, 412-416, 426-428
dubitative, 196-199
past, 181-185

Buffer consonants, 29-30

Case. See Ablative case, Dative case, Genitive case, Locative case, Objective case
Causative, 343-349
with other derivational suffixes, 358-359, 369-370
Classifiers. See Counting words
Complements. See Noun phrase complements
Compound verbs, 246-248
Conditional auxiliary, 412-416, 426-428
Conditional tense, 411-416
Conjunction, 81-84
Consonants, 4-13. See also Stops
front and back k, g, l, 7-10
yumuşak ge, 10-12
Consonant clusters, in final position, 105-107, 246
Consonant harmony, 30
Converbs. See Adverbial constructions
Counting words, 126-129

Dates, 151-152
Dative case, 67-68
in causatives, 347
in prices, 172-174
for purpose, 311
Definite past tense, 48
Definiteness
effect on choice of participle, 300-301

Definiteness (continued)
in the noun phrase, 38
effect on word order, 71-72, 102, 300-301
Demonstratives, 121-124
in adverbs of place, 136-139
böyle, şöyle, öyle, 160-161
Derivation
of adjectives, 391-393
of adverbs, 337-338
of nouns, 338, 350-351, 359-361
of verbs, 370-372
of intransitive from transitive, 336-337
of transitive from intransitive, 347-348, 372
-DIr, 32-33, 207-209
Direct quotations, 431-432
Dubitative auxiliary, 195-199

Epenthesis, 105-107
Existential particles, 101-105

Fractions, 139-140
Future tense, 135-136

Genitive case, 91-92
Gerunds. See Adverbial constructions
Glottal stops, 382-383

Imperative, 421-423
third person. See Optative
Indefinite article (bir), use of, 38-40, 102-103
Indefinite expressions and pronouns, 257-262
Indirect commands, 311-312
Indirect questions, 325-326
Indirect quotations, 321-324, 432
Infinitive, 47, 310-312
Interrogatives. See also Questions
hangi, 81
kaç, 129
kim, 107
ne, 69-70
with postpositions, 161-162
Izafet. See Possessive compounds, Possessive constructions

Locative case, 79-80
in dates, 151-152
in fractions, 140

Names, 201-202
Narrative past tense, 169-171
Necessitative, 425-426
Negative expressions and pronouns, 262-265
Negatives
nonverbal (değil), 40
verbal (-mE), 57, 402-403
Nominalizations, 321-326
Noun phrase
composition of, 37-38
as predicate, 39
Noun phrase complements, 307-312, 321-324, 433-435
Numbers
cardinal, 124-129
distributive, 199-200
ordinal, 187-188
Numerical expressions. See Dates, Fractions, Numbers, Prices, Times

Objective case, 50-51

Objects
 obligatory with transitive verbs, 52, 118
 position in verb phrase, 49-50, 71
Optative, 423-425

Participles, 273-276
 object, 287-292, 297-303
 subject, 276-282, 297-301
Passive, 331-337
 with other derivational suffixes, 349, 358-359, 369-370
Past auxiliary, 181-185
Percentages, 140
Periphrastic constructions, 403-405
Personal endings, 31, 48-50, 92-93, 114-116
 predicative vs. possessive endings, 114-116
Phonemic transcription, 1-4
Plural, 33
 in adverbs of place, 136-139
 with indefinite nouns, 102-103
 with names, 201-202
 with numbers, 125-129
 with predicates, 40
Possessive compounds, 93-96
Possessive constructions, 90-97
 with var and yok, 104-105
Possessive suffixes, 92-93, 114-116
Possibility and impossibility, 402-404
Postpositional constructions, 234-239, 248-249, 393-394, 417
Postpositions, 157-158
 with the ablative, 219-224
 with the dative, 171-172
 with the nominative/genitive, 158-160
 use with adverbial constructions, 388-390
 use with nominalizations, 324-325
 use with object participles, 303
 use (için) with verbal nouns, 311-312
Predicate, 30-31. See also Verb phrase
 noun phrase as, 39-40
Predicative endings, 31, 114-116
Prefixes, 436-438
Present tense, 145-149
Prices, 172-174
Progressive tense, 112-114
 journalistic progressive (-mEktEdIr), 313-314
Pronominal n, 90
Pronouns, 32
Proper nouns
 accent, 61
 personal names, 201-202
 spelling, 43

Questions, yes-or-no (mI), 58-60. See also Interrogatives
 with auxiliaries, 184-197
 with -Iyor, 113-114
 with var and yok, 103-104

Reciprocal pronoun and verb, 365-370
Reduplication, 436-438
Reflexive pronoun and verb, 355-359

Relative clauses, 273-282, 287-292, 297-303
Relative suffix (-ki), 209-212

Stops
 aspiration, 12-13
 in final position, 41-43
Stress. See Accent
Subject, 30-31
 position of indefinite, 72, 102
Subjunctive. See Optative
Subordinating conjunctions, 433-436
Subordination. See Adverbial constructions, Nominalizations, Relative clauses, Subordinating conjunctions, Verbal nouns

Tense. See Conditional tense, Definite past tense, Future tense, Narrative past tense, Necessitative, Optative, Present tense, Progressive tense
Times, 162-163

Unaccented suffixes, 34

Variation in stems
 double final consonants, 246
 final clusters, 105-107
 final g, 42
 final long vowels, 174-175
 final voiced stops, 41-42
 glottal stops, 382-383
 pronominal n, 90
 su and ne, 105
 y conditioning (raising), 111-112
Variation in suffixes
 buffer consonants, 29-30
 consonant harmony, 30
 vowel dropping, 89-90
 vowel harmony, 23-27
Verb phrase, 49-50
Verbal nouns, 307-314, 323-324
 use with lâzım, 314-315
Vocative, 61-62
Vowels, 13-18
 long, 17-18
  in last syllable of stem, 174-175
 system of, 23-25
Vowel dropping, 89-90
Vowel harmony, 23-27

Word order in sentence, 70-73